COMPUTATIONAL MODELING
IN COGNITION

COMPUTATIONAL MODELING IN COGNITION PRINCIPLES AND PRACTICE

STEPHAN LEWANDOWSKY
University of Western Australia

SIMON FARRELL
University of Bristol

Los Angeles | London | New Delhi
Singapore | Washington DC

For information:

SAGE Publications, Inc.
2455 Teller Road
Thousand Oaks, California 91320
E-mail: order@sagepub.com

SAGE Publications India Pvt. Ltd.
B 1/I 1 Mohan Cooperative
   Industrial Area
Mathura Road, New Delhi 110 044
India

SAGE Publications Ltd.
1 Oliver's Yard
55 City Road, London, EC1Y 1SP
United Kingdom

SAGE Publications Asia-Pacific
   Pte. Ltd.
33 Pekin Street #02-01
Far East Square
Singapore 048763

Printed and bound by CPI Group (UK) Ltd, Croydon, CR0 4YY

Library of Congress Cataloging-in-Publication Data

Lewandowsky, Stephan.
Computational modeling in cognition : principles and practice / Stephan Lewandowsky and Simon Farrell.
     p. cm.
Includes bibliographical references and index.
ISBN 978-1-4129-7076-1 (pbk.)
   1. Cognition—Mathematical models. I. Farrell, Simon, 1976- II. Title.

BF311.L467 2011
153.01'5118—dc22   2010029246

This book is printed on acid-free paper.

10   11   12   13   14   10 9 8 7 6 5 4 3 2 1

Acquisitions Editor:	Christine Cardone
Editorial Assistant:	Sarita Sarak
Production Editor:	Brittany Bauhaus
Permissions Editor:	Karen Ehrmann
Copy Editor:	Gillian Dickens
Typesetter:	C&M Digitals (P) Ltd.
Proofreader:	Sally Jaskold
Cover Designer:	Gail Buschman
Marketing Manager:	Dory Schrader

Contents

Preface

The rapid progress in cognitive science during the past decade is intimately linked to three exciting and particularly active areas of research: computational and quantitative modeling of cognition, advances in the neurosciences, and the emphasis on Bayesian techniques as a tool to describe human behavior and to analyze data. Each of those areas is sufficiently broad to fill (at least one) textbook. This volume therefore focuses exclusively on cognitive modeling: We do not consider current research in the neurosciences or Bayesian techniques for data analysis and modeling because we cannot do justice to those additional topics in a single volume. Instead, this book is best considered an introductory stepping stone for further reading: Many of the issues discussed in this book constitute basic knowledge for the Bayesian data analyst and modeler.

What do you need to read this book? We have aimed this volume at an audience with only a limited background in mathematics. For example, we expect you to know the difference between a scalar, a vector, and a matrix, but we do not expect you to be an expert in matrix algebra.

In addition, we rely throughout on MATLAB to illustrate the core concepts with programming examples. If you want to follow those examples—and we strongly recommend that you do—then you will need access to MATLAB, and you need some prior knowledge of how to program in that language. If you have no background at all in programming, then you need to acquire some basic skills before you can tackle this book. Computational modeling, after all, involves computing.

Our intention was to write a book that would allow a junior Ph.D. student or a researcher without background in modeling to begin to acquire the skills necessary for cognitive modeling. Similarly, this book is suitable for use in an advanced undergraduate course on modeling if accompanied by suitable tuition. We also expect that many experts may find it a useful reference guide; however, to do justice to our primary intended target audience, there are many issues that we— reluctantly—had to omit from this volume. Accordingly, we have not covered such topics as Bayesian parameter estimation or multilevel modelling. Applying the

Pareto principle, we believe that 80% of our readership will be interested in 20% of the field—and so we focused on making those 20% particularly accessible.

There are several ways in which this book can be used and perused. The order of our chapters is dictated by logic, and we thus present basic modeling tools before turning to model selection and so on. However, the chapters can be read in a number of different orders, depending on one's background and intentions.

For example, readers with very little background in modeling may wish to begin by reading Chapters 1, 2, and 3, followed by the first part of Chapter 7 and all of Chapter 8. Then, you may wish to go back and read Chapters 4, 5, and 6. In contrast, if this book is used for formal tuition in a course, then we suggest that the chapters be assigned in the order in which they are presented; in our experience, this order follows the most logical progression in which the knowledge is presented.

This project would not have been possible without support and assistance from many sources. We are particularly grateful to Klaus Oberauer, John Dunn, E.-J. Wagenmakers, Jeff Rouder, Lael Schooler, and Roger Ratcliff for comments and clarifications on parts of this book.

—Stephan Lewandowsky
—Simon Farrell
Perth and Bristol,
April 2010

1

Introduction

1.1 Models and Theories in Science

Cognitive scientists seek to understand how the mind works. That is, we want to *describe* and *predict* people's behavior, and we ultimately wish to *explain* it, in the same way that physicists predict the motion of an apple that is dislodged from its tree (and can accurately describe its downward path) and explain its trajectory (by appealing to gravity). For example, if you forget someone's name when you are distracted seconds after being introduced to her, we would like to know what cognitive process is responsible for this failure. Was it lack of attention? Forgetting over time? Can we know ahead of time whether or not you will remember that person's name?

The central thesis of this book is that to answer questions such as these, cognitive scientists must rely on quantitative mathematical models, just like physicists who research gravity. We suggest that to expand our knowledge of the human mind, consideration of the data and verbal theorizing are insufficient on their own.

This thesis is best illustrated by considering something that is (just a little) simpler and more readily understood than the mind. Have a look at the data shown in Figure 1.1, which represent the position of planets in the night sky over time.

How might one describe this peculiar pattern of motion? How would you explain it? The strange loops in the otherwise consistently curvilinear paths describe the famous "retrograde motion" of the planets—that is, their propensity to suddenly reverse direction (viewed against the fixed background of stars) for some time before resuming their initial path. What explains retrograde motion? It took more than a thousand years for a satisfactory answer to that question to become

Figure 1.1 An example of data that defy easy description and explanation without a quantitative model.

available, when Copernicus replaced the geocentric Ptolemaic system with a heliocentric model: Today, we know that retrograde motion arises from the fact that the planets travel at different speeds along their orbits; hence, as Earth "overtakes" Mars, for example, the red planet will appear to reverse direction as it falls behind the speeding Earth.

This example permits several conclusions that will be relevant throughout the remainder of this book. First, the pattern of data shown in Figure 1.1 defies description and explanation unless one has a *model* of the underlying process. It is only with the aid of a model that one can describe and explain planetary motion, even at a verbal level (readers who doubt this conclusion may wish to invite friends or colleagues to make sense of the data without knowing their source).

Second, any model that explains the data is itself unobservable. That is, although the Copernican model is readily communicated and represented (so readily, in fact, that we decided to omit the standard figure showing a set of concentric circles), it cannot be directly observed. Instead, the model is an abstract explanatory device that "exists" primarily in the minds of the people who use it to describe, predict, and explain the data.

Third, there nearly always are *several* possible models that can explain a given data set. This point is worth exploring in a bit more detail. The overwhelming

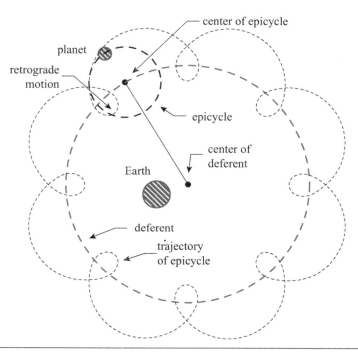

Figure 1.2 The geocentric model of the solar system developed by Ptolemy. It was the predominant model for some 1,300 years.

success of the heliocentric model often obscures the fact that, at the time of Copernicus's discovery, there existed a moderately successful alternative—namely, the geocentric model of Ptolemy shown in Figure 1.2. The model explained retrograde motion by postulating that while orbiting around the Earth, the planets also circle around a point along their orbit. On the additional, arguably somewhat inelegant, assumption that the Earth is slightly offset from the center of the planets' orbit, this model provides a reasonable account of the data, limiting the positional discrepancies between predicted and actual locations of, say, Mars to about 1° (Hoyle, 1974). Why, then, did the heliocentric model so rapidly and thoroughly replace the Ptolemaic system?[1]

The answer to this question is quite fascinating and requires that we move toward a *quantitative* level of modeling.

1.2   Why Quantitative Modeling?

Conventional wisdom holds that the Copernican model replaced geocentric notions of the solar system because it provided a better account of the data.

But what does "better" mean? Surely it means that the Copernican system predicted the motion of planets with less quantitative error—that is, less than the 1° error for Mars just mentioned—than its Ptolemaic counterpart? Intriguingly, this conventional wisdom is only partially correct: Yes, the Copernican model predicted the planets' motion in latitude better than the Ptolemaic theory, but this difference was slight compared to the overall success of both models in predicting motion in longitude (Hoyle, 1974). What gave Copernicus the edge, then, was not "goodness of fit" alone[2] but also the intrinsic elegance and simplicity of his model—compare the Copernican account by a set of concentric circles with the complexity of Figure 1.2, which only describes the motion of a single planet.

There is an important lesson to be drawn from this fact: The choice among competing models—and remember, there are always several to choose from—inevitably involves an *intellectual judgment* in addition to quantitative examination. Of course, the quantitative performance of a model is at least as important as are its intellectual attributes. Copernicus would not be commemorated today had the predictions of his model been *inferior* to those of Ptolemy; it was only because the two competing models were on an essentially equal quantitative footing that other intellectual judgments, such as a preference for simplicity over complexity, came into play.

If the Ptolemaic and Copernican models were quantitatively comparable, why do we use them to illustrate our central thesis that a purely verbal level of explanation for natural phenomena is insufficient and that all sciences must seek explanations at a quantitative level? The answer is contained in the crucial modification to the heliocentric model offered by Johannes Kepler nearly a century later. Kepler replaced the circular orbits in the Copernican model by ellipses with differing eccentricities (or "egg-shapedness") for the various planets. By this straightforward mathematical modification, Kepler achieved a virtually perfect fit of the heliocentric model with near-zero quantitative error. There no longer was any appreciable quantitative discrepancy between the model's predictions and the observed paths of planets. Kepler's model has remained in force essentially unchanged for more than four centuries.

The acceptance of Kepler's model permits two related conclusions, one that is obvious and one that is equally important but perhaps less obvious. First, if two models are equally simple and elegant (or nearly so), the one that provides the better quantitative account will be preferred. Second, the predictions of the Copernican and Keplerian models cannot be differentiated by verbal interpretation alone. Both models explain retrograde motion by the fact that Earth "overtakes" some planets during its orbit, and the differentiating feature of the two models—whether orbits are presumed to be circular or elliptical—does not entail any differences in predictions that can be appreciated by purely verbal analysis.

That is, although one can talk about circles and ellipses (e.g., "one is round, the other one egg shaped"), those verbalizations cannot be turned into testable predictions: Remember, Kepler reduced the error for Mars from 1° to virtually zero, and we challenge you to achieve this by verbal means alone.

Let us summarize the points we have made so far:

1. Data never speak for themselves but require a model to be understood and to be explained.

2. Verbal theorizing alone ultimately cannot substitute for quantitative analysis.

3. There are always several alternative models that vie for explanation of data, and we must select among them.

4. Model selection rests on both quantitative evaluation and intellectual and scholarly judgment.

All of these points will be explored in the remainder of this book. We next turn our attention from the night sky to the inner workings of our mind, first by showing that the preceding conclusions apply in full force to cognitive scientists and then by considering an additional issue that is of particular concern to scholars of the human mind.

1.3   Quantitative Modeling in Cognition

1.3.1   Models and Data

Let's try this again: Have a look at the data in Figure 1.3. Does it remind you of planetary motion? Probably not, but it should be at least equally challenging to discern a meaningful pattern in this case at it was in the earlier example. Perhaps the pattern will become recognizable if we tell you about the experiment conducted by Nosofsky (1991) from which these data are taken. In that experiment, people were trained to classify a small set of cartoon faces into two arbitrary categories (we might call them the Campbells and the MacDonalds, and members of the two categories might differ on a set of facial features such as length of nose and eye separation).

On a subsequent transfer test, people were presented with a larger set of faces, including those used at training plus a set of new ones. For each face, people had to make two decisions: which category the face belonged to and the confidence of that decision (called "classification" in the figure, shown on the x-axis), and whether or not it had been shown during training ("recognition," on

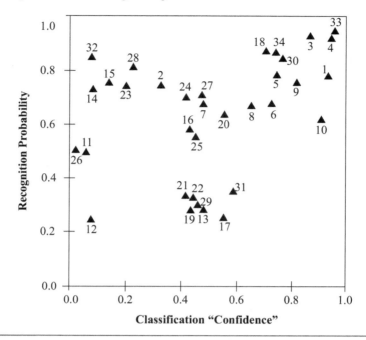

Figure 1.3 Observed recognition scores as a function of observed classification confidence for the same stimuli (each number identifies a unique stimulus). See text for details. Figure reprinted from Nosofsky, R. M. (1991). Tests of an exemplar mode for relating perceptual classification and recognition memory. *Journal of Experimental Psychology: Human Perception and Performance, 17*, 3–27. Published by the American Psychological Association; reprinted with permission.

the *y*-axis). Each data point in the figure, then, represents those two responses, averaged across participants, for a given face (identified by ID number, which can be safely ignored). The correlation between those two measures was found to be $r = .36$.

Before we move on, see if you can draw some conclusions from the pattern in Figure 1.3. Do you think that the two tasks have much to do with each other? Or would you think that classification and recognition are largely unrelated and that knowledge of one response would tell you very little about what response to expect on the other task? After all, if $r = .36$, then knowledge of one response reduces uncertainty about the other one by only 13%, leaving a full 87% unexplained, right?

Wrong. There is at least one quantitative cognitive model (called the GCM and described a little later), which can relate those two types of responses with considerable certainty. This is shown in Figure 1.4, which separates classification and recognition judgments into two separate panels, each showing the

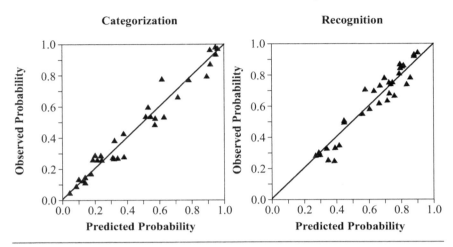

Figure 1.4 Observed and predicted classification (left panel) and recognition (right panel). Predictions are provided by the GCM; see text for details. Perfect prediction is represented by the diagonal lines. Figure reprinted from Nosofsky, R. M. (1991). Tests of an exemplar mode for relating perceptual classification and recognition memory. *Journal of Experimental Psychology: Human Perception and Performance, 17*, 3–27. Published by the American Psychological Association; reprinted with permission.

relationship between observed responses (on the y-axis) and the predictions of the GCM (x-axis). To clarify, each point in Figure 1.3 is shown twice in Figure 1.4—once in each panel and in each instance plotted as a function of the *predicted* response obtained from the model.

The precision of predictions in each panel is remarkable: If the model's predictions were absolutely 100% perfect, then all points would fall on the diagonal. They do not, but they come close (accounting for 96% and 91% of the variance in classification and recognition, respectively). The fact that these accurate predictions were provided by the same model tells us that classification and recognition can be understood and related to each other within a common psychological theory. Thus, notwithstanding the low correlation between the two measures, there is an underlying model that explains how both tasks are related and permits accurate prediction of one response from knowledge of the other. This model will be presented in detail later in this chapter (Section 1.4.4); for now, it suffices to acknowledge that the model relies on the comparison between each test stimulus and all previously encountered exemplars in memory.

The two figures enforce a compelling conclusion: "The initial scatterplot ... revealed little relation between classification and recognition performance. At that limited level of analysis, one might have concluded that there was little in common between the fundamental processes of classification and recognition. Under the guidance of the formal model, however, a unified account of these processes is achieved" (Nosofsky, 1991, p. 9). Exactly paralleling the developments in 16th-century astronomy, data in contemporary psychology are ultimately only fully interpretable with the aid of a quantitative model. We can thus reiterate our first two conclusions from above and confirm that they apply to cognitive psychology in full force—namely, that *data never speak for themselves but require a model to be understood and to be explained* and that *verbal theorizing alone cannot substitute for quantitative analysis*. But what about the remaining earlier conclusions concerning model selection?

Nosofsky's (1991) modeling included a comparison between his favored exemplar model, whose predictions are shown in Figure 1.4, and an alternative "prototype" model. The details of the two models are not relevant here; it suffices to note that the prototype model compares a test stimulus to the *average* of all previously encountered exemplars, whereas the exemplar model performs the comparison one by one between the test stimulus and each exemplar and sums the result.[3] Nosofsky found that the prototype model provided a less satisfactory account of the data, explaining only 92% and 87% of the classification and recognition variance, respectively, or about 5% less than the exemplar model. Hence, the earlier conclusions about model selection apply in this instance as well: There were several alternative models, and the choice between them was based on clear quantitative criteria.

1.3.2   From Ideas to Models

So far, we initiated our discussions with the data and we then ...poof! ...revealed a quantitative model that spectacularly turned an empirical mystery or mess into theoretical currency. Let us now invert this process and begin with an idea, that is, some psychological process that you think might be worthy of exploration and perhaps even empirical test. Needless to say, we expect you to convert this idea into a quantitative model. This raises at least two obvious questions: First, how would one do this? Second, does this process have implications concerning the role of modeling other than those we have already discussed? These questions are sufficiently complex to warrant their own chapter (Chapter 2), although we briefly survey the latter here.

Consider the simple and elegant notion of rehearsal, which is at the heart of much theorizing in cognition (e.g., A. D. Baddeley, 2003). We have all engaged in rehearsal, for example, when we try to retain a phone number long enough to enter it into our SIM cards. Several theorists believe that such subvocal—or sometimes overt—rehearsal can prevent the "decay" of verbal short-term memory traces, and introspection suggests that repeated recitation of a phone number is a good means to avoid forgetting. Perhaps because of the overwhelming intuitive appeal of the notion and its introspective reality, there have been few if any attempts to embody rehearsal in a computational model. It is therefore of some interest that one recent attempt to explicitly model rehearsal (Oberauer & Lewandowsky, 2008) found it to be detrimental to memory performance under many circumstances rather than beneficial. Specifically, because rehearsal necessarily involves retrieval from memory—how else would an item be articulated if not by retrieving it from memory?—it is subject to the same vagaries that beset memory retrieval during regular recall. In consequence, repeated rehearsal is likely to first introduce and then compound retrieval errors, such as ordinal transpositions of list items, thus likely offsetting any benefit that might be derived from restoring the strength of rehearsed information. Oberauer and Lewandowsky (2008) found that the exact consequences of rehearsal depended on circumstances—in a small number of specific conditions, rehearsal was beneficial—but this only amplifies the point we are making here: Even intuitively attractive notions may fail to provide the desired explanation for behavior once subjected to the rigorous analysis required by a computational model.[4] As noted by Fum, Del Missier, and Stocco (2007), "Verbally expressed statements are sometimes flawed by internal inconsistencies, logical contradictions, theoretical weaknesses and gaps. A running computational model, on the other hand, can be considered as a sufficiency proof of the internal coherence and completeness of the ideas it is based upon" (p. 136). In Chapter 2, we further explore this notion and the mechanics of model development by developing a computational instantiation of Baddeley's (e.g., 2003) rehearsal model.

Examples that underscore the theoretical rigor afforded by quantitative models abound: Lewandowsky (1993) reviewed one example in detail that involved construction of a model of word recognition. Shiffrin and Nobel (1997) described the long and informative behind-the-scenes history of the development of a model of episodic recognition.

Finally, theoreticians who ignore the rigor of quantitative modeling do so at their own peril. Hunt (2007) relates the tale of the 17th-century Swedish king and his desire to add another deck of guns to the *Vasa*, the stupendous new flagship of his fleet. What the king wanted, the king got, and the results are history: The *Vasa* set sail on her maiden voyage and remained proudly upright for, well, nearly half an hour before capsizing and sinking in Stockholm harbor. Lest one think that such follies are the preserve of heads of state, consider the claim in a textbook on learning: "While adultery rates for men and women may be equalizing, men still have more partners than women do, and they are more likely to have one-night stands; the roving male seeks sex, the female is looking for a better partner" (Leahey & Harris, 1989, pp. 317–318). Hintzman (1991) issued a challenge to set up a model consistent with this claim—that is, "there must be equal numbers of men and women, but men must have more heterosexual partners than women do" (p. 41). Needless to say, the challenge has not been met because the claim is mathematically impossible; the obvious lesson here is that verbal theories may not only be difficult to implement, as shown by Oberauer and Lewandowsky (2008), but may even turn out to be scientifically untenable.

1.3.3   Summary

We conclude this section by summarizing our main conclusions:

1. Data never speak for themselves but require a model to be understood and to be explained.

2. Verbal theorizing alone cannot substitute for quantitative analysis.

3. There are always several alternative models that vie for explanation of data, and we must compare those alternatives.

4. Model comparison rests on both quantitative evaluation and intellectual and scholarly judgment.

5. Even seemingly intuitive verbal theories can turn out to be incoherent or ill-specified.

6. Only instantiation in a quantitative model ensures that all assumptions of a theory have been identified and tested.

If you are interested in expanding on these conclusions and finding out more about fascinating aspects of modeling, we recommend that you consider the studies by Estes (1975), Lewandowsky (1993), Lewandowsky and Heit (2006), Norris (2005), and Ratcliff (1998).

1.4   The Ideas Underlying Modeling and Its Distinct Applications

We have shown that quantitative modeling is an indispensable component of successful research in cognition. To make this point without getting bogged down in too many details, we have so far sidestepped a number of fundamental issues. For example, we have yet to define what a model actually is and what common ground all psychological models may share—and, conversely, how they might differ. We now take up those foundational issues.[5]

1.4.1   Elements of Models

What exactly is a model, anyway? At its most basic, a model is an abstract structure that captures structure in the data (cf. Luce, 1995). For example, a good model for the set of numbers {2, 3, 4} is their mean—namely, 3. A good model for the relationship between a society's happiness and its economic wealth is a negatively accelerated function, such that happiness rises steeply as one moves from poverty to a modest level of economic security, but further increases in happiness with increasing material wealth get smaller and smaller as one moves to the richest societies (Inglehart, Foa, Peterson, & Welzel, 2008). Those models are *descriptive* in nature, and they are sufficiently important to merit their own section (Section 1.4.2).

Needless to say, scientists want to do more than describe the data. At the very least, we want to *predict* new observations; for example, we might want to predict how much happiness is likely to increase if we manage to expand the gross national product by another zillion dollars (if you live in a rich country, the answer is "not much"). In principle, any type of model permits prediction, and although prediction is an important part of the scientific endeavor (and probably the only ability of consideration for stockbrokers and investment bankers), it is not the whole story. For example, imagine that your next-door neighbor, a car mechanic by trade, were able to predict with uncanny accuracy the outcome of every conceivable experiment on some aspect of human cognition (a scenario discussed by K. I. Forster, 1994). Would you be satisfied with this state of affairs? Would your neighbor be a good model of human cognition? Clearly the answer is no; in addition to robotic predictions, you also want an *explanation* for the phenomena under consideration (Norris, 2005). *Why* does this particular outcome obtain in that experiment rather than some other result?

It follows that most cognitive modeling goes beyond mere description and seeks to permit prediction and explanation of behavior. The latter, explanatory role is the exclusive domain of models that we refer to as providing a process characterization and process explanation, respectively.

When models are used as an explanatory device, one other attribute becomes particularly relevant: Models are intended to be simpler and more abstract versions of the system—in our case, human cognition—they are trying to explain (Fum et al., 2007). Models seek to retain the essential features of the system while discarding unnecessary details. By definition, the complexity of models will thus never match the complexity of human cognition–and nor should it, because there is no point in replacing one thing we do not understand with another (Norris, 2005).

1.4.2   Data Description

Knowingly or not, we have all used models to describe or summarize data, and at first glance, this appears quite straightforward. For example, we probably would not hesitate to describe the salaries of all 150 members of the Australian House of Representatives by their average because in this case, there is little doubt that the mean is the proper "model" of the data (notwithstanding the extra allowances bestowed upon ministers). Why would we want to "model" the data in this way? Because we are replacing the data points ($N = 150$ in this instance) with a single estimated "parameter."[6] In this instance, the parameter is the sample mean, and reducing 150 points into one facilitates understanding and efficient communication of the data.

However, we must not become complacent in light of the apparent ease with which we can model data by their average. As a case in point, consider U.S. President Bush's 2003 statement in promotion of his tax cut, that "under this plan, 92 million Americans receive an average tax cut of $1,083." Although this number, strictly speaking, was not incorrect, it arguably did not represent the best model of the proposed tax cut, given that 80% of taxpayers would receive less than this cut, and nearly half (i.e., some 45 million people) would receive less than $100 (Verzani, 2004). The distribution of tax cuts was so skewed (bottom 20% of income earners slated to receive $6 compared to $30,127 for the top 1%) that the median or a trimmed mean would have been the preferable model of the proposed legislation in this instance.

Controversies about the proper model with which to describe data also arise in cognitive science, although fortunately with more transparency and less disingenuousness than in the political scene. In fact, data description, by itself, can have considerable psychological impact. As a case in point, consider the debate on whether learning of a new skill is best understood as following a "power law" or is better described by an exponential improvement (Heathcote, Brown, & Mewhort, 2000). There is no doubt that the benefits from practice accrue in a nonlinear fashion: The first time you try your hands at a new skill (for example, creating an Ikebana arrangement), things take seemingly forever (and the output may not be worth writing home about). The second and third time round, you will notice vast improvements, but eventually, after some dozens of trials, chances are that all further improvements are small indeed.

What is the exact functional form of this pervasive empirical regularity? For several decades, the prevailing opinion had been that the effect of practice is best captured by a power law—that is, by the function (shown here in its simplest possible form),

$$RT = N^{-\beta}, \tag{1.1}$$

where RT represents the time to perform the task, N represents the number of learning trials to date, and β is the learning rate. Figure 1.5 shows sample data, taken from Palmeri's (1997) Experiment 3, with the appropriate best-fitting power function superimposed as a dashed line.

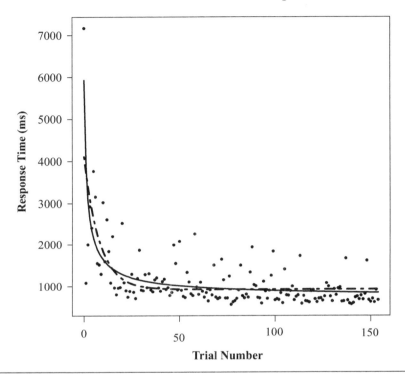

Figure 1.5 Sample power law learning function (dashed line) and alternative exponential function (solid line) fitted to the same data. Data are represented by dots and are taken from Palmeri's (1997) Experiment 3 (Subject 3, Pattern 13). To fit the data, the power and exponential functions were a bit more complex than described in Equations 1.1 and 1.2 because they also contained an asymptote (A) and a multiplier (B). Hence, the power function took the form $RT = A_P + B_P \times (N + 1)^{-\beta}$, and the exponential function was $RT = A_E + B_E \times e^{-\alpha N}$.

Heathcote et al. (2000) argued that the data are better described by an exponential function given by (again in its simplest possible form)

$$RT = e^{-\alpha N}, \tag{1.2}$$

where N is as before and α the learning rate. The best-fitting exponential function is shown by the solid line in Figure 1.5; you will note that the two competing descriptions or models do not appear to differ much. The power function captures the data well, but so does the exponential function, and there is not much to tell between them: The residual mean squared deviation (RMSD), which represents the average deviation of the data points from the predicted function, was 482.4 for the power function compared to 526.9 for the exponential. Thus, in this instance, the power function fits "better" (by providing some 50 ms less error in its predictions than the exponential), but given that RT's range is from somewhere less than 1000 ms to 7 seconds, this difference is not particularly striking.

So, why would this issue be of any import? Granted, we wish to describe the data by the appropriate model, but surely neither of the models in Figure 1.5 misrepresents essential features of the data anywhere near as much as U.S. President Bush did by reporting only the average implication of his proposed tax cut. The answer is that the choice of the correct descriptive model, in this instance, carries important implications about the psychological nature of learning. As shown in detail by Heathcote et al. (2000), the mathematical form of the exponential function necessarily implies that the learning rate, relative to what remains to be learned, is constant throughout practice. That is, no matter how much practice you have had, learning continues by enhancing your performance by a constant fraction. By contrast, the mathematics of the power function imply that the relative learning rate is slowing down as practice increases. That is, although you continue to show improvements throughout, the rate of learning *decreases* with increasing practice. It follows that the proper characterization of skill acquisition data by a descriptive model, in and of itself, has considerable psychological implications (we do not explore those implications here; see Heathcote et al., 2000, for pointers to the background).

Just to wrap up this example, Heathcote et al. (2000) concluded after reanalyzing a large body of existing data that the exponential function provided a better description of skill acquisition than the hitherto presumed power law. For our purposes, their analysis permits the following conclusions: First, quantitative description of data, by itself, can have considerable psychological implications because it prescribes crucial features of the learning process. Second, the example underscores the importance of model selection that we alluded to earlier; in this instance, one model was chosen over another on the basis of strict quantitative criteria. We revisit this issue in Chapter 5. Third, the fact that Heathcote et al.'s model selection considered the data of individual subjects, rather than the average across participants, identifies a new issue—namely, the most appropriate way in which to apply a model to the data from more than one individual—that we consider in Chapter 3.

The selection among competing functions is not limited to the effects of practice. Debates about the correct descriptive function have also figured prominently in the study of forgetting. Does the rate of forgetting differ with the extent of learning? Is the rate of information loss constant over time? Although the complete pattern of results is fairly complex, two conclusions appear warranted (Wixted, 2004a): First, the degree of learning does not affect the rate of forgetting. Hence, irrespective of how much you cram for an exam, you will lose the information at the same rate—but of course this is not an argument against dedicated study; if you learn more, you will also retain more, irrespective of the fact that the rate of loss per unit of time remains the same. Second, the rate of forgetting *decelerates* over time. That is, whereas you might lose some 30% of the information on the first day, on the second day, the loss may be down to 20%, then 10%, and so on. Again, as in the case of practice, two conclusions are relevant here: First, quantitative comparison among competing descriptive models was required to choose the appropriate function (it is a power function, or something very close to it). Second, although the shape of the "correct" function has considerable theoretical import because it may imply that memories are "consolidated" over time *after* study (see Wixted, 2004a, 2004b, for a detailed consideration, and see G. D. A. Brown & Lewandowsky, 2010, for a contrary view), the function itself has no psychological content.

The mere description of data can also have psychological implications when the behavior it describes is contrasted to *normative* expectations (Luce, 1995). Normative behavior refers to how people would behave if they conformed to the rules of logic or probability. For example, consider the following syllogism involving two premises (P) and a conclusion (C). P1: All polar bears are animals. P2: Some animals are white. C: Therefore, some polar bears are white. Is this argument valid? There is a 75% to 80% chance that you might endorse this conclusion (e.g., Helsabeck, 1975), even though it is logically false (to see why, replace *white* with *brown* in P2 and C). This example shows that people tend to violate normative expectations even in very simple situations. In this instance, the only descriptive model that is required to capture people's behavior—and to notice the normative violation—is a simple proportion (i.e., .75–.80 of people commit this logical error). In other, more realistic instances, people's normatively irrational behavior is best captured by a rather more complex descriptive model (e.g., Tversky & Kahneman, 1992).

We have presented several descriptive models and have shown how they can inform psychological theorizing. Before we move on, it is important to identify the common threads among those diverse examples. One attribute of descriptive models is that they are explicitly devoid of psychological *content*; for example, although the existence of an exponential practice function constrains possible learning mechanisms, the function itself has no psychological content. It is merely concerned with describing the data.

For the remainder of this chapter, we will be considering models that have increasingly more psychological content. In the next section, we consider models that characterize cognitive processes at a highly abstract level, thus going beyond data description, but that do not go so far as to explain those processes in detail. The final section considers models that go beyond characterization and explain the cognitive processes.

1.4.3   Process Characterization

What does it mean to characterize a cognitive process? There are two relevant attributes: First, models that characterize processes peek inside the "black box" that is the mind and postulate—and then measure—distinct cognitive components. Unlike descriptive models, their explanatory power thus rests on hypothetical constructs within the mind rather than within the data to be explained. Second, these models do not go beyond identification of those constructs or processes; that is, they remain neutral with respect to specific instantiations and explanations underpinning the cognitive processes they characterize. (Providing those explanations is the domain of the last class of models, to be considered in the next section.)

We illustrate this class of models using the multinomial processing tree (MPT) approach (Batchelder & Riefer, 1999; see also Riefer & Batchelder, 1988). The MPT approach makes the uncontroversial assumption that psychological data often result from multiple cognitive processes and provides a technique to disentangle and measure the relative contributions of these underlying processes. To do so, an MPT model postulates a sequence of processing stages and connects them by a variety of paths that can give rise to the observed behavioral outcome. While this may sound complicated, it is actually quite simple once shown graphically: Figure 1.6 contains a multinomial processing tree proposed by Schweickert (1993) to characterize recall from short-term memory.

The model postulates two ways in which recall can be successful: First, if the information in memory is intact (with probability I), then the item is recalled directly. Second, if the memorial representation is not intact (probability $1 - I$), then an item might nonetheless be "redintegrated" (with probability R). The redintegration stage refers to some reconstruction process that fills in the missing bits of a partially forgotten item on the basis of, say, information in long-term memory; for example, knowledge of the word *hippopotamus* will enable you to recall a memorized item even if all you can remember is something like "h_p_ _ _ _tam_ _." Only if redintegration also fails (with probability $1 - R$), then recall will be unsuccessful.

Let us trace these possible outcomes in Figure 1.6: We enter the tree at the top, and depending on whether the trace is intact, we branch right (with probability I) or left ($1 - I$). In the former case, the item is recalled, and outcome "C" (for "correct" recall) is obtained. In the latter case, the second stage kicks in, and we ask whether the item—not being intact—can nonetheless be successfully

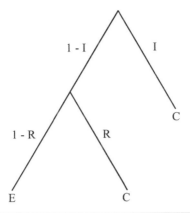

Figure 1.6 A simple multinomial processing tree model proposed by Schweickert (1993) for recall from short-term memory.

redintegrated (with probability R; branch right) or not $(1 - R$; keep going left). In the former case, we score another correct response; in the latter, we commit an error (E). The overall predictions of the model—for correct responses and errors, respectively—are thus given by $C = I + (1 - I) \times R$ and $E = (1 - I) \times (1 - R)$.

You are likely to ask at least two questions at this point: First, why are those components multiplied together, and second, how do we know what the values are of I and R?

The former question is answered by noting that each branch in the tree builds on the previous one; that is, redintegration (R) only takes place if the item was not intact $(1 - I)$ in the first place. Because the two stages are assumed to be independent, their probabilities of occurrence are multiplied together (for further discussion, see first part of Chapter 4). It follows that one possible way in which a response may be correct, via the path *left-right*, is given by $(1 - I) \times R$. This outcome is then added to the other way in which one can be correct, along the simple path *right*, which is given by I. Analogously, an error can only occur via the path *left-left*, which is thus given by $(1 - I) \times (1 - R)$.

The latter question, concerning the values of I and R, has both a simple and also a very involved answer. The simple answer is that those quantities are parameters that are estimated from the data, similar to the way in which we compute a sample mean to estimate the central tendency of the data. In contrast to the purely descriptive mean, however, the quantities I and R have psychological meaning and characterize two presumed cognitive processes—namely, memory storage (intact or not) and redintegration (successful or not). The more involved answer concerns the technical issues surrounding parameter estimation, and we will explore that answer in several of the following chapters in great detail.[7]

This is a good opportunity for recapitulation. We have presented a simple MPT model that characterizes the presumed processes operating in recall from short-term memory. Like the descriptive models in the preceding section, this model replaces the data by parameters. Unlike descriptive models, however, the parameters in the present case (I and R) have a psychological interpretation and characterize postulated cognitive processes.

To illustrate the way in which these types of models can provide a peek inside our minds, consider an application of Schweickert's (1993) model to the recall of lists containing words of different natural-language frequencies by Hulme et al. (1997). Hulme et al. compared lists composed of high-frequency words (e.g., *cat*, *dog*) and low-frequency words (*buttress*, *kumquat*) and examined performance as a function of each item's serial position in the list (i.e., whether it was presented first, second, and so on). What might the MPT model shown in Figure 1.6 predict for this experiment?

Hulme et al. (1997) reasoned that the redintegration process would operate more successfully on high-frequency words than low-frequency words because the former's representations in long-term memory are more easily accessed by partial information—and hence are more likely to contribute to reconstruction. Accordingly, R should be greater for high- than for low-frequency items. Does it follow that high-frequency items should always be recalled better than their low-frequency counterparts? No, because redintegration is only required if information in memory is no longer intact. It follows that early list items, which are less subject to degradation during recall, will be largely intact; because they thus bypass the redintegration stage, their frequency should matter little. Later list items, by contrast, are degraded more by the time they are recalled, and hence redintegration becomes more important for them—and with it, the effect of word frequency should emerge. This is precisely what Hulme et al. found: High-frequency words were recalled better than low-frequency words, but that effect was primarily confined to later list positions. The data, when interpreted within the MPT model in Figure 1.6, therefore support the notion that word frequency affects the success of reconstruction of partially degraded memory traces but not their retention in short-term memory. Given the utmost simplicity of the MPT model, this is quite an interesting insight—and not one that can be confidently inferred from inspection of the data. Instead, Hulme et al. buttressed their conclusions by quantitatively examining the correspondence between the model's predictions and the data.

That said, the limitations of the MPT model are also noteworthy—and they set the stage for discussion of the next class of model. The MPT model may have identified and characterized a cognitive process known as redintegration, but it neither described nor explained that process. Is this even possible? Can we know more about redintegration? The answer is a clear yes, and providing that additional knowledge is the domain of process explanation models that we consider next. To wrap up this example, we briefly note that Lewandowsky (1999) and Lewandowsky and Farrell (2000) provided a detailed process account of redintegration that explains exactly how partial traces can be reconstructed. The Lewandowsky and Farrell model consists of a network of interconnected units that bounce information back and forth between them, adding bits and pieces from long-term memory to the degraded memory trace at each step, until the original item is perfectly reconstructed (instantiating R, in the MPT model's terminology) or another item is produced, in which case an error has occurred $(1 - R)$.[8] We now consider this class of models that not only identify processes but also explain them.

1.4.4   Process Explanation

What does it mean to explain, rather than merely characterize, a cognitive process? First, explanatory models provide the most close-up view inside the "black box" that is possible with current psychological techniques. Like characterization models, their power rests on hypothetical cognitive constructs, but by providing a detailed explanation of those constructs, they are no longer neutral. That is, whereas the MPT model in the previous section identified the redintegration stage but then remained neutral with respect to how exactly that reconstruction might occur, an explanatory process model (e.g., Lewandowsky & Farrell, 2000) goes further and removes any ambiguity about how that stage might operate.

At first glance, one might wonder why not every model belongs to this class: After all, if one can specify a process, why not do that rather than just identify and characterize it? The answer is twofold. First, it is not always possible to specify a presumed process at the level of detail required for an explanatory model, and in that case, a model such as the earlier MPT model might be a valuable alternative. Second, there are cases in which a coarse characterization may be preferable to a detailed specification. For example, it is vastly more important for a weatherman to know whether it is raining or snowing, rather than being confronted with the exact details of the water molecules' Brownian motion. Likewise, in psychology, modeling at this level has allowed theorists to identify common principles across seemingly disparate areas (G. D. A. Brown, Neath, & Chater, 2007).

That said, we believe that in most instances, cognitive scientists would ultimately prefer an explanatory process model over mere characterization, and the remainder of this book is thus largely (though not exclusively) devoted to that type of model.

There are countless explanatory models of cognitive phenomena ranging from reasoning through short-term memory to categorization, and we will be touching on many of those during the remaining chapters.

We begin our discussion by presenting a close-up of the exemplar model of categorization first presented in Section 1.3.1. We choose this model, known as the generalized context model (GCM; see, e.g., Nosofsky, 1986), for three reasons: First, it is undoubtedly one of the most influential and successful existing models of categorization. Second, its basic architecture is quite straightforward and readily implemented in something as simple as Microsoft Excel. Third, some of the GCM architecture also contributes to other important models of cognition, which we will consider in later chapters (e.g., SIMPLE in Chapter 4).

We already know that GCM is an exemplar model. As implied by that name, GCM stores every category exemplar encountered during training in memory. We mentioned an experiment earlier in which people learned to classify cartoon faces; in GCM, this procedure would be implemented by adding each stimulus to the pile of faces belonging to the same category. Remember that each response during training is followed by feedback, so people know whether a face belongs to a MacDonald or a Campbell at the end of each trial. Following training, GCM has thus built two sets of exemplars, one for each category, and all subsequent test stimuli are classified by referring to those memorized ensembles. This is where things get really interesting (and, refreshingly, a bit more complicated, but nothing you can't handle).

First, we need some terminology. Let us call a particular test stimulus i, and let us refer to the stored exemplars as the set $\mathfrak{J}$ with members $j = 1, 2, \ldots, J$, hence $j \in \mathfrak{J}$. This notation may seem like a bit of an overkill at first glance, but in fact it is useful to clarify a few things at the outset that we will use for the remainder of the book. Note that we use lowercase letters (e.g., i, j, $\ldots$) to identify specific elements of a set and that the number of elements in that set is identified by the same uppercase letters (I, J, $\ldots$), whereas the set itself is identified by the "Fraktur" version of the letter ($\mathfrak{I}$, $\mathfrak{J}$, $\ldots$). So, we have a single thing called i (or j or whatever), which is one of I elements of a set $\mathfrak{I}$.

We are now ready to consider the effects of presenting stimulus i. In a nutshell, a test stimulus "activates" all stored exemplars (remember, that's $j \in \mathfrak{J}$) to an extent that is determined by the *similarity* between i and each j. What exactly is similarity? GCM assumes that stimuli are represented in a perceptual space and that proximity within that space translates into similarity. To illustrate, consider the left panel (A) in Figure 1.7, which shows the perceptual representation of three hypothetical stimuli that differ along a single dimension—in this case, line length. The broken line labeled d represents the distance between two of those stimuli. It is easy to see that the greater this distance is, the *less* similar the two stimuli are. Conversely, the closer together two stimuli are, the greater their similarity.

Now consider Panel B. Here again we have three hypothetical stimuli, but this time they differ along two dimensions simultaneously—namely, distance and

A 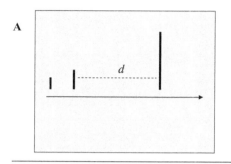   B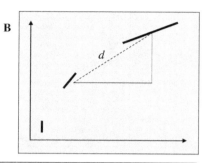

Figure 1.7 The representational assumptions underlying the generalized context model (GCM). Panel A shows stimuli that differ along one dimension only (line length), and Panel B shows stimuli that differ along two dimensions (line length and angle). In both panels, a representative distance (d) between two stimuli is shown by the broken line.

angle. Panel B again shows the distance (d) between two stimuli, which is formally given by the following equation:

$$d_{ij} = \left(\sum_{k=1}^{K} |x_{ik} - x_{jk}|^2 \right)^{\frac{1}{2}}, \tag{1.3}$$

where x_{ik} is the value of dimension k for test item i (let's say that's the middle stimulus in Panel B of Figure 1.7), and x_{jk} is the value of dimension k for the stored exemplar j (say, the right-most stimulus in the panel). The number of dimensions that enter into computation of the distance is arbitrary; the cartoon faces were characterized by four dimensions, but of course we cannot easily show more than two dimensions at a time. Those dimensions were eye height, eye separation, nose length, and mouth height. [9]

An easy way to understand Equation 1.3 is by realizing that it merely restates the familiar Pythagorean theorem (i.e., $d^2 = a^2 + b^2$), where a and b are the thin solid lines in Panel B of Figure 1.7, which are represented by the more general notation of dimensional differences (i.e., $x_{ik} - x_{jk}$) in the equation.

How, then, does distance relate to similarity? It is intuitively obvious that greater distances imply lesser similarity, but GCM explicitly postulates an exponential relationship of the following form:

$$s_{ij} = exp(-c \cdot d_{ij}), \tag{1.4}$$

where c is a parameter and d_{ij} the distance as just defined. Figure 1.8 (see page 22) visualizes this function and shows how the activation of an exemplar (i.e., s_{ij}) declines as a function of the distance (d_{ij}) between that exemplar and the test

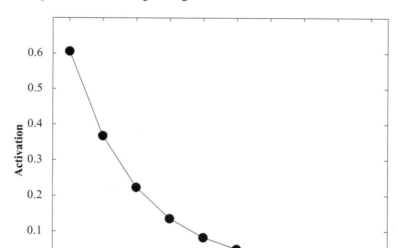

Figure 1.8 The effects of distance on activation in the GCM. Activation (i.e., s_{ij}) is shown as a function of distance (d_{ij}). The parameter c (see Equation 1.4) is set to .5.

stimulus. You may recognize that this function looks much like the famous generalization gradient that is observed in most situations involving discrimination (in species ranging from pigeons to humans; Shepard, 1987): This similarity is no coincidence; rather, it motivates the functional form of the similarity function in Equation 1.4. This similarity function is central to GCM's ability to generalize learned responses (i.e., cartoon faces seen during study) to novel stimuli (never-before-seen cartoon faces presented at test only).

It turns out that there is little left to do: Having presented a mechanism by which a test stimulus activates an exemplar according to its proximity in psychological space, we now compute those activations for *all* memorized exemplars. That is, we compute the distance d_{ij} between i and each $j \in \mathfrak{J}$ as given by Equation 1.3 and derive from that the activation s_{ij} as given by Equation 1.4. The next step is to convert the entire set of resulting activations into an explicit decision: Which category does the stimulus belong to? To accomplish this, the activations are summed separately across exemplars within each of the two categories. The relative magnitude of those two sums directly translates into response probabilities as follows:

$$P(R_i = A|i) = \frac{\left(\sum\limits_{j \in A} s_{ij}\right)}{\left(\sum\limits_{j \in A} s_{ij}\right) + \left(\sum\limits_{j \in B} s_{ij}\right)},$$ (1.5)

where A and B refer to the two possible categories, and $P(R_i = A|i)$ means "the probability of classifying stimulus i into category A." It follows that application of Equations 1.3 through 1.5 permits us to derive classification predictions from the GCM. It is those predictions that were plotted on the abscissa (x-axis) in the left panel of the earlier Figure 1.4, and it is those predictions that were found to be in such close accord with the data.

If this is your first exposure to quantitative explanatory models, the GCM may appear daunting at first glance. We therefore wrap up this section by taking a second tour through the GCM that connects the model more directly to the cartoon face experiment.

Figure 1.9 shows the stimuli used during training. Each of those faces corresponds to a memorized exemplar j that is represented by a set of dimensional values $\{x_{j1}, x_{j2}, \dots\}$, where each x_{jk} is the numeric value associated with dimension k. For example, if the nose of exemplar j has length 5, then $x_{j1} = 5$ on the assumption that the first dimension (arbitrarily) represents the length of the nose.

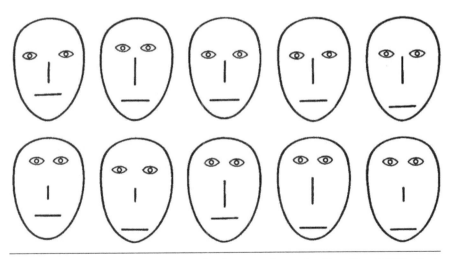

Figure 1.9 Stimuli used in a classification experiment by Nosofsky (1991). Each row shows training faces from one of the two categories. Figure reprinted from Nosofsky, R. M. (1991). Tests of an exemplar mode for relating perceptual classification and recognition memory. *Journal of Experimental Psychology: Human Perception and Performance, 17,* 3–27. Published by the American Psychological Association; reprinted with permission.

To obtain predictions from the model, we then present test stimuli (those shown in Figure 1.9 but also new ones to test the model's ability to generalize). Those test stimuli are coded in the same way as training stimuli—namely, by a set of dimensional values. For each test stimulus i, we first compute the distance between it and exemplar j (Equation 1.3). We next convert that distance to an activation of the memorized exemplar j (Equation 1.4) before summing across exemplars within each category (Equation 1.5) to obtain a predicted response probability. Do this for each stimulus in turn, and bingo, you have the model's complete set of predictions shown in Figure 1.4. How exactly are these computations performed? A whole range of options exists: If the number of exemplars and dimensions is small, a simple calculator, paper, and a pencil will do. More than likely, though, you will be using a computer package (such as a suitable worksheet in Excel) or a computer program (e.g., written in a language such as MATLAB or R). Regardless of how we perform these computations, we are assuming that they represent an analog of the processes used by people. That is, we presume that people remember exemplars and base their judgments on those memories alone, without access to rules or other abstractions.

At this point, one can usefully ponder two questions. First, why would we focus on an experiment that involves rather artificial cartoon faces? Do these stimuli and the associated data and modeling have any bearing on classification of "real-life" stimuli? Yes, in several ways. Not only can the GCM handle performance with large and ill-defined perceptual categories (McKinley & Nosofsky, 1995), but recent extensions of the model have been successfully applied to the study of natural concepts, such as fruits and vegetables (Verbeemen, Vanpaemel, Pattyn, Storms, & Verguts, 2007). The GCM thus handles a wide variety of both artificial and naturalistic categorizations. Second, one might wonder about the motivation underlying the equations that define the GCM. Why is distance related to similarity via an exponential function (Equation 1.4)? Why are responses determined in the manner shown in Equation 1.5? It turns out that for any good model—and the GCM is a good model—the choice of mathematics is not at all arbitrary but derived from some deeper theoretical principle. For example, the distance-similarity relationship in the GCM incorporates our knowledge about the "universal law of generalization" (Shepard, 1987), and the choice of response implements a theoretical approach first developed by Luce (1963).

What do you now know and what is left to do? You have managed to study your (possibly) first explanatory process model, and you should understand how the model can predict results for specific stimuli in a very specific experiment. However, a few obstacles remain to be overcome, most of which relate to the "how" of applying the model to data. Needless to say, those topics will be covered in subsequent chapters.

1.4.5   Classes of Models

We sketched out three broad classes of models. We considered descriptive models whose sole purpose it is to replace the intricacies of a full data set with a simpler representation in terms of the model's parameters. Although those models themselves have no psychological content, they may well have compelling psychological implications.

We then considered two classes of models that both seek to illuminate the workings of the mind, rather than data, but do so to a greatly varying extent. Models that characterize processes identify and measure cognitive stages, but they are neutral with respect to the exact mechanics of those stages. Explanatory models, by contrast, describe all cognitive processes in great detail and leave nothing within their scope unspecified.[10]

Other distinctions between models are possible and have been proposed (e.g., Luce, 1995; Marr, 1982; Sun, Coward, & Zenzen, 2005), and we make no claim that our classification is better than other accounts. Unlike other accounts, however, our three classes of models map into three distinct tasks that confront cognitive scientists: Do we want to describe data? Do we want to identify and characterize broad stages of processing? Do we want to explain how exactly a set of postulated cognitive processes interact to produce the behavior of interest?

1.5   What Can We Expect From Models?

We have explored some of the powerful insights that are afforded by quantitative modeling. However, all examples so far were demonstrations that one model or another could provide a good quantitative account of otherwise inexplicable data—impressive, perhaps, but is that all we can expect from models? Is a "good fit" between a model's predictions and the data the one and only goal of modeling? The answer is no; there are several other ways in which models can inform scientific progress.

1.5.1   Classification of Phenomena

It is intuitively obvious that, at least at the current level of understanding in our science, all models will necessarily be limited in their explanatory power. Every model will be confronted sooner or later with data that it cannot accommodate. So, if every model is doomed to fail, why spend considerable time and effort on its development in the first place? One answer to this conundrum was provided by Estes (1975), who suggested that even the mere classification of phenomena into those that fall within and those that fall outside a model's scope can be very informative: "What we hope for primarily from models is that they will bring out relationships between experiments or sets of data that we would not otherwise have perceived. The fruit of an interaction between model and data should be a new categorization of phenomena in which observations are organized in terms of a rational scheme in contrast to the surface demarcations manifest in data" (p. 271).

Even if we find that it takes two different models to handle two distinct subclasses of phenomena, this need not be at all bad but may in fact crystallize an interesting question. In physics, for example, for a very long time, light was alternately considered as a wave or a stream of particles. The two models were able to capture a different subset of phenomena, with no cross-linkage between those sets of phenomena and the two theories. Although this state was perhaps not entirely satisfactory, it clearly did not retard progress in physics.

In psychology, we suggest that models have similarly permitted a classification of phenomena in categorization. We noted earlier that the GCM is a powerful model that has had a profound impact on our understanding of how people classify stimuli. However, there are also clear limits on the applicability of the GCM. For example, Rouder and Ratcliff (2004) showed that the GCM captures people's behavior only when the stimuli are few and highly discriminable. When there is a large ensemble of confusable stimuli, by contrast, people's behavior is better captured by a rule model rather than the GCM's exemplar representation (more on this in Chapter 7). Likewise, Little and Lewandowsky (2009) showed that in a complex probabilistic categorization task, some people will build an exemplar representation, whereas others will create an ensemble of partial rules; the former were described well by the GCM, but the latter were best described by a rule model. Taken together, those studies serve to delineate the applicability of two competing theoretical approaches—namely, rules versus exemplars—somewhat akin to the differentiation between wave and particle theories of light.

1.5.2   Emergence of Understanding

The models we consider in this book are, almost by definition, always implemented as a computer program. Computers, however, only do as they are programmed to do—does it not follow that our models, unlike behavioral experiments, will never generate anything truly novel or unexpected? Indeed, some time ago, this opinion appeared to reflect accepted practice (e.g., Reitman, 1965). Since then, it has become apparent that this opinion is flawed. There have been innumerable instances in which models have generated novel insights in nontrivial ways, many of which involved artificial neural networks. (Networks contain many interconnected units that process and transmit information.) For example,

Seidenberg and McClelland (1989) presented a network that could learn to pronounce both regular (*lint*) and irregular (*pint*) words from printed input: It was not at all clear prior to the modeling being conducted that a uniform architecture could handle both types of words. Indeed, a "central dogma" (Seidenberg & McClelland, 1989, p. 525) of earlier models had been that two processes were required to accommodate irregular words (via lexical lookup) and regular (non)words (via pronunciation rules).

As another example, Botvinick and Plaut (2006) recently presented a network model of short-term memory that was able to learn the highly abstract ability of "seriation"—namely, the ability to reproduce *novel random sequences* of stimuli. Thus, after learning the skill, the model was capable of reproducing short serial lists. Thus, when presented with "A K P Q B," the model would reproduce that sequence after a single presentation with roughly the same accuracy and subject to the same performance constraints as humans. This might appear like a trivial feat at first glance, but it is not: It is insufficient to learn pairwise contingencies such as "A precedes B" because in a random list, A might precede B as frequently as B precedes A. Likewise, it is insufficient to learn that "A occurs in position 1" because in fact A could occur in any position, and so on for any other specific arrangements of letters (triplets, quadruplets, etc.). Instead, the model had to learn the highly abstract ability "whatever I see I will try to reproduce in the same order" from a small subset of all possible sequences. This abstract ability, once learned, could then be transferred to novel sequences.

In summary, the point that models can yield unexpected and novel insights was perhaps best summed up by Fum et al. (2007): "New ways of understanding may assume several forms. They can derive, for instance, from the discovery of a single unifying principle that will explain a set of hitherto seemingly unrelated facts. They can lead to the emergence of complex, holistic forms of behavior from the specification of simple local rules of interaction. New ways of understanding can arise from unexpected results that defy the modelers intuition" (p. 136).

1.5.3   Exploration of Implications

Unlike people, models can quite literally be taken apart. For example, we can "lesion" models to observe the outcome on behavior of certain localized dysfunctions. As a case in point, consider the model by Hinton and Shallice (1991), which was trained to map a set of orthographic representations into semantic features, so that presentation of a spelling pattern would activate the correct "word" at the semantic output level of their network. After training, Hinton and Shallice lesioned their model in various ways—for example, by removing units, by contaminating the connections between units with random noise, or by eliminating some connections altogether.

Hinton and Shallice found that virtually any such lesioning of their network, irrespective of location, led to a persistent co-occurrence of visual (*cat* read as *mat*) and semantic (*peach* read as *apricot*) errors. This generality elegantly explained why this mix of visual and semantic errors is common across a wide range of patients whose performance deficits differ considerably in other respects.

We can draw two conclusions from this example: First, it clarifies the in-principle point that one can do things to models that one cannot do to people, and that those lesioning experiments can yield valuable knowledge. Second, the fact that the results in this instance were surprising lends further support to the point made in the previous section—namely, that models can show emergent properties that are not at all apparent by verbal analysis alone.

1.6   Potential Problems

We conclude by discussing two issues that must be considered to ensure a complete understanding of the basic principles of modeling.

1.6.1   Scope and Testability

Suppose you are a venture capitalist and a scientist approaches you for funding to develop a new theory that will revolutionize gambling. A first version of the theory exists, and it has been extremely successful because it probabilistically characterized the outcomes of 20 successive rolls of a die. In quantitative terms, the theory anticipated each individual outcome with $P = 1/6$. Would you be impressed? We trust that you are not, because any theory that predicts any possible outcome with equal facility is of little scientific interest, even if it happens to be in complete accord with the data (e.g., Roberts & Pashler, 2000). This is quite obvious with our fictitious "theory" of gambling, but it is less obvious—though nonetheless equally applicable—with psychological theories.

Let us reconsider one of the earlier examples: Nosofsky (1991) showed that an exemplar model (the GCM) can integrate people's recognition and classification responses under a common theoretical umbrella (see Figure 1.4). We considered this to be impressive, especially because the GCM performed better than a competing prototype theory, but was our satisfaction justified? What if the exemplar model could have equally explained any other possible relationship between recognition and classification and not just the one shown in Figure 1.3? Indeed, in that case, one would need to be quite concerned about the exemplar model's viability as a testable and falsifiable psychological theory.[11] Fortunately, however, these concerns can be allayed by the fact that the exemplar model is at least in principle subject to falsification, as revealed by some of the results mentioned earlier that place limits on the GCM's applicability (e.g., Little & Lewandowsky, 2009; Rouder & Ratcliff, 2004; Yang & Lewandowsky, 2004).

We are now faced with a conundrum: On the one hand, we want our theories to explain data. We want powerful theories, such as Kepler's, that explain fundamental aspects of our universe. We want powerful theories, such as Darwin's, to explain the diversity of life. On the other hand, we want the theories to be falsifiable—that is, we want to be assured that there are at least *hypothetical* outcomes that, if they are ever observed, *would* falsify a theory. For example, Darwin's theory of evolution predicts a strict sequence in which species evolved; hence, any observation to the contrary in the fossil record—for example, human bones co-occurring with dinosaur remains in the same geological strata (e.g., Root-Bernstein, 1981)—would seriously challenge the theory. This point is sufficiently important to bear repetition: Even though we are convinced that Darwin's theory of evolution, one of the most elegant and powerful achievements of human thought, is true, we simultaneously also want it to be falsifiable—falsi*fiable*, not false.[12] Likewise, we are committed to the idea that the earth orbits around the sun, rather than the other way round, but as scientists, we accept that fact only because it is based on a theory that is falsifiable—again, falsi*fiable*, not false.

Roberts and Pashler (2000) considered the issue of falsifiability and scope with reference to psychological models and provided an elegant graphical summary that is reproduced in Figure 1.10. The figure shows four hypothetical outcome spaces that are formed by two behavioral measures. What those measures represent is totally arbitrary; they could be trials to a criterion in a memory experiment and a final recognition score or any other pair of measures of interest.

Within each panel, the dotted area represents all possible predictions that are within the scope of a psychological theory. The top row of panels represents some hypothetical theory whose predictions are constrained to a narrow range of outcomes; any outcome outside the dotted sliver would constitute contrary evidence, and only the narrow range of values within the sliver would constitute supporting evidence. Now compare that sliver to the bottom row of panels with its very generous dotted areas; the theory shown here is compatible with nearly all possible outcomes. It follows that any observed outcome that falls within a dotted area would offer greater support for the theory in the top row than the bottom row, simply because the likelihood of falsification is greater for the former than the latter, thus rendering the match between data and predictions far less likely—and hence more informative when it occurs (see Dunn, 2000, for a similar but more formalized view). Ideally, we would want our theories to occupy only a small region of the outcome space but for all observed outcomes to fall within that region—as they do for Kepler's and Darwin's theories.[13]

Another important aspect of Figure 1.10 concerns the quality of the data, which is represented by the columns of panels. The data (shown by the single

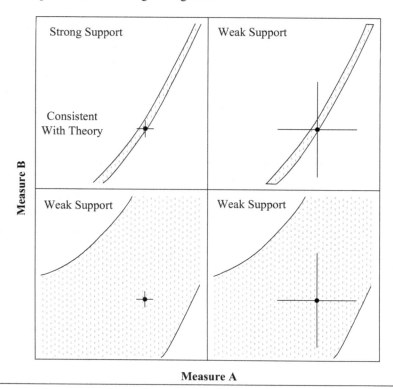

Figure 1.10 Four possible hypothetical relationships between theory and data involving two measures of behavior (A and B). Each panel describes a hypothetical outcome space permitted by the two measures. The shaded areas represent the predictions of a theory that differs in predictive scope (narrow and broad in the top and bottom panels, respectively). The error bars represent the precision of the observed data (represented by the black dot). See text for details. Figure reprinted from Roberts, S., & Pashler, H. (2000). How persuasive is a good fit? A comment on theory testing. *Psychological Review, 107,* 358–367. Published by the American Psychological Association; reprinted with permission.

black point bracketed by error bars) exhibit less variability in the left column of panels than in the right. For now, we note briefly that support for the theory is thus strongest in the top left panel; beyond that, we defer discussion of the important role of data to Chapter 6. That chapter will also provide another in-depth and more formal look at the issue of testability and falsifiability.

Let us now turn from the abstract representation in Figure 1.10 to a specific recent instance in which two theories were compared by exploration of an outcome space. Howard, Jing, Rao, Provyn, and Datey (2009) examined the nature of associations among list items. Their study was quite complex, but their central question of interest can be stated quite simply: Are associations between list items symmetrical or asymmetrical? That is, given a to-be-memorized list such

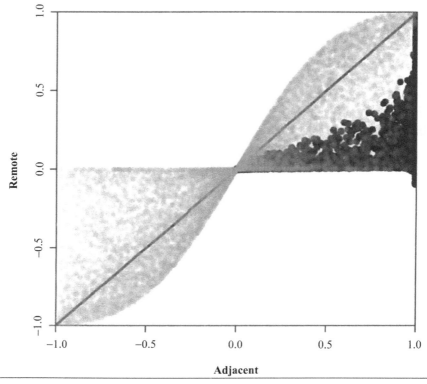

Figure 1.11 Outcome space covered by two models examined by Howard, Jing, Rao, Provyn, and Datey (2009). An index of remote asymmetry is shown as a function of an index of adjacent asymmetry for a variety of parameter values for two models (referred to here as "black" and "gray," corresponding to the color of their plotting symbols). See text for details. Figure reprinted from Howard, M. W., Jing, B., Rao, V. A., Provyn, J. P., & Datey, A. V. (2009). Bridging the gap: Transitive associations between items presented in similar temporal contexts. *Journal of Experimental Psychology: Learning, Memory & Cognition, 35*, 391–407. Published by the American Psychological Association; reprinted with permission.

as "A B C D," is the association from A to B as strong as the association from B to A? Can you recall B when given A as a cue with equal facility as recalling A when given B? And how does the extent of symmetry vary with list position? Empirically, it turns out that adjacent associations (such as between A and B) are asymmetric and stronger in a forward direction, whereas remote associations (such as between A and D) are symmetrical. Howard et al. (2009) compared the abilities of two theories (whose identity is irrelevant in this context) to capture this pattern of symmetries; the pattern of predictions for the two rival theories is shown in Figure 1.11.

The figure shows an outcome space involving two measures—namely, indices of symmetry for adjacent and remote associations. In Howard et al.'s (2009) experiment, the observed values were .25 and .03, respectively. The dark and gray point clouds in the figure, respectively, represent the possible predictions of the two models under consideration. The figure suggests the following conclusions: First, both models can handle the data (i.e., their prediction regions contain the point .25, .03). Second, the "gray" model covers a much larger region of the outcome space than the "black" model, including regions in which remote asymmetry is greater than adjacent symmetry, something that has never been observed in the data. Third, it follows that the "black" model is supported more by these data than the "gray" model. (This conclusion is also supported by other results not shown in the figure, but for present purposes, we focus only on the trade-off between scope and falsifiability.) Note how the large area covered by the "gray" model corresponds to the hypothetical situation in the bottom panels of Figure 1.10, whereas the small area covered by the "black" model corresponds to the situation in the top panels.

1.6.2   Identification and Truth

Throughout our discussion, we have emphasized the existence of multiple alternative models to explain the same data. We considered the Ptolemaic and the Copernican system, we contrasted Nosofsky's (1986) GCM exemplar theory with a prototype model, and we repeatedly underscored the need for model selection. Our discussion entailed two tacit assumptions: first, that we can identify the "correct" model and, second, that there is such a thing as a "true" model. It turns out that both of those assumptions are most likely wrong. So why do we nonetheless advocate modeling? What are the implications of the fact that models may be neither identifiable nor true?

Let us first clarify what exactly the problem concerning model identification does and does not imply. First, it is important to realize that this problem is not unique to psychology but applies to all sciences; we noted earlier that in addition to Kepler's model, an *infinite number of equivalent models* can adequately capture planetary motion. Does this invalidate our view of the solar system? No, it does not, because as we also noted earlier, criteria other than goodness of fit help differentiate between models. So, the fact that in cognitive science, just like in astronomy, "there undoubtedly exists a very diverse set of models, but all equivalent in that they predict the behavior of humans at cognitive tasks" (J. R. Anderson, 1976, p. 4) is true in principle but not particularly troubling.

Second, the fact that there exist, in principle, many equivalent models does not imply that *all* models are equally capable. Indeed, we have shown throughout this chapter that some models handle the data better than others. It is therefore clearly possible to choose one model over another, even if (in principle) the chosen model is equivalent to many unknown others. Simply put, the fact that there are many good models out there does not prevent us from rejecting the bad ones.

Third, the mere existence of equivalent models does not imply that they have been—or indeed will be—discovered. In our experience, it is difficult enough to select a single suitable model, let alone worry about the existence of an infinite number of equivalent competitors.

Finally, even supposing that we must select from among a number of competing models of equivalent capability (i.e., equal goodness of fit), some fairly straightforward considerations have been put forward to achieve this (see, e.g., Fum et al., 2007). We revisit this issue in detail in Chapter 5.

Now let us turn to the issue concerning the "truth" of a model. Is there such a thing as one true model? And if not, what are the implications of that? The answer to the first question is strongly implied by the preceding discussion, and it was most clearly stated by MacCallum (2003): "Regardless of their form or function, or the area in which they are used, it is safe to say that these models all have one thing in common: *They are all wrong*" (p. 114). Now what?

To answer this question, we again briefly digress into astronomy by noting that Kepler's model, being based on Newtonian physics, is—you guessed it—wrong. We now know that Newtonian physics is "wrong" because it does not capture the phenomena associated with relativity. Does this mean that the earth is in fact not orbiting around the sun? No, it does not, because Kepler's model is nonetheless useful because within the realm for which it was designed—planetary motion— Newtonian physics holds to an acceptable degree. Likewise, in psychology, our wrong models can nonetheless be useful (MacCallum, 2003). We show exactly how wrong models can still be useful at the end of the next chapter, after we introduce a few more essential tools and concepts.

Notes

1. Lest one think that the heliocentric and geocentric models exhaust all possible views of the solar system, it is worth clarifying that there is an infinite number of equivalent models that can adequately capture planetary motion because relative motion can be described with respect to *any* possible vantage point.

2. *Goodness of fit* is a term for the degree of quantitative error between a model's predictions and the data; this important term and many others are discussed in detail in Chapter 2.

3. Astute readers may wonder how the two could possibly differ. The answer lies in the fact that the similarity rule involved in the comparisons by the exemplar model is nonlinear; hence, the summed individual similarities differ from that involving the average. This nonlinearity turns out to be crucial to the model's overall power. The fact that subtle matters of arithmetic can have such drastic consequences further reinforces the notion that purely verbal theorizing is of limited value.

4. Another lesson that can be drawn from this example is a rejoinder to the popular but largely misplaced criticism that with enough ingenuity and patience, a modeler can always get a model to work.

5. Several distinctions between models have been proposed (e.g., Luce, 1995); ours differs from relevant precedents by being explicitly psychological and being driven entirely by considerations that are relevant to the cognitive researcher.

6. We will provide a detailed definition of what a parameter is in Chapter 2. For now, it suffices to think of a parameter as a number that carries important information and that determines the behavior of the model.

7. Some readers may have noticed that in this instance, there are two parameters (I and R) and two data points (proportion correct and errors; C and R), which renders the model nonidentifiable. We ignore this issue here for simplicity of exposition; for a solution, see Hulme et al. (1997).

8. This model is a connectionist model, and these are discussed further in Chapter 8.

9. For simplicity, we omit discussion of how these *psychological* distances relate to the physical measurement (e.g., line length in cm) of the stimuli; these issues are covered in, for example, Nosofsky (1986).

10. Of course, a cognitive model may leave other levels of explanation unspecified, for example, the underlying neural circuitry. However, at the level of abstraction within which the model is formulated, nothing can be left unspecified.

11. Throughout this book, we use the terms *falsifiable* and *testable* interchangeably to denote the same idea—namely, that at least in principle, there are some possible outcome(s) that are incompatible with the theory's predictions.

12. Despite its falsifiability, Darwin's theory has a perfect track record of its predictions being uniformly confirmed; Coyne (2009) provides an insightful account of the impressive list of successes.

13. It is important to clarify that, in our view, this argument should apply only with respect to a particular measurement. That is, for any given measurement, we prefer theories that could have only predicted a subset of all possible observations over theories that could have predicted pretty much any outcome. However, it does not follow that we prefer theories that are so narrow in scope that they only apply to a single experiment; on the contrary, we prefer theories that apply to a range of different situations.

2

From Words to Models: Building a Toolkit

Let us turn some of the ideas of the preceding chapter into practice. We begin by presenting an influential model of working memory that has been stated at a verbal level (A. D. Baddeley, 1986), and we then take you through the steps required to instantiate this verbal model in a computer simulation. Along the way, we introduce you to MATLAB, which is a programming environment that is particularly suitable for developing computer simulations. We conclude the chapter with a toolkit of terms and concepts and some further thoughts about modeling that are essential for your understanding of the remainder of the book.

2.1 Working Memory

The munchies strike. Time for a pizza. Your roommate recites the number of her favorite delivery outlet and you proceed to dial it, only to discover that you can remember no more than the first 3 digits. Or imagine you are at a party and someone introduces you to another visitor (the 14th person you meet that night). You get distracted briefly and, oops, what was his name again? We are all familiar with situations like these, in which we (sometimes too) briefly remember snippets of information—an ability that is the domain of "short-term" or "working" memory and that turns out to be central to much of human cognition. For example, mental arithmetic would be impossible without memory for intermediate sums, and we can only understand a spoken sentence such as "while Bob hunted the deer ran into the woods" by reexamining already heard material to resolve our initially incorrect understanding. It is perhaps unsurprising, therefore, that the capacity of our working memories predicts higher level cognitive abilities with considerable precision (e.g., Oberauer, Süß, Wilhelm, & Sander, 2007).

The importance of working memory is reflected in the large number of models that describe and explain its functioning (e.g., A. D. Baddeley, 1986; G. D. A. Brown et al., 2007; Burgess & Hitch, 1999; Lewandowsky & Farrell, 2008b; Oberauer & Kliegl, 2006). Here, we focus on the highly influential model by Baddeley (e.g., 1986; see also A. D. Baddeley & Hitch, 1974). The model assumes that working memory consists of several interacting components, most crucially a "visuospatial sketchpad" that is dedicated to the processing of visual (as opposed to verbal) information and a "phonological loop" that is dedicated to the retention of verbal information. The model contains a number of additional components, such as a "central executive" and a (recently added) "episodic buffer," but for present purposes, we restrict consideration to the phonological loop.

2.1.1   The Phonological Loop

The phonological loop rests on two elegant and simple assumptions: Information that has entered the loop is subject to rapid temporal decay. Decay cannot be prevented, but the contents of memory can be refreshed by (overt or subvocal) articulatory rehearsal. With the aid of these two opposing processes, the model can accommodate a surprisingly wide range of findings. For example, the fact that recall of verbal lists declines dramatically when people pronounce irrelevant material during encoding (a manipulation known as "articulatory suppression") follows directly from the fact that rehearsal is prevented by articulation, thus revealing the underlying inexorable temporal decay. Conversely, when rehearsal is possible, the model can accommodate the pervasive finding (e.g., A. D. Baddeley, Thomson, & Buchanan, 1975; Mueller, Seymour, Kieras, & Meyer, 2003) that lists composed of long words (e.g., *hippopotamus*, *helicopter*) are recalled less accurately than lists of short words (e.g., *pig*, *bus*). The poorer memory for long words than short words has been taken to reflect the fact that in comparison to short words, fewer long words can be recalled or refreshed by rehearsal in the limited time before decay has rendered the trace irrecoverable.

This so-called word length effect (WLE from here on) is very robust, and it is generally the case that words containing more syllables are recalled more poorly than words with few syllables.[1] Illustrative data that show this effect are shown in Figure 2.1, which plots performance on a five-item list as a function of "speech rate." Speech rate is the number of times that words of a given number of syllables can be spoken aloud in one second. High speech rates correspond to short words (and low rates to long words), which explains why performance increases with speech rate (and by implication decreases with word length).

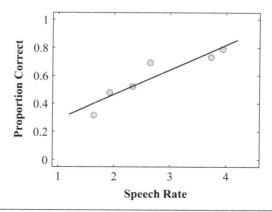

Figure 2.1 Memory performance on a five-item list as a function of speech rate for 7- and 10-year-olds. Long words such as *helicopter* translate into a low speech rate (because few long words can be articulated in a second), and shorter words (*e.g., bus*) translate into high speech rates. The solid line is the regression line. Data taken from Hulme, C., & Tordoff, V. (1989). Working memory development: The effects of speech rate, word-length, and acoustic similarity on serial recall. *Journal of Experimental Child Psychology, 47,* 72–87.

These data strongly imply that your social graces will be greatly facilitated if the people you meet at a party are called Bob, Pat, Ben, or Buzz, rather than Vladimir, Chathuranga, Konstantin, or Phillipa. What was that guy standing next to Vladimir called again?

2.1.2   Theoretical Accounts of the Word Length Effect

At first glance, the case appears closed: We have an elegant model that proposes that information rapidly decays from memory unless refreshed by rehearsal, and we have supporting data that show that memory declines with the time it takes to pronounce (and thus rehearse) words. Upon closer inspection, however, this seemingly shut case is just the beginning of an exciting empirical and theoretical journey. We summarize this journey in Figure 2.2. Our departure point is the situation shown in panel (a)—namely, a one-to-one mapping between a model and a key piece of supporting evidence. There are two major problems with this scenario.

First, at an empirical level, words such as *helicopter* differ from their shorter counterparts in more ways than just pronunciation duration. For example, they contain more syllables, they may be less frequently used during normal speech, and so on. This is an in-principle problem, because try as you might, you can never be sure that short and long words *only* differ in pronunciation duration but nothing

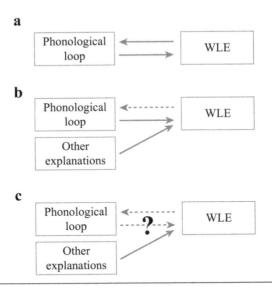

Figure 2.2 The evolution of our understanding of the relationship between a model (in this instance, the phonological loop) and a key piece of supporting data (in this case, the word length effect or WLE). Panel (a) shows the initially presumed situation in which the model predicts the WLE and is, in turn, uniquely supported by those data. Panel (b) shows that the supporting role of the data is weakened by the existence of alternative explanations. Panel (c) shows that the phonological loop may not even predict the WLE in the first place. See text for details.

else, given the many variables along which words differ in natural language. It follows that—notwithstanding its ubiquity—the WLE may be of limited theoretical diagnosticity because it can arise from processes other than decay (e.g., differing levels of phonological complexity; for details, see Lewandowsky & Oberauer, 2008).

Second, at a theoretical level, it is known that the data in Figure 2.1 can be explained by models that do not rely on decay (e.g., G. D. A. Brown & Hulme, 1995; Lewandowsky & Farrell, 2000). The existence of alternative explanations, then, creates the situation in panel (b) in Figure 2.2: The supporting link between the data and the model is weakened because the WLE is no longer uniquely and exclusively compatible with the phonological loop.

In fact, we may take an even more radical step by asking whether the phonological loop model even predicts the very data that constitute its principal support. Although this question might seem awfully contrived at first glance, you may remember that we began this book with a chapter devoted to demonstrating the vagaries of verbal theorizing; might this be another instance in which a verbal model behaves differently from what is expected at first glance?

To address this issue, we now illuminate the steps involved in constructing a computer simulation of the phonological loop. This step-by-step process converges on two principal conclusions that we foreshadow here: First, we will find that it is *possible* to instantiate the phonological loop in a computer simulation that reproduces the crucial data in Figure 2.1. This is not surprising, given that several such simulation models already exist (e.g., Burgess & Hitch, 1999; Page & Norris, 1998b), and it underscores one of the benefits of computational modeling—namely, that it forces us to instantiate all postulated mechanisms with great exactitude.

Second, we will discover that there are *many* possible instantiations of the phonological loop, all of which plausibly implement the axioms of the verbal model, but each of which is based on a different set of decisions about the exact mechanisms. Thus, A. D. Baddeley's (1986) verbal theory of working memory actually constitutes an entire *family* of possible models. Although we cannot explore this entire family here, we show that at least some models in this family make predictions that diverge from the data, thus creating the situation shown in panel (c) in Figure 2.2. The fact that the verbal model as originally formulated may not even predict the data that constitute its central support suggests that it may be resistant to empirical constraints or falsification.

2.2 The Phonological Loop: 144 Models of Working Memory

How can we implement the phonological loop in a computer model? This turns out to be far from straightforward because the verbal model leaves many things unspecified. For example, it does not explain how the order among items is represented—it merely *assumes* that they can be recycled in the correct order during rehearsal or recall. The model also does not tell us what it is that actually decays; surely it cannot be your knowledge of the word *helicopter*, but if that does not decay, what does? Conversely, what does rehearsal actually do? Surely it does not make you more knowledgeable about helicopters, so what does it do?

Instantiating the verbal model therefore requires making a large number of decisions to fill in those blanks. Some of those decisions may have far-reaching consequences, and none are constrained by the verbal model. There are two classes of decisions: First, we must resolve "deep" representational issues. For example, we must decide whether to use a "localized" representation (whereby each item is stored in a unique location) or a "distributed" scheme (whereby an item's representation is spread across numerous locations, and it is the collective overall pattern that identifies the item). For present purposes, we chose to represent list

Table 2.1 Summary of Decisions Necessary to Implement the Phonological Loop Model in a Simulation

Decision Point	N Alternatives	Our Decision
(1) Begin of decay	2	After list
(2) Decay function	3	Linear
(3) Decay rate	2	Variable [a]
(4) Recall success	2	Thresholded
(5) Recall errors	3	Omissions only
(6) Rehearsal sequence	2	Ordered

[a]We explore this choice point below by comparing several alternative simulations.

items in a localized manner, by the activation of single dedicated units. For simplicity, we represented order among the items by using their subscripts in the memory array as "positional markers." Another simplifying assumption was that all items were assumed to be encoded with equal strength.

The second class of decisions involves more technical issues, such as the exact mechanics of rehearsal and decay. We highlight these technical issues because they illustrate the necessary decision-making process particularly well. To provide a road map for what follows, we summarize our technical decisions in Table 2.1. The pattern of our decisions (right-most column) describes our preferred instantiation of the phonological loop; that is, if this particular set of decisions is taken, then, as you will see shortly, the resulting computer simulation will reproduce the data in Figure 2.1. The table also contains a column that lists the number of possible alternatives at each choice point.[2] Because the choices are for the most part independent, the total number of distinct models that could have been constructed to instantiate the phonological loop model is given by their product—namely, 144.

2.2.1   Decay Process

The phonological loop model postulates that memory representations decay rapidly. But when does decay commence? Immediately upon encoding of each item, irrespective of how many others have already been encoded? Or only once list presentation is complete? Once decay commences, does it continue unabated during rehearsal or recall? Perhaps the most elegant assumption is to postulate that each item, once encoded, inexorably decays until it is forgotten or recalled and that any intervening rehearsal briefly "resets" the decay. Alas, this mechanism is prohibitively sophisticated for one's first simulation, and we therefore make the simplifying assumption that decay does not commence until list presentation is complete. Lest one think that this assumption is unduly simplistic, it should be noted that it is shared by at least one other instantiation of the phonological loop (Page & Norris, 1998b).[3]

We must next consider the exact functional form of decay. In a simulation, it is insufficient to speak of "decay" without specifying a function: That is, for each second delay, is there a constant loss of information (i.e., a linear decay function), or is the loss proportional (i.e., exponential)? Most decay models assume that decay is exponential (e.g., Page & Norris, 1998b); indeed, a linear decay function makes limited sense because, unless accompanied by a lower bound, it necessarily predicts that long temporal delays can result in "negative memories." Nonetheless, bearing in mind this caveat, we chose a linear decay function for simplicity.

Finally, we must decide whether the decay is constant or variable. That is, does each item for each participant decay at the same rate, or is there some variability? This decision turns out to be crucial, and we will therefore explore more than one option below; we begin by assuming that decay is constant across items and people.

2.2.2   Recall Process

How do memory representations get accessed during recall, and how are they converted into performance? The decisions made thus far constrain the recall process considerably; in particular, the use of positional markers implies that recall involves interrogation of each marker and retrieval of the associated item. Nonetheless, several decisions remain to be made concerning the nature of errors. First, is it *always* possible to retrieve an item? Or is there some minimum threshold below which we consider an item to have been forgotten? This decision is straightforward because it makes little sense to assume that items decay without also assuming that they decay to a point at which retrieval becomes impossible. Hence, we assume that there is an activation threshold below which an item will not be recalled.

Second, people on occasion recall items that were not in fact on the list. How might this be possible in our simulation? People also frequently report list items in the wrong order (Henson, Norris, Page, & Baddeley, 1996); how might this be modeled? It turns out that modeling of intrusions (i.e., report of extra-list items) and transpositions (e.g., report in incorrect order) requires more complex assumptions than we can make here in this introductory example. We therefore do not model transpositions or intrusions in these first simulations.

2.2.3   Rehearsal

Did you keep track of how many decisions we have made so far? If you have tracked our progress through Table 2.1, you will have noticed that we have journeyed past 5 choice points and that we have selected one particular model from among 72 options. And we had to do this simply to implement the postulate of the phonological-loop model that information in short-term memory decays rapidly—a seemingly straightforward postulate that turns out to be compatible with not one but more than 70 actual models. We return to the implications of this many-to-one mapping after we present our simulation results.

Let us now turn to the second postulate of the phonological-loop model; namely, that decay can be counteracted by articulatory rehearsal. What exactly is rehearsal? There is considerable evidence that rehearsal can take several different forms (e.g., Hudjetz & Oberauer, 2007); namely, one that is verbal-articulatory and another that is non-verbal and "attentional." Within the phonological-loop framework, rehearsal is considered to be articulatory and we inherit this assumption here. Moreover, following much precedent (see Tan & Ward, 2008, for a brief review), we assume that rehearsal is equivalent to recall; that is, recitation of a list during rehearsal is nothing but repeated recall of that list (albeit subvocally in most cases). This assumption simplifies our modeling decisions considerably because, having already specified a recall process, we can readily adapt it for rehearsal.

In particular, we assume that rehearsal is ordered (i.e., people rehearse in order, from the beginning of the list to the end), an assumption supported by data (Tan & Ward, 2008).[4] We furthermore assume that rehearsal restores the memory representations to their original state—in that sense, rehearsal is not only identical to recall but also isomorphic to a further presentation of the list. As during recall, only those items are restored that have not been completely forgotten. Likewise, as in recall, any items not completely forgotten are restored in their correct position, and no extra-list intrusions are possible.

This, then, finalizes our decisions about how to implement the phonological-loop model. We have settled on one of at least 144 possible instantiations of the verbal model by making the sequence of decisions just outlined. It is important to note that we make no claim that those were the only possible decisions; on the contrary, our decisions were guided primarily by the desire to keep things tractable rather than by the intention to maximize psychological plausibility. Let's see whether our decisions still produced a plausible model.

2.3   Building a Simulation

2.3.1   MATLAB

There are numerous ways in which models can be instantiated in a computer simulation. We rely on the popular MATLAB programming language, and all examples in this book assume that you have access to MATLAB and that you have at least some limited knowledge of how to use it.

We cannot teach you MATLAB programming from the ground up in this book. However, all programming examples that we provide in this book are extensively commented, and it should require only some limited assistance for you to reproduce those examples, even if you have no programming background at all. All of our programs are available at the supporting webpage, http://www.cogsciwa.com, which also contains external links to other important and useful sites. One such external site is "MATLAB Central," which is a facility maintained by Mathworks Inc., the company that produces and maintains MATLAB. This site contains a huge (and growing) archive of numerous MATLAB programs that are contributed by programmers from around the world; we will occasionally refer to MATLAB Central in the remaining chapters. You can browse to MATLAB Central via our supporting webpage.

In addition, there are numerous books available that can assist you in learning MATLAB. Rosenbaum's (2007) book is aimed specifically at behavioral scientists and may therefore be of particular value; we also link to a number of other texts at our supporting webpage.

Why did we choose MATLAB? Why do we think it is worth your while to learn it? We chose MATLAB because it provides a vast array of functions that can perform many of the operations required in computer simulations (e.g., drawing random numbers from a variety of distributions) with great ease. The existence of those functions allows programmers to focus on the crucial elements of their modeling without having to worry about nitty-gritty details. We will next see exactly how that is done.

2.3.2 The Target Methodology

To provide a specific context for the simulation, we first revisit the exact method underlying the results shown in Figure 2.1. Hulme and Tordoff (1989) were interested in the development of the phonological loop in children, and they examined the effects of speech rate in 4-, 7-, and 10-year-olds. Here, we focus on the 7- and 10-year-old children who were presented with lists of five words. Words were presented at the rate of one per second, and the child verbally recalled the list immediately after presentation in the order presented, saying "blank" if a word could not be recalled. The average proportion of words (out of a possible five) that were recalled in their correct position is shown on the ordinate in Figure 2.1.

The pronunciation duration of the words varied between lists and was short (*egg, pig, bus, car, fish*; high speech rate), medium (*rocket, monkey, tiger, apple, Indian*; medium speech rate), or long (*elephant, umbrella, helicopter, banana, kangaroo*; low speech rate). The values for speech rate were obtained from the same participants after they completed the recall phase by averaging the time required for 10 overt recitations of word triplets at each pronunciation duration. Those averages were converted to speech rates and are plotted on the abscissa in Figure 2.1.

The simulation that we now develop instantiates this experimental procedure with one important exception that we note below. We present this program in separate listings (each listing is like a figure, except that it contains programming code rather than a graph). Each listing is followed by an explanation of what this particular segment of code accomplishes.

2.3.3   Setting Up the Simulation

We begin by presenting a snippet of MATLAB code that sets up the simulation.

Listing 2.1 Setting Up the Simulation

```
 1 % Implementation of the phonological loop for
 2 % Lewandowsky and Farrell's
 3 % "Computational Modeling in Cognition: Principles ↩
        and Practice''
 4 % Sage publishing.
 5 clear all
 6
 7 nReps = 1000;            %number of replications
 8
 9 listLength = 5;          %number of list items
10 initAct = 1;             %initial activation of items
11 dRate = .8;              %decay rate (per second)
12 delay = 5;               %retention interval (seconds)
13 minAct = .0;             %minimum activation for recall
```

Where exactly did the preceding segment come from? It represents the first handful of lines of a MATLAB program that we typed into the program editor that forms part of the MATLAB package; as we noted earlier, we cannot help you with setting up MATLAB and we are assuming that if you want to reproduce our simulation, you will learn how to use the MATLAB environment (including its editor) on your own.

The first four lines of code are comments that are not addressed to the computer but a human reader; they tell you what the program is about. You will find that all programs in this book are extensively commented. Comments are an indispensable part of a program because even if you have written it yourself, rest assured that you will forget what it does in a frighteningly short time—hence, any time invested in commenting is time saved later on when you are trying to figure out your own brilliant coding (let alone when other scientists want to read your code).

Lines 7 to 13 declare various parameters that are explained in the accompanying comments. To understand what those variables do, let's consider the next listing.

Listing 2.2 The Overall Framework

```
14  rRange = linspace(1.5,4.,15);
15  tRange = 1./rRange;
16  pCor = zeros(size(rRange));
17
18  i=1;                     %index for word lengths
19  for tPerWord=tRange
20
21      for rep=1:nReps
22          actVals = ones(1,listLength)*initAct;
```

```
41              pCor(i) = pCor(i) + ↵
                    (sum(actVals>minAct)./listLength);
42
43      end
44      i=i+1;
45  end
46
47  scatter(rRange,pCor./nReps,'s','filled',...
48          'MarkerFaceColor','k')
49  xlim([0  4.5])
50  ylim([0  1])
51  xlabel('Speech Rate')
52  ylabel('Proportion Correct')
```

Note how Listing 2.2 is broken into two panels; this is because there is a lot of code in between the two panels that contains the core components of the simulations, and that is omitted here (this also explains the discontiguous line numbers in the two panels). Because those core components only make sense if one understands the frame into which they are embedded, we will consider lines 14 to 22 and 41 to 52 on their own before looking at the important bits in between.

First, lines 14 to 18 define the principal "experimental manipulation" that we are interested in—namely, the effects of word length or speech rate. Accordingly, to create different speech rates, we first define the variable rRange by calling the function linspace(1.5, 4, 15). This function call provides us with 15 equally spaced values between 1.5 and 4 that represent the desired speech rates. (If this seems mysterious to you, check the MATLAB help pages for linspace.

Things will become instantly obvious.) A brief glance at the abscissa in Figure 2.1 confirms that these values span the experimentally obtained range. You will also note that we cover the range at a finer level of grain than is possible in a behavioral experiment; this is one of the advantages of a simulation.

The speech rates are then converted into the time that it takes to pronounce each word by simple inversion, and the results are stored in the variable tRange. Note how we exploit the ability of MATLAB to operate on entire vectors of numbers all at the same time; we just had to use the "./" notation (instead of "/") to ensure that the operation was done on each element in the vector.

Finally, we set aside a vector for the results (pCor), which has a subscript i to record data for each speech rate.

The following lines contain two nested loops that govern the simulation: The first one, for tPerWord=tRange, goes through all the speech rates, one at a time, and the second one, for rep=1:nReps, goes through the replications for each level of speech rate. Each of those replications can be understood to represent a different trial (i.e., a different set of words) or a different participant or indeed both. We should briefly explain why we used 1,000 replications here, rather than a more modest number that is comparable to the number of subjects in the experiment. We did this because to compare the simulation results to the data, we want to maximize the reliability of the former. Ideally, we want the simulation to yield predictions with negligible or no error (which can be achieved by cranking the number of replications up to 1,000,000 or more) so we can see if they fall within the standard error of the data. In essence, we can consider the simulation to represent an (error-free) population prediction against which we compare the data. (Exceptions arise when we also seek to capture individual variation in our results; we revisit those exceptions in the next few chapters.)

We next consider what happens within each of the 1,000 replications.

The single statement in line 22 encodes all items by setting them equal to the value of initAct, which was defined at the outset (Listing 2.1). Having encoded the list, you may wonder how it can be retrieved from memory. The answer is given in line 41. This single line of code is more sophisticated than first meets the eye. The statement determines which items have an activation value that exceeds minAct, which represents a threshold activation that was defined at the outset (Listing 2.1). This comparison is achieved by making use of "positional markers," because each item in memory is addressed by its position, and its activation is interrogated to see if it exceeds the threshold; again, we exploit MATLAB's ability to operate on entire vectors by reducing this sequential comparison to the simple expression actVals>minAct. By summing the comparison, we count the number of items correctly recalled—remember that we do not model transpositions or intrusions; hence, any item whose activation is above threshold is considered to be retrieved—and we then add that sum (converted to a proportion correct by dividing by listLength) to the data for that speech rate.

Note how the index `i` is set to 1 initially and is then incremented by 1 at every end of the speech rate loop; hence, `i` points to the current value of speech rate in the vector `pCor`, which keeps track of the proportion correct.

The final set of lines in the bottom panel of Listing 2.2 simply plots the predictions (the contents of `pCor` averaged across replications) against the set of speech rates. Below, we will show some of the results from this simulation.

Before we can report any simulation results, we need to consider the missing bit of code that was excised from the preceding listing. This code is shown in Listing 2.3 below. Remember that this code segment is immediately preceded by encoding (line 22 above) and immediately followed by retrieval (41 above); hence, the code below instantiates forgetting and rehearsal in our model.

Listing 2.3 The Core: Rehearsal and Decay

```
23      cT = 0;
24      itemReh = 0; % start rehearsal
25                   % with beginning of list
26      while cT < delay
27
28          intact = find(actVals>minAct);
29          % find the next item still accessible
30          itemReh = intact(find(intact>itemReh, 1));
31          % rehearse or return to beginning of list
32          if isempty(itemReh)
33              itemReh=1;
34          end
35          actVals(itemReh) = initAct;
36
37
38          % everything decays
39          actVals = actVals - (dRate.*tPerWord);
40          cT=cT+tPerWord;
41      end
```

The core of Listing 2.3 is the while `cT < delay` loop, which is executed as many times as steps of duration `tPerWord` fit within `delay`—in other words, this loop rehearses as many list items as can be articulated within the total retention interval. This is the one place where our simulation deviates from the method of Hulme and Tordoff (1989) that gave rise to the data in Figure 2.1: Whereas recall in the experiment was immediate (hence the retention interval was zero, or close to it), we introduced a delay of 5 seconds (see Listing 2.1). The reason for this deviation is that given our decision not to commence decay until after list presentation (Decision 1 in Table 2.1), we require some nonzero interval during which decay and compensatory rehearsal can exert their opposing effects. This is perfectly fine for present purposes, but we would not want to publish the simulation results with this deviation between actual and simulated methodologies.

Let us resume our discussion of rehearsal in the simulation. The duration of each articulation is given by tPerWord, which changes with speech rate as shown earlier in Listing 2.2. The number of rehearsals thus depends on word length, exactly as it should. Within the while loop, we first locate the next item that is still accessible (because its activation exceeds minAct) and then restore its activation to its initial value in line 35. The order in which items are rehearsed is from the beginning of the list to the end, skipping over items that have been completely forgotten and wrapping around at the end, for a renewed cycle of rehearsal, if time permits. This mechanism conforms to our decision earlier that rehearsal should be ordered (Decision 6, Table 2.1). (If you find it difficult to figure out how this mechanism operates, we suggest that you study the MATLAB help pages for find and isempty; those are the two functions used to select items for rehearsal.)

At each rehearsal step, the contents of memory decay in the linear and constant manner decided upon earlier (Decisions 2 and 3 in Table 2.1), using the statement in line 39. The decay process deserves several comments. First, it does not occur until after encoding is complete (Decision 1). Second, the extent of decay varies with word length, with longer words providing more opportunity for decay than shorter words. Third, decay affects *all* items, including the one just rehearsed. That is, the boost in activation resulting from rehearsal is immediately counteracted by decay, reflecting the fact that decay is a continuous and uninterruptable process. This is another arbitrary decision that was required to instantiate the model. If you prefer, the just-rehearsed item can be exempted from decay by changing line 39 to read actVals((1:listLength)~=itemReh)=actVals ((1:listLength)~=itemReh)−(dRate.*tPerWord);.

The relationship between rehearsal and decay deserves to be examined more closely because it reveals an extremely important property of simulations. You may have noted that the statement that instantiates decay (line 39) *follows* the line that instantiates rehearsal (line 35). Does this mean that rehearsal precedes decay? No; the two processes actually occur at the *same* (simulated) time. In a simulation, time always needs to be advanced explicitly, which in our case happens in line 40. It follows that everything in between increments of the variable cT takes place at the same (simulated) time; hence, rehearsal and decay occur simultaneously, notwithstanding the fact that one statement follows the other in the program. This property of simulated time is true for any simulation involving a temporal component.

Our journey is almost complete: We have taken a slow but informative trip through the processes involved in translating a verbal model into a computer simulation. We have presented and discussed the simulation program, which provides one of a multitude of possible instantiations of the phonological loop model.

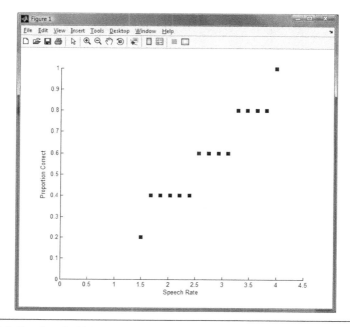

Figure 2.3 Results of a MATLAB simulation of the phonological loop. See text and Listings 2.1 through 2.3 for details.

Let us now see how well this model works. Can we reproduce the speech rate function in Figure 2.1?

2.3.4   Some Unanticipated Results

When we run the program shown in Listings 2.1 through 2.3 (by clicking on the green arrow at the top in the MATLAB editor, in case you are wondering), we obtain the graph that is shown in Figure 2.3. We have retained the entire window created by MATLAB to underscore the link between these results and the preceding program and to encourage you to reproduce them on your own.

The results are striking. First, there is an overall increase in performance with speech rate; that is, the more quickly words can be articulated, the better they are retained after a 5-second delay, exactly as predicted by the verbal model. Second, this increase is entirely discontinuous, and the speech rate function consists of a series of flat plateaus—quite unlike the data.

So does our simulation support the notion of the phonological loop? Yes and no. On the one hand, the basic pattern is right, but on the other hand, the predictions of the simulation are clearly at odds with the data. The predictions are

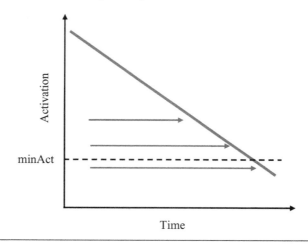

Figure 2.4 The implications of the decay function assumed in our simulation. The thick solid line is the decay function relating activation to time. The broken horizontal line indicates the minimum activation value; any item whose activation falls below that line is considered to have been forgotten. The horizontal arrows represent hypothetical rehearsal durations. See text for details.

also at odds with what we might expect from the verbal description of the phonological loop; there is really nothing in the verbal model that would lead one to believe that the speech rate function should be discontinuous. What went wrong?

In a sense, nothing "went wrong." Our particular instantiation of the phonological loop is as legitimate—that is, it is as compatible with the verbal theory—as any of the other 143 we could have created. Hence, rather than asking what went wrong, it is more appropriate to ask what the reasons are for the discontinuity in the predicted speech rate function. The answer to this question is provided in Figure 2.4.

The figure shows the relationship between an item's level of activation and time in our simulation by the thick decreasing function. As an exercise, refer to Listing 2.1 to determine the slope of this function. If you cannot figure it out, read the footnote.[5] The figure also shows the minimum activation level (the broken horizontal line at minAct) below which an item is considered to have been forgotten. Once an item is below that line, it can be neither recalled nor rehearsed.

The joint implications of this threshold and the decay function are illustrated by the horizontal arrows, which represent several hypothetical rehearsal durations. As we noted earlier, decay continues throughout rehearsal, so although rehearsal restores an item's activation, all items that are not currently being rehearsed continue to decay along the function shown in the figure.

The unequal lengths of the arrows represent different speech rates; remember that shorter words can be rehearsed more quickly than longer words. Now, bearing in mind that any above-threshold activation translates into a correct recall (or successful rehearsal), note how the length of the arrows does not affect recall for any item whose activation remains above threshold throughout. That is, up to a point, it does not matter how long it takes to rehearse a given list item because the next one will nonetheless remain above threshold and will thus be available for rehearsal (or recall). This explains the plateaus that are obtained with a range of speech rates. It is only when the additional rehearsal time permits all (or some) of the remaining items to decay below threshold that an item is irrevocably lost—and it is this loss of an item that explains the steps in between plateaus in Figure 2.3.

The preceding analysis is informative in two ways: First, it reveals that our simulation can be readily understood and that its predictions are not mysterious. Second, it points to a way in which the simulation can be revised so that its predictions are more in line with the data.

2.3.5   Variability in Decay

The problem we have identified is that minor variations in speech rate are either amplified or nullified, depending on whether or not those speech rates straddle the recall threshold. There is a fairly straightforward way in which this problem can be resolved. Listing 2.4 below contains a revised simulation, which differs from the preceding variant by exactly three lines of code. The listing is complete, with the exception of the final few statements that plot the data.

The crucial addition to this simulation is in line 18, which computes the decay rate (dRate) anew for each replication. The decay rate is based on two components: a constant that is represented by the variable decRate, defined in line 5, plus a random component with standard deviation decSD, defined in line 6. The random component is normally distributed with mean zero, and those random numbers are supplied by the MATLAB function randn. This then implements our Decision 3 in Table 2.1.

What is the intention behind introducing this variability in decay rate? And what are the likely consequences? First, the assumption that a psychological process has some variability, both within and across individuals, is entirely plausible and pervasive (e.g., McNicol, 1972). Indeed, psychologically it is *more* plausible to assume the presence of variability than its absence. Second, variable decay rates imply that the single decay function in Figure 2.4 is replaced by a family of functions with a common intercept whose slopes form a probability distribution. (As an exercise, do you know what the intercept and mean and standard deviation of the slopes are? If not, read the footnote.)[6] This variability in decay rate can be expected to "wash out" the discontinuities in the speech rate function across replications.

Listing 2.4 The Second Simulation: Variable Decay Rates

```
1  clear all
2  nReps = 1000;          %number of replications
3  listLength = 5;        %number of list items
4  initAct = 1;           %initial activation of items
5  decRate = .8;          %mean decay rate (per second)
6  decSD = .1;            %standard deviation of decay rate
7  delay = 5;             %retention interval (seconds)
8  minAct = .0;           %minimum activation for recall
9  rRange = linspace(1.5,4.,15);
10 tRange = 1./rRange;
11 pCor = zeros(size(rRange));
12
13 i=1;                   %index for word lengths
14 for tPerWord=tRange
15
16     for rep=1:nReps
17         actVals = ones(1,listLength)*initAct;
18         dRate = decRate+randn*decSD;
19
20         cT = 0;
21         itemReh = 0;
22         while cT < delay
23             intact = find(actVals>minAct);
24             itemReh = intact(find(intact>itemReh, 1));
25             if isempty(itemReh)
26                 itemReh=1;
27             end
28             actVals(itemReh) = initAct;
29
30             % everything decays
31             actVals = actVals - (dRate.*tPerWord);
32             cT=cT+tPerWord;
33         end
34         pCor(i) = pCor(i) + ↵
               (sum(actVals>minAct)./listLength);
35     end
36     i=i+1;
37 end
```

Figure 2.5 confirms that this is exactly what happens. The figure contains the results of a run of the second version of our simulation shown in Listing 2.4. It is clear that these results are much more in accord with the data shown at the outset

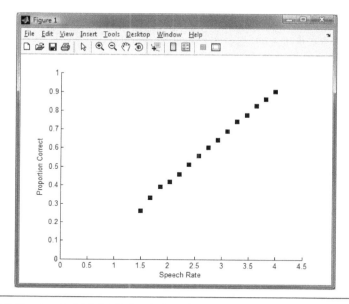

Figure 2.5 Results of a MATLAB simulation of the phonological loop with variable decay rates. See text and Listing 2.4 for details.

(Figure 2.1). The results also conform far better to one's intuitions about what the phonological loop model ought to predict.

Our technical journey is now complete. We commenced our journey by considering the empirical speech rate function; we then derived a simulation from a verbally stated theory. The simulation implemented a process model of the phonological loop and applied it to a speech rate experiment, and finally, we obtained predictions from a simulation that closely mirrored the original data. We now analyze the conceptual lessons that can be drawn from our exercise.

2.4   What Can We Learn From These Simulations?

2.4.1   The Phonological Loop Model Instantiated

One clear conclusion that can be drawn from our simulations is that Baddeley's phonological loop model *can* be implemented in a simulation model and that the simulation can predict the empirically observed shape of the speech rate function. This is not altogether surprising because other computational instantiations of the phonological loop already exist (e.g., Burgess & Hitch, 1999; Page & Norris, 1998b).

Let us explore what options would now lie ahead if our simulations had been "serious" rather than a pedagogical exercise. What might we do next to explore our phonological loop instantiation? One obvious avenue for exploration is gradually to relax the design decisions (see Table 2.1) that were made primarily for simplicity's sake; for example, the linear decay assumption might be replaced by a more realistic exponential function.[7]

A further avenue for exploration is to introduce a mechanism that can give rise to transpositions and intrusions. This is a matter of central importance; a serious model of short-term memory must explain why people so frequently transpose the order of list items. If you are curious about how such a mechanism might be added to the present model, Neath (2000) presents a relevant precedent involving the "feature model," which broadly resembles our simulations.

Two other constraints of the present simulation that ought to be explored relate to the ordering of items during rehearsal and the encoding strengths. Concerning the former, it would be worthwhile to examine what happens if list items are rehearsed in a random order rather than in strict forward sequence. Concerning the latter, many models assume that early list items are encoded more strongly than later items (e.g., G. D. A. Brown, Preece, & Hulme, 2000; Page & Norris, 1998b), and the effects of this so-called primacy gradient should also be examined in our simulation. Our supporting website, http://www.cogsciwa.com, also contains those additional explorations.

2.4.2   Testability and Falsifiability

There is a second set of important conclusions that can be drawn from our simulations. These revolve around the testability of our instantiations and the testability and falsifiability of the verbal version of the phonological loop model. The previous chapter concluded with a discussion of how the scope of a theory interacts with the quality of the data to determine its falsifiability. The simulations developed in this chapter illustrate this issue further.

Our first simulation (Listings 2.1–2.3) was found to be at least partially inconsistent with the data. We therefore rejected that variant of the phonological loop model and replaced it with another variant (Listing 2.4) that introduced variability into the decay rates. The fact that we rejected the first simulation establishes its falsifiability as well as its inadequacy. The fact that the second simulation reproduced the data suggests that its assumptions were more appropriate—but can we say anything about its falsifiability? In the previous chapter, we examined the argument by Roberts and Pashler (2000) that the extent of support provided by a model's fit to the data depends on the total breadth of findings that it is capable of predicting (see Figure 1.10). There are formal techniques that permit an examination of a model's likely scope (e.g., Li, Lewandowsky, & DeBrunner, 1996), but they are too involved for the present introductory chapter. Instead, we merely note that our explorations (not reported in detail here) reveal the second simulation's predictions to be quite robust; that is, several other features of the model can be changed without affecting the shape of the predicted speech rate function. We therefore at least cautiously conclude that the support for our second model is gratifyingly strong because the model's predictions do not represent just one of many possible predicted outcomes; given the known stability of the speech rate data, our second simulation therefore likely instantiates the top-left panel in Figure 1.10.

What are the implications of our simulations for the verbal model of the phonological loop as initially formulated by Baddeley (e.g., 1986)? There are two reasons to suggest that support for the verbal model is not terribly strong. First, we established that the verbal model can be instantiated in more than a hundred possible ways. Second, we explored two of those possible instantiations and found the results to be relatively divergent. Although we cannot anticipate exactly how many different results can be predicted by the remaining 140 or so possible instantiations, the fact that a subset of two can create divergent predictions suggests that the overall ensemble will likely generate even greater heterogeneity. It follows that the state of the verbal model is more likely to be characterized by the bottom-left panel in Figure 1.10: The data are precise, but the theory would have been compatible with outcomes other than those that were observed, and hence support for it is weak.

Is this to be taken as a criticism of verbal models in general or the working memory model in particular? No, not at all. Verbal models can have enormous impact and can stimulate much valuable and informative research—indeed, the working memory model rightfully ranks among the leading theories of memory. However, to achieve a detailed understanding of the underlying psychological processes, a verbal model must *ultimately* be implemented in a computational model—as indeed has been the case for the working memory model (e.g., Burgess & Hitch, 1999; Page & Norris, 1998b).

2.4.3   Revisiting Model Design: Foundational Decisions

The preceding discussion of our simulations skimmed over several important conceptual decisions in an effort to shorten the journey from the verbal model to the simulation results. For example, we merely stated that we would rely on localist token representations without considering any alternative rabbits in our hat.

Having presented our first simulations, we now briefly revisit those more fundamental issues. Unlike the technical decisions that were relevant only to the phonological loop model, those foundational decisions about representations and basic architecture must precede *any* modeling in cognition, irrespective of the particular model or domain in question. Table 2.2 lists some of these issues together with pointers to the literature or other places within this book that contain further discussion.

Table 2.2 Some Foundational Decisions That Precede Model Instantiation

Decision	Alternatives	Further Discussion in
Nature of data or measures	Accuracies	Chapter 4
	Latencies	Chapter 4; Luce (1986)
Resolution of data	Aggregate (group)	Chapter 3; Cohen, Sanbom, and Shiffrin (2008)
	Individual participants	Chapter 3; Cohen et al. (2008)
Level of modeling	Data description	Chapter 1
	Process characterization	Chapter 1
	Process explanation	Chapter 1
Class of architecture	Symbolic	J. R. Anderson (1996)
	Connectionist	J. A. Anderson (1995)
	Hybrid	Sun, Slusarz, and Terry (2005)
	Informed by neuroscience	Meeter and Murre (2005)
Type of representation	Token	Nosofsky (1986)
	Type	Ashby and Gott (1988)
	Localist	Page (2000)
	Distributed	J. McClelland and Rumelhart (1986)

For now, the important thing to bear in mind is that the technical issues involved in model building are always embedded in a broader theoretical context. The links between the broader theoretical context and your decisions about a model can often be tacit; for example, it may not occur to you that your model of short-term memory could rely on anything but a token representation. Alternatively, you may have subscribed to a particular theoretical outlook—for example, connectionism—some time ago, and hence you will naturally approach any further modeling from that perspective and may not consider symbolic alternatives.

Because those foundational decisions are often subjective, this initial phase of model development has been referred to as an "art" rather than science (Shiffrin & Nobel, 1997). Shiffrin and Nobel (1997) provide an extended discussion of this foundational phase of model development, and we refer the interested reader to their paper.

2.5   The Basic Toolkit

In the remainder of this chapter, we provide you with a basic toolkit that is required to understand all subsequent material. We introduce the notion of parameters, discrepancy functions, and parameter estimation techniques, and we briefly foreshadow the issue of model selection. We also examine the conceptual issues surrounding parameter estimation to place the subsequent material on a firm theoretical footing.

With the completion of this toolkit, you will be ready to embark on serious modeling in the subsequent chapters. Be forewarned that you are about to encounter a toolkit, not a complete workshop; all the concepts we introduce here will be developed more fully throughout the remainder of the book.

2.5.1 Parameters

Let us briefly reconsider Listing 2.1, which set up some of the variables that governed the behavior of our simulation (e.g., initAct, dRate, minAct). Those variables are called *parameters*. What is the role of parameters? Parameters can be understood as "tuning knobs" that fine-tune the behavior of a model once its architecture (i.e., basic principles) has been specified. A good analogy is your car radio, which has "knobs" (or their high-tech digital equivalent) that determine the volume and the station; those knobs determine the behavior of your radio without changing its architecture.

In our model of the phonological loop, dRate was one important parameter: Varying its value affects the overall performance of the model: As dRate decreases, performance increases (because there is less forgetting) and the effect of speech rate is diminished (because the effects of word length depend on the existence of decay). In the extreme case, when dRate=0, performance will be perfect irrespective of speech rate. Changing the decay rate does not change the architecture of our simulation, but it certainly changes its behavior. Usually, our models involve more than a single parameter. It is helpful to introduce some notation to refer to the parameters of a model: For the remainder of the book, we will use θ ("theta") to denote the vector of all parameter values of a model.

2.5.1.1 *Flexibility Versus Testability Once Again*

Yes, the issue of flexibility versus testability raises its head again: If you can "turn off" forgetting in a simulation by adjusting the decay rate parameter, does it not follow that the model is capable of a broad range of predictions (including some very implausible ones)? And does this not imply that support for the model is weak (bottom panels of Figure 1.10)? Perhaps, but not necessarily.

We begin by postulating some ideal state of affairs, the modeler's Nirvana as it were. In this Nirvana, the model predicts the data, with quantitative precision, without any parameters at all. If there are no parameters, there is nothing to tune with, and hence whatever the model's predictions may be, they are inevitable. How would a model do this? What is left of a model if there are no parameters;

wouldn't this be like getting a plane to fly without wings and a fuselage? No, it is more like listening to a radio that is permanently tuned to one station: Its *architecture* is still intact, and hence it is able to receive the signal and amplify it and so on. What is lost is the ability to tune into different stations. But is it a "loss"? No, if you *like* listening to that station (and that station only), then nothing has been lost—and by exact analogy, nothing has been lost if a model has no parameters but it nonetheless predicts the observed data. Quite to the contrary, if a model handles the data notwithstanding the absence of parameters, then we have amassed the strongest possible support for a model; by definition, the model's predictions cannot be altered (because there are no parameters), and we are therefore firmly anchored in the top row of panels in Figure 1.10. (Or indeed in a hypothetical row of panels floating above the figure in which there is a single point corresponding to both data and predictions.)

Can this Nirvana be attained in practice? Yes, but not very often. One example is shown in Figure 2.6, which shows a subset of the results of an experiment by Lewandowsky, Griffiths, and Kalish (2009). The details of the model and the study can be largely glossed over; suffice it to say that we asked people to predict the total duration of the reign of an Egyptian pharaoh in response to a (quasi-random) cue. For example, given that a pharaoh has been ruling for 5 years, how long will his total reign be? People responded to multiple such cues, and their distribution of responses was compared to the distribution predicted by a Bayesian model without any parameters. This comparison is shown in the figure, which shows that the quantiles of the two distributions are very similar to each other (perfect agreement is represented by the diagonal), suggesting that the model captured people's performance. So yes, there are occasions in which support for a model can be extremely strong because its predictions involve no free parameters.

To clarify what a parameter-free model looks like, we reproduce Lewandowsky et al.'s (2009) Bayesian model in the following equation:

$$p(t_{total}|t) \propto p(t|t_{total})p(t_{total}), \qquad (2.1)$$

where $p(t_{total})$ is the prior distribution of quantities (in this instance, the distribution of the reigns of Egyptian pharaohs, gleaned from a historical database), $p(t|t_{total})$ is the likelihood of encountering any particular probe value t (assumed to be uniformly distributed), and $p(t_{total}|t)$ is the predicted posterior distribution. The quantiles of that posterior distribution are compared to the data in Figure 2.6.

If this terse description of the model leaves you baffled and mystified, we can comfort you by noting that what is important here are not the details of the model but the fact that there are no parameters in Equation 2.1: The predictions result from the prior distribution, which is independently known, and the assumption that any value of t from that prior distribution is equally likely to be encountered (as indeed was the case in the experiment). So, the predictions of the model

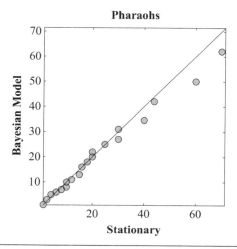

Figure 2.6 Snapshot of results from an experiment that tested the predictions of a Bayesian model with no parameters. The ordinate plots quantiles of the predicted distribution, and the abscissa plots the obtained quantiles. Figure from Lewandowsky, S., Griffiths, T. L., & Kalish, M. L. (2009). The wisdom of individuals: Exploring people's knowledge about everyday events using iterated learning. *Cognitive Science*, *33*, 969–998. Copyright by the Cognitive Science Society; reprinted with permission.

were *inevitable*, arising from its architecture in Equation 2.1 alone. It follows that the model would have been challenged had the data come out even slightly differently.[8]

Returning from Nirvana to more common pastures, what about the present simulations, where altering the value of the decay parameter noticeably affected the model's predictions? Does this mean the support for the model is weak? Well, it is *weaker* than the support for the Bayesian model just discussed, but it need not be weak. For example, although the reduction in decay rate reduces the slope of the predicted speech rate function, it will never reverse it. (We are disallowing the possibility of "antidecay," or the increase in memory strength with time, by reducing the decay rate below zero.) In consequence, our simulation model remains falsifiable because it would be incompatible with a reversed word length effect. (Lest you think that a reversed word length effect is absurd, this finding is not altogether unknown; see Lewandowsky & Oberauer, 2008, for a review and analysis.)

You may have already guessed, then, that the issue of testability and flexibility is tied to the presence of parameters—and in particular to their effects on a model's prediction—but that it is considerably more complex than a simple postulate such as "parameters prevent testability." There is an old saying, attributed to

John von Neumann (Dyson, 2004, p. 297), that "with four parameters I can fit an elephant, and with five I can make him wiggle his trunk." In actual fact, the truth could not be more different: Wei (1975) showed that it takes 30 (!) parameters to fit an elephant. We explore the notion of testability and how it relates to the number of parameters in detail in Chapter 6.

A more relevant question, then, is how many free parameters it takes to characterize a verbal model. Could we escape the problem of model flexibility by returning to a verbal model? No, because as we have just seen, a verbal model leaves open many important issues, and indeed the decision points in Table 2.1 are best considered free parameters.

2.5.1.2   Types of Parameters

If parameters are tuning knobs, how are their values set? How do you tune your car radio to a new station?. . . Exactly, you adjust the frequency knob until the hiss has been replaced by Moz[9] or Mozart. Likewise, there is a class of parameters in cognitive models that are adjusted until the predictions are in line with the data to the extent possible. Those parameters are known as *free* parameters. In our preceding simulations, the decay rate and its variability were free parameters. The process by which the parameters are adjusted is known as parameter estimation or, sometimes, model fitting. The resulting estimates are known as the "best-fitting" parameter values.

Free parameters are usually estimated from the data that the model seeks to explain. In Chapter 1, we proposed that the salary of Australian members of parliament can be summarized by a single parameter—namely, the mean. We estimated that parameter by simply computing the average of the data. Things are a little more complicated if we fit a regression model to some bivariate data, in which case we estimate two parameters—slope and intercept. And things get more complicated still for psychological process models—sufficiently complicated, in fact, for us to devote the next two chapters to this issue.

Because the predictions of the model depend on its specific parameter values, a fair assessment of the model's adequacy requires that we give it the "best shot" to account for the data. For that reason, we *estimate* the free parameters from the data by finding those values that maximally align the model's predictions with the data. Those parameter estimates often (though not necessarily) vary between different data sets to which the model is applied.

Generally, as we have seen in the previous section, modelers seek to limit the number of free parameters because the larger their number, the greater the model's flexibility—and as we discussed in some detail in Chapter 1, we want to place bounds on that flexibility. That said, we also want our models to be powerful and to accommodate many different data sets: It follows that we must satisfy a delicate trade-off between flexibility and testability in which free parameters play a crucial role. This trade-off is examined in detail in Chapter 5.

There is another class of parameters, known as *fixed*, that are not estimated from the data and hence are invariant across data sets. In our simulations, the initial encoding strengths (variable `minAct`) were a fixed parameter. The role of fixed parameters is primarily to "get the model off the ground" by providing some meaningful values for its components where necessary. In the radio analogy, the wattage of the speaker and its resistance are fixed parameters: Both can in principle be changed, but equally, keeping them constant does not prevent your radio from receiving a variety of stations at a volume of your choice. Although parsimony dictates that models should have few fixed parameters, modelers are less concerned about their number than they are about minimizing the number of free parameters.

2.5.2   Discrepancy Function

You now know that the goal of parameter estimation is to maximize the alignment between the model's predictions and the data. Most parameter estimation procedures prefer the equivalent way of stating this—namely, that we seek to *minimize* the discrepancy between predictions and data. Minimization requires a continuous *discrepancy function* that condenses the discrepancy between predictions and data into a single number. That discrepancy function is minimized by gradual and iterative adjustment of the parameters. The discrepancy function is also variously known as objective function, cost function, or error function, and we will consider a few such functions along the way.

To illustrate, consider the speech rate data and the corresponding predictions from our simulation, which are shown together in Figure 2.7. To facilitate comparison, we tweaked the simulation a tiny bit by obtaining predictions for the exact values of speech rates that were observed in the data; hence, there are some gaps between the small open circles in this figure that were absent in Figure 2.5. We achieved this by changing line 9 in Listing 2.4 to `rRange=` [1.64 1.92 2.33 2.64 3.73 3.94]; where the numbers inside the [...] happen to be the observed speech rates.

A discrepancy function expresses the deviation between the two sets of numbers in a single numeric value. A popular and simple discrepancy function for continuous data is the (square root of the) average of the squared deviations (or root mean squared deviation [RMSD]) between data and predictions. Formally,

$$RMSD = \sqrt{\frac{\sum_{j=1}^{J} (d_j - p_j)^2}{J}}, \qquad (2.2)$$

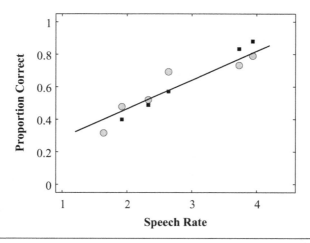

Figure 2.7 Speech rate data (large gray plotting symbols), taken from Figure 2.1, and simulation predictions (small black squares), produced by the simulation in Listing 2.4 for the exact speech rates observed in the data.

where J is the number of data points over which the sum is taken, and d and p represent data and predictions, respectively. For Figure 2.7, the RMSD turns out to be .082. In other words, the simulation predictions differ from the data by 8 percentage points on average. Note that the "data points" that contributed to the RMSD were the means in the figure, rather than the underlying individual observations. This is frequently the case when we fit group averages rather than individual subjects (which is why we used J in the denominator rather than N, which is the notation of choice to refer to the number of observations).[10]

If the data are discrete—for example, when the number of responses is constant, but each response can fall into one of several different categories (e.g., whether an item is recalled in its correct position or 1, 2, ..., positions away)—then a χ^2 or G^2 discrepancy measure is more appropriate (e.g., Lamberts, 2005). The χ^2 is defined as

$$\chi^2 = \sum_{j=1}^{J} \frac{(O_j - N \cdot p_j)^2}{N \cdot p_j}, \tag{2.3}$$

where J refers to the number of response categories, N refers to the total number of observed responses, and O_j refers to the number of observed responses within each category j. Note that the sum of all O_js is N, and note that the model predictions, p_j, are assumed to be probabilities rather than counts, as one would commonly expect from a model (hence the need to multiply each p_j with N, in order to place the observed and expected values on an equivalent scale).

The G^2 measure, also known as the log-likelihood ratio, is given by

$$G^2 = 2 \sum_{j=1}^{J} O_j \log\{O_j/(N \cdot p_j)\}, \qquad (2.4)$$

using the same notation as in Equation 2.3.

One sometimes desirable attribute of χ^2 and G^2 is that they can be interpreted as test statistics because both have an asymptotic χ^2 distribution with $df = J - n_p - 1$, where n_p is the number of free parameters being estimated. When the χ^2 (or G^2) is "significant," this indicates that the model significantly deviates from the data—hence, unlike in conventional hypothesis testing, modelers do not necessarily desire a significant result. However, in most circumstances, one is more likely to be interested in the *relative* fit of the various models; Chapter 5 discusses techniques for that type of comparison.

The χ^2 discrepancy function has two attributes that need to be considered. First, caution is advised if the number of observed or expected responses in a category falls below 5. Where possible, a solution in those cases may involve the collapsing of several small response categories into a larger one (e.g., Van Zandt, 2000). Second, even when the number of degrees of freedom remains constant, increasing the sample size (N) can increase the magnitude of χ^2 because even small variations that are due to noise are amplified by a factor N during computation of the χ^2. (To see why, compute the χ^2 component for $p_j = .8$ when N is 10 and O_j is 9, versus when $N = 100$ and $O_j = 90$, respectively.) In consequence, when the χ^2 discrepancy is used as a statistical test, it has enormous power and may detect even slight departures of the predictions from the data.

Several other discrepancy functions may be of interest to psychologists. A useful discussion can be found in Chechile (1998, 1999).

2.5.3   Parameter Estimation and Model-Fitting Techniques

How do we minimize the discrepancy function? Two basic approaches exist, known as *least squares* and *maximum likelihood estimation*. Although the mechanics of those two approaches are quite similar, their underlying motivation and properties differ considerably.

In a least squares approach, the emphasis is on goodness of fit; that is, the goal of parameter estimation is to minimize the discrepancy between the model predictions and the data. Some suitable discrepancy function (usually the RMSD) is defined, and all that matters is that its value be minimized by adjusting the parameters. All of the next chapter (Chapter 3) is devoted to the least squares approach.

The advantage of the least squares approach is its conceptual simplicity: It is intuitively obvious that one wants to minimize the discrepancy between the model and the data, and least squares does just that. However, this simplicity comes at a cost: Least squares techniques typically have no known statistical properties. For example, we generally cannot tell whether a model's deviation from the data is likely to reflect mere chance fluctuation in the data or whether it is more serious. Is the RMSD for Figure 2.7 "good" or "bad"; is a value as great as .082 to be expected by chance, or does it imply that the model is inadequate? Likewise, if two models differ in their least squares fit, we generally cannot make a statistical comparison between the two; one may fit better than the other, but again we cannot be certain whether this represents chance or a real difference between the two models in their proximity to the data. Finally, the parameter estimates generally have no obvious statistical properties; we do not know what confidence one can place in the estimate, and we cannot predict how likely it is that a replication of the experiment would yield similar parameter values.

In contrast to least squares, the maximum likelihood approach is entirely statistical. Although maximum likelihood estimation also minimizes the discrepancy between predictions and data, the discrepancy function takes into account the statistical nature of the data and thus has some powerful statistical properties that are explored in Chapter 4. Specifically, the goal of maximum likelihood estimation is to find those parameter values that are maximally likely in light of the data. In consequence, the predictions obtained under maximum likelihood parameter estimates are the best predictions available for future replications of an identical (or similar) experiment. Likewise, the goodness of fit of the model can be assessed statistically; for example, it is possible to conduct hypothesis testing on the model's fit. We can also place confidence bounds on each estimated parameter value, and by extension, we can conduct statistical comparisons between models and select the one that fits "significantly better" than another one. This process is known as model selection and will be discussed in Chapter 5. Model selection is a very active research area, and new techniques—most of them based on maximum likelihood estimation—continue to be developed. Common to all those techniques is to balance the goodness of fit of a model with its complexity (e.g., the number of free parameters) and hence with its flexibility. Chapter 5 will therefore provide closure on one of the central issues raised so far—namely, the trade-off between testability and flexibility.

2.6   Models and Data: Sufficiency and Explanation

We have covered much ground in the first two chapters. We have explained the basic tools and concepts involved in modeling, and we have provided an

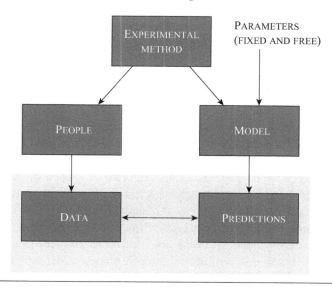

Figure 2.8 The basic idea: We seek to connect model predictions to the data from our experiment(s). This process involves the observables in the gray area at the bottom of the figure. The area at the top shows the origin of data and predictions, as well as the auxiliary role of the model parameters.

illustrative example of what is involved in cognitive model construction. Let us now step back for a moment and take another look at the global picture: We know that the basic aim of modeling is to connect the model's predictions with our data; this idea is illustrated in Figure 2.8, which also shows the origin and the variables that determine the data and the predictions.

We know from Chapter 1 (in particular Figure 1.10 and the discussion surrounding it in Section 1.6.1) that we want the connection between predictions and data to be taut; that is, we want the data to be precise and the possible predictions of the model to be confined to a subset of all possible outcomes.

Let's suppose, then, that our model's predictions and the data have those desirable properties. What exactly are the implications of a successful model fit? What conclusions can be legitimately drawn from successful modeling? We briefly discussed this at the end of the previous chapter, but the issue is sufficiently important to deserve more careful analysis.

2.6.1   Sufficiency of a Model

A successful model fit implies that the model's predictions, most likely with the aid of some estimated parameters, mirror the data quantitatively (within some reasonable tolerance). The fact that a model fits the data implies that it is *sufficient* to explain those data. Does it follow that the model is also *necessary*—that is, that the model provides the sole unique explanation for the data? No, not at all, in the same way that the fact that you flew from Lagos to Tripoli on your last African trip does not rule out that you could have taken an overland caravan. This rather painful—but frequently forgotten—fact deserves to be fleshed out.

It follows that a successful fit of your model to the available data represents, alas, fairly weak evidence in its favor: Although a successful fit shows that your model is a *possible* explanation for the data, it does not identify your model as *the only* possible explanation. This is an in-principle problem that has nothing to do with the quality of the data and the model: The case was stated strongly and eloquently by J. R. Anderson (1990), who concluded, "It is just not possible to use behavioral data to develop a theory of the implementation level in the concrete and specific terms to which we have aspired" (p. 24). By implication, irrespective of how good and how large our behavioral database is, Anderson suggested that there would always be *multiple* different possible models of the internal processes that produce those data (models of internal processes are at the "implementation level," and this most closely corresponds to our view of "process explanation" as developed in Section 1.4.4). We agree with Anderson, and we agree that for any successful model that handles the data, there exist an unknown and unknowable number of equally capable alternative models—thus, our seemingly trivial Figure 2.8 is actually quite complex because the single "Model" node on the right is hiding an infinity of equally powerful (but unknown) alternatives. It follows that the data never necessarily imply or identify one and only one model.

What are we to do in light of this indeterminacy, which is often referred to as the "identifiability problem"? We begin by noting that J. R. Anderson (1990) proposed two solutions to the identifiability problem. The first one abandoned the idea of process modeling altogether and replaced it by a "rational analysis" of behavior that sought to identify the linkages between the demands of the environment and human adaptation to those demands (e.g., J. R. Anderson & Schooler, 1991) A defining feature of rational analysis is that it explicitly eschews the modeling of cognitive processes and remains at a level that we would consider to be descriptive (see Sections 1.4.2 and 1.4.3). Anderson's second solution invoked the constraints that could be provided by physiological data, which were said to permit a "one-to-one tracing of the implementation level" (J. R. Anderson, 1990, p. 25). Recently, J. R. Anderson (2007) has argued that this additional constraint—in the form of brain imaging data—has now been achieved or is at least near, thus putting a solution to the identification problem tantalizingly within reach (a view that resonates with at least some philosophers of science; Bechtel, 2008). We revisit the role of neuroscientific data in Chapter 8, where we consider some neurally inspired models in greater detail.

Our preferred response to the identifiability problem is to acknowledge its existence while also putting the problem into its proper context by noting what it does *not* imply. First, the fact that many potentially realizable models exist in principle that can handle the available data does not imply that any of those models are trivial or easy to come by—quite on the contrary, as we have shown in the first two chapters, constructing cognitive models is an effortful and painstaking process that is far from trivial. Second, the existence of an unknown number of potential models does not preclude comparison and selection from among a limited set of instantiated models—we noted in Chapter 1 that there is an infinite number of possible models of planetary motion; however, this has not precluded selection of a preferred model that is now universally accepted. Third, the fact that whatever model we select will ultimately turn out to be wrong—a fate of which all cognitive models can be virtually assured (see Chapter 1)—does not preclude it from being potentially very useful. We thus address the identification problem by defanging its implications rather than by refuting it.

This approach, however, creates a new conundrum: If we grant that even our "best" model is false, in addition to being accompanied by an infinity of invisible potential alternatives, how exactly can it be useful? If we wish to explain cognition, how can we do so on the basis of something that is known to be wrong?

2.6.2   Verisimilitude Versus Truth

Suppose you read a newspaper report of a car accident of which you have first-hand knowledge. You find that all the details are correct, except the middle initial of one of the people involved. You pick up another paper, a flashy tabloid, and you find that its report of the accident places the event in the wrong place at the wrong time, with the identity of the drivers and vehicles randomly mixed up.[11] Technically speaking, neither report is completely true—yet, most people would likely consider the former to be more truthful than the latter. Popper (1963) coined the term *verisimilitude* to refer to this "partial truth value" that can be associated with rival accounts.[12]

If we accept the notion of verisimilitude—and we do— then we are warranted to continue using models that we know to be—literally—false. How can we ensure that this approach does not degenerate into issuing our model with a blank check that eternally protects it against falsification?

We propose a solution along the lines advanced by Meehl (1990). On this account, we can continue to use a theory, and we may even legitimately continue to make modifications to it in response to empirical challenges, provided the theory has accumulated credit by strong successes, by "having lots of money in the bank" (Meehl, 1990, p. 115). How does one get money in the bank? By "predicting facts that, absent the theory, would be antecedently improbable" (Meehl, 1990, p. 115). Thus, the more a model has succeeded in making counterintuitive predictions, the greater its verisimilitude, and hence the more entitled we are to continue using it even though we know it to be (literally) false.

2.6.3   The Nature of Explanations

No exploration of modeling can be complete without discussing the concept of an explanation. What does it mean to *explain* something? In modern science, an "explanation" is commonly interpreted as identifying causes for an event or phenomenon of interest (Sun et al., 2005); accordingly, in Chapter 1, we alluded to explanations in the context of identifying the psychological processes that cause an outcome. The fact that those processes are unobservable is not necessarily of concern; contemporary physics, too, relies increasingly on unobservable constructs (e.g., quarks, leptons, or mesons) whose names are only slightly more magical and esoteric than their properties. Trout (2007) cited other elements of what makes a good scientific explanation, such as the unification of disparate phenomena, and a (typically) logical relation between the explanation's propositions and what it seeks to explain.

There is a final attribute of scientific explanations that is rarely made explicit: Explanations can "be epistemically valuable only if we could, implicitly or explicitly, understand them. As a result, explanation must maintain some contact with our psychological powers of understanding" (Trout, 2007, p. 565). It follows that *any* scientific explanation—be it in astronomy, biology, or particle physics—must necessarily also be evaluated with respect to its *psychological* properties. This rather striking insight has numerous implications.

First, an explanation that cannot be understood is not an explanation. It follows that some facts of the universe may remain irreducibly mysterious to humans—not because explanations do not exist in principle but because they cannot be humanly understood and hence cannot be formulated (Trout, 2007). It also follows that models in psychology benefit from *simplifying* the reality they seek to explain even though this simplification would likely render the model wrong. At the risk of being provocative, we would even argue that models are useful *only because* they are wrong. This is because of something known as Bonini's paradox (Dutton & Starbuck, 1971), which holds that as a model more closely approximates reality, it becomes less understandable. In the extreme case, the model may become just as difficult to understand as that which it is supposed to explain—in which case, nothing has been gained!

Second, when there are multiple potentially understandable explanations, some are preferred over others for reasons that are exclusively psychological and have nothing to do with their objective properties. In an article that was evocatively titled "Explanation as Orgasm," Gopnik (1998) highlighted the distinctive phenomenology (i.e., subjective feeling) associated with explanations; specifically, she proposed that the gratifying sense that accompanies the discovery of an explanation (the "aha," p. 108) may be evolution's mechanism to ensure the impetus for continued search and discovery—in the same way that orgasms may deliver the necessary impetus for reproduction. Although this "cognitive emotion" may deliver benefits to the species as a whole, by ensuring continued exploration of the environment, it does not ensure that people—including people who are scientists—will necessarily accept the best available explanation. Thus, Trout (2007) identifies several cognitive factors, such as hindsight bias and overconfidence, that can lead to a false or exaggerated sense of intellectual satisfaction (the earth actually did *not* move) when a scientist selects an explanation. Similarly, people generally have been found to prefer simple explanations to a greater extent than warranted by the data (Lombrozo, 2007), and they tend to cling to seductive adaptationist explanations (e.g., that animals have large eyes because they are better for seeing in the dark; Lombrozo, 2005). Hintzman (1991) even suggested that people will accept mere acronyms as an explanation for something, even if the acronym implies that the phenomenon is unexplained (e.g., UFO).

Are there any safeguards against these psychological risks that are associated with the pursuit of scientific explanations? Yes, and the best safeguard is to seek explanations that are embodied within the type of models discussed in this book. This case was argued very eloquently by Hintzman (1991), who listed 10 attributes of human reasoning that are likely contributors to errors in scientific reasoning and showed how those potential weaknesses can be counteracted by the use of quantitative models. Quantitative models are therefore preferable to verbal models not only for the reasons discussed throughout the first two chapters but also because they provide a "cognitive prosthesis" for our own human insufficiencies during theory construction itself. Farrell and Lewandowsky (in press) provide further analysis of how models can serve as a prosthesis to aid in scientific reasoning.

Notes

1. Readers familiar with the literature on the word length effect may object that only certain select stimuli give rise to the effect, whereas the majority of words do not; Bireta, Neath, and Surprenant (2006); Neath, Bireta, and Surprenant (2003). We agree entirely (Lewandowsky & Oberauer, 2008). However, our discussion here is limited to the *syllabic* word length effect using *pure* lists (i.e., all words on a given list are either all short or all long). Under those circumstances, the word length effect is robust and replicable (Bireta et al., 2006).

2. These numbers are conservative and represent the minimum number of choices available; for example, there are an infinite number of possible decay functions, and we assume here that only three are worthy of serious consideration (power, exponential, and linear).

3. Page and Norris (1998b) postulate that decay occurs during list presentation, but their assumption that *all* items have been rehearsed (and their activation has thus been restored to their encoded values) at the end of list presentation is formally identical to the assumption that decay does not commence until after the list has been presented.

4. This is an over-simplification because ordered rehearsal breaks down at some point. Nonetheless, for present purposes we retain this simple assumption.

5. The slope is (minus) the decay rate, which is defined to be dRate = .8;. Do not use the figure to infer the slope because the axes are not labeled—hence, the $45°$ angle of the line is entirely arbitrary.

6. The common intercept is the variable initAct, and the slopes have mean (minus) decRate and standard deviation decSD.

7. In fact, we have explored exponential decay, and it makes no difference to the results shown in Figures 2.3 and 2.5. Without variability in decay rate, the speech rate function is discontinuous.

8. Returning to our earlier analogy, the parameter-free radio can also be horrifically unsatisfying if you consider its instantiation in contemporary elevators.

9. Morrissey, erstwhile member of the band The Smiths.

10. Because the RMSD computes a continuous deviation between predictions and data, it assumes that the data are measured at least on an interval scale. Use of nominal measures (e.g., a Likert-type rating scale) is inappropriate because the meaning of a given deviation varies across the scale (Schunn & Wallach, 2005).

11. Meehl (1990) employed this analogy.

12. Formal analysis of verisimilitude, in particular a principled comparison between the values of rival theories, has proven to be surprisingly difficult (see, e.g., Gerla, 2007).

3

Basic Parameter Estimation Techniques

There is little doubt that even before you started reading this book, you had already fit many models to data. No one who has completed an introductory statistics course can escape learning about linear regression. It turns out that every time you computed a regression line, you were actually fitting a model—namely, the regression line with its two parameters, slope and intercept—to the data.

3.1   Fitting Models to Data: Parameter Estimation

For familiarity's sake, we therefore initiate our discussion of parameter estimation within the linear regression framework. Specifically, we begin by defining the "model" $y_i = b_0 + b_1 x_i + e_i$, which expresses each observation y_i as a function of the measurement of the independent variable x_i and two to-be-estimated parameters (intercept b_0 and slope b_1), plus an error term e_i. A more efficient representation of the same model is possible in matrix notation:

$$y = X b + e, \qquad (3.1)$$

where the two elements of the vector $\mathbf{b}$ are the parameters (b_0 and b_1) whose values we wish to obtain and where $\mathbf{X}$ is a two-column matrix. The first column consists of 1s (to represent the constant intercept for all observations) and the second column of the observed values of our independent variable. You may remember from your statistics background that the parameters can be computed by rearranging Equation 3.1:

71

$$b = (X^T X)^{-1} X^T y, \qquad\qquad (3.2)$$

where the superscripts T and -1 refer to the matrix transpose and matrix inverse operators, respectively.

In MATLAB, Equation 3.2 can be trivially implemented by the single statement b = x\y, where y is a vector of y values, and x is the two-column matrix just discussed. The "\" operator is shorthand for "matrix left division" and implements the operations required for a linear regression.

Given the availability of this simple solution in MATLAB, why do we devote an entire chapter to the process of fitting a model to data? The answer is that unlike linear regression, the parameters for most psychological models cannot be computed directly, by a single statement or a single equation such as Equation 3.2, because their complexity prevents a direct algebraic solution. Instead, parameters must be estimated iteratively. Several parameter estimation techniques exist, and although they differ in important ways, they also share many features in common. Let's begin by establishing those before we turn to the more technical details.

3.1.1   Visualizing Modeling

The first thing to note is that parameter estimation techniques provide a toolbox of considerable generality that can be applied to *any* modeling problem. That is, irrespective of the specifics of your model and the data to which you want to apply it, the techniques presented in this chapter can estimate the best-fitting parameter values. How is this possible? The answer is quite straightforward and is graphically illustrated in Figure 3.1.

The figure shows an "error surface" for a modeling problem involving two parameters. For now, we can ignore what those parameters mean, we can ignore the nature of the model, and we can even ignore the data—but don't worry, we'll get around to all of that soon.

Each point on the surface shows the extent of discrepancy between the predictions of the model and the data (measured by the root mean squared deviation [RMSD]; see Section 2.5.2) as a function of the model's two parameters. This implies that to generate the surface in the figure, the model's predictions had to be compared to the data for all possible combinations of parameter values; this is indeed how this figure was generated. Note that the surface has a point at the center at which its height is minimized: The parameter values associated with that point—most readily identified by the "bull's-eye" formed by the contour projection onto the two-dimensional basis space—are the "best-fitting parameter estimates." The goal of fitting a model to data is to obtain those estimates. Once the estimates have been obtained, the predictions of the model can be examined, and one can determine if the model provides an adequate account of the data. Note

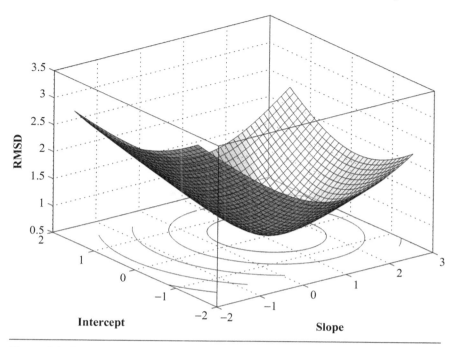

Figure 3.1 An "error surface" for a linear regression model given by $\mathbf{y} = \mathbf{X}\mathbf{b} + \mathbf{e}$. The discrepancy between data and predictions is shown on the vertical axis (using the root mean squared deviation [RMSD] as a discrepancy function) as a function of the two parameters (slope, b_1, and intercept, b_0). The underlying data consist of observations sampled from two normal distributions (one for x and one for y) with means 0 and standard deviations 1 and correlation $\rho = .8$. The contours projected onto the two-dimensional basis space identify the minimum of the error surface at $b_1 = .74$ and $b_0 = -.11$. See text for details.

that there is no guarantee that a model can handle the data to which it is applied: Even though the error surface *will* have a minimum (or indeed more than one), and even though best-fitting parameter values can always be estimated, the minimum discrepancy between predictions and data may nonetheless be too great—and hence its goodness of fit poor—for the model to be of much use. We will continue to return to this issue of assessing the goodness of fit of a model later, but for now, we need to ask how exactly the best-fitting estimates of the parameters are obtained.

One possibility, of course, is to do what we did for Figure 3.1 and to examine all possible combinations of parameter values (with some degree of granularity because we cannot explore the infinite number of combinations of continuous parameter values). By keeping track of the lowest discrepancy, we can then simply read off the best-fitting parameter estimates when we are done. This procedure is known as a "grid search" and can be useful in certain circumstances. However, in most instances, this approach is not feasible: The surface in our figure was drawn using some 1,600 discrepancy values, and this number increases to 2.5 *million* if we need to examine four rather than two parameters (keeping granularity constant).

Fortunately, there is an alternative approach that readily suggests itself if you pretend that the error surface in Figure 3.1 is carved out of wood or some other hard material. Suppose you dropped a marble onto the surface at any random point, what would happen? Exactly; driven by gravity, the marble would very quickly come to rest at the lowest point of the surface. In this particular example, it would not matter where exactly you dropped the marble; it would reach the same minimum from *any* starting point on the surface. This simple physical analogy is embodied in nearly all parameter estimation techniques: One begins by determining "starting values" for the parameters (either randomly or, more commonly, by educated guesswork), and the parameter estimation technique then iteratively adjusts the parameters such that the value of the discrepancy function is reduced at each step until no further improvement is possible.[1] At that point, the best-fitting estimates have been obtained. This mechanism implies that in reality, the error surface shown in Figure 3.1 is never instantiated (or known) in its entirety; instead, the parameter estimation traces out a single path across the surface from the starting point to the minimum. All other values on the error surface remain un-instantiated and hence unknown.

Although this visualization of parameter estimation is conceptually quite simple, considerable technical sophistication underlies the choice of parameter adjustments at each step down the error surface. We will turn to those technical issues after we reveal the details of the model that gave rise to Figure 3.1.

3.1.2   An Example

You may have already guessed that the model underlying our error surface is a simple linear regression involving two variables that were related by the standard two-parameter model $y_i = b_0 + b_1 x_i + e_i$. For our example, the data for each variable were generated by randomly sampling 20 observations from a normal distribution with mean $\mu = 0$ and standard deviation $\sigma = 1$. The correlation between the two variables was $\rho = .8$, and the best-fitting regression line for the data underlying our error surface was $y_i = -.11 + .74\, x_i$. The best-fitting parameter values were computed by the MATLAB statement mentioned earlier—namely, b = x\y. The RMSD (see Equation 2.2) between model predictions—that is, the fitted values $\hat{y}_i$—and the data was .46 for the best-fitting parameter values; this represents the value on the ordinate at the minimum of the surface in Figure 3.1.

What does this have to do with parameter estimation techniques in cognitive modeling? The answer is provided in the following program listings, which show the MATLAB code for estimating the parameters in the way just described—that is, by starting at an arbitrary location on the error surface and then moving toward the minimum. Remember that we said earlier that the techniques presented in this chapter are extremely general and can handle *any* estimation problem? Indeed— and that means the parameter estimation techniques can also handle linear regression, thus permitting a direct comparison of the results to those obtained by conventional computation.[2]

Listing 3.1 Computing and Estimating Regression Parameters

```
1  nDataPts = 20;
2  rho = .8;
3  intercept = .0;
4
5  %generate simulated data
6  data=zeros(nDataPts,2);
7  data(:,2) = randn (nDataPts,1) ;
8  data(:,1) = randn (nDataPts,1) .* sqrt(1.0-rho^2) + ↩
        (data (:,2).*rho) + intercept;
9
10 %do conventional regression analysis and compute ↩
        parameters
11 bigX = [ones(nDataPts,1) data(:,2)];
12 y = data (:,1);
13 b = bigX\y
14
15 %assign and display starting values and call ↩
        parameter-estimation function
16 startParms = [-1., .2]
17 [finalParms,finDiscrepancy] = ↩
        wrapper4fmin(startParms,data)
```

Consider first the program in Listing 3.1, which spans only a few lines but accomplishes three major tasks: First, it generates data, then it performs a regression analysis, and finally it repeats the regression but this time by calling a function that estimates the parameters using the procedure just described. Let's go through those steps in detail.

The first line of interest is line 7, which fills the second column of a rectangular matrix (called `data`) with samples from a random normal distribution. Those are our values for the independent variable, x. The next line, line 8, does almost the same thing: It samples random-normal values, but it also ensures that those values are correlated with the first set (i.e., x) to the extent determined by the variable `rho`. The resulting samples are put into the first column of the data matrix, and they represent our values of y. It is important to realize that those two lines of code draw *random samples* from two distributions with known means (μ), standard deviations (σ), and correlation (ρ); thus, we expect the sample statistics (namely, $\overline{X}$, s, and r) to be approximately equal to those population values, but it would be surprising indeed if they turned out to be exactly equal. (In reality, of course, we would replace these lines with the code required to read our data of interest into the program. Here we generated synthetic data because we can then determine their properties and examine how well our fit recovers those known properties.)

Having thus generated the data, we next generate a "design matrix" for the regression by adding a column of 1s in front of our values of x. This is done in line 11 and results in a matrix called bigX, which we need to compute the regression parameters using the statement already discussed. Note that the column of 1s represents the regression intercept, which is constant and does not depend on x—hence the use of a column of constant values. Note the absence of a ";" at the end of line 13 that computes the actual regression. MATLAB prints out the end result of any statement that is not terminated by a ";" and this ensures that you can see the parameter estimates (in the vector b) on the screen.

Now let's turn to the most interesting and novel part, which commences in line 16. That line assigns starting values to the two parameters—namely, slope (b_1) and intercept (b_0), which are represented in a single vector in that order. (The order was determined by the programmer and is arbitrary, but once it's been decided, it is important to keep it consistent.) Note that the starting value for the slope is -1, which is exactly opposite to the true slope value implied by our data generation in line 8, so these starting values are nowhere near the true result. Although we chose these starting values mainly for illustrative purposes, it also reflects real life where we often have no inkling of the true parameter values. Later, we discuss the issue of finding suitable starting values for parameters.

The final line of the program, line 17, hands over control to another function, called wrapper4fmin, and passes the parameters and the data as arguments to that function. The function returns two values that are printed out (if you don't know why they are printed, reread the preceding paragraph) and that contain the final best-fitting parameter estimates and the final value of the discrepancy function (i.e., its achieved minimum).

Seem simple? It is—almost. Just like in the examples in the previous chapter, we call a function to do most of the work for us. This function appears to take the data and starting values and then returns the best-fitting parameter estimates. How does it know what model and what discrepancy function to use? The function knows because we wrote it; unlike the functions from the previous chapter, this one is not built into MATLAB.

One of the more powerful features of MATLAB (and of most other programming languages) is that we can write new functions ourselves. Listing 3.2 shows this function, which is defined in a separate file that must be available in the same directory on your disk as the preceding program or available in the MATLAB path. (By the way, the file's name must be "wrapper4fmin.m" because MATLAB expects each function to be contained in a file with the same name.)

Listing 3.2 The Core Function for Parameter Estimation

```
 1 function [x,fVal] = wrapper4fmin(pArray,data)
 2
 3 [x,fVal] = fminsearch(@bof,pArray);
 4
 5 %nested function 'bof' inherits 'data' and argument ↩
       'parms'
 6 %is provided by fminsearch
 7       function rmsd=bof(parms)
 8
 9          predictions=getregpred(parms, data);
10          sd=(predictions-data(:,1)).^2;
11          rmsd=sqrt(sum(sd)/numel(sd));
12       end
13 end
```

The listing is rather short because the function accomplishes only two things: First, in line 3, it calls the MATLAB function fminsearch, which performs the actual parameter estimation. Note that fminsearch is passed the starting parameter values (in the array pArray) and something called @bof. The latter is of particular interest, and we will discuss it in a moment—but first, note that fminsearch returns two variables (x and fVal), which are also the return arguments of the function wrapper4fmin itself. You can tell they are return arguments because they appear on the left-hand side of the so-called "function header" in line 1. So it appears that our function merely takes information, passes it on to another function, and then returns that other function's result itself—so what's the point?

The answer lies in the variable @bof, which is a special variable known as a *function handle*. Unlike other variables that contain standard information such as parameter values or the results of computations, this variable contains the name of a function. Function handles are identified by a leading "@" symbol, and they permit MATLAB to call a function by referencing the function handle. The great advantage of this is that MATLAB need not know about the actual function—all it needs is the function handle. (We recommend that you consult the MATLAB documentation at this point if you need a more detailed description of function

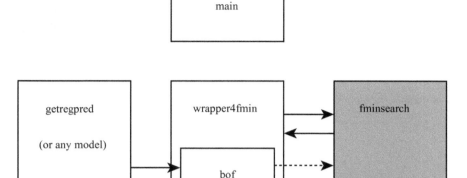

Figure 3.2   The relationship between the MATLAB functions used in Listings 3.1 through 3.3. The names in each box refer to the function name, and the arrows refer to exchanges of information (function calls and returns). Solid arrows represent information exchange that is entirely managed by the programmer, whereas broken arrows represent exchanges managed by MATLAB. Shading of a box indicates that the function is provided by MATLAB and does not require programming. See text for details.

handles.) Thus, the second main task of our function `wrapper4fmin` is to define another function, called `bof`, in lines 7 through 12. This function is called an "embedded" function (because it is itself wholly contained within a function), and it is not called directly by any of our own functions—instead, the embedded function `bof` is called from within MATLAB's `fminsearch`, which knows about it because we pass `fminsearch` the function handle `@bof`.

Because this calling sequence is somewhat complex, we have illustrated the overall relationship between the various functions in Figure 3.2. In the figure, the box labeled "main" refers to the program in listing 3.1, and the other boxes refer to the various functions. Note the arrows that connect the box "main" with "wrapper4fmin" and the latter to "fminsearch." This indicates that those functions communicate directly with each other in the manner controlled by us, the programmers (or you, eventually!). This communication is done by passing values as function arguments or by accepting return values from functions (or by inheriting variables from containing functions, as noted below). Note also that "fminsearch" and "bof" are connected by dotted arrows—this is to indicate that those calls are under the control of MATLAB rather than the programmer.

Which brings us to the really nifty bit. MATLAB's `fminsearch` will estimate the parameters for *any* model—all that `fminsearch` needs is (a) what starting values to use for the parameters and (b) the handle of some function (in this instance, bof) that can return the discrepancy between that model's predictions and the data. Before we move on, it is important to focus your understanding on the most crucial part: The function bof is never invoked directly, but only indirectly, via the MATLAB built-in function fminsearch. The two listings we have discussed so far (3.1 and 3.2) set up the scaffolding around bof that permits this indirect call (hence the dotted arrows in Figure 3.2) to happen.

Let's have a closer look at bof. Figure 3.2 tells us that bof calls a function named getregpred; this happens in line 9. Although we haven't shown you getregpred yet, we can tell you that it takes the current parameter values and returns the predictions of the model. In this instance, the model predictions are the fitted values ($\hat{y}$) provided by the regression line. The two lines following the function call take those predictions and compare them to the data by computing the RMSD (see Section 2.5.2). That value of RMSD is the return argument of bof. Two further points are noteworthy: First, the values of the parameters passed in parms are constantly changing during calls to bof. Their values will resemble the starting values at the outset, and they will ultimately end up being the best-fitting estimates, with fminsearch providing the path from the former to the latter set of values. Second, did you notice that bof used the array data in line 9? This may have escaped your notice because it is not terribly remarkable at first glance; however, it is quite important to realize that this is possible only because bof is embedded within wrapper4fmin and hence inherits all variables that are known to wrapper4fmin. Thus, by passing data to wrapper4fmin as an argument, we also make it automatically available to bof—notwithstanding the fact that we do not pass that variable as an argument. In general, the fact that an embedded function has access to all variables in the surrounding function provides a direct path of communication with bof in addition to the indirect calls via fminsearch.

We have almost completed our discussion of this example. Listing 3.3 shows the final function, getregpred, which computes predictions from the current parameter values whenever it is called by bof. The function is simplicity itself, with line 4 taking the parameters b_0 and b_1 and the values of x (in the second column of data; see line 7 in listing 3.1) to compute the fitted values ($\hat{y}$).

The remainder of the function plots the data and the current predictions (i.e., the current estimate of the best-fitting regression line) before waiting for a keypress to proceed. (The pause and the plotting at each step are done for didactic purposes only; except for this introductory example, we would not slow the process down in this fashion.) There is no pressing need to discuss those lines here, although you may wish to consult them for a number of informative details about MATLAB's plotting capabilities (which are considerable; many of the figures in this book were produced by MATLAB).

Listing 3.3 Computing Predictions From Parameters

```
1  function preds = getregpred (parms,data)
2  b1 = parms(1);
3  b0 = parms(2);
4  preds = b0 + (b1 .* data(:,2));
5
6  %plot current predictions and data and wait for keypress
7  clf
8  hold on
9  plot (data(:,2),data(:,1), 'o', ←
          'MarkerFaceColor',[0.4 0.4 ←
          0.4],'MarkerEdgeColor','black');
10 plot (data(:,2),preds, '-k');
11 axis([-2 2 -2 2]);
12 xlabel('X','FontSize',18,'FontWeight','b');
13 ylabel('Y','FontSize',18,'FontWeight','b');
14 set(gca,'Ytick',[-2:2],'Xtick',[-2:2])
15 box on
16 pause
```

We are done! Figure 3.3 provides two snapshots of what happens when we run the programs just discussed. The top panel shows the data together with a regression line during the opening stages of parameter estimation, whereas the bottom panel shows the same data with another regression line toward the end of the parameter estimation. Altogether, when we ran the program, 88 such graphs were produced, each resulting from one call to `bof` by `fminsearch`. In other words, it took 88 steps to descend the error surface from the starting values to the minimum.

As we noted earlier, the starting values were very different from what we knew to be the true values: We chose those rather poor values to ensure that the early snapshot in Figure 3.3 would look spectacular. Had we chosen better starting values, the optimization would have taken fewer steps—but even the 88 steps here are a vast improvement over the roughly 1,600 predictions we had to compute to trace out the entire surface in Figure 3.1. By the way, reassuringly, the final estimates for b_0 and b_1 returned by our program were identical to those computed in the conventional manner at the outset.

Let us recapitulate once more. We first visualized the mechanism by which parameters are estimated when direct analytical solution is impossible (i.e., in the vast majority of cases in cognitive modeling). We then provided an instantiation of parameter estimation in MATLAB. What remains to be clarified is that our MATLAB code was far more powerful than it might appear at first glance. Although we "only" estimated parameters for a simple regression line, the framework provided in Listings 3.1 through 3.3 can be extended to far more complex modeling: Just

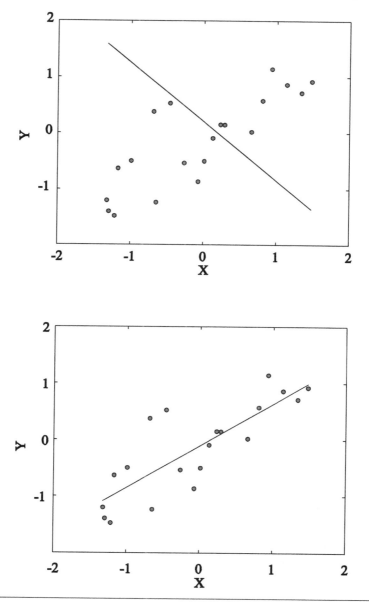

Figure 3.3 Two snapshots during parameter estimation. Each panel shows the data (plotting symbols) and the current predictions provided by the regression parameters (solid line). The top panel shows a snapshot early on, and the bottom panel shows a snapshot toward the end of parameter estimation.

replace line 4 in Listing 3.3 with your favorite cognitive model (which of course may stretch over dozens if not hundreds of lines of code) and our programs will estimate that model's parameters for you. A later chapter of this book (Chapter 7) contains two examples that do exactly that, but before we can discuss those, we need to deal with several important technical issues.

3.1.3   Inside the Box: Parameter Estimation Techniques

How exactly does a parameter estimation technique find its way to the bottom of the error surface? Several techniques are available, and we begin by examining the *Simplex* method of Nelder and Mead (1965). This method underlies MATLAB's fminsearch function and was thus used in the preceding example.

3.1.3.1   Simplex

The workings of Simplex. A simplex is a geometrical figure that consists of an arbitrary number of interconnected points in an arbitrary number of dimensions. For example, a triangle and a pyramid represent a simplex in two and three dimensions, respectively.[3] In Nelder and Mead's (1965) algorithm, which is also known as a polytope algorithm, the dimensionality of the simplex corresponds to the dimensionality of the parameter space, and the number of points in the simplex is one greater than the number of parameters. Hence, the preceding example involved a two-dimensional simplex consisting of three points—that is, a triangle. Each point of the simplex corresponds to a conjunction of parameter values; in the earlier example, that vector contained the slope and intercept. Thus, for the preceding example, the simplex is a triangle that is projected onto the X-Y space in Figure 3.1. At the outset, a simplex is created at a location given by the starting values, and the discrepancy function is evaluated for each point of the simplex. From then on, the simplex moves through the parameter space by taking one of two possible steps (the choice among them is governed by an algorithm that is not relevant here). First, the simplex may be reflected, which means that the point with the greatest discrepancy (worst fit) is flipped to the opposite side, thus performing a downhill somersault. If the somersault is in a particularly rewarding direction, it may be accompanied by an expansion of the simplex (thus covering more ground). Second, the simplex may be contracted by moving the point (or points) with the worst fit closer toward the center. These reflections and contractions continue until the simplex has tumbled down the error surface and comes to rest at the bottom.

This process is illustrated in Figure 3.4, which shows a two-dimensional projection of our earlier error surface with the degree of shading representing the values of the discrepancy function (i.e., RMSD in this case). The figure contains three

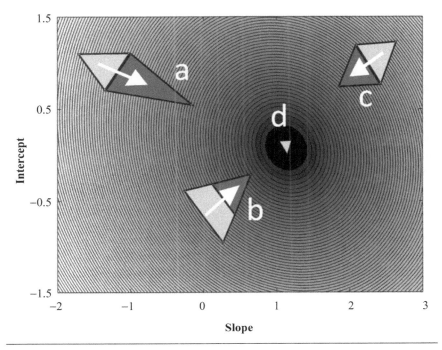

Figure 3.4 Two-dimensional projection of the error surface in Figure 3.1. Values of RMSD are represented by degree of shading, with lower values of RMSD corresponding to darker shades of gray. The three large simplexes illustrate possible moves down the error surface. (a) Reflection accompanied by expansion. (b) Contraction along two dimensions (shrinkage). (c) Reflection without expansion. Note that the locations of those points are arbitrary and for illustration only. The tiny simplex at point d represents the final state when the best-fitting parameter values are returned. See text for details.

hypothetical points during parameter estimation (locations a, b, and c) that illustrate the behavior of the simplex as it tumbles down the surface. At each point, the simplex will move closer to the minimum (the obvious "bull's eye") by variously reflecting (a and c) or contracting (b). The process will end when the simplex has reached point d, where it will continually contract until it has collapsed onto a single point,[4] whose location corresponds to the best-fitting parameter estimates. That point is known as a minimum on the error surface.

The Simplex algorithm reaches the minimum of the error surface without any knowledge of the function whose parameters it is estimating and without regard to the number of parameters involved. All that the algorithm requires is knowledge of the parameter values and an evaluation of the discrepancy function at each step.

Limitations of Simplex. Although Simplex[5] works well in many circumstances, it suffers from a number of limitations and drawbacks. First, although the simplex tumbles in discrete steps, it nonetheless requires all parameters to be continuous. Thus, Simplex cannot estimate parameters that are constrained to be integers (e.g., the number of times people are assumed to rehearse an item before recalling it). In those cases, one can combine a grid search for the integers with Simplex estimation of the remainder. Alternatively, the model must be reparameterized such that a parameter that is continuous with respect to Simplex will take on a discrete function within the model (e.g., a value of 1.3 for the number of rehearsals may be taken to represent the average prediction of 7 runs with 1 rehearsal and 3 runs with 2 rehearsals).

A related problem involves the fact that most model parameters are at least tacitly constrained to be within a certain range. For example, it would make no sense for a forgetting rate to be greater than 1, and hence Simplex must be made aware of this constraint. One way in which this can be achieved is by assigning a large discrepancy value to the model's predictions (irrespective of what they actually are) whenever the constraint is violated. Ideally, this will be implemented as a "barrier function" such that the penalty grows continuously and rapidly as the boundary of legitimate parameter values is approached (and beyond, to penalize particularly outrageous values). While this technique succeeds in keeping parameter estimates within bounds, it may cause the simplex to collapse prematurely into a subspace, thus returning inappropriate parameter estimates (Rowan, 1990). Alternatively, you may use a version of `fminsearch` that explicitly handles boundaries on parameter values. This alternative version, `fminsearchbnd`, is not part of a standard MATLAB installation but can be readily downloaded from MATLAB Central (recall that Section 2.3.1 contains instructions about how to access MATLAB Central). One of the examples in Chapter 7 will make use of `fminsearchbnd`.

Third, although there is no in-principle limit on the number of parameters that can be estimated, Simplex is known to be quite inefficient when the number of parameters is large. Specifically, if there are more than five parameters, efficient estimation becomes problematic (Box, 1966). Even when the number of parameters is as small as two, there may be instances in which Simplex fails to converge onto the minimum of even a well-behaved (i.e., "convex") function (Lagarias et al., 1998).

Fourth, Simplex will only work well if the discrepancy function is deterministically related to the model's parameters. That is, Simplex will encounter difficulties if the same parameter values yield different predictions every time the model is evaluated. You might wonder how this could possibly occur, but in fact it is quite common: Any model that includes a random component—such as our instantiation of the phonological loop with variable decay rate in the previous chapter—will necessarily yield variable predictions under identical parameter values. This random variation can be thought to reflect trial-to-trial "noise" within a participant or individual differences between participants or both. The presence of random variation in the model's predictions is no trivial matter because it turns the error surface into a randomly "bubbling goo" in which dimples and peaks appear and disappear in an instant. It takes little imagination to realize that this would present a major challenge to Simplex. The bubbling can be reduced by running numerous replications of the model each time it is called, thus averaging out random error. (When this is done, it is advantageous to reseed the random number generator each time Simplex calls your model because this eliminates an unnecessary source of noise; more on that in Chapter 7.) [6]

A general limitation of parameter estimation. A final problem, which applies to *all* parameter estimation techniques, arises when the error surface has a more challenging shape. Until now, we have considered an error surface that is smooth and gradual (Figure 3.1), but there is no guarantee that the surface associated with our model is equally well behaved. In fact, there is every probability that it is not: Complex models tend to have surfaces with many dimples, valleys, plateaus, or ridges. Given what you now know about parameter estimation, the adverse implications of such surfaces should be clear from a moment's thought. Specifically, there is the possibility that Simplex will descend into a *local* minimum rather than the *global* minimum. This problem is readily visualized if you imagine an empty egg carton that is held at an angle: Although there will be one minimum that is lowest in absolute terms—namely, the cup whose bottom happens to be the lowest, depending on which way you point the carton—there are many other minima (all other cups) that are terribly tempting to a tumbling simplex. Because the simplex knows nothing about the error landscape other than what it can "see" in its immediate vicinity, it can be trapped in a local minimum. Being stuck in a local minimum has serious adverse consequences because it may obscure the true power of the model. Imagine the egg carton being held at a very steep angle, with the lowest cup being near zero on the discrepancy function—but you end up in the top cup whose discrepancy is vast. You would think that the model cannot handle the data, when in fact it could if you could only find the right parameter values. Likewise, being stuck in a local minimum compromises any meaningful interpretation of parameter values because they are not the "right" (i.e., best-fitting) estimates.

The local-minima problem is pervasive and, alas, unsolvable. That is, there is never any guarantee that your obtained minimum is the global minimum, although your confidence in it being a global minimum can be enhanced in a number of ways. First, if the parameter estimation is repeated with a number of different starting values, and one always ends up with the same estimates, then there is a good chance that these estimates represent a global minimum. By contrast, if the estimates differ with each set of starting values, then you may be faced with an egg carton. In that instance, a second alternative is to abandon Simplex altogether and to use an alternative parameter estimation technique that can alleviate—though not eliminate—the local-minimum problem by allowing the procedure to "jump" out of local minima. This technique is known as simulated annealing (Kirkpatrick, Gelatt, & Vecchi, 1983).

3.1.3.2   Simulated Annealing

Thus far, our discussion of parameter estimation has rested on the seemingly inevitable assumption that we follow a *downward* trajectory on the error surface. At first glance, it seems inadvisable to relax that assumption—how could an *upward* movement possibly be advantageous? On closer inspection, however, an occasional upward movement turns out to be indispensable if one wishes to avoid local minima. After all, the only way in which a local minimum can be avoided is by "climbing" out of it first, before one can descend to a lower point. This recognition is embodied in the *simulated annealing* approach to parameter estimation (e.g., Kirkpatrick et al., 1983; Vanderbilt & Louie, 1984).

Simulated annealing (SA) is based on a physical analogy: If a hot liquid is allowed to cool rapidly, the resulting crystal will have many imperfections. If the liquid is instead cooled slowly, and much time is spent in the vicinity of the freezing point, the resulting crystal will be far more uniform. All you need to know about crystals for now is that they represent a state of minimum energy— replace the word *energy* with *discrepancy*, and think of molecules as parameters and, presto, parameter estimation isn't just cool but also cooling.

The crucial attribute of SA is that at any iteration, when the current parameter estimates are updated, the algorithm may sometimes accept a new point in parameter space with *greater* discrepancy than the current one. Specifically, suppose $\theta^{(t)}$ represents our current (i.e., at iteration t) vector of parameter values. We first generate a *candidate* update according to

$$\theta_c^{(t+1)} = D(\theta^{(t)}), \tag{3.3}$$

where D is a "candidate function" whose mechanics we discuss later. For now, all we need to know is that D, unlike the techniques considered earlier, does not ensure that the new parameter vector necessarily yields a lower discrepancy. This provides the opportunity for the following stochastic decision step:

$$\theta^{(t+1)} = \begin{cases} A(\theta_c^{(t+1)}, \theta^{(t)}, T^{(t)}) & \text{if } \Delta f > 0 \\ \theta_c^{(t+1)} & \text{if } \Delta f \leq 0, \end{cases} \tag{3.4}$$

where Δf is a shorthand way of saying "the difference in the discrepancy value between the candidate parameter vector, $\theta_c^{(t+1)}$, and the original vector, $\theta^{(t)}$." Thus, any value of Δf below zero represents an improvement, and Equation 3.4 tells us that this candidate is always accepted. In that case, the new parameter vector $(\theta^{(t+1)})$ is set to the value of the candidate $(\theta_c^{(t+1)})$. What happens if the candidate does not represent an improvement but actually makes things worse? In that case, the new parameter vector takes on the value of an "acceptance function," A, which takes as arguments the new candidate, the current parameter vector, and a parameter $T^{(t)}$ that we explain below. The acceptance function, in turn, is given by

$$A(\theta_c^{(t+1)}, \theta^{(t)}, T^{(t)}) = \begin{cases} \theta_c^{(t+1)} & \text{if } p < e^{-\Delta f/T^{(t)}} \\ \theta^{(t)} & \text{otherwise,} \end{cases} \tag{3.5}$$

where p is a sample from a uniform distribution in $[0, 1]$. Put simply, the acceptance function returns one of two possible outcomes: It either returns the current parameter vector, in which case the candidate is rejected and the process continues and another candidate is drawn anew using Equation 3.3, or it returns the candidate parameter vector despite the fact that it increases the discrepancy function. The probability of this seemingly paradoxical uphill movement is determined by two quantities: the extent to which the discrepancy gets worse (Δf) and the current "temperature" of the annealing process ($T^{(t)}$).

Let us consider the implications of Equations 3.4 and 3.5. First, note that the acceptance function is only relevant if the candidate makes things worse (i.e., $\Delta f > 0$)—otherwise, no decision is to be made, and the improved candidate vector is accepted. The fact that $\Delta f > 0$ whenever the acceptance function is called implies that the quantity $e^{-\Delta f/T^{(t)}}$ in Equation 3.5 is always < 1 and will tend toward zero as Δf increases. In consequence, large steps up the error surface are quite unlikely to be accepted, whereas tiny uphill steps have a much greater acceptance probability. This relationship between step size and acceptance probability is further modulated by the temperature, $T^{(t)}$, such that high temperatures make it more likely for a given step uphill to be accepted than lower temperatures. Figure 3.5 shows the interplay between those two variables.

The figure clarifies that when the temperature is high, even large movements up the error surface become possible, whereas as things cool down, the probability of an upward movement decreases. In the limit, when the temperature is very low, no movement up the error surface, however small, is likely to be accepted. This makes intuitive sense if one thinks of temperature as a Brownian motion: The more things heat up, the more erratically everything jumps up and down, whereas less and less motion occurs as things cool down. By implication, we are unlikely to get stuck in a local minimum when the temperature is high (because

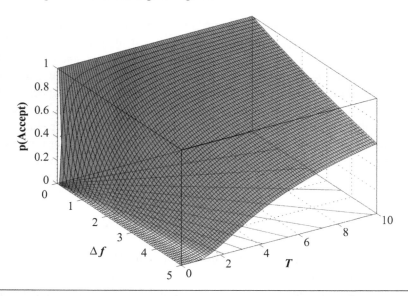

Figure 3.5 Probability with which a worse fit is accepted during simulated annealing as a function of the increase in discrepancy (Δf) and the temperature parameter (T). The data are hypothetical but illustrate the interplay between the two relevant variables. The range of temperatures follows precedent (Nourani & Andresen, 1998). See text for details.

we have a good chance of jumping out of it despite a positive Δf). That is of course desirable, but it is also problematic because it implies that we are equally likely to jump around in the vicinity of a *global* minimum without settling onto the lowest possible point. There is an obvious solution: Start out the search with a high temperature, thus avoiding local minima along the way, and reduce the temperature so we can settle within the (hopefully) global minimum later on. All SA algorithms include a cooling schedule along those lines, which gradually decreases the temperature across iterations (hence the superscript t).

To complete our discussion, we therefore need to do two more things: First, what is the initial value of the temperature and how does it cool down? Second, how are candidate vectors ($\theta_c^{(t+1)}$) generated by the function D? Those two issues turn out to be intimately related and are the subject of much research and discussion (e.g., Locatelli, 2002; Nourani & Andresen, 1998). For present purposes, we briefly discuss a very common—but not necessarily optimal (see Nourani and Andresen, 1998)—cooling schedule and candidate function.

Kirkpatrick et al. (1983) proposed two cooling schedules that have been used widely: an exponential schedule given by

$$T^{(t)} = T_0 \, \alpha^t \tag{3.6}$$

and a linear schedule given by

$$T^{(t)} = T_0 - \eta\,t, \tag{3.7}$$

where α and η are fixed parameters, and T_0 represents the initial temperature of the system. (The choice of T_0 is crucial and depends on the nature of the discrepancy function, which may be ascertained by computing the discrepancies for a sample of randomly chosen parameter values; Locatelli, 2002.) Whichever cooling schedule is used, Equations 3.6 and 3.7 imply that across iterations, the SA process gradually moves toward the left in Figure 3.5, and the system becomes more and more stable until it finally settles and no further uphill movement is possible. (Quick test: Is the surface in Figure 3.5 an error surface, such as those discussed earlier in connection with Simplex? If you were tempted to say yes, you should reread this section—the two surfaces represent quite different concepts.) Finally, then, where do the candidates $\boldsymbol{\theta}_c^{(t)}$ come from? Perhaps surprisingly, it is not uncommon to generate the next candidate by taking a step in a random direction from the current point:

$$D(\boldsymbol{\theta}^{(t)}) = \boldsymbol{\theta}^{(t)} + s\,\boldsymbol{\theta}_r, \tag{3.8}$$

where s is a step size parameter and $\boldsymbol{\theta}_r$ is a vector of *random* parameter values constrained to be of unit length (i.e., $\|\boldsymbol{\theta}_r\| = 1$). Equation 3.8 defines the candidate function D that we used as a "black box" at the outset (Equation 3.3) to generate a candidate. Thus, at any given point, the SA algorithm takes a step in a random direction, which is then accepted or rejected according to Equations 3.4 and 3.5.[7]

One last issue remains to be clarified: In the discussion so far, we have used the same superscript (t) to refer to the iterations that give rise to new candidates and to the cooling schedule across those iterations. This choice was made to facilitate presentation; many actual SA algorithms will generate multiple candidates at each temperature, and the cooling is much slower than the movement through the parameter space. Simulated annealing is now quite commonly used in cognitive modeling; for example, Erickson and Kruschke (2002) used SA to fit two categorization models to their data.

A visually striking interactive exploration of simulated annealing was created by Goldstone and Sakamoto (2003): Their study contains links to a webpage where you can interactively explore the workings of simulated annealing by drawing your own error surface and by adjusting the parameters just discussed (our supporting website, http://www.cogsciwa.com, contains a direct link to their simulations). We highly recommend that you explore their simulation because it is striking to see how simulated annealing can avoid getting stuck in even fairly deep local minima.

Simulated-annealing algorithms are not built into MATLAB but can be downloaded from MATLAB Central (see Section 2.3.1 for instructions). Once downloaded, the MATLAB implementations of SA can be called and used in much the same way as `fminsearch`. Alternatively, if you have access to the "Genetic Algorithm and Direct Search Toolbox" for MATLAB, which can be purchased as an add-on to the basic MATLAB package, then you will have immediate access to SA functions as well as the genetic algorithms that we discuss in the next section.

3.1.3.3   Genetic Algorithms

We briefly consider another class of estimation techniques that are based on evolutionary genetics. These *genetic algorithms* rival simulated annealing in their ability to resist local minima and noise (Buckles & Petry, 1992), but they are based on a completely different approach to "search"—so different, in fact, that we put "search" in quotation marks.[8]

We take a first stab at introducing the technique by retaining the (pseudo) genetic language within which it is commonly couched. At the heart of a genetic algorithm is the idea of a population of organisms that evolves across generations. Transmission across generations involves mating, where the choice of potential mates is tied to their fitness. Reproduction is imperfect, involving the occasional random mutation as well as more systematic crossovers between pairs of parents. This process repeats across generations until an organism has evolved whose fitness satisfies some target criterion.

Now let's translate this into modeling terminology. The population of organisms in a genetic algorithm involves representations of candidate parameter values. Specifically, each organism represents a θ_c; that is, a complete set of candidate values for all parameters that are being estimated. Each organism's fitness, therefore, relates to the value of our standard discrepancy function, f, for those parameter values (because the algorithm relies on maximizing fitness rather than minimizing discrepancy, we must invert the value of f so it points in the required direction). At each generational cycle, organisms are selected for mating with replacement on the basis of their fitness—that is, the fitter an organism is, the more likely it is to "mate," and because sampling occurs with replacement, any organism can contribute more than once. Once mates have been selected, the next generation (which contains the same number of organisms as before) is derived from the mating set by one of three processes that are chosen at random and on the basis of some preset probabilities: (a) An exact copy of an organism is made, (b) a random mutation occurs during copying, or (c) a crossover occurs in which two parents exchange part of their genetic material to form two offspring. The new population, thus derived, replaces the old one, and the process continues until a satisfactory solution has been attained as determined by some appropriate stopping rule.

Stated at this level, the mechanics of a genetic algorithm are easy to grasp, and its elegance is readily apparent. What remains to be seen, though, is how exactly this can work—in particular, how can parameter values "mutate" or "cross over" to generate "offspring"? To understand this core process, we need to examine all steps involved in a genetic algorithm in some more detail. Note that the following presentation is highly "generic" (e.g., Chong & Zak, 1996; Mitchell, 1996) and that actual implementations of the algorithm are likely to differ slightly from our description.

Representation. We begin by examining the way in which the candidate parameter values, θ_c, are represented in an organism. Each organism consists of (usually) a single chromosome, which in turn consists of a large number, L, of alleles. For present purposes, each allele is thought to consist of a single bit that can be either 0 or 1. Hence, the string 010011001 forms a chromosome with $L = 9$. How can this chromosome possibly represent a conjunction of parameter values, such as the values $\{.74, -.11\}$, which were the best-fitting intercept and slope estimates for the introductory example in this chapter?

The surprising answer is that the mapping between the parameter space represented by θ_c and the chromosome space can be largely arbitrary (provided it is consistent). One way in which this mapping can be achieved is by rescaling the range of possible parameter values into a binary representation of some suitable length. For example, suppose we constrain the possible values of our intercept to the range $[-5, 1.5]$, and suppose furthermore that we set aside eight alleles to represent it within the chromosome, and then we linearly transform the range $[-5, 1.5]$ to the binary range $[0, 2^8 - 1]$, which creates a binary scale that can represent any permissible parameter value (with some granularity) by a string of 0s and 1s. For example, the value .74 would translate into the allele sequence 10011110. Once we have thus converted all parameter values in θ_c to their binary allele equivalent, we simply concatenate the allele strings to form the final chromosome of length L. Thus, the set of parameter values $\{.74, -.11\}$ might be represented by the chromosome 10011110110010. (For simplicity, we put the same bounds on the slope parameter.) Crucially, as we show later, much of the work within a genetic algorithm involves this chromosome representation without any regard whatsoever to its mapping into the parameter space.

Selection. Suppose we have created an initial population (call that $P^{(0)}$) of organisms, each capturing a different random set of starting values for the parameters. The next step involves the creation of a mating set, $M^{(0)}$. The mating set involves the same *number* of organisms as the population, but it need not include all members of the population—instead, some members of $P^{(0)}$ may be represented multiple times in $M^{(0)}$, and others may be entirely absent. The reason for this is that each member of $M^{(0)}$ is sampled from $P^{(0)}$ with replacement and on the basis of its fitness. Specifically, each member $m^{(0)}$ of $M^{(0)}$ is set equal to some $x^{(0)}$ in $P^{(0)}$ with probability[9]

$$f(x^{(0)})/F^{(0)}, \tag{3.9}$$

where

$$F^{(0)} = \sum f(x^{(0)}), \tag{3.10}$$

with the sum taken over all organisms in $P^{(0)}$. This ensures that each organism is recruited for mating with a probability that is proportional to its fitness.

Note that the fitness evaluation required for selection takes place at the level of parameter space, not chromosome space. This means that, implicitly within the function f, each organism's chromosome is converted into a vector $\boldsymbol{\theta}_c$ to evaluate its fitness—in the same way that the evolution of a live organism depends on its fitness with respect to the environment rather than on direct analysis of its genes.

Once $M^{(0)}$ has been thus created, the next generation $P^{(1)}$ is derived from the mating set as follows.

Crossover. With probability p_c, two randomly chosen members of $M^{(0)}$ are designated as "parents," which means that they cross over their alleles from a randomly determined point (in the range $1 - L$ with uniform probability) to form two offspring. For example, the chromosomes 11111 and 00000 might form the offspring 11000 and 00111 after a crossover in the third position.

With probability $1 - p_c$, the crossover is skipped, and parents generate offspring by passing on an exact copy.

Mutation. Each offspring may then undergo a further mutation, by randomly "flipping" each of the bits in its chromosome with probability p_m. The value of p_m is typically very small, in the order of .001 (Mitchell, 1996). Mutation occurs at the level of each allele, so in some rare instances, more than one bit in a chromosome may be flipped.

Stopping rule. Once all offspring have been created, the initial population $P^{(0)}$ is replaced by $P^{(1)}$, and the process continues with renewed selection of members for the mating set $M^{(1)}$ and so on for generations $1, 2, \ldots, k, \ldots N$. Across generations, the fitness of the various organisms will (in all likelihood) improve, and the process is terminated based on some stopping rule.

A variety of stopping rules have been proposed; for example, Kaelo and Ali (2007) suggested a rule based on the best and the worst point. That is, if the absolute difference in fitness between the best and the worst organism in a generation falls below some suitable threshold, evolution terminates because all organisms have optimally adapted to the environment. Note the resemblance between this stopping rule and its equivalent in Simplex (when the simplex collapses toward a single point, all vertices have the same discrepancy). Tsoulos (2008) additionally considered the variance of the best organism across generations; if the fitness of the best point no longer changes across generations, thus reducing its intergenerational variance, then the algorithm stops because further improvement is unlikely.

Why does it work? The most stunning aspect of genetic algorithms is that they actually work. In fact, they can work extremely well, and sometimes better than simulated annealing (Thompson & Bilbro, 2000). But why? After all, we take our parameters, convert them to concatenated binary strings, and then we (a) randomly flip bits within the strings or (b) randomly exchange portions of those strings between organisms. While the latter might seem plausible if the crossover point were always at the boundary between parameters, it is more difficult to intuit why if a parameter happens to have the values 2.34 and 6.98 across two organisms, exchanging the ".34" with the ".98" would enhance the fitness of one or both of them. This acknowledged (potential) mystery has been widely researched (e.g., Schmitt, 2001; Whitley, 1994), and here we briefly illustrate the crucial insight—namely, that genetic algorithms implement a *hyperplane sampling* approach to optimization.

We begin by noting the fact that if our chromosomes are of length L (and binary, as we assume throughout), then the total search space is an L-dimensional hyperspace with 2^L vertices or possible values. Our task thus is to find that one point out of 2^L points that has maximal fitness. Lest you consider this task trivial, bear in mind that realistic applications may have values of $L = 70$ (Mitchell, 1996), which translates into roughly $1.18 \times 10,000,000,000,000,000,000,000$ points—we do not recommend that you (or your children, grandchildren, and great-grandchildren) attempt to search them one by one.

To introduce the idea of hyperspace sampling, Figure 3.6 shows a three-dimensional search space (i.e., $L = 3$) in which all possible points are labeled with their allele code. Hence, each vertex of the cube represents one organism that may potentially be a member of our population, $P^{(k)}$, at some generation k. The figure also introduces the concept of a *schema*. A schema is a string in which some values are fixed but others are arbitrary; the latter are represented by asterisks and stand for "I do not care." Hence, in this instance, all points on the gray frontal plane are represented by the string $0**$. Any string that can be created by replacing an asterisk with either 0 or 1 conforms to that schema; hence, 010 and 011 do, but 111 does not.

Why would we care about schemata? The answer is implied by the fitness values associated with each point, which are also shown in the figure (in parentheses next to each vertex). The bottom-left point on the frontal plane is clearly the "best" solution because it has the highest fitness value. Hence, to hone in on this point, we would want organisms that conform to that schema (010 and so on)

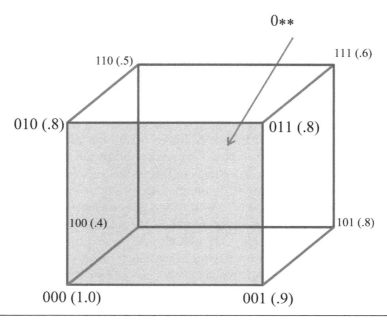

Figure 3.6 A three-dimensional space spanned by chromosomes with $L = 3$. Each vertex is labeled by the complete set of allele values (and fitness value in parentheses); size of font is larger for points on the front of the cube than the back. The gray frontal surface represents the hyperplane defined by $0 * *$. See text for details.

to be preferentially represented in our population, and those that do not conform we would want to drop out of the pool across generations.

It turns out that a genetic algorithm achieves precisely that; when evaluating organisms for inclusion in the mating set, $M^{(k)}$, "the schemata of competing hyperplanes increase or decrease their representation in the population according to the relative fitness of the strings that lie in those hyperplane partitions" (Whitley, 1994, p. 69). Thus, the selection step is not just recruiting fit *individuals* for procreation, but it is also considering those individuals as samples of an entire partition of the search space—in our example, the organism 010 would be considered as representative of the frontal plane $0**$ of the cube in Figure 3.6.

What, then, is the function of crossover and mutation? Ideally, across generations, one would like to sample more and more new organisms that conform to the most promising schema. In practice, alas, this is not possible because the algorithm does not know *which* schema is instantiated by the organisms that are in the mating set. For example, the organisms 010 and 011 might equally correspond to $0 * *$ or $*1*$: Remember that it is only in the context of our constructed example that we know which schema (namely, the gray plane) contained the point of maximal fitness. In reality, we do not know *why* the selected points have a high fitness.

The role of crossover, then, is to further narrow down the subspace in which fitness is maximal. Of course, crossover is frequently going to generate offspring that fall outside the most promising schema; if that happens, they are unlikely to be included in future generations, and hence there is no lasting damage. If, by contrast, crossover generates offspring that fall within a more narrow schema of equal or greater promise, then those will be more likely to carry their information into future generations. Effectively, across generations, this process will gradually replace all asterisks in a schema with 0s or 1s because only those organisms make it into the next generation whose alleles conform to the most promising schema.

This tendency toward narrowing of the schema is slowed and counteracted by the random mutation. The role of mutation is therefore similar to the role of the occasional acceptance of "uphill" steps in simulated annealing; it helps prevent premature convergence onto a suboptimal solution (Whitley, 1994).

Genetic algorithms are not built into MATLAB but can also be downloaded from MATLAB Central (see Section 2.3.1 for instructions). Once downloaded, the genetic algorithm can be called and used in much the same way as `fminsearch`.

3.1.3.4 *Relative Merits of Parameter Estimation Techniques*

We have discussed three algorithms for parameter estimation: Simplex, simulated annealing, and genetic algorithms. For a thorough and detailed review of alternative approaches, consult Kolda, Lewis, and Torczon (2003).

What are the relative merits of those three approaches? In a nutshell, Simplex is easy to use and understand, and it is highly efficient. In many cases, Simplex only requires a single evaluation of the discrepancy function to determine the direction of its next somersault. By way of trade-off, Simplex does not work well for high-dimensional parameter spaces, and it is susceptible to local minima.

The relative merits of the other two techniques are largely the converse. Simulated annealing and genetic algorithms are somewhat more complex and require more attention during program preparation and execution than Simplex. Moreover, they are not nearly as efficient and require many more function evaluations. However, compared to Simplex, they are considerably less likely to get stuck in local minima, and they also handle high-dimensional problems with aplomb. Although there are some suggestions that genetic algorithms outperform simulated annealing (Thompson & Bilbro, 2000), we suggest that the jury is still out on their relative merits.

On balance, Simplex is preferable for small parameter spaces that need to be explored quickly and simply. For all other applications, simulated annealing or genetic algorithms are preferable. In the cognitive literature, all three approaches are used widely. One word of caution: The time taken to estimate parameters can be far greater for simulated annealing and genetic algorithms than for Simplex. Although this difference may be negligible for simple models that are rapidly evaluated—such as our introductory regression example—the time difference may be significant when more complex models are involved. Clearly, it makes a huge pragmatic difference whether a parameter estimation takes several hours or a week![10]

3.2   Considering the Data: What Level of Analysis?

What have we achieved so far in this chapter? You have learned about the basics of model fitting, and you have been alerted to common pitfalls and problems, so you are almost ready to apply a "real" model to data. We will do just that in all remaining chapters (with particularly detailed examples in Chapter 7), but first we must talk about the data—specifically, we need to sort out *what kind of data* a model should be applied to.[11]

Let's begin our consideration of the data with a politically charged and highly emotive problem. Suppose you are an affirmative action officer at a major university and you learn that of the nearly 13,000 applicants to your institution's graduate programs, 8,442 were men and 4,321 were women. Suppose furthermore that 44% of the men but only 35% of the women were admitted. Red alert! Isn't this clear evidence of a gender bias in admissions? Your suspicions are confirmed when you conduct a statistical test on these data to detect whether there is a relationship between gender and admission rates and find $\chi^2(1) = 110.8$, with a p value that's nearly indistinguishable from zero. Surely you must now act and identify the culprit or culprits—that is, the departments that discriminate against women—so that corrective action can be taken.

We did not make up these numbers; they represent the real admissions data of the University of California at Berkeley in 1973 (Bickel, Hammel, & O'Connell, 1975). And as you might expect, those data (quite justifiably) caused much concern and consternation, and the university embarked on an examination of the admission records of individual departments. A snapshot of the outcome of this further examination, taken from Freedman, Pisani, Purves, and Adhikari (1991), is shown in Table 3.1. The table shows the number of applicants to each department, broken down by gender, and the percentage of applicants who were admitted.

What is going on here? Not one department can be faulted for a bias against women—indeed, if anything, the men have something to complain about because their admission rates are (slightly) lower than those of women. This table is representative of all departments and, no, we did not tweak the snapshot to make a point; instead, the reason that the apparent gender bias disappears when

Table 3.1 Berkeley Admission Data Broken Down by Department

Department[a]	Men		Women	
	Number of Applicants	Number Admitted	Number of Applicants	Number Admitted
A	825	511 (62%)	108	89 (82%)
B	560	353 (63%)	25	17 (68%)
C	325	120 (37%)	593	225 (38%)
D	191	53 (28%)	393	114 (29%)

[a]Departments are known by code letter only.

considered at the level of individual departments is that women primarily tend to apply to competitive programs that are difficult to get into (labeled C and D in the table), whereas men tend to apply to "easier" programs with higher admission rates (A and B). When this important correlation between gender and preference is ignored, consideration of the aggregate data yields a completely mistaken impression of the true situation. (Just sum the numbers—*not* percentages—for each of the columns and then compute the percentages on the sums. The bias reemerges in an instant!)[12] This pernicious problem, which has nothing to do with sexism or discrimination, is known as "Simpson's paradox," and it may occur whenever data are carelessly aggregated. Unfortunately, Simpson's paradox is not limited to the political arena, but it also arises in cognitive experimentation. Hintzman (1980) provides a thorough treatment of this issue and its ramifications in the context of contingency tables.

You may be tempted to think that Simpson's paradox represents an extreme consequence of aggregating that occurs only in isolated cases and hence has no implications for cognitive modeling in general. Unfortunately, this is not the case. Aggregation of data can have several other adverse consequences, and even quite "benign" variations between individual participants, or between different stimuli in an experiment, may contribute to a misleading picture of the data. In fact, as we show next, simple averaging across subjects can be fraught with problems.

3.2.1   Implications of Averaging

Most psychological experiments report data at the group level, usually after averaging the responses from many subjects in a condition. What could be wrong with that? Lots, it turns out. Averaging the data from different individuals may create a strikingly misleading picture of what is happening in your experiment. We illustrate this problem first by simulation. In our simulation, subjects must learn some task over the course of 120 trials. We do not care what the task is, we do not care who the subjects are, but we do specify that subjects initially hover

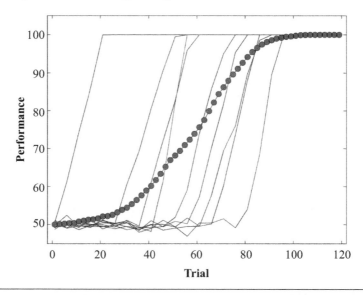

Figure 3.7 Simulated consequences of averaging of learning curves. The thin solid lines represent the individual performance of a randomly chosen subset of 100 simulated subjects. Each subject learns linearly, and across subjects, there is a slight variation in learning rate but considerable variation in the onset of learning. The solid line and filled circles represent average simulated performance across all 100 subjects.

at chance (50% in this instance) before they commence learning at some point s at a linear rate of improvement r. We assume that there is considerable variation across subjects in s ($\sigma_s = 20$) but only small variation across subjects in r ($\sigma_r = 1.5$). Our assumptions embody the idea that learning is accompanied by an "aha" experience; that is, a problem may initially appear unsolvable, but at some point or another, there is a sudden "insight" that kick-starts the then very rapid learning.

The results of our simulation are shown in Figure 3.7. The figure shows the individual data for a handful of randomly chosen subjects (each subject is represented by one of the thin solid lines). The variation among individuals is obvious, with one subject commencing learning virtually instantaneously, whereas the last subject in our sample requires 80 trials to get going. However, there is also considerable similarity between subjects: Once learning commences, there is a nearly constant increment in performance at each trial. Now consider the thick filled circles: They represent average performance across all 100 simulated subjects. Does the average adequately characterize the process of learning? No, not at all. The average seems to suggest that learning commences right from the outset and is smooth, gradual, and highly nonlinear. Alas, every single one of those attributes is an artifact of averaging, and not a single subject learns in the manner assumed by the average learning curve.

One might object that the figure plots simulation results and that "real" data might behave very differently. Sadly, this objection cannot be sustained: Our simulation results are almost identical to behavioral results reported by Hayes (1953) in an experiment involving brightness discrimination learning in rats. (This is not surprising because we designed the simulation to act just like the rats in that study.) Moreover, it is not just rats whose behavior can be misrepresented by the average: You may recall that in Section 1.4.2, we discussed the study by Heathcote et al. (2000) that compared different functions for capturing people's learning performance in skill acquisition experiments. Heathcote et al. concluded that the hitherto popular "power law" of practice was incorrect and that the data were best described by an exponential learning function instead. In the present context, it is particularly relevant that their conclusions were based on examination of *individual* performance rather than the average. Heathcote et al. explicitly ascribed the earlier prominence of the power law to an inopportune reliance on averaged data. This is no isolated case; the vagaries of aggregating have been noted repeatedly (e.g., Ashby, Maddox, & Lee, 1994; Curran & Hintzman, 1995; Estes, 1956).

Where does this leave us, and where do we go from here? First, we must acknowledge that we have a potentially serious problem to contend with. This may appear obvious to you now, but much contemporary practice seems oblivious to it. Second, it is important to recognize that this problem is *not* (just) the modeler's problem but a problem that affects anyone dealing with psychological data—as evidenced by the decade-long practice to fit power functions to average learning data. Hence, although as modelers we must be particularly aware of the problem, we cannot avoid it simply by giving up modeling.

Fortunately, the problems associated with data aggregation are not insurmountable. One solution relies on the recognition that although the problem is pervasive, it is not ubiquitous. Estes (1956) provides mathematical rules that permit identification of the circumstances in which averaging of data across individuals is likely to be problematic. Specifically, if the function characterizing individual performance is known, then one can readily determine whether that functional form will look different after averaging. For a variety of functions, averaging does not present a problem, including nonlinear functions such as $y = a \log x$ and $y = a + bx + cx^2$ (where x is the independent variable, for example trials, and a, b, and c are parameters describing the function).[13] Then there are other functions, such as $y = a + b\,e^{-cx}$, whose shape does change with averaging. Of course, this mathematical information is of limited use if the function describing individual behavior is unknown; however, if one is entertaining several candidate functions and seeks to differentiate between them, then information about their shape invariance is crucial. For example, the fact that an exponential learning function does *not* retain its shape upon averaging should caution against fitting a (quite similar) power function to average learning data.

More recently, J. B. Smith and Batchelder (2008) provided statistical methods for the detection of participant heterogeneity that may prevent averaging. Those tests can be applied to the data prior to modeling to determine the correct level at which a model should be applied. When the tests reveal heterogeneity, fitting at the aggregate level is inadvisable. When the tests fail to detect heterogeneity, fitting at the aggregate level may be permissible. We now turn to a discussion of the relative merits of the three principal approaches to fitting data.

3.2.2   Fitting Individual Participants

In an ideal world, the issue of data aggregation could be readily avoided by fitting models to the data of individual subjects. Specifically, using the techniques outlined in this chapter, we could estimate parameters for each subject in our experiment, and we could assess the success of our endeavor by examining the average goodness of fit of the model. (Note that for the reasons just discussed, the average goodness of fit represents a very different quantity from the goodness of fit to the average; if you find this puzzling, reread the preceding discussion surrounding Figure 3.7.)

3.2.2.1   Advantages

The individual approach has some deep theoretical advantages that go beyond resolution of the aggregation problem. For example, capturing the behavior of individuals within a cognitive model opens a window into cognition that cannot be obtained by other means. It has long been known that individual differences provide a "crucible in theory construction" (Underwood, 1975, p. 128), and there is a plethora of research on individual differences in cognition (e.g., Oberauer, Süß, Schulze, Wilhelm, & Wittmann, 2000). That research has served to constrain and inform our understanding of numerous cognitive processes (e.g., Miyake, Friedman, Emerson, Witzki, & Howerter, 2000). Traditionally, this research has been conducted by behavioral means. It is only recently that those investigations have begun to be accompanied by theoretical analysis. For example, Schmiedek, Oberauer, Wilhelm, Süß, and Wittmann (2007) fitted two models to the response time distributions of a large sample of participants, thus obtaining separate parameter estimates for each subject for a variety of cognitive tasks (e.g., a speeded decision about the number of syllables in a word). Analysis of the variation of those parameter values across individuals revealed that only some model parameters covaried with people's "working memory" capacity (WMC).[14] Specifically,

Schmiedek et al. found that a parameter reflecting the speed of evidence accumulation in a popular decision-making model (Ratcliff & Rouder, 1998) was highly correlated with WMC, whereas a parameter reflecting the time for encoding of a stimulus was not. Thus, by fitting individual data and analyzing the resultant parameter values across subjects, Schmiedek et al. were able to link a particular stage of a decision model to a cognitive construct that is a powerful predictor of reasoning ability.

Another advantage of fitting models to individual data is that it may reveal boundaries of the applicability of a model. Simply put, a model may fit some subjects but not others, or it may describe behavior in one condition but not another. Although such heterogeneity may present a source of frustration for a modeler who is interested in making general statements about human behavior, it can also be extremely illuminating. A particularly striking case was reported in a visual signal detection study by Wandell (1977), who used a descriptive model (namely, signal detection theory) to infer how people interpret spikes of neural activity in a visual channel to detect a signal. Specifically, when presented with a weak signal that results in infrequent neural activity, people have a choice between counting the number of spikes that are received in a constant time period (and deciding that a signal is present when the number is sufficiently large) or waiting for a fixed number of spikes to be detected (and deciding that a signal is present because that number is reached within a reasonable waiting period). It turns out that those two distinct mechanisms make differing predictions about the time to respond and the relationship between "hits" (successful detections of the signal) and "false alarms" (erroneously reporting a signal when it was not there). Wandell (1977) showed that people predictably alternated between those decision modes in response to an experimental manipulation (the details of which are not relevant here), and he was also able to pinpoint individual departures from the expected model (see Luce, 1995, p. 11, for further details). What can we learn from this example? As Luce (1995) put it, "People typically have several qualitatively different ways of coping with a situation. If we ... elect to ignore ... them, we are likely to become confused by the data" (Luce, 1995, p. 12). In the example just discussed, reliance on a descriptive model permitted Wandell (1977) to avoid such confusion by identifying (and manipulating) each person's decision strategy.

3.2.2.2 Disadvantages

At first glance, it might appear that there are no disadvantages associated with fitting of individuals. This perspective would be overly optimistic because several potentially troublesome exceptions can be cited.

First, it is quite common for modelers to apply their theories to archival data (which, in the extreme case, may have been extracted from a published plot). In those cases, it may simply be impossible to fit the data at the individual level because that information may no longer be available. Needless to say, in those cases, the best one can do is to fit the available aggregate data with the appropriate caution (more on that later).

Second, a related problem arises even with "new" data when the experimental methodology does not permit multiple observations to be drawn. For example, mirroring real-life police procedures, eyewitness identification experiments necessarily involve just a single lineup and a single response from each participant. Clearly, in those circumstances, no modeling at the individual level is possible, and the data must be considered in the aggregate (i.e., by computing the proportion of participants who picked the culprit or any of the various foils from the lineup). We will present an in-depth example of a model of eyewitness identification in Chapter 7 that illustrates this approach to modeling.

The third problem is similar and involves experiments in which the number of observations per participant is greater than one but nonetheless small. This situation may occur in experiments with "special" populations, such as infants or clinical samples, that cannot be tested extensively for ethical or pragmatic reasons. It may also occur if pragmatic constraints (such as fatigue) prevent repeated testing of the same person. Although it is technically possible in these circumstances to fit individuals, is this advisable? How stable would parameter estimates be in those circumstances, and how much insight can we expect from the modeling? Cohen, Sanborn, and Shiffrin (2008) conducted a massive study—involving nearly half a *million* simulated experiments—that sought answers to those questions using the model recovery technique discussed later in Chapter 6 (see Figure 6.2). That is, Cohen et al. used a number of competing models to generate data for simulated subjects and then tested whether the correct model was recovered, varying the number of (simulated) observations per subject and the number of (simulated) subjects. Although Cohen, Sanborn, and Shiffrin's results are so complex that it is risky to condense them into a simple recommendation, in our view, it appears inadvisable to fit individuals whenever the number of observations per participant falls below 10. Cohen et al. showed that in many—but not all—cases with fewer than 10 observations per subject, the model that generated the data was more likely to be correctly recovered from the aggregate data than from fits to individuals.[15]

A related problem arises when the number of observations per participant is moderate (i.e., > 10) but not large ($<< 500$; Farrell & Ludwig, 2008). Although fits to individual participants may be quite successful under those circumstances, the distribution of estimated parameter values across individuals may be overdispersed—that is, the variance among parameter estimates is greater than the true variance among those parameters (Farrell & Ludwig, 2008; Rouder & Lu, 2005). This overdispersion problem arises because each individual estimate is subject to sampling variability or "noise" within a participant, which may cause contamination of those individual estimates.

3.2.3   Fitting Subgroups of Data

Suppose you have decided that fitting of individuals is inadvisable or impossible. Suppose furthermore that you suspect that there might be some relevant heterogeneity in your sample; for example, you may suspect that some subjects use one strategy, whereas another subgroup of participants uses an alternative strategy, making averaging across all participants inappropriate. What can you do?

One solution involves further "preprocessing" of the data by statistical means, for example, by conducting a cluster analysis (Everitt, 1993). There are a variety of such techniques, all of which classify the units of interest—in this case, individual participants—so as to maximize within-cluster similarity while minimizing between-cluster similarity. Once clusters have been identified, the model(s) can be fit to the data aggregated across subjects within each subgroup. This technique alleviates the pitfalls associated with overall aggregation while also overcoming the pragmatic problems that may prevent fitting of individual subjects.

A good illustration of this approach can be found in Yang and Lewandowsky (2004), who discovered that different groups of people used very different classification strategies for an identical categorization problem. When people were grouped together on the basis of a cluster analysis, it turned out that a different model was required to accommodate each of the two primary groups of interest. Clearly, it would have been inappropriate to lump those qualitatively different individuals together into a single analysis, as the average across participants would not be representative of most (or indeed any) individuals. In addition, the finding that different groups of individuals were best captured by two different models was of considerable theoretical interest. Thus, as we already noted, far from being a "nuisance" variable, individual differences—in this case, qualitative differences—can be highly informative and theoretically interesting.

3.2.4   Fitting Aggregate Data

We have talked about "aggregating" data throughout this chapter. It is now time to pin down its meaning more precisely. Generally, aggregating occurs when the data from all participants (or all participants in a subgroup) are considered together, but this can be done in several ways.

Not surprisingly, the most common means of aggregation involves averaging across subjects. On this approach, the data are treated as though they were generated by a single source (i.e., a single participant), and each to-be-fitted observation is formed by averaging (or equivalently, summing) the underlying data across subjects. For example, if we are fitting data from a categorization experiment, in which each subject classifies a stimulus as belonging to category A or B, we may sum response frequencies across participants and fit the resulting cell frequencies (or proportions of "A" responses). Similarly, when modeling response latencies, we may choose to estimate a single set of parameters to capture the average latency across trials in some skill acquisition experiment.

An alternative approach to aggregation goes beyond simple averaging and seeks to retain information about the underlying structure of each participant's responses. This is best illustrated by considering cases in which responses are represented in distributions. One case where this approach is often used is in analyzing and modeling response times (RTs). RT distributions have played an important role in cognitive psychology, and we will introduce them in greater detail in Chapter 4. For now, it suffices to know that a person's response times can be "binned," by linear interpolation, into quantiles (e.g., the latency values cutting off 10%, 30%, 50%, 70%, and 90% of the distribution below; Ratcliff & Smith, 2004), and we can then average the observations within each quantile across participants to obtain average quantiles whose location, relative to each other, preserves the shape of the distribution of each individual (e.g., Andrews & Heathcote, 2001; Jiang, Rouder, & Speckman, 2004; Ratcliff, 1979).

This procedure, known as "Vincentizing" (Ratcliff, 1979), is a particularly useful aggregating tool: Like simple averaging, it yields a single set of scores that we can fit, but unlike averaging, those scores retain information about the individual RT distributions that would be lost if all observations were lumped together. That is, in the same way that the average learning curve in Figure 3.7 does not represent any of the underlying individual curves, the distribution of all observed RTs across subjects is unlikely to resemble any of the underlying individual distributions. If those distributions are Vincentized before being averaged, their shape is retained. We recommend Vincentizing techniques for any situation involving distributions or functions whose shape is of interest and should be preserved during aggregation.[16] Van Zandt (2000) provides an extremely detailed treatise of Vincentizing and other ways in which RT distributions can be fit.

3.2.5   Having Your Cake and Eating It: Multilevel Modeling

We would be remiss not to mention a recent and exciting development that combines the advantages of fitting aggregate and individual data. This technique is known as multilevel (or hierarchical) modeling and has been popular for some time among statisticians. In this approach, parameters are estimated for each subject, but those parameters are simultaneously constrained to be drawn from a distribution that defines the variation across individuals (see, e.g., Farrell & Ludwig, 2008; Lee & Webb, 2005; Morey, Pratte, & Rouder, 2008; Rouder, Lu, Speckman, Sun, & Jiang, 2005).

This type of modeling is known as "multilevel" because the parameters are estimated at two levels: first at the level of individual subjects (base level) and second at a superordinate level that determines the relationship (e.g., variance) among base-level parameters. Those techniques have considerable promise but are beyond the scope of the present volume.

3.2.6   Recommendations

We have surveyed the three major options open to modelers and have found that each approach comes with its own set of advantages and difficulties. Is it possible to condense this discussion into a clear set of recommendations? Specifically, under what conditions should we fit a model to individual participants' data, and when should we fit aggregate or average data and estimate a single set of parameters? Although we can offer a set of decision guidelines based on current practice, the rapidly evolving nature of the field and the heterogeneity of prevailing opinions renders our advice suggestive rather than conclusive.

3.2.6.1   Fit Individuals If Possible

The problems associated with aggregating usually outweigh the drawbacks of fitting individual data (Cohen et al., 2008). Thus, unless there are compelling reasons to the contrary (e.g., insufficient data per participant, computationally expensive model), we recommend that models should be fit to the data from individual subjects. This holds in particular when there is a known nonlinear relationship between the estimates of parameters and the parameters themselves; the classic case involves standard signal detection theory, whose parameters (d' and the criterion) are nonlinearly related to hit rates and false alarm rates (Wickens, 2002; see also Morey et al., 2008). Hence, averaging of hit and false alarm rates before computing d' is very different from averaging each person's own d'. Accordingly, much of the modeling in the next chapter is devoted to fitting at the individual level.

One pragmatic constraint that may dictate a departure from this recommendation involves the amount of computing time that is required to fit individual subjects: If it takes 5 hours to fit one subject, then it may simply not be feasible to fit all 100 subjects individually (absent some other solution, such as a grid of computers).

3.2.6.2   Let the Data Determine the Level of Aggregation

If the number of observations per subject is small, fitting group data is advisable. We recommend that the level of aggregation be determined by analysis of the data; for example, if there are identifiable subgroups of individuals, each group should be considered on its own by aggregating across subjects within it and then fitting the model(s) to each group separately.

Irrespective of the level of aggregation, data should be combined in a manner that preserves important features (e.g., by Vincentizing). Likewise, irrespective of the level of aggregation, one should apply diagnostic tests such as those developed by J. B. Smith and Batchelder (2008) to ascertain that aggregation is advisable. What is one to do if aggregation appears statistically inadvisable but, for one reason or another, fitting the model to individual participants is infeasible? One solution is to examine the robustness of one's model to heterogeneity in the data via simulation (J. B. Smith & Batchelder, 2008).

3.2.6.3   Doing It Both Ways: The Joint Acceptance Hypothesis

The results of Cohen et al.'s (2008) large simulation study were complex and somewhat heterogeneous; however, the study also yielded one highly consistent outcome. Cohen et al. found that in all cases, the best outcome was obtained when the fits to individuals as well as to the aggregated data pointed in the same direction. That is, whenever a model was identified as fitting the data best on the basis of both methods, that identification was almost universally correct.

In practice, this implies that it may be advisable to fit one's models to both individual data and aggregate data; if both yield the same result, one can have increased confidence in the outcome. If they diverge, one ought to rely on the fit to individuals rather than the aggregate.

Notes

1. The rolling marble is not a perfect analogy because it continuously rolls down the error surface, whereas parameter estimation typically proceeds in discrete steps. A more accurate analogy might therefore involve a blind parachutist who is dropped onto a mountain behind enemy lines on a secret mission and must reach the bottom of the valley by making successive downward steps.

2. By implication, the same parameter estimation techniques can also be applied to psychological models that *are* analytically tractable, just like regression.

3. To satisfy your curiosity, a four-dimensional simplex is called a pentachoron, and a five-dimensional simplex is a hexateron.

4. In actual fact, the simplex will never be a point, but it will have a very small diameter. The size of that diameter is determined by the convergence tolerance, which can be set in

MATLAB via a call to the function optimset; see the MATLAB documentation for details. Lagarias, Reeds, Wright, and Wright (1998) provide a rigorous examination of the convergence properties of Simplex.

5. For brevity, from here on we will refer to the algorithm by capitalizing its name ("Simplex") while reserving the lowercase ("simplex") to refer to the geometrical figure.

6. Brief mention must be made of an alternative technique, known as *Subplex* (Rowan, 1990), which was developed as an alternative to Simplex for situations involving large numbers of parameters, noisy predictions (i.e., models involving random sampling), and the frequent need to dismiss certain combinations of parameter values as unacceptable (Rowan, 1990). As implied by the name, Subplex divides the parameter space into sub-spaces, each of which is then independently (and partially) optimized by standard Simplex.

7. In order to focus the discussion and keep it simple, we considered only very simple cooling schedules and a trivial candidate function. More sophisticated alternatives are discussed by Locatelli (2002) and Nourani and Andresen (1998).

8. At a mathematical level, one can in fact draw a plausible connection between genetic algorithms and simulated annealing because both involve the exploration of randomly chosen points. We do not consider this connection here and focus on the overriding conceptual differences between the two.

9. Because the parameter values at this stage have been converted to chromosome strings, we refer to the organisms by the notation x (or $\boldsymbol{x}$) rather than $\boldsymbol{\theta}$.

10. In this context, it is also worth noting that MATLAB may evaluate models more slowly than other, "low-level" languages such as C. If execution time presents a problem, it may therefore be worthwhile to rewrite your model in another language, such as C, provided you save more in program execution time than you spend to rewrite your model in another language.

11. If you are really keen to sink your teeth into a "real" model, you can proceed from the end of this chapter directly to Chapter 7; Section 7.1 does not require knowledge of the material in the intervening Chapters 4 and 5.

12. The table contains only a snapshot of the situation, and hence the totals will not yield the exact percentages reported by Bickel et al. (1975).

13. Estes (1956) offers the following heuristic to identify this class of functions: "What they all have in common is that each parameter in the function appears either alone or as a coefficient multiplying a quantity which depends only on the independent variable x" (p. 136).

14. Working memory is closely related to the concept of short-term memory. However, unlike tests of short-term memory that rely on memorization and recall alone, examinations of working memory typically involve some additional cognitive processes. For example, in one favored working memory task, study items may alternate with, say, mental arithmetic problems (Turner & Engle, 1989). People might process a sequence such as $2 + 3 = 5$?, $A, 5 + 1 = 7$?, $B, \ldots$, where the equations have to be judged for correctness and the letters must be memorized for immediate serial recall after the sequence has been completed. The capacity of working memory, as measured by performance in the complex span task, accounts for a whopping half of the variance among individuals in measures of general fluid abilities (i.e., intelligence; see, e.g., Kane, Hambrick, & Conway, 2005).

15. Cohen et al. (2008) identified a situation in which fitting of the aggregate data was *always* more likely to recover the correct model than fits to individuals, irrespective of the number of observations per participant and the overall number of participants. This situation involved forgetting data, in which individual subjects (simulated or real) often

scored 0% recall; those extreme scores uniquely favored one of the models under consideration (even if it had not generated the data), thus enabling that model (whose details are not relevant here) to do particularly well when applied to individual data. Upon aggregation, the individual 0s were absorbed into the group average, thus leveling the playing field and enabling better identification of the correct model.

16. As an exercise, you may wish to figure out a way in which the learning curves in Figure 3.7 can be aggregated so that they retain their shape. If you find this difficult, consult Addis and Kahana (2004).

4

Maximum Likelihood Estimation

In the previous chapters, we encountered one of the key issues in computational modeling: A full, quantitative specification of a model involves not just a description of the model (in the form of algorithms or equations) but also a specification of the parameters of the model and their values. Although in some cases, we can use known parameter values (e.g., those determined from previous applications of the model; see, e.g., Oberauer & Lewandowsky, 2008), in most cases we must estimate those parameters from the data. Chapter 3 described the basics of estimating parameters by varying the parameters to minimize the root mean squared deviation (RMSD) between the data and the model's predictions. Chapter 4 deals with a principled and popular approach to parameter estimation called maximum likelihood estimation.

Unlike many modeling applications, which have a very practical aim, maximum likelihood estimation is deeply rooted in statistical theory. Maximum likelihood estimators have known properties that cannot be accorded to estimates obtained via minimizing RMSD (except under specific situations detailed later); for example, maximum likelihood estimates are guaranteed to become more accurate on average with increasing sample size. In addition, likelihood can be treated as the relative weight of evidence for a particular hypothesis, either about the value of a particular parameter or about a model as a whole. This lays the groundwork for the discussion of model comparison in the next chapter, where we will combine the idea of likelihood as the strength of evidence with the principle of parsimony to develop a deep and rigorous technique for comparing scientific models.

4.1   Basics of Probabilities

4.1.1   Defining Probability

The term *likelihood* in common parlance is used interchangeably with *probability*; we might consider the likelihood of it raining tomorrow (which varies considerably between the two authors, who live in Australia and the United Kingdom) or the likelihood that an individual randomly selected from the population will live past the age of 80. When considering statistical or computational modeling, the term *likelihood* takes on a very strict meaning, which is subtly—but fundamentally—different from that of *probability*.

The best way to define likelihood and to distinguish it from probability is to start with the concept of probability itself. We all have some intuitive notion of what a probability is, and these intuitions probably make some connection with the formal definitions we will introduce here. A strict definition of probability relies on the notion of *samples*, *events*, and *outcomes*. Think of the casino game of *roulette*, in which a wheel containing slots corresponding to numbers is spun, and a ball is thrown in; the game consists of gambling on (i.e., guessing) the slot into which the ball will land. Each time the croupier spins the wheel, and the ball is thrown in and settles in a slot, constitutes a *sample*. The *outcome* for a spin would specify into which slot the ball finally fell, from the *sample space* of all possible slots. We can also define an *event*, which is simply a subset of the sample space, by considering the various gambles I could have made. Indeed, I have a large number of possible gambles I could make in roulette; I could bet on a single number (straight up) but could also bet on an even number coming up, or a number between 1 and 18 (inclusive), or that the color of the number is red. Each of these refers to an event, which is effectively a possible set of outcomes for the experiment. For example, the event "odd number" consists of the outcomes number 1, number 3, number 5, and so on, all the way up to number 35 (the largest odd number possible in roulette). Later on, we will consider cases where the outcomes are not enumerable (e.g., probabilities on continuous dimensions such as distance and time).

Assigning a probability $P(a)$ to an event a involves giving it a numerical value reflecting our expectation of the event. There has been, and continues to be, a great deal of debate over the nature of these values and how they relate to affairs in the world (e.g., Jeffrey, 2004; Keynes, 1921; Venn, 1888). In being more concerned with the mathematics of probabilities than their interpretation, we will follow the lead of early pioneers in the world of probability such as Pascal, Fermat, and Newton, who were concerned with the application of chance and probabilities (specifically, gambling; David, 1962). We are interested in probability theory in order to build a foundation for inference from computational models.

4.1.2   Properties of Probabilities

The language of probability is a strict formal system known as probability theory or the calculus of probability (e.g., Jaynes, 2003; Jeffreys, 1961). Probability theory starts off with the following axioms:

1. Probabilities of events must lie between 0 and 1 (inclusive).

2. The probabilities of all possible outcomes must sum exactly to 1.

3. In the case of *mutually exclusive* events (i.e., two events that cannot both occur simultaneously, such as the ball in roulette settling on both an odd and an even number), the probability of either of the events occurring is equal to the sum of their individual probabilities.

These few starting assumptions give us a number of other useful properties of probabilities. One is the notion of a *joint probability*, denoted $P(a, b)$, which gives the probability that both a and b occur (for example, that tomorrow it will be dry in Perth and rainy in Bristol). Joint probabilities allow us to formally define the concept of mutual exclusivity, introduced in the third axiom above: Two events are mutually exclusive if $P(a, b) = 0$. Be careful to note that the joint probability $P(a, b)$ can never exceed the individual probabilities $P(a)$ and $P(b)$.

An idea that will be critical for our discussion of likelihoods is that of *conditional probability*. The conditional probability of a given b, denoted $P(a|b)$, tells us the probability of observing a given that we have observed b. If a and b are independent, the probability of observing event a is unaffected by whether or not we observed b; that is, $P(a|b) = P(a)$. This formally states what psychologists usually assume when performing standard statistical tests such as the t test: The probability of observing a particular pattern of data in a particular participant does not depend on the observations we collected from other participants. If a and b are not independent, b gives us some information about a and therefore changes the probability that we will observe a.

Conditional dependence is essential for reasoning with mathematical or computational models since we are usually concerned with some conditional relationship between data and model. Specifically, we are usually concerned with the probability of observing a set of data given a particular model. This relationship is important for telling us how consistent some data are with a particular theory; a fully specified model will make predictions about data we have not yet collected, and we can then use the conditional probability $P(data|model)$ to assess the extent to which the data were predicted by (i.e., consistent with) the model.

There are several relationships between joint and conditional probabilities that are additionally useful for modelers of cognition. First, if two outcomes are independent (as defined using conditional probabilities above), then their joint probability is computed simply by multiplying their individual probabilities:

$$P(a, b) = P(a)P(b). \tag{4.1}$$

More generally, if a and b are not independent, and if we know the conditional relationship $a|b$ between a and b, the joint probability is given by

$$P(a, b) = P(a|b)P(b). \tag{4.2}$$

This relationship is of interest in cases where contingencies exist in experimental data. For example, in some developmental experiments, a child is tested on some easy pass/fail task and is then presented with some more difficult task only if the easier test is passed (Hood, 1995; Hughes, Russell, & Robbins, 1994). Because of the contingent nature of the experiment (the probability of passing the second test given the first test was failed is 0, since the child is never given the chance to pass the test), the joint probability of passing both tests is then more properly conceptualized by Equation 4.2 than by Equation 4.1.

Before we can begin to relate probability models to data in detail, we first need to discuss how we formulate the predictions of models. We need some way of saying how consistent the unobserved data are with the model, and we need to do this for all possible data sets we could observe. This comes down to specifying a predicted probability for all possible outcomes in the experiment to which the model is being applied. Accordingly, we start by considering all the possible hypothetical sets of data that the model can predict.

4.1.3   Probability Functions

When working with models in the maximum likelihood framework, we will usually consider all the possible events the model could predict and an associated measure of their probability. In this book, we will refer to these functions generally as *probability functions*. It turns out there are several probability functions we might use to characterize a model, depending on the nature of the data. In the case where events are discrete, the probabilities are specified as a *probability mass function*. There are many examples of discrete measures in psychology: for example, the number of trials on which a participant provided a correct answer, whether a child passes or fails a developmental test, or the rating of a statement on a Likert scale.

A probability mass function is shown in Figure 4.1 for the example of serial recall of a single list of eight words following some delay activity (e.g., Farrell & Lelièvre, 2009). The probabilities shown in Figure 4.1 are those predicted by

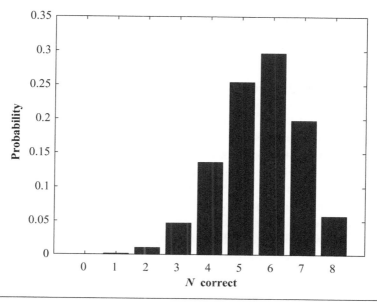

Figure 4.1 An example probability mass function: the probability of correctly recalling N out of eight items, where the probability of correctly recalling any particular item is $p_{correct}=.7$.

a statistical model called the binomial function; we will examine this model in more detail later. For the moment, we can see in Figure 4.1 that the binomial model assigns a probability to each possible outcome from the experiment. The only assumption that has been made here is that the probability of correctly recalling each of the eight items, which we label $p_{correct}$, is equal to .7; as we will see later, $p_{correct}$ is a parameter of the binomial model.[1] The distribution of probabilities across different possible values of N reflects the assumed variability in responding: Although on average a person is predicted to get a proportion of .7 of items correct, by chance she may get only three correct, or maybe all eight items correct. Note that all the probabilities in Figure 4.1 add to 1, consistent with the second axiom of probability theory. This is because we have examined the entire sample space for N: An individual could recall a minimum of zero and a maximum of eight items correctly from an eight-item list, and all intermediate values of N are shown in Figure 4.1.

We were able to plot probability values in Figure 4.1 because there are a finite number of discrete outcomes, each with an associated probability of occurrence. What about the case where variables are continuous rather than discrete? Continuous variables in psychology include direct measures such as response latencies (e.g., Luce, 1986), galvanic skin response (e.g., Bartels & Zeki, 2000), and neural firing rates (e.g., Hanes & Schall, 1996), as well as indirect measures such as latent variables from structural equation models (Schmiedek et al., 2007). Accuracies are also often treated as continuous variables when a large number of observations have been collected or when we have calculated mean accuracy.

One property of a continuous variable is that, as long as we do not round our observations (and thus turn it into a discrete variable), the probability of observing a specific value is effectively 0. That is, although we might record a latency of 784.5 ms, for a fully continuous variable, it would always in theory be possible to examine this latency to another decimal place (784.52 ms), and another (784.524 ms), and another (784.5244 ms). Accordingly, we need some way of representing information about probabilities even though we cannot meaningfully refer to the probabilities of individual outcomes.

There are two useful ways of representing probability distributions for continuous variables. The first is the cumulative density function (CDF; also called the cumulative probability function and, confusingly, the probability distribution function). An example CDF is shown in Figure 4.2, which gives a CDF predicted by a popular model of response times called the ex-Gaussian. We will come back to this model later and look at its insides; for the moment, we will treat the model as a black box and simply note that when we feed a certain set of parameters into the model, the predicted CDF shown in Figure 4.2 is produced. To give this some context, let's imagine we are modeling the time taken to make a decision, such as deciding which of two faces on the computer screen is more attractive (e.g., Shimojo, Simion, Shimojo, & Scheier, 2003). This decision latency t is measured as the time in seconds between the appearance of the pair of faces and the keypress indicating which face is judged more attractive. The abscissa gives our continuous variable of time t; along the ordinate axis, we have the probability that a decision latency x will fall below (or be equal to) time t; formally,

$$f(t) = P(x \leq t). \tag{4.3}$$

Note that the ordinate is a probability and so is constrained to lie between 0 and 1 (or equal to 0 or 1), consistent with our first axiom of probability.

Another representation of probability for continuous variables, and one critical to the likelihood framework, is the probability density function (PDF), or simply probability density. Figure 4.3 plots the probability density function for latencies predicted by the ex-Gaussian, using the same parameters as were used to generate the CDF in Figure 4.2. The exact form of this density is not important for the moment, except that it shows the positively skewed shape typically associated with latencies in many tasks (see, e.g., Luce, 1986; Wixted & Rohrer, 1994). What is important is what we can read off from this function. Although it

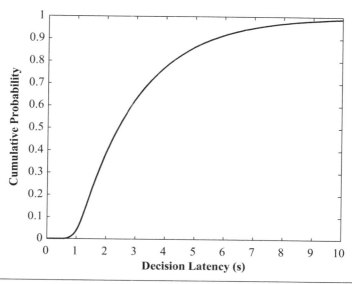

Figure 4.2 An example cumulative distribution function (CDF). For a particular value along the x-axis, the function gives the probability of observing a latency less than or equal to that value.

might be tempting to try and interpret the y-axis directly as a probability (as in Figure 4.1), we cannot: Because we are treating latency as a continuous dimension, there are effectively an infinite number of precise latency values along that dimension, which consequently means that the probability of a particular latency value is vanishingly small. Nonetheless, the height of the PDF can be interpreted as the relative probability of observing each possible latency. Putting these two things together, we can see why the function is called a probability *density* function. Although a particular point along the time dimension itself has no "width," we can calculate a probability by looking across a range of time values. That is, it is meaningful to ask what the probability is of observing a latency between, say, 2 and 3 seconds. We can do this by calculating the area under the curve between those two values. This gives the probability density function its name: It provides a value for the height (density) of the function along the entire dimension of the variable (in this case, time), and this density can then be turned into an area, and thus a probability, by specifying the range for which the area should be calculated. As a real-world example, think about a cake. Although making a single cut in a cake does not actually have any dimensionality (the cut cannot be eaten), if we make two cuts, we can remove the area of cake sliced out by the cuts and devour it. The height of the curve corresponds to the height of a cake: A taller

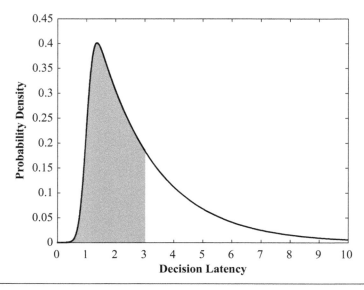

Figure 4.3 An example probability density function (PDF). See text for details.

cake will give us more cake if we make two cuts spaced a specific distance apart (e.g., 3 cm).

Formally, the PDF is the derivative of the CDF (taken with respect to the dependent variable, in this case t); that is, it gives the rate of change in the cumulative probability as we move along the horizontal axis in Figure 4.2. To make this more concrete, imagine Figure 4.2 plots the total distance covered in a 100-m sprint (instead of probability) as a function of time; as time passes, the sprinter will have covered more and more distance from the beginning of the sprint. In this case, the PDF in Figure 4.3 would give the instantaneous velocity of the sprinter at any point in time in the race. According to Figure 4.3, this would mean the sprinter started off slowly, sped up to some peak velocity at around 1.5 seconds, and then slowed down again. We can also flip this around: The CDF is obtained by integrating (i.e., adding up) the PDF from the minimum possible value to the current value. For example, the value of the CDF at a value of 3 seconds is obtained by integrating the PDF from 0 to 3 seconds or, equivalently, working out the area under the PDF between 0 and 3 seconds, which in turn gives us the probability of observing a latency between 0 and 3 seconds; this is the area shaded in light gray in Figure 4.3.

Because the probability of an observation on a continuous variable is effectively 0, the scale of the ordinate in the PDF is in some sense arbitrary. However, an important constraint in order to give the relationship between the CDF and the PDF is that the area under the PDF is equal to 1, just as probabilities are constrained to add up to 1. This means that if the scale of the measurement is changed (e.g., we measure latencies in milliseconds rather than seconds), the values on the ordinate of the PDF will also change, even if the function itself does not. Again, this means that the scale in Figure 4.3 cannot be interpreted directly as a probability, but it does preserve relative relationships, such that more likely outcomes will have higher values. We can also talk about the probability of recording a particular observation with some error ϵ, such that the probability of recording a latency of 784.52 ms is equal to the probability that a latency will fall in the window 784.52 ms $\pm\epsilon$ (Pawitan, 2001). This equates to measuring the area under the density function that is cut off by the lower limit of 784.52 ms $-\epsilon$ and the upper limit of 784.52 ms $+\epsilon$.

Before moving on, let us reiterate what is shown in Figures 4.1 to 4.3. Each of these figures shows the predictions of a model given a particular set of parameter values. Because of the variability inherent in the model and in the sampling process (i.e., the process of sampling participants from a population and data from each participant; we tease these sources of variability apart later in this chapter), the models' predictions are spread across a range of possible outcomes: number of items correct, or latency in seconds for the examples in Figure 4.1 and Figures 4.2 to 4.3, respectively. What the model does is to assign a probability (in the case of discrete outcomes) or probability density (in the case of continuous outcomes) to each possible outcome. This means that although the model effectively predicts a number of different outcomes, it predicts that some outcomes are more likely than others, which, as we will see next, will be critical when relating the model to data we have actually observed.

4.2   What Is a Likelihood?

So far, we have dealt purely with model predictions. The models we have skimmed over so far entertain a number of possible outcomes and assign each of those outcomes a probability or probability density; these, in turn, represent the extent to which the model expects those outcomes to be observed in future samples. The next step is to ask: how do we relate those parallel worlds of possible outcomes to an actual data set obtained from an experiment? We now come to the concept of the likelihood, where we will see how we can relate probabilities and probability densities to the actual outcome we have observed when we run an experiment and analyze the data.

The first important thing to grasp when dealing with likelihoods is that the distribution and density functions we have looked at so far (those shown in Figures 4.1 to 4.3) are actually conditional. Specifically, they show the predicted distribution or density function given (a) a model and (b) a specific set of parameters for that model. For a single data point y, the model M, and a vector of parameter values $\boldsymbol{\theta}$, we will therefore refer to the probability or probability density for an observed data point given the model and parameter values as $f(y|\boldsymbol{\theta}, M)$, where f is the probability mass function or probability density function.[2] We will assume for the rest of the chapter that we are reasoning with respect to a particular model and will leave M out of the following equations, although you should read any of those equations as being implicitly conditional on M. We will return to M in Chapter 5, where we will look at comparing different mathematical or computational models on their account for a set of data.

Rather than considering all possible values of y, as in Figure 4.3, we are now interested in the probability (discrete) or probability density (continuous variable) for the data y we have actually observed. To illustrate, Figure 4.4 shows some obtained data points, represented by stars, for the examples we have looked at so far. In the top panel, we see a single data point, five out of eight items correct, from a single participant in our serial recall experiment, along with a depiction of reading off the probability of getting five items correct according to the model (which is equal to .25). In practice, we do not determine this value graphically but will feed our data y and parameters $\boldsymbol{\theta}$ into the function $f(y|\boldsymbol{\theta}, M)$ and obtain a probability.

In the bottom panel of Figure 4.4, we see the case where we have obtained six latencies in the attractiveness decision experiment considered earlier. Again, a graphical depiction of the relationship between one of the data points and its probability density is shown in this panel. When we have a number of data points (as we usually will in psychology experiments), we can obtain a joint probability or probability density for the data in the vector $\mathbf{y}$ by multiplying together the individual probabilities or probability densities, under the assumption that the observations in $\mathbf{y}$ are independent:

$$f(\mathbf{y}) = \prod^{k} f(y_k|\boldsymbol{\theta}), \tag{4.4}$$

where k indexes the individual observations y_k in the data vector $\mathbf{y}$ (remember, this is also implicitly conditional on our particular model M).

Now that we have explicitly recognized that we can relate collected data to a model through a probability function, we can now answer the question heading up this section: What is a likelihood? The likelihood involves the same function as the probability density but expresses things in the opposite direction. As we discuss later, this is not strictly the reverse conditional probability $f(\boldsymbol{\theta}|y)$ but does involve a reversal in the direction of inference. Rather than keeping the model and the parameter values fixed and looking at what happens to the probability function or probability density across different possible data points, we instead

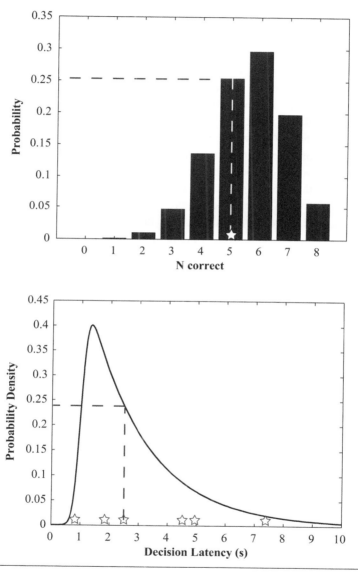

Figure 4.4 Reading off the probability of discrete data (top panel) or the probability density for continuous data (bottom panel). The stars in each panel show example data points, and the dashed lines describe what we are doing when we calculate a probability or probability density for some data.

keep the data and the model fixed and observe changes in *likelihood* values as the parameter values change. That is, we get some measure of how likely each possible parameter value is given our observed data. This is of obvious utility when modeling data: We usually have collected some data and now wish to know what the values of the parameters are.

To understand the relationship between probabilities and likelihoods and how they differ, let's look at the latencies in the attractiveness choice example again. As discussed above, latency probability densities tend to be positively skewed. One simple model of latencies that nicely captures the general shape of latency distributions is the ex-Gaussian distribution. This model assumes that each latency produced by a participant in any simple choice experiment can be broken down into two independent components (see Figure 4.5). The first of these is the time taken to make the decision, which is assumed to be distributed according to an exponential function (left panel of Figure 4.5). The assumption of an exponential is made to capture the extended tail of latency distributions and because it is naturally interpreted as reflecting the time of information processing in many areas of psychology (e.g., Andrews & Heathcote, 2001; Balota, Yap, Cortese, & Watson, 2008; Hohle, 1965; Luce, 1986). The second component is assumed to be processes supplementary to the information processing of interest, including the time to encode a stimulus and initiate motor movement (Luce, 1986). This second component (middle panel of Figure 4.5) is assumed to be Gaussian (i.e., a normal distribution) for convenience and because it follows from the assumption that a number of different processes and stages contribute to this residual time (the Gaussian shape then following from the central limit theorem). The ex-Gaussian has three parameters: the mean μ and standard deviation σ of the Gaussian distribution and the parameter τ governing the rate of drop-off of the exponential function.

Let's consider the case where we have collected a single latency from a participant and where we know the values of σ and τ but μ is unknown. This is just for demonstration purposes; usually all the parameters will have unknown values, and we will certainly want to estimate those parameters from more than a single observation. (Just like multiple regression, it is important that we have a reasonable number of data points per free parameter in our model.)

The top panel of Figure 4.6 plots the probability density $f(y|\mu)$ as a function of the single data point y and the single parameter μ; both axes are expressed in units of seconds. Each contour in the figure is a probability density function, plotting out the probability density function for a particular value of μ. We've only plotted some of the infinite number of possible probability density functions (keep in mind μ is a continuous parameter). As an illustration, a particular probability density function $f(y|\mu = 2)$ is marked out as a gray line on the surface in the

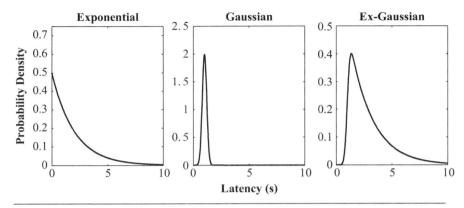

Figure 4.5 Building up the ex-Gaussian model. When independent samples are taken from a Gaussian PDF (left panel) and an exponential PDF (middle panel) and summed, the resulting values are distributed according to the ex-Gaussian PDF (right panel).

top panel, running perpendicular to the μ axis at $\mu = 2$; the corresponding cross section through the surface is plotted in the middle panel.

Also marked out in the top panel of Figure 4.6 is a heavy line running perpendicular to the data axis at $y = 3$. This line, plotted as a cross section of the surface in the bottom panel of Figure 4.6, gives the likelihood function for μ given a fixed value of $y = 3$, denoted $L(\mu|y)$. This shows us the state of affairs we would usually have in estimating a parameter, where we have collected some data (in this case, a single data point) and have some uncertainty about the value of the parameters. Just as for the probability density/mass function, the likelihood function tells us about possible states of the world; the difference is that these states here refer to different possible parameter values, and the likelihood function tells us about how likely each of those parameter values is given the data we have observed. In that sense, the likelihood function is a little bit like a probability density for the parameters rather than the data. This is heuristically true, in that the likelihood function tells us about the relative plausibility of different parameter values; however, as we discuss in the next section, we cannot treat the likelihood function exactly like a probability density.

All this can be a little confusing because in both the probability density function and the likelihood function, the value of the function is given by the probability density $f(y|\mu)$ (and should properly be written in as the label on the vertical axis in the top panel of Figure 4.6; we have omitted it to avoid confusion). The probability density function and likelihood function in this case are distinguished by whether μ is fixed and y traces out the function (the probability density function) or y is fixed and μ traces out the function (the likelihood function).

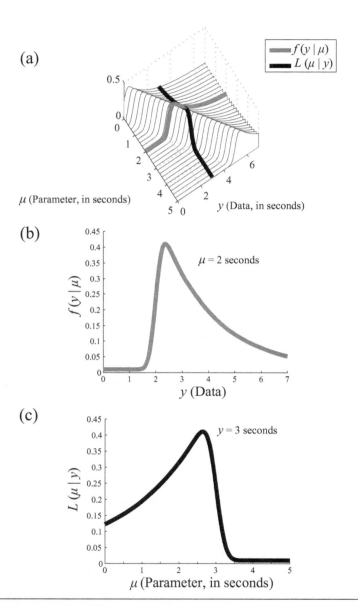

Figure 4.6 Distinguishing between probabilities and likelihoods. The top panel plots the probability density as a function of the single ex-Gaussian model parameter μ and a single data point y. Also shown are cross sections corresponding to a probability density (gray line) and likelihood function (dark line), which are respectively shown in profile in the middle and bottom panels. See text for further details.

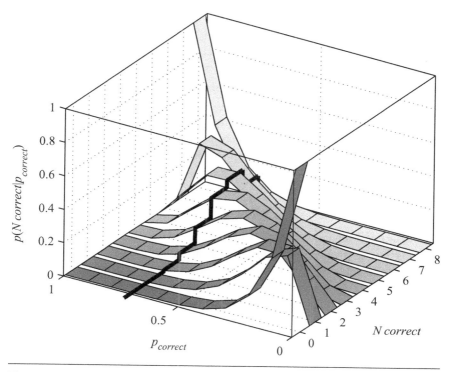

Figure 4.7 The probability of a data point under the binomial model, as a function of the model parameter $p_{correct}$ and the data point N correct. The solid line shows the probability mass function for a particular value of $p_{correct}$, while each of the strips represents a continuous likelihood function.

As another example, and to reinforce this distinction, Figure 4.7 plots a similar surface, this time for the example of the binomial distribution given in Figure 4.1. As mentioned earlier, the binomial distribution tells us the probability with which we should expect each possible outcome in terms of number of items correctly recalled (N correct). The binomial distribution assigns these probabilities on the basis of the number of items that could be correctly recalled ($N=8$) and the parameter $p_{correct}$, which represents the probability of recalling any single item correctly. (The parameter $p_{correct}$ has no psychological import for the moment but will be associated with a psychological model later in the chapter.) The surface in Figure 4.7, which plots $f(N correct | p_{correct})$ for different combinations of N correct (the data) and $p_{correct}$ (the binomial model parameter), looks irregular because we are considering a discrete variable. The parameter $p_{correct}$, by contrast, is continuous because it can lie anywhere between (and including) 0 and 1.

Each cut of this surface perpendicular to the $p_{correct}$ axis in Figure 4.7 gives us the binomial probability mass function $f(N correct | p_{correct})$ for a particular value of $p_{correct}$. As an example, the heavy line on the surface traces out the probability mass function for $p_{correct} = 0.7$; this function is identical to the one in Figure 4.1. In contrast, each ribbon in Figure 4.7 traces out the likelihood function for each value of N correct, $L(p_{correct} | N correct)$; that is, N correct is fixed and $p_{correct}$ is allowed to vary. The difference between the likelihood and the probability functions is evident from their different characteristics; each probability mass function in Figure 4.7 is composed of a series of steps (being a discrete function), while the likelihood functions are smoothly varying (being continuous).

4.2.1   Inverse Probability and Likelihood

Talking about likelihoods allows us to reason backwards: We can take a known function giving precise predictions based on parameter values—$P(y|\theta)$—and reverse the direction of the conditional to work out how likely different parameter values are based on observed data, $L(\theta|y)$.[3] In the latter case, why do we refer to likelihoods rather than probabilities? Isn't the likelihood simply the probability of the parameters given the data, $P(\theta|y)$? The answer is no. Above, we briefly visited the relationship between joint probabilities and conditional probabilities and found that $P(a, b) = P(a|b)P(b)$; equivalently, $P(a, b) = P(b|a)P(a)$. If we put these all in the one equation and reformulate in terms of data and the parameters (i.e., we replace a with the data y and b with the parameter θ), we get $P(y|\theta)P(\theta) = P(\theta|y)P(y)$. Rearranging, we get

$$P(\theta|y) = \frac{P(y|\theta)P(\theta)}{P(y)}. \tag{4.5}$$

Equation 4.5 is known as *Bayes' theorem* and forms the basis of Bayesian parameter estimation and model selection. We will not cover the Bayesian approach to modeling in this book but note here that Bayes' theorem tells us that the likelihood—which appears as $P(y|\theta)$ in Equation 4.5 (and which is equal to $L(\theta|y)$ as discussed above)—does not give us enough information in order to calculate the probability of the parameters given the data. First, we need to know $P(\theta)$, the prior probability of the parameter before observing the data y. Second, we need to know the probability $P(y)$, which serves the purpose of normalizing the likelihood function to ensure it adds to one (in line with the fundamental assumptions of probability theory). Nonetheless, we hope to show you that simply knowing the likelihood of the data given the model, $L(\theta|y)$, gives us a lot of mileage in estimating parameters and making inferences from models. In particular, and as you may have guessed from the name, we can work out the most likely parameter values given the data, or *maximum likelihood* estimates. We'll get to this shortly (in Section 4.4). For the moment, we first need to talk about a critical step along the way: actually specifying a probability function.

4.3 Defining a Probability Function

Before we can use the likelihood function to fit a model to data, the probability distribution first needs to be specified, whether it be a probability mass function ($P(y|\theta)$) or probability density function ($f(y|\theta)$). A model that does not predict any noise in the data will not be able to take advantage of likelihood methods; if the model predicts a deterministic outcome based on a particular set of parameter values, our PDF would have a singularity (i.e., would go to infinity) at the predicted data value and would be zero otherwise. In the case of a probability mass function, we would have one outcome predicted with probability one and all other outcomes associated with a probability of zero. Accordingly, it is critical that our model specifies some probability function across all the possible data values that could be observed. As should be obvious from our discussion so far, the critical role of the probability function is to map parameter(s) into an assignment of probability or probability density for every possible data value.

In some cases, specification of a probability function is not only required for the reasons just outlined but is itself the goal of the modeling. A number of theorists and experimenters in psychology are interested in the dynamics of behavior and are specifically interested in the characterization of the distribution of response times or choice times (e.g., Balota et al., 2008; S. Brown & Heathcote, 2005; Carpenter & Williams, 1995; Ratcliff, 1998; Usher & McClelland, 2001; Wixted & Rohrer, 1994; see Luce, 1986, for a review). Applying models of response time distributions to data is informative because different parameters in response time models, tied to particular psychological processes, will tend to systematically map to different aspects of the distributions. Accordingly, by estimating the parameters of a model distribution or by looking at the change in the location, shape, and skew of the data themselves and linking these to a model (e.g., Andrews & Heathcote, 2001), researchers can make inferences about the underlying processes.

But where do these probability functions come from? How do we arrive at an appropriate probability function for a particular data set? For the examples we looked at earlier, where did those binomial and ex-Gaussian functions come from, and why did we focus on those functions in particular? Let's focus on developing a probability density for a single observation for the moment; we will then move on to consider modeling data from multiple observations and participants. An appropriate probability distribution for data from a single individual can be obtained by considering (a) the nature of the dependent variable to which the model is being fit or compared and (b) the probability distribution predicted by the model. The nature of the dependent variable tells us whether a probability mass function or a PDF will be more appropriate, which depends on whether our dependent variable is discrete or continuous. Second, the probability distribution predicted by our model, together with the nature of the data, tells us whether we can apply the model to the data directly or whether we need to introduce some intermediate probability function first.

4.3.1 Probability Functions Specified by the Psychological Model

The response time models just discussed are a good example of a case where the probability density function is fully specified by the model. A PDF commonly assumed is the ex-Gaussian distribution, the convolution of an exponential distribution and a normal distribution, that we covered earlier. The equation for the PDF for the ex-Gaussian is as follows:

$$f(y_k|\mu, \sigma, \tau) = \frac{1}{\tau} \exp\left(\frac{\mu - y_k}{\tau} + \frac{\sigma^2}{2\tau^2}\right) \Phi\left(\frac{y_k - \mu}{\sigma} - \frac{\sigma}{\tau}\right), \qquad (4.6)$$

where μ, σ, and τ are the three parameters of the probability density function; y_k is a single data point (response time); and Φ is the Gaussian cumulative distribution function.

Implementing this function in MATLAB is straightforward, as shown in Listing 4.1. The last factor in the listing (beginning with the multiplication by .5) computes the cumulative normal from scratch by relying on the relation

$$\Phi(x) = .5\left(1 + \left(\text{erf}\left(\frac{x}{\sqrt{2}}\right)\right)\right), \qquad (4.7)$$

where erf refers to the "error function" that is built into MATLAB.

Listing 4.1 Calculation of Density for the Ex-Gaussian

```
1  function dens = exGaussPDF(y, mu, sigma, tau)
2
3  dens = (1./tau).*...
4    exp(((mu−y)./tau)+((sigma.^2)./(2.*tau.^2))).*.5
5      .*(1+erf(((((y−mu)./sigma)−(sigma./tau))./sqrt(2)));
```

To remind yourself what the ex-Gaussian PDF looks like, refer back to Figure 4.6. Using Equation 4.6, we can calculate a probability density for each of the data points in the data vector **y** directly from the values for μ, σ, and τ. In this case, the probability density function is itself the model of behavior, and no further assumptions are needed to relate the model to the data.

4.3.2   Probability Functions via Data Models

However, not all models are like the ex-Gaussian in this respect. In some situations, a model may only make predictions about mean performance and will not be cast in a way that allows the model to directly predict an entire PDF. In such situations, the probability function is specified by the data themselves. Let us consider again the case of the serial recall experiment, in which participants are presented with short lists of stimuli (e.g., words) to remember and recall in their order of original presentation. We wish to fit a particular model to the accuracy serial position function from a single participant (for another example, see Myung, 2003). The model we will consider is the SIMPLE model (Scale-Invariant Memory, Perception and LEearning) of G. D. A. Brown et al. (2007). SIMPLE is a distinctiveness model, meaning that the accuracy of recall of an item depends on the extent to which it can be discriminated from other potential recall candidates. SIMPLE's primary claim is that list items in serial recall are distinguished along the dimension of time: When we recall something, we are looking back along the dimension of time and trying to pick out the target memory from other memories that occurred around the same time of the target memory. This means that separation of events in time determines the accuracy of their recall. Another assumption of SIMPLE is that time is logarithmically compressed: As items recede into the past, they become more squashed together, just as telephone poles become more squashed as they recede into the distance when viewed from the rear of a moving car.

Let's express SIMPLE mathematically (for a more elaborate and principled description of SIMPLE, see G. D. A. Brown et al., 2007). We will denote the current time, the time of retrieval, as T_r. Now let's take two arbitrary events that have occurred in the recent past; in our serial recall example, these would be items in the list just presented. We will label these events i and j and denote the respective times at which they were presented as T_i and T_j. The psychological distance between the present time and the time at which event i occurred—we'll call this M_i following G. D. A. Brown et al. (2007)—is given by $M_i = \log(T_r - T_i)$; similarly, $M_j = \log(T_r - T_j)$. The form of this equation should be fairly obvious: We are looking at the difference in time between the original event and the time of retrieval and then logarithmically compressing this distance using the log function.

The similarity of memory for the two events is then given by

$$\eta_{ij} = \exp(-c|M_i - M_j|), \tag{4.8}$$

where c is a scaling parameter. Based on the ηs given by Equation 4.8, the probability of recalling item j given the temporal probe i is given by

$$p(j|i) = \frac{\eta_{ij}}{\sum_k \eta_{ik}}, \qquad (4.9)$$

where k is an index for all possible recall candidates (i.e., list items, in the present instance). You may recognize the preceding equations from our discussion of GCM in Chapter 1. SIMPLE can be thought of as an extension of GCM to phenomena in memory and perception, where the dimensions of the category space are replaced by the temporal dimension.

Based on Equation 4.9, the probability of correctly recalling an item is obtained by setting j equal to i; since the similarity of an item to itself, η_{ii}, is equal to 1,[4] this is given by

$$p_{correct}(i) = \frac{1}{\sum_k \eta_{ik}}, \qquad (4.10)$$

where $p_{correct}$ is the predicted proportion correct at position i.

Listing 4.2 gives some MATLAB code for the SIMPLE model. The function `SIMPLEserial` takes four arguments. The first is the parameter c from Equation 4.8. The last three arguments are details of the experiment needed to obtain predictions for a specific experiment. The first of these, `presTime`, is the time separating the onset of items in the experiment; this is used to give the times of presentation T_i used to calculate M. The third argument `recTime` determines how quickly time passes during retrieval and is used to calculate the retrieval times T_r. This argument could be estimated from the experiment if latency data are available; otherwise, we could assume some reasonable value characterizing participants' actual recall times (G. D. A. Brown et al., 2007) or leave it as a free parameter in fitting the model to data (Farrell, 2010). Finally, the argument `J` is the constant length of the lists used in the experiment. The first several lines in the code initialize the vector `pcor` and calculate the presentation times T_i and recall times T_r from the arguments `presTime` and `recTime`. The for loop cycles across output position, and at each position i we probe for that item in the list. Line 12 calculates a vector of Ms (the log-transformed temporal displacement of all items from the present) and then calculates the similarity between the cued item i and all other items (including itself) in a vectorized form of Equation 4.8 in line 13. These statements exploit the facility of MATLAB to combine vectors and scalars into a single expression; thus, the expression `Tr(i)−Ti` will take a scalar (`Tr(i)`) and will subtract from it a vector of quantities (`Ti`), thereby creating another vector. Whenever a single scalar enters into an expression with a vector, the scalar is implicitly "replicated" as many times as is necessary to match it up with every element in the vector. The final line of the loop calculates a predicted proportion

Listing 4.2 Code for the Basic SIMPLE Model of Serial Recall

```
1  function pcor = SIMPLEserial(c, presTime, recTime, J)
2  % c is the single parameter of SIMPLE
3  % presTime and recTime are the effective temporal
4  % separation of items at input and output
5  % J is the length of the list
6
7  pcor = zeros(1,J);
8  Ti = cumsum(repmat(presTime,1,J));
9  Tr = Ti(end) + cumsum(repmat(recTime,1,J));
10
11  for i=1:J % i indexes output + probe position
12      M = log(Tr(i)-Ti);
13      eta = exp(-c*abs(M(i)-M));
14      pcor(i) = 1./sum(eta);
15  end
```

correct at position i using Equation 4.10, the vector `pcor` then being returned as the output of the function.

The output of the code in Listing 4.2 presents us with a problem when modeling the accuracy serial position function: We have a predicted probability of correct recall for the item at a particular serial position i, but we have not specified a full probability function. This is because SIMPLE predicts a single number, a single probability correct, for each set of parameter values. We need some way of assigning a probability (or probability density) to all possible outcomes; in this case, this means all possible values of proportion correct will have some probability of occurrence predicted by SIMPLE. To solve this issue, it helps to step back and consider why SIMPLE does not produce a range of possible outcomes, whereas we know that if we ran this experiment on people that we would get a range of different outcomes. The answer is that the variability in our data is due to sampling variability: Although *on average* a person may recall half of the items correctly, by chance that same person may remember 60% of items correctly on one trial and only 40% on the next. An even clearer case is a fair coin: A coin is not subject to fluctuations in motivation, blood sugar levels, and so on, but each time we toss the coin a fixed number of times, we are not surprised to see that the coin does not always give the same number of tails each time.

Does this sound familiar? It should. Look back to Figure 4.1 and the discussion around that figure, where we discussed the same issue. The implication is that it is possible for a model like SIMPLE to predict a specific probability of correct recall, but for the *observed* proportion correct to vary from trial to trial because of sampling variability, as on some trials a participant will correctly recall the item at a particular serial position, and at other times will fail to recall the corresponding item. If we have N trials, we will have $N_C(i)$ correct recalls and $N_F(i)$ failures to recall at a particular serial position i, where $N_C(i) + N_F(i) = N$. (This assumes there are no missing data; if there were, we would need to specify N for each individual serial position, such that $N_C(i) + N_F(i) = N(i)$.) As we discussed in the context of Figure 4.1, this situation is formally identical to the case where we flip a weighted coin N times and record the number of heads (correct recalls) and tails (failures to recall). Given the coin has a probability p_{heads} of coming up heads, the probability distribution across all possible numbers of heads (out of N) is given by the following binomial distribution:

$$p(k|p_{heads}, N) = \binom{N}{k} p_{heads}{}^k (1 - p_{heads})^{N-k}, \tag{4.11}$$

where $p(k)$ is the probability of observing exactly k out of N coin tosses come up as heads, and $\binom{N}{k}$ is the combinatorial function *from N choose k*, giving the total number of ways in which k out of N tosses could come up heads (if this is unfamiliar, permutations and combinations are covered in most introductory books on probability). Listing 4.3 gives MATLAB code corresponding to Equation 4.11.

Listing 4.3 The Binomial Probability Mass Function

```
1  function pMass = binomPMF(k, N, p)
2
3  % this code is vectorized , so we can
4  % pass a vector of p's and obtain
5  % a vector of probability masses back
6  % k cannot be a vector; instead ,  use
7  % binopdf in the Mathworks Statistics Toolbox
8  pMass = nchoosek(N,k).* p.^k .*(1−p).^(N−k);
```

Replacing the variables in Equation 4.11 with those from our serial recall experiment, we get

$$p\left(N_C(i)|p_{correct}(i), N\right) = \binom{N}{N_C(i)} p_{correct}(i)^{N_C(i)} (1 - p_{correct}(i))^{N - N_C(i)}. \tag{4.12}$$

Given the probability of correctly recalling item i, $p_{correct}(i)$, and that the person completed N trials, this gives us the probability of correctly recalling item i on N_C trials, out of a maximum of N. This function is plotted in Figure 4.1 for $p_{correct}(i) = .7$ and $N=8$. This means that we can take predicted proportion correct $p_{correct}(i)$ from any model (in this case, SIMPLE) and obtain a full probability mass function based only on the number of trials! We therefore turn a model's point prediction into a distribution of predictions not by exploiting natural variability within the model but by modeling the stochastic process that we presume generates the data.

Listing 4.4 gives a modification of the code in Listing 4.2 to obtain a probability mass function for SIMPLE. The main change is that the function accepts additional parameters Nc and N; these are, respectively, a vector of the number of correctly recalled items N_C (each element in the vector corresponding to a serial position) and a scalar value indicating the total number of trials (i.e., the total number of observations at each serial position). Accordingly, if we feed in the SIMPLE parameters, as well as values for Nc and N, we get back the predicted probability of observing Nc correct recalls (out of a maximum possible N) for each serial position.

Listing 4.4 Code for Obtaining Predicted Probability Masses From SIMPLE

```
1  function pmf = SIMPLEserialBinoPMF(c, presTime, ↩
       recTime, J, Nc, N)
2  % c is the parameter of SIMPLE
3  % presTime and recTime are the effective temporal
4  % separation of items at input and output
5  % J is the length of the list
6  % Nc (a vector) is the number of items correctly ↩
       recalled at each position
7  % N is the number of trials at each position
8
9  pmf = zeros(1,J);
10 Ti = cumsum(repmat(presTime,1,J));
11 Tr = Ti(end) + cumsum(repmat(recTime,1,J));
12
13 for i=1:J % i indexes output + probe position
14     M = log(Tr(i)-Ti);
15     eta = exp(-c*abs(M(i)-M));
16     pcor = 1./sum(eta);
17     pmf(i) = binomPMF(Nc(i), N, pcor);
18 end
```

Note that we have two levels of function parameters in the above example. On one hand, we have the model parameters of SIMPLE; in this basic version, that's the single parameter c in Equation 4.8.[5] These are used to calculate $p_{correct}(i)$ using the equations for SIMPLE presented above. Each $p_{correct}(i)$ is then used as a parameter for the binomial distribution function in Equation 4.12. We are really only interested in c as the model parameter, as it fully determines the binomial density function via Equations 4.8 and 4.10, but we should be aware that we are using the binomial function as an intermediate function connecting the model to the data, based on assumptions about the way the data were sampled (specifically, how many trials there were in the experiment: N). From here on, we will refer to this intermediate function as the *data model*, to reflect its role in relating the psychological model to the data, and because it is effectively a model of the sampling process we assume is generating the data in the experiment being modeled.

4.3.3   Two Types of Probability Functions

The case of SIMPLE can be contrasted with the ex-Gaussian, which, as discussed, directly predicts a full probability density function. The contrasting situations are made explicit in Figure 4.8.

On the left of the figure, we show the case of a model like the ex-Gaussian, which is a psychological model but also describes the sampling process that allows the model to be directly related to the data, as it produces a full probability function.

The right of Figure 4.8 shows the other scenario in which a model's predictions are fed into the data model, along with other information about the assumed sampling process in the experiment; that data model is then used to generate a full probability function.

In the end, the data model is not of theoretical interest, and we are instead interested in treating the combination of functions on the right in Figure 4.8 as a single "black box" function; in the case of the binomial function applied to SIMPLE, black box gives us the probability of various values of N_C given our parameter c, with the intermediate point prediction of SIMPLE, $p_{correct}(i)$, hidden inside the black box. Since this means that the black box really provides us with a probability mass function $p(N_C|c)$, we can flip this around to refer to the likelihood of the parameters given the observed data, $L(c|N_C)$. As we saw in Section 4.2, specifically in Figures 4.6 and 4.7, the computations of $p(N_C|c)$ and $L(c|N_C)$ are identical; the difference is whether we are interested in estimating some unknown parameters based on data (the likelihood) or working out what types of data we might expect to observe in the future given a set of known parameter values.

Figure 4.8 also makes clear the importance of distinguishing between different types of probability. In the case of the SIMPLE model with a binomial data model, we can talk about a number of different probabilities:

1. The probability $p_{correct}(i)$, the probability of correct recall predicted by SIMPLE

2. The probability of correct recall in the data, obtained by dividing N_C by N

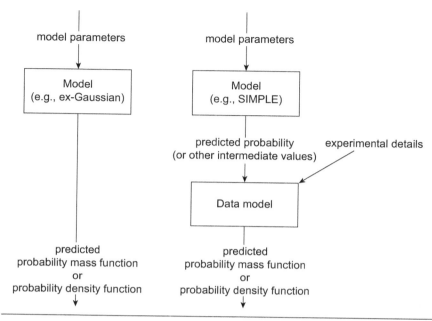

Figure 4.8 Different ways of predicting a probability function, depending on the nature of the model and the dependent variable. On the left, the model parameters and the model are together sufficient to predict a full probability function. This usually applies to the case where the dependent variable is continuous and the model is explicitly developed to predict probability functions (e.g., response time models). On the right, the model parameters and the model predict some intermediate value(s), such as proportion correct. Together with other assumptions about the sampling process, these intermediate values are used to specify a full probability function via the data model.

3. The probability of each of the possible outcomes N_C predicted by SIMPLE after applying the data model in Equation 4.12 (i.e., the ordinate in Figure 4.1)

Whenever working with models like this, it is important not to get these different types of probabilities confused. To keep these probabilities distinct in your head, it might help to think about where these different probabilities slot in Figure 4.8 (going from model parameters to a full probability function) and Figure 2.8 (relating the model to the data).

4.3.4   Extending the Data Model

Although we said above that the data model is not of theoretical interest, the consideration of the sampling process required to implement a data model can open up some further opportunities for modeling. In the preceding example, we were interested simply in accounting for overall accuracy. However, we may also be interested in accounting for the distribution of errors. In the serial recall literature, researchers are often interested in the *displacement* of an erroneously recalled item by comparing the sequence presented to the participant with the sequence produced by the individual at recall. That is, if a person recalls an item in the incorrect position in the serial recall task, what is the difference between the *list* position (j) of the recalled item and its output position (i; i.e., the ordinal position in the person's sequence of output)? We are then interested in examining the probability distribution (specifically, the probability mass function) across all possible transposition displacements. We may ask this question in even more detail, by examining the probability of recalling each possible item j at each output position i. That is, for the second output position, what is the probability of recalling item 1, item 2, item 3, and so on? As you may have guessed, what we wish to do is specify a probability distribution across all possible recallable items at each output position (Farrell & Lelièvre, 2009).

In both cases (looking at displacements overall and breaking down displacements by output position), we can use an extension of the binomial distribution called the multinomial distribution. The multinomial distribution works in the same manner but extends to a dependent variable with more than two possible categorical outcomes. If we have J categories of responses, then we are interested in the number of observations N_j in each category j, $j = 1 \ldots J$. We will represent the N_js together in the vector **N**. The multinomial distribution relates these frequencies to the probability that a particular observation will fall in category j, p_j; we will represent these probabilities together in the vector **p**. As an analogy, we can think of our categories as buckets and observations as balls that we throw into the buckets, with each ball landing in one (and only one) bucket. We are then interested in how the balls are distributed across the buckets.

To reiterate, both **N** (the number of balls landing in each bucket) and **p** (the predicted probability of a ball landing in each bucket) are vectors, with each element in the vector referring to a category and each vector containing J elements. Because we have a fixed total number of observations to be distributed across the categories (we'll call this N_T for total number of observations), the elements in **N** must add up to N_T, that is, $\sum^J N_j = N_T$. Similarly, our probabilities will necessarily add up to 1: $\sum^J p_j = 1$. (Remember why? If not, it may be worth your while to revisit the introductory statements about probabilities.) The multinomial function then tells us the probability of observing the frequencies in the categories, **N**, given the probability that an observation will fall in each category, **p**. The general form of the multinomial distribution is as follows:

$$p(\mathbf{N}|\mathbf{p}, N_T) = \frac{N_T!}{N_1!N_2!\ldots N_J!} p_1{}^{N_1} p_2{}^{N_2} \ldots p_J{}^{N_J}, \qquad (4.13)$$

with $\mathbf{N}$, $\mathbf{p}$, N_T, and J as described above. The exclamation marks in Equation 4.13 do not express surprise but instead denote the factorial function $k! = 1 \times 2 \times 3 \times \ldots \times k$. It turns out that the multinomial function is similar in form to the binomial function in Equation 4.11. Equation 4.11 is a simplification of another way of expressing the binomial distribution function:

$$p(N|p, N_T) = \frac{N_T!}{N!(N_T - N)!}p^N(1 - P)^{N_T-N}, \qquad (4.14)$$

where the variables and parameters from Equation 4.11 have been replaced with N, p, and N_T. You'll notice that Equations 4.13 and 4.14 are similar in form; in fact, the binomial distribution is simply the multinomial distribution obtained when we have only two categories (e.g., heads vs. tails or correct vs. incorrect). Equation 4.14 simplifies Equation 4.13 by taking advantage of the constraint that the probabilities of the two outcomes must add up to 1: If we are correct with probability p, then we must necessarily be incorrect with probability $1 - p$.

Let's consider how we might use the multinomial model to apply SIMPLE to serial recall data in more detail. As above, for each output position i, we may ask the probability of recalling each item j, $1 \leq j \leq J$, where J is the length of the list (i.e., we assume that participants only recall list items). The predicted probability of making each response, $p(j|i)$, is given by Equation 4.9, which in turn depends on the values of the SIMPLE parameters via Equation 4.8. For a particular probe (i.e., output position) i, we can then rewrite Equation 4.13 in the language of SIMPLE:

$$p(\mathbf{N}(i)|\mathbf{p}(i), N_T) = \frac{N_T!}{N(i)_1!N(i)_2!\ldots N(i)_J!}p(i)_1{}^{N(i)_1}p(i)_2{}^{N(i)_2}\ldots p(i)_J{}^{N(i)_J},$$
$$(4.15)$$

where N_T is the number of trials (i.e., the number of total responses made at each output position), $\mathbf{N}(i)$ is the vector containing the number of times each response j was produced at the ith output position, and $\mathbf{p}(i)$ is the probability with which SIMPLE predicts each response j will be produced at the ith output position. The end product is a single number, probability $p(\mathbf{N}(i)|\mathbf{p}(i))$, of observing the frequencies in $\mathbf{N}(i)$ given the predicted probabilities $\mathbf{p}(i)$ and the total number of responses N_T. We will defer providing code for this function until later in the chapter, where we will see how we can simplify Equation 4.15 and make this job easier.[6]

When should we use the multinomial distribution in preference to its simpler sibling, the binomial distribution? This depends on the question we are asking. If we are simply interested in fitting accuracies (e.g., the accuracy serial position curve), then we can define our events of interest as *correct* and its complement *incorrect*; in this case, the binomial will be sufficient to produce a likelihood.

If we are interested in fitting the distribution of all possible responses in detail, then we have a larger number of possible events, and the multinomial function is necessary (e.g., Busemeyer & Stout, 2002; Farrell & Lelièvre, 2009; Farrell & Lewandowsky, 2008; Nosofsky, 1989). The multinomial can be of help even if our theoretical interest classically lies in response accuracies. For example, although SIMPLE and another serial recall model (see, e.g., G. D. A. Brown et al., 2000; Burgess & Hitch, 1999; Lewandowsky & Farrell, 2008b; Page & Norris, 1998b) may be able to closely capture the serial position curve, the entire transposition matrix will present a greater challenge that may allow the models to be teased apart (e.g., Farrell & Lelièvre, 2009; see Chapter 5 on using multinomial distributions to distinguish between models).

4.3.5   Extension to Multiple Data Points and Multiple Parameters

The examples plotted in Figures 4.6 and 4.7 are simple examples that would not warrant such a thorough treatment in practice. Usually, we will have a number of data points and a number of parameters to estimate (and, as discussed in Chapter 3, the data will come from a number of participants). Nevertheless, the principles just outlined extend to these cases. In the case where we have a number of data points in a data vector $\mathbf{y}$, if we assume that the data points are independent, then we can follow Equation 4.1 and calculate a *joint likelihood* by multiplying together the likelihoods for individual observations, just as we multiply joint probabilities together to obtain a joint probability (Equation 4.4). That is,

$$L(\theta|\mathbf{y}) = \prod_{k}^{k} L(\theta|y_k), \qquad (4.16)$$

where k indexes the individual observations. We can then reconceptualize Figures 4.6 and 4.7 as plotting the joint probability $p(\mathbf{y}|\mu)$ on the vertical axis.

This also applies to more complicated examples. For example, Equation 4.15 gives the probability of observing a certain number of observations in each category given the outcome probabilities predicted by SIMPLE. Treating the multinomial function as a "black box" (Figure 4.8), we can talk more generally about the likelihood of the SIMPLE parameter c given the obtained category frequencies in $N(i)$, where i refers to a specific output position. Of course, we would usually want to calculate a joint likelihood across all output positions, easily done using Equation 4.16 with k indexing output position.

What about the case where we have data from multiple participants? Can we obtain a joint likelihood across participants in a similar fashion? The short answer is yes. However, were we to do this, we would be making the strong assumption that the participants could be jointly characterized by a single set of parameter values; that is, we would assume that there is no variability between participants except for that introduced by sampling variability within each participant. As discussed in Chapter 3, we would usually prefer to fit the data from individual participants unless circumstances prohibited us from doing so. We return to maximum likelihood estimation for multiple participants in Section 4.5.

Not only will we usually have multiple data points, but we will also usually have multiple parameters. This doesn't affect our likelihood calculations but does mean that we should be clear about our conceptualization of such models. In the case where we have multiple parameters, Figures 4.6 and 4.7 will incorporate a separate dimension for each parameter. As an example, let's return to the ex-Gaussian model that we covered earlier in the chapter and, in particular, panel c in Figure 4.6; as a reminder, this plots out the likelihood of the ex-Gaussian parameter μ for a fixed, single observation $y = 3$. Figure 4.9 develops this further by plotting the joint likelihood for the data vector $\mathbf{y} = [3\ 4\ 4\ 4\ 4\ 5\ 5\ 6\ 6\ 7\ 8\ 9]$ (all are response times in seconds from a single participant) as a function of two parameters of the ex-Gaussian model, μ and τ; the other ex-Gaussian parameter σ is fixed to the value of 0.1. (We have no specific reason for fixing the value of σ here except that adding it as an additional dimension to Figure 4.9 would give us a four-dimensional figure, which is not easily conceptualized on the printed page!) Together, μ and τ make the parameter vector $\boldsymbol{\theta}$, such that the value plotted along the vertical axis is the joint likelihood $L(\boldsymbol{\theta}|\mathbf{y})$, calculated using Equation 4.16. Note the size of the units along this axis; because we have multiplied together a number of likelihood values (as per Equation 4.16), we end up with very small numbers, as they are in units of 10^{-10}. This surface is called a likelihood surface (as is panel c in Figure 4.6) and plots the joint likelihood $L(\boldsymbol{\theta}|\mathbf{y})$ as a function of the model parameters. To show how this figure was generated, the code used to generate Figure 4.9 (and an accompanying log-likelihood surface; see below) is presented in Listing 4.5.

Listing 4.5 MATLAB Script for Generating Likelihood and Log-Likelihood Surfaces for the μ and τ Parameters of the Ex-Gaussian Model

```
1  mMu = 5; mTau= 5; muN=50; tauN=50; %range and ↩
       resolution of points along each dimension
2  mu = linspace(0,mMu,muN);
3  tau = linspace(0,mTau,tauN);
4
5  rt = [3 4 4 4 4 5 5 6 6 7 8 9];
6
7  i=1;
8  lsurf = zeros(tauN,muN);
9  % nested loops across mu and tau
10 % calculate a joint likelihood for each parameter ↩
       combination
11 for muloop=mu
```

(Continued)

(Continued)

```
12    j=1;
13    for tauloop = tau
14        lsurf(j,i)=prod(exGaussPDF(rt,muloop, .1 , ←↩
              tauloop));
15        lnLsurf(j,i) = sum(log(exGaussPDF(rt,muloop, ←↩
              .1, tauloop)));
16        j=j+1;
17    end
18    i=i+1;
19 end
20
21 %likelihood surface
22 colormap(gray(1)+.1)
23 mesh(tau, mu, lsurf);
24 xlabel('\tau (s)');
25 ylabel('\mu (s)');
26 zlabel('L(y|\theta)');
27 xlim([0 mTau]);
28 ylim([0 mMu]);
29
30 figure
31 %log-likelihood surface
32 colormap(gray(1)+.1)
33 mesh(tau, mu, lnLsurf);
34 xlabel('\tau (s)');
35 ylabel('\mu (s)');
36 zlabel('ln L(y|\theta)');
37 xlim([0 mTau]);
38 ylim([0 mMu]);
```

4.4   Finding the Maximum Likelihood

The likelihood surface in Figure 4.9 (see also panel c of Figure 4.6) plots the likelihood of a parameter given some data—specifically, $L(\mu, \tau|\mathbf{y})$—for all possible values of μ and τ. Often, we are not interested in all these possible values but simply wish to know those parameters that give the best fit to the data. Looking at Figure 4.9, how would you identify those best-fitting parameters? You may not be surprised to learn that we wish to find those parameters with the highest likelihood; that is, we wish to obtain *maximum likelihood parameter estimates*. Maximum likelihood (ML) estimation is a *modal* method: We are looking for the mode (i.e., peak) of the likelihood function.

One way to find the maximum would be to plot likelihood surfaces such as those in Figures 4.6 and 4.9 and identify that combination of parameters that gives

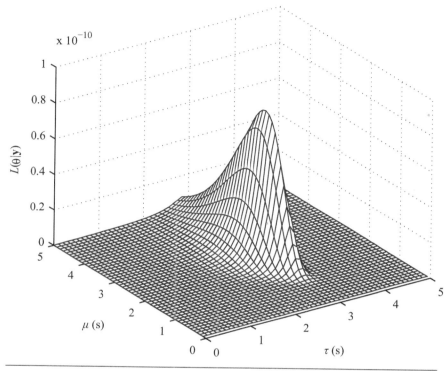

Figure 4.9 The joint likelihood of the parameters of the ex-Gaussian given the data in the vector **y**. The likelihood is shown as a function of two of the ex-Gaussian parameters, μ and τ.

the highest point on the surface (e.g., Eliason, 1993). However, this would be an exhaustive and inefficient strategy and would certainly be impractical when more than a few free parameters need to be estimated. As discussed in Chapter 3, a more practical method is to use an algorithm such as the Simplex algorithm of Nelder and Mead (1965) to search the parameter space for the best-fitting parameters. Indeed, all the methods discussed in Chapter 3 apply directly to maximum likelihood estimation.

One caveat on using the routines discussed in Chapter 3 is that they are geared toward minimization, meaning that we will need to reverse the sign on the likelihood when returning that value to the optimization function. In fact, there are a few other changes we can make to the likelihoods to follow convention and to make our job of fitting the data easier. One convention usually adopted is to measure *log* likelihoods rather than straightforward likelihoods, by taking the natural log, *ln*, of the likelihood (e.g., the `log` function in MATLAB). There are a number of reasons this makes estimation and communication easier. The first is that many analytic models are exponential in nature. That is, many of the probability densities we would wish to specify in psychology come from the exponential family of probability distributions. These include probability mass functions such as the binomial, the multinomial, and the Poisson and probability density functions such as the exponential, the normal/Gaussian, the gamma, and the Weibull. The log and the exponential have a special relationship, in that they are inverse functions. That is, the log and the exponential cancel out each other: $\ln(\exp(x)) = \exp(\ln(x)) = x$. One consequence is that any parts of a probability function that are encapsulated in an exponential function are unpacked; this makes them easier to read and understand and can also have the pleasant result of revealing a polynomial relationship between parameters of interest and the log-likelihood, making minimization easier. The natural log is also useful for turning products into sums:

$$\ln\left(\prod_{k=1}^{K} f(k)\right) = \sum_{k=1}^{K} \ln\left(f(k)\right) \tag{4.17}$$

Similarly, the log turns division into subtraction. As well as being useful for simplifying likelihood functions (as we'll see shortly), this deals with a nasty problem: The likelihood for a large number of observations can sometimes go outside the range of possible values that can be represented on a modern computer since each extra observation multiplies the likelihood by a value usually much greater or smaller than 1! The log acts to compress the values and keep them in reasonable ranges. The log also makes combining information across observations or participants easier since we can simply add the log-likelihoods from independent observations or participants to obtain a joint log-likelihood (cf. Equation 4.16):

$$\ln\left(L(\boldsymbol{\theta}|\mathbf{y})\right) = \sum_{k=1}^{K} \ln\left(L(\boldsymbol{\theta}|y_k)\right), \tag{4.18}$$

where k might index observations (in order to obtain a sum across observations for a single participant) or participants (in order to obtain a joint—that is, summed—log-likelihood for all participants).

As an example of several of these advantages of dealing with log-likelihoods, consider the normal distribution, the familiar bell-shaped probability density usually assumed as the distribution of responses in psychology:

$$p(y|\mu, \sigma) = \frac{1}{\sqrt{2\pi\sigma^2}} \exp\left(-\frac{(y-\mu)^2}{2\sigma^2}\right). \tag{4.19}$$

Taking this as our likelihood function $L(\mu, \sigma|y)$, we can obtain the following log-likelihood function:

$$\ln L(\mu, \sigma | y) = \ln(1) - \ln(\sqrt{2\pi\sigma^2}) - \frac{(y-\mu)^2}{2\sigma^2}. \tag{4.20}$$

Whether attempting to solve this analytically or using an algorithm such as the Simplex algorithm discussed in Chapter 3, expressing things in this manner makes it easier to read the equation and see cases where we could cancel out unneeded calculations. For example, the first term, $\ln(1)$, actually works out to be 0 and so can be discarded. In addition, if we were not concerned with estimating σ and only estimating μ, the second term $\ln(\sqrt{2\pi\sigma^2})$ could also be removed. This is because this term does not depend on μ and therefore acts as a constant in the equation. If we knew the value of σ, this would make μ very easy to estimate since only the third and final term would remain, where the log-likelihood is related to μ by a simple quadratic function. This means that whatever value of μ was the best estimate for the entire equation would also be the best with the first and second term as constants.

Similarly, taking the probability mass function for the multinomial (Equation 4.13) and turning it into a log-likelihood, we get

$$\ln L(\mathbf{p}|\mathbf{N}) = \ln(N_T!) - \sum^{J} \ln N_j! + \sum^{J} N_j \ln p_j, \tag{4.21}$$

where J refers to the number of categories into which the responses can fall. In this case, the first two terms can be discarded. The term $\ln(N_T!)$ depends only on the number of observations and therefore acts as a constant for the log-likelihood. Similarly, $\sum^{J} \ln N_j!$ depends only on our observed data (the number of observations falling into each category) and can also be treated as a constant (remember, the data are fixed and the parameters vary when talking about likelihoods). Only the final term $\sum^{J} N_j \ln p_j$ depends on the model parameters (via $\mathbf{p}$) and is therefore important for estimating the parameters. Listing 4.6 shows how this simplified multinomial log-likelihood function can be incorporated into the SIMPLE code we've presented earlier. Note that the code produces a log-likelihood value for each output position; to obtain a single joint log-likelihood, we would need to sum the values returned in the lnL vector.

In this case, note that the log-likelihood values will be negative because $p < 1$, meaning that $\log(p) < 0$. Because we wish to maximize the log-likelihood, that means we want the number to get closer to 0 (i.e., less negative), even though that means its absolute value will thereby get smaller. Note, however, that it is possible for values from a probability density function to lie above 1 depending on the scale of the variable along the abscissa, meaning that our log-likelihood values are also positive. Consider, for example, a uniform distribution with lower and upper bounds of 0 and 0.1, respectively. For the area under the function to be 1 (i.e., for the probability density to integrate to 1), we need the value of the probability density to be a constant value of 10 across that range.

Listing 4.6 Obtaining a Multinomial Log-Likelihood From the SIMPLE Model

```
 1 function lnL = SIMPLEmultinomLnL(c,  presTime, ↩
      recTime, J, k)
 2 % c is the parameter of SIMPLE
 3 % presTime and recTime are the effective temporal
 4 %     separation of items at input and output
 5 % J is the length of the list
 6 % k is a matrix; each row i corresponds to an output ↩
      position,
 7 %     and element j in the row gives the number of times
 8 %     item j was recalled at position i
 9
10 pmf = zeros(1,J);
11 Ti = cumsum(repmat(presTime,1,J));
12 Tr = Ti(end) + cumsum(repmat(recTime,1,J));
13
14 for i=1:J % i indexes output + probe position
15     M = log(Tr(i)-Ti);
16     eta = exp(-c*abs(M(i)-M));
17     pall = eta./sum(eta);
18     lnL(i) = sum(k(i,:).*log(pall));
19 end
```

A final advantage of dealing with log-likelihoods is their statistical interpretation. The next chapter is dedicated to using the log-likelihood as a measure of statistical information. There, we will use the value $-2 \ln L$, which is usually referred to as the *deviance* of the model, to assess the fit of models and to compare models on the basis of their fit. Note that the minus sign flips the interpretation of the $\ln L$ around: A higher deviance means a worse fit to the data whereas a more negative $\ln L$ corresponds to a worse fit. You can see that it is quite important to keep an eye on your log-likelihoods, to make sure that you are not trying to minimize when you should be maximizing, and to ensure that the log-likelihood values that you carry forward to the analyses that we discuss in Chapter 5 are correct.

4.5   Maximum Likelihood Estimation for Multiple Participants

As discussed in Chapter 3, we will usually wish to estimate parameters for more than a single participant. There are a number of ways to approach this problem, the choice of the approach really depending on features of the experiment and the conclusions we wish to draw. Generally, this choice will be between estimating parameters for individual participants and estimating a single set of parameters for all participants.

4.5.1   Estimation for Individual Participants

Maximum likelihood parameter estimation for individuals follows from what we've presented so far in Chapters 3 and 4. An appropriate probability function is specified, either directly or by using a data model, and a set of maximum likelihood estimators is obtained by fitting the model to each participant's data in isolation. Once estimation has been carried out for all participants, the results of the fitting can be presented in a number of ways. We may wish to plot histograms of parameter estimates or compare the estimates to some expected value using a t test (see Chapter 5). We can also take advantage of the unique properties of log-likelihoods and obtain an overall measure of fit by summing the $\ln L$s across participants. This relies on the additivity of $\ln L$s discussed earlier and is one example of the advantage of MLE over more generic discrepancy functions like the RMSD.[7]

4.5.2   Estimating a Single Set of Parameters

Although fitting the data of individual participants is a good method for obtaining maximum likelihood estimates, we discussed situations in Chapter 3 where we may wish to estimate a single set of parameters for all participants. When fitting the data from multiple participants simultaneously, MLE demands some additional considerations that are not of issue when fitting using RMSD. These additional considerations follow directly from the discussion surrounding Figure 4.8: We must think carefully about the exact nature of the data we are fitting and what the appropriate data model would be.

One option we discussed in Chapter 3 is to combine information across participants in a way that retains information about the distribution of individual participants' data. This is of particular relevance for MLE, where a probability distribution is a necessary requirement for calculating a likelihood. The combining of information across participants in this manner should also be more concrete given our discussion of several types of probability distributions in this chapter. For example, if we are fitting discrete data (i.e., data distributed binomially or multinomially), we may sum response frequencies in each response bin across participants and then fit the resulting cell frequencies. Similarly, when modeling latencies, we may choose to estimate a single set of parameters for the ex-Gaussian for all response data by "vincentizing" (e.g., Rohrer, 2002). In such cases, our assumed probability function is identical to the one that we would adopt if fitting the data of individual participants. One undesirable consequence of this method is that we lose any information about the distributions of individual participants. An alternative is to calculate a log-likelihood for each participant and then sum these log-likelihoods across participants but under the assumption that all participants' behavior can be captured by a single set of parameter values. Indeed, in both these cases, we are treating the data as though they have been generated by a single source (i.e., a single participant).

An alternative is to fit average data, an approach often adopted in psychology when performing statistical analysis. Take the example of the binomial above, where we were interested in fitting a model to response frequencies; specifically, we wished to account for the frequencies of correct and incorrect responses at different serial positions in a memory experiment. Rather than fitting these data from individuals, we can instead calculate an average number or proportion correct at each serial position and fit these averaged data. Note that our dependent variable has changed (from frequencies of responses to *mean* number or proportion correct), and a model like SIMPLE is now being treated as a model of average data, not as a model of the behavior of individuals.

Because our analysis of the data has changed, we need a new data model to connect SIMPLE to the data. What is the appropriate probability distribution for this or any other case we might come across? Regardless of what is being averaged (response proportions, latencies, pupil dilation, etc.), a fundamental theorem in statistics called the central limit theorem guarantees that as we average across more and more data (i.e., as sample size increases), the probability density for the mean will become more normally distributed. With enough participants, we can assume our mean is normally distributed and adopt Equation 4.19, the Gaussian PDF, as our probability function. The one difference between the binomial data model and the Gaussian data model is that the standard deviation of the Gaussian distribution is not specified by the experiment or the psychological model (e.g., SIMPLE) and will need to be estimated from the data as an additional parameter. One beneficial side effect of fitting averaged data is that there is a fortuitous and simple relationship between RMSD and maximum likelihood with a normal (Gaussian) probability function: Minimizing RMSD is equivalent to finding ML parameter estimates with an assumed normal PDF. This means that we can fit averaged data using methods outlined in Chapter 3, with RMSD as our measure of goodness of fit, and treat our obtained parameter estimates as ML parameter estimates! We can also obtain the log-likelihood associated with the ML parameter estimates by transforming the minimized RMSD; see Glover and Dixon (2004) and Burnham and Anderson (2002) for details. Although this relationship is useful, we should keep in mind that this averaging will obscure any heterogeneity between participants that isn't due to normal continuous variance in the data means; see discussion in Chapter 3.

4.6   Properties of Maximum Likelihood Estimators

Maximum likelihood estimation has a firm footing in statistical theory. As a consequence, ML parameter estimates have some desirable properties that rely on a few easily met assumptions about the regularity of the likelihood function, such that it is fully continuous and that all parameters are identifiable (essentially, the likelihood function is not flat with respect to a particular parameter). We point out a few of these features below. For more on the regularity conditions on which these properties rely and other properties of ML estimators we do not discuss below, see Spanos (1999).

One useful property of maximum likelihood estimates is that of parameterization invariance: If we apply some transformation function g to a parameter, then finding the maximum likelihood estimate of the transformed variable, $g(\theta)$, is equivalent to first finding the ML estimate of θ and then applying the transform g (DeGroot, 1989; Spanos, 1999). Transforming parameters can be appropriate when a model is easier to understand in one formulation but easier to implement and fit to data in another. As an example, Farrell and Ludwig (2008) reparameterized the exponential component of the ex-Gaussian distribution with a new parameter $\lambda = 1/\tau$, to facilitate comparison of MLE with a Bayesian approach to estimate response time distributions, under which the inverse transform of τ facilitates combining likelihoods with prior probabilities. Parameterization invariance allowed Farrell and Ludwig (2008) to find the MLE of λ and then take the inverse of this estimate to give the MLE for the original parameter τ.

Two additional and popular properties of ML estimators are those of *consistency* and *efficiency* (Eliason, 1993; Severini, 2000). Consistency means that as we collect larger and larger samples, the probability that the difference between the "real" parameter value and the estimated value is larger than some small arbitrary value that approaches zero; in other words, our estimates get more accurate on average as our sample size increases, or they will be less biased. Efficiency means that, given an estimator has a particular consistency, ML estimation will deliver the least variable parameter estimates. These properties mean that an ML estimate will be easy to find (since efficiency means the likelihood function will be sharply peaked around the maximum; see Eliason, 1993 and Chapter 5) and that our obtained estimate will on average be as close as we could expect to the "true" value.

A final property of ML estimates is that they are asymptotically normally distributed; that is, the more data we have, the closer the variability in our estimates will come to look like a normal distribution. As we discuss in Chapter 5, this is based on changes in the shape of the likelihood function with increasing sample size and leads to some handy methods for estimating standard errors on our parameter estimates.

One property that ML estimators do not in general possess is that of *unbiasedness* (Edwards, 1992; Spanos, 1999). That is, if we generate a number of random samples from a model with a known single parameter and estimate that parameter (using maximum likelihood estimation) for the individual samples, we may find that the average of the estimated parameters deviates from the known value in the generating model. In practice, this is of little concern, as any biases will tend to be drowned out by variability in estimates between samples, such that ML estimators can be treated as effectively unbiased for most purposes. The property of consistency also means that ML estimates will behave more like unbiased estimates as sample size increases (Eliason, 1993); since most psychologists are aware of power issues, they are likely to have collected data from a sufficiently sized sample. In addition, it has been argued that requiring estimates to be strictly unbiased can lead to a loss of properties like parameterization invariance and to unusual parameter behavior for specific samples (Pawitan, 2001).

One other note of caution is that although ML estimates are efficient, they tend to be *overdispersed*. Imagine a case where we want to examine the variability of some parameter in a population (for example, some measure of processing speed, such as drift rate in the diffusion model of response times; Schmiedek et al., 2007). From simulation studies, we know that the ML estimates of that parameter will tend to be more variable between individuals than the known variability in that parameter (e.g., Farrell & Ludwig, 2008; Rouder et al., 2005). As we touched on in the previous chapter, this has led to the use of modeling methods that constrain the variability in parameters by employing a hierarchical modeling structure that provides some top-down constraints on the parameter estimates for individual participants (e.g., Farrell & Ludwig, 2008; Oberauer & Kliegl, 2006; Rouder et al., 2005).

Finally, ML estimation is so popular because it allows us to systematically compare different models on their fit to the data and use such comparisons to make inferences about the psychological mechanisms or representations in the models' domain of application. This process of model comparison and drawing inferences from models is the topic of the next chapter.

Notes

1. We make the simplifying assumption that accuracy of recall is independent; in practice, the recall of one item will modify the probabilities for next recall of all items (e.g., Schweickert, Chen, & Poirier, 1999).

2. f could also represent a CDF, but we will rarely refer to the CDF when working with likelihoods.

3. We are using P to denote probabilities generally. In many cases, the functions will be continuous probability densities, which we would usually denote f following the terminology adopted in this book.

4. To see why, try setting the distance to 0 in Equation 4.8 and working out the similarity.

5. The full version of SIMPLE also allows for the case where people may fail to recall any item from the list, which is captured in SIMPLE by introducing a threshold function similar to that we used in our model of the phonological loop in Chapter 2. We've omitted discussion of that threshold here to simplify presentation of the model.

6. Alternatively, if you are desperate, the multinomial PMF is available as the function mnpdf in the Statistics Toolbox.

7. This property of additivity does extend to the χ^2 statistic, which is closely related to the deviance ($-2 \ln L$) introduced earlier.

5

Parameter Uncertainty and Model Comparison

Chapter 4 dealt with full specification of a model, including a probability distribution, and estimating the parameters of the model using maximum likelihood estimation (MLE). If we had run an experiment and collected some data, fitting the model to those data using MLE would produce two end products: a vector of ML parameter estimates, and the value of the maximized log-likelihood. Although the obtained estimates are in most respects the best estimates, and the globally maximized log-likelihood is by definition the best (in that it is the highest possible log-likelihood for that model), we haven't really given attention to how these estimates are affected by variability.

As we've discussed in Chapter 4, variability creeps into our model through the stochastic nature of many models and through the random sampling process underlying the generation of the empirical data (as captured by our data model; see Chapter 4). This variability leads to a general problem of *uncertainty* in modeling. This concept of uncertainty is intimately tied to both the ML parameter estimates and the maximized log-likelihood. In the case of parameter estimates, although we may have found what look like the best parameter estimates, the stochastic nature of data collection means that if we run our experiment again and fit the model to the newly collected data, we are likely to obtain a different set of values for our parameter estimates. Accordingly, our ML parameter estimates are subject to uncertainty, and it would be useful to have some measure of that uncertainty.

More generally, there is also uncertainty about the models themselves. If we have a set of candidate models in some domain, then any of those models could potentially provide a "true" account of the data. We then have the problem of determining which model is most likely to have generated the data and a further problem of quantifying our confidence in that model being the best one. (By "best," we mean the model that best characterizes the psychological processes that generated the data.) It turns out that maximized log-likelihood can be used to quantify uncertainty about models and that this in turn leads to a natural mechanism for making statistical and theoretical inferences from models and to differentiate between multiple candidates.

This chapter gives an introduction to model selection and model inference in the likelihood framework. We will discuss the uncertainty surrounding parameter estimates and outline methods for quantifying this uncertainty and using it to make inferences from parameter estimates. We will then step through the theoretical basis of model selection[1] and discuss its practical application in psychology. By the end of this chapter, you should be equipped to interpret reports of parameter uncertainty and model selection in psychology (including the use of information criteria and information weights) and to apply this knowledge by following the methods that we introduce.

5.1   Error on Maximum Likelihood Estimates

Maximum likelihood parameter estimates are point estimates: As covered in Chapter 4, we obtain a single vector of parameter values that maximizes the probability of observing the data given the specified model [remember, the likelihood function $L(\theta|\mathbf{y})$ is actually provided by the density $f(\mathbf{y}|\theta)$]. However, we shouldn't put absolute trust in these estimates, as they are subject to uncertainty. One critical part of our training as experimental psychologists is to recognize that estimators in all areas of statistics—including standard estimators of central tendency such as the mean and median—have some error attached to them, and that we need some way of quantifying this error. We usually do this by providing a single number, such as the standard error of the mean, and perhaps by plotting a confidence interval around the mean.

Fortunately, we can obtain standard errors and confidence limits on our ML parameter estimates just like for those conventional estimators in statistics. These measures of parameter variability can be used to show the uncertainty on the ML parameter estimates and to draw inferences from the models. For example, just as for conventional statistical models such as a regression line, we may compare an estimated parameter value to some expected value under the null hypothesis. We will look at three different methods for obtaining information about parameter uncertainty.

5.1.1   Standard Errors Across Participants

If we are fitting our model to data from individual participants, we will often want to present the mean estimate for the parameters, averaging across participants. As long as these participants can be considered separate and independent samples, we can obtain a confidence interval on this mean parameter estimate using standard statistical practice. As an example, Ludwig, Farrell, Ellis, and Gilchrist (2009) were interested in the processes underlying visual search, a task we often perform in our everyday lives in which we must locate a target item (e.g., a book about computational modeling) among distractors (e.g., all the other materials, including other books, on our desk). It has been suggested that visual search takes advantage of regularities in the environment (e.g., Chun & Jiang, 1998; Walthew & Gilchrist, 2006). One of these assumed regularities is temporal: The world tends not to change incredibly rapidly, such that a location that has just been inspected is unlikely to contain any new information on an immediate reinspection (Klein & MacInnes, 1999). This manifests itself as inhibition of saccadic return (ISR): When the eye movements of participants are tracked using eye-tracking equipment, it has been found that the fixation times preceding movement of gaze back to a location that has recently been visited ("return" saccades) are longer than those preceding saccades to a location that has not been recently fixated ("new" saccades; Hooge & Frens, 2000; Klein & MacInnes, 1999). Previous work has suggested that fixation times reflect a decision-making process, where the decision is about where to move the eyes next. Following on from this suggestion, Ludwig et al. (2009) applied a simple model of choice decision making called the Linear Ballistic Accumulator model (LBA; S. D. Brown & Heathcote, 2008) to eye movement data.

In the LBA, units representing the alternatives (called *accumulators*) are assumed to race: Specifically, they increase their activations linearly over time until one of the accumulators' activations passes a threshold, at which point it is taken as being the "winner" and given as a response. Variability in the fixation times is assumed to reflect both the variability between accumulators in where they start the race and variability in the rate at which each accumulator races toward the threshold. Ludwig et al. (2009) were interested in determining whether the longer fixations preceding "return" saccades were due to those locations having a longer distance to travel in the race or whether those locations started out with the same activation but accumulated at a slower rate on average. Ludwig et al. (2009) fit the LBA model to the distributions of fixation times preceding "return" and "new" saccades using maximum likelihood estimation, with a free parameter representing each of the two alternatives just outlined. After calculating the mean parameter estimates and the variability on those estimates across participants, Ludwig et al. (2009) found that the observed slowing of responses when revisiting a location (compared to fixating on a new one) was uniquely linked to a change in the rate of accumulation of evidence in the LBA model. That is, the parameter capturing the *change* in accumulation rate between "return" and "new" saccades was significantly different from 0. The other parameter that might have potentially changed between conditions (e.g., the distance needed to travel), by contrast, did not differ significantly from 0. Thus, Ludwig et al. (2009) were able to use the variability around the mean parameter estimates—which represented the differences between conditions—to determine which process was modulated by the recent history of saccades.

In general, we can submit individual ML parameter estimates to inferential tests using standard statistical procedures such as the analysis of variance (ANOVA). Consider again the ex-Gaussian model, which we discussed in Chapter 4 as a model of response latency distributions. Balota et al. (2008) applied the ex-Gaussian model to latency distributions involving *semantic priming* in tasks such as lexical decision and word naming. Briefly, semantic priming refers to the fact that processing of a word (e.g., *doctor*) is facilitated if it is preceded by a related item (e.g., *nurse*) as compared to an unrelated item (e.g., *bread*). Priming effects are highly diagnostic and can help reveal the structure of semantic knowledge (e.g., Hutchison, 2003) and episodic memory (e.g., Lewandowsky, 1986).

Balota et al. (2008) were particularly interested in the effect of prime-target relatedness on the time to name target words and the interaction of prime-target relatedness with variables such as stimulus onset asynchrony (SOA; the time between onset of the prime and onset of the target) and target degradation (rapidly alternating the target word with a nonsense string of the same length; e.g., @#\$&%). For each cell in their factorial experimental designs, Balota et al. (2008) estimated values of μ, σ, and τ for individual participants using MLE. The μ, σ, and τ parameter estimates were then treated as dependent variables and entered into an ANOVA with, for example, prime-target relatedness and target degradation as factors. Balota et al. found that, sometimes, the semantic priming effect was linked to μ, indicating that primes gave related words a "head start," leading to a constant shift in the naming latency distribution. However, when the targets were degraded, an additional pattern of results emerged because τ (and thus the rate of information processing) then also varied across prime-target relatedness. Thus, depending on the visual quality of the stimuli, priming either provided a "head start" to processing or affected the information accumulation itself. Without a descriptive model and interpretation of its parameter values, those conclusions could not have been derived by analysis of the behavioral data alone.

Similar approaches have been used to make inferences from models of signal detection theory (Grider & Malmberg, 2008) and to make inferences from computational models of decision-making deficits in patients with neuropsychological disorders such as Huntington's and Parkinson's disease (Busemeyer & Stout, 2002; Yechiam, Busemeyer, Stout, & Bechara, 2005). As well as simply calculating the standard error around a mean parameter estimate, it can also be instructive to plot a histogram of parameter estimates. For example, Farrell and Lelièvre (2009) were interested in people's tendency to spontaneously group sequences of items into subsequences when performing a serial recall task. Farrell and Lelièvre (2009) estimated a parameter measuring the tendency for such spontaneous grouping on a participant-by-participant basis and observed in a histogram that this tendency varied widely between individuals: Several participants appeared never to spontaneously group, whereas other participants almost always spontaneously grouped the sequences.

Finally, the *co*variance in parameters can be usefully examined in an individual differences setting. For example, Schmiedek et al. (2007) were interested in working memory, a system presumed to support the short-term retention and manipulation of information, and its relation to other measures such as reasoning and reaction times. As well as obtaining measures of reasoning and working memory capacity, Schmiedek et al. (2007) gave participants eight reaction time tasks and fit the ex-Gaussian model to obtain an estimate of μ, σ, and τ for each reaction time task for each participant. Schmiedek et al. (2007) then examined the correlation between these estimates and the measures of reasoning abilities and working memory capacity and observed that the estimates of τ had the strongest relationship with working memory and reasoning.

5.1.2   Curvature of the Likelihood Surface

This section starts with a warning: We rely heavily on the ex-Gaussian model in the following. If you are unsure what that is, please refamiliarize yourself with the ex-Gaussian by looking at Section 4.2 in the previous chapter. In addition, this section relies on some conceptual understanding of calculus; if it's been a while since you engaged with this, you might benefit from referring to an introductory book on calculus for some of the material below. If you still find this section daunting even after referring to an introductory calculus book, then it can be safely skipped for now.

Although we have so far been interested only in the *mode* of the likelihood surface—that is, the point at which the likelihood or log-likelihood is maximized— the entire likelihood function contains information useful for model inference (Pawitan, 2001). The likelihood function reflects uncertainty about the parameter values; the maximum likelihood values give the best estimate of the "true" parameter values, but other values are also possible, particularly when they lie close to the maximum likelihood estimate. For example, consider the two hypothetical log-likelihood functions for the τ parameter of the ex-Gaussian function in Figure 5.1 (the code for the log-likelihood function for the ex-Gaussian model is given in Listing 5.1). Although the two functions peak at the same value of τ, with the same ln L, the darker function is more peaked at the maximum. In other

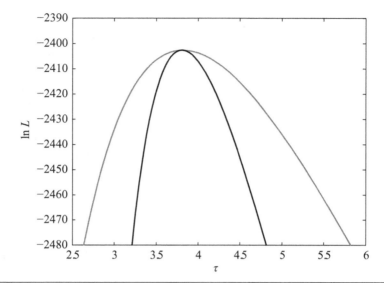

Figure 5.1 Two log-likelihood surfaces from the ex-Gaussian density, displayed with respect to the τ parameter. Both surfaces have the same maximum log-likelihood at the same value of τ (approximately 3.8); the surfaces differ in their curvature (the extent to which they are peaked) at that maximum. Note that this is an artificially constructed example: For a specific model, if we collect more data, both the extent of peaking and the maximum log-likelihood will change.

words, the range in which we could reasonably consider τ to potentially lie is larger for the more shallow function (in gray). As in standard statistical practice, we can quantify this uncertainty and use it as a tool for statistical inference.

Listing 5.1 Log-Likelihood Function for the Ex-Gaussian Model

```
1  function fval = exGausslnL(y, mu, sigma, tau)
2
3  fval = log(1./tau)+...
4      (((mu-y)./tau)+((sigma.^2)./(2.*tau.^2)))...
5      +log(.5)...
6      +log(1+erf(((((y-mu)./sigma)-(sigma./tau))./sqrt(2)));
```

A key step in using the likelihood function for inference lies in recognizing that a more peaked likelihood function reflects greater confidence in the maximum likelihood parameter estimate. A greater curvature indicates that as we move away from the maximum likelihood estimate (i.e., away from the peak of the likelihood function), the likelihood of those other parameter values given the data falls off faster. For the purposes of inference, we can quantify this curvature using the partial derivatives of the log-likelihood surface. The *partial derivatives* of a function (which are themselves functions) specify how much the value of a function changes as each of the variables entering into the function changes.

Another way of thinking about partial derivatives is that they specify the tangent of the function with respect to the different variables entering into the function. For example, if a likelihood function represents two parameters (say, *a* and *b*), then the partial derivative with respect to *a* corresponds to the tangent of a cross section of the surface at some constant value of *b*. In general, when several free parameters are being estimated, the *first partial derivatives* will be contained in a vector, with each element of the vector corresponding to the partial derivative of the log-likelihood surface with respect to a particular parameter. In the case of the likelihood function, the function giving the vector of partial derivatives is given a special name, the *score* function (e.g., Edwards, 1992; Pawitan, 2001).

To make this a bit more concrete, the top row of Figure 5.2 plots the log-likelihood function across the three parameters of the ex-Gaussian model, μ, σ, and τ, for a set of 1,000 observations that were themselves generated from the ex-Gaussian models with $\mu = 1, \sigma = .25, \tau = 4$. These functions are effectively cuts through the full multidimensional log-likelihood surface: For each parameter, we have traced out the log-likelihood as a function of that parameter and with the other two parameters held at their ML estimates. The middle row shows the first derivative of each of the corresponding log-likelihood functions. Notice that when the first derivative is above 0, the log-likelihood function is increasing, and when the first derivative is below 0, the log-likelihood function is decreasing. These functions were obtained analytically, by explicitly calculating each first derivative from the original log-likelihood function.

To examine the curvature of the log-likelihood surface, we need to go even further and either calculate or estimate the *second partial derivatives* of the surface. A second partial derivative is simply obtained by taking the derivative of a function that is itself a first derivative function; for the ex-Gaussian model, this would mean calculating the derivatives of the functions in the middle row of Figure 5.2. While the first derivatives tell us how the likelihood surface is changing (i.e., whether it is increasing or decreasing), the second partial derivatives tell us directly about the curvature of the likelihood surface: how fast the likelihood surface changes as each parameter changes.

Let's see how this proceeds. To start off with, let's establish some terminology. Let's take the ex-Gaussian parameters μ, σ, and τ and represent them jointly in the parameter vector θ. If we have collected some data (stored in the vector **y**), we will have three first partial derivative functions, labeled as

$$\frac{\partial \ln L(\theta|\mathbf{y})}{\partial \mu},$$

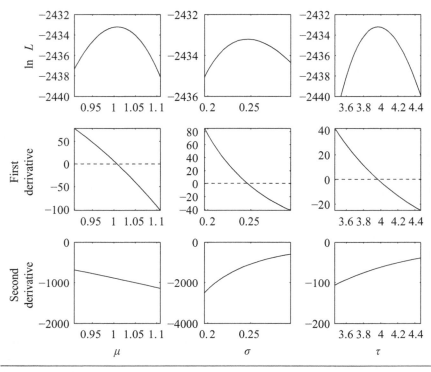

Figure 5.2 Log-likelihood (top row) surfaces for the μ (left column), σ (middle column), and τ (right column) parameters of the ex-Gaussian model. In the middle row, the first derivatives of the log-likelihood functions are plotted (also called score functions), and in the bottom panel, the second partial derivatives are plotted from the diagonal of the Hessian matrix (see text for details).

the change in the log-likelihood as μ changes;

$$\frac{\partial \ln L(\boldsymbol{\theta} \,|\, \mathbf{y})}{\partial \sigma},$$

the change in the log-likelihood as σ changes; and

$$\frac{\partial \ln L(\boldsymbol{\theta} \,|\, \mathbf{y})}{\partial \tau},$$

the change in the log-likelihood as τ changes; these are the three functions plotted in the middle row of Figure 5.2. For each of these first derivative (or score) functions, we can then take the next step of finding the derivative of any of these three functions with respect to any of the three parameters, giving nine possible combinations. For example, if we calculate the derivative of

$$\frac{\partial \ln L(\boldsymbol{\theta} \,|\, \mathbf{y})}{\partial \mu}$$

(which is itself a function) with respect to τ, we end up with the second partial
derivative:

$$\frac{\partial^2 \ln L(\theta|\mathbf{y})}{\partial \tau \partial \mu}.$$

The second partial derivatives are represented by a matrix called the *Hessian*
matrix, where each element (i, j) in the matrix gives the partial derivative,
with respect to i, of the partial derivative function of the log-likelihood with
respect to j:

$$\frac{\partial^2 \ln L(\theta|\mathbf{y})}{\partial i \partial j},$$

where i and j point to particular parameters in the parameter vector θ (read that
sentence a few times to get it clear in your head). One property of second partial
derivatives is that they are generally invariant to the order of application of the
derivatives: Taking the derivative of function f with respect to parameter x and
then taking the derivative of that derivative function with respect to y gives the
same result as taking the derivative of f with respect to y and then taking the
derivative of that function with respect to x. That is,

$$\frac{\partial^2 f}{\partial i \partial j} = \frac{\partial^2 f}{\partial j \partial i},$$

which means that the Hessian matrix is symmetric around the main diagonal. In
fact, the main diagonal is arguably the most interesting part of the Hessian matrix:
It contains the second partial derivatives obtained by taking the derivative of the
log-likelihood function twice with respect to the same parameter. Accordingly,
these entries in the Hessian matrix tell us how quickly the likelihood surface is
changing as each parameter is changing: the curvature of the log-likelihood functions. The bottom row of Figure 5.2 plots these second partial derivatives for the
parameters of the ex-Gaussian model. Notice that the function values are consistently negative and indicate a consistent downward accelerative force on the
log-likelihood functions in the top row. This means that the log-likelihood function is concave (has an upside-down U shape), which in turn means that we will
be able to find a maximum for this function.

5.1.2.1   Using Derivatives to Quantify Uncertainty
About Parameter Estimates

That all seems pretty technical; how can we use all this information in a practical setting? We now know that the second partial derivatives in the Hessian
matrix are directly related to the curvature of the log-likelihood surface: The bigger the number we see in a cell of the Hessian matrix, the more pointy is the

log-likelihood function along that variable or pair of variables. In fact, Fisher suggested the curvature as a measure of the *information* in the parameter estimate; a more peaked function means that the maximum likelihood parameter estimate gives us more information about where the "true" parameter value actually lies. In likelihood theory, *Fisher information* measures the variance of the score (the first derivative) and turns out to be equal to the negative of the Hessian matrix of the log-likelihood. The observed Fisher information matrix (or simply the observed information matrix) is the information matrix calculated at the maximum likelihood parameter estimate (e.g., Edwards, 1992; Pawitan, 2001).

The Hessian and information matrices may seem like fairly abstract concepts, but they are really just tools to get what we really want: an estimate of variability around the parameters. From the Hessian matrix, we can calculate a standard error, and thus a confidence interval, on our parameter estimate. The fundamental requirement is that our log-likelihood surface is approximately quadratic in shape around the maximum likelihood estimate. Why this seemingly arbitrary assumption? This is because the log-likelihood function for the mean of the normal distribution is exactly quadratic in shape. To confirm this, have a look back at Equation 4.20 in Chapter 4, which gives the log-likelihood function for the normal distribution. Recall that the first two terms in this equation act as constants. This leaves the third term

$$\frac{(y - \mu)^2}{2\sigma^2},$$

which gives a quadratic relationship between μ and the log-likelihood. If we were to take the exponential of this function (to "undo" the log and revert to the raw likelihood), we would obtain something like Equation 4.19, which is the formula for the probability density function (PDF) of the normal distribution.[2] Furthermore, if we take the derivative of the normal log-likelihood twice with respect to μ, we find this is equal to $-N/\sigma^2$ (e.g., Eliason, 1993). Since we know that the standard error of the mean of a sample is equal to $\sigma/\sqrt{N}$ and thus that the variance in our estimate of the mean (the square of the standard error) is equal to σ^2/N, then there is a nice, simple relationship between the variance in the estimate of μ and the second derivative: Each can be obtained by taking the inverse of the negative of the other!

In practice, this means that once we have our Hessian matrix for any model (with an approximately quadratic log-likelihood function), we can obtain a covariance matrix by simply taking the inverse of the Hessian matrix if we have minimized the negative log-likelihood or by taking the inverse of the negative Hessian matrix if we have maximized the log-likelihood (in other words, watch the sign!).[3] We can then read the values of the diagonal of the covariance matrix to get the variances around individual parameters and take the square root of these to obtain standard errors. Note that when we have estimated the value of more than one parameter (i.e., the Hessian really is a matrix and not just a single number), we need to take the matrix inverse and not simply take the inverse of individual elements in the matrix.

How do we know if our log-likelihood function is quadratic? It turns out that one property of likelihoods is that the likelihood function is asymptotically normal in shape (i.e., with a large sample; Pawitan, 2001). This means that if we have a reasonable number of data points, we can make the assumption that our log-likelihood function is approximately quadratic and obtain reasonable estimates of parameter variability. Conversely, in cases where the log-likelihood function is not quadratic in shape, obtaining a covariance matrix from the Hessian may give unreliable estimates (see, e.g., Pawitan, 2001; Riefer & Batchelder, 1988; Visser, Raijmakers, & Molenaar, 2000). What sample size counts as being sufficient for assuming asymptotic normality will vary between models and applications. Also note that it is sufficient to assume that our likelihood function is approximately normal, which will then give us approximate confidence intervals. Figure 5.2 shows a case where the quadratic assumption does not exactly hold; although the log-likelihood functions in the top row look fairly close to being quadratic, the second derivatives in the bottom panel are not constant, as they would be if the quadratic assumption was exactly met. Nonetheless, the sample size is probably sufficient. For a discussion of the role of sample size in the context of multinomial tree models and an empirical demonstration about the consequences of small sample sizes, see Riefer and Batchelder (1988).

5.1.2.2   Obtaining and Using the Hessian Matrix

One aspect that we have glossed over so far is how we actually obtain the Hessian matrix. This depends on the exact nature of the model we are using. If we are lucky and our model is simple and not highly nonlinear, we will be able to obtain the second partial derivatives analytically (see, e.g., Heathcote, 2004). In most cases, however, an analytic solution will not be obtainable (or will not be worth spending the time to obtain and check for errors), and we will compute the Hessian matrix by numerical approximation. There is a general family of methods called differencing methods available for obtaining derivatives in this manner. These methods examine the local change in the surface around the minimum/maximum. When examining second partial derivatives for the purposes of obtaining a covariance matrix, we can calculate the $< i, j >$th element of the Hessian as

$$\frac{\partial^2 \ln L(\theta|\mathbf{y})}{\partial i \, \partial j} \approx \frac{C}{4\delta^2}, \tag{5.1}$$

where

$$
\begin{aligned}
C = \; & \ln L(\boldsymbol{\theta} + \mathbf{e}_i + \mathbf{e}_j | \mathbf{y}) - \ln L(\boldsymbol{\theta} + \mathbf{e}_i - \mathbf{e}_j | \mathbf{y}) \\
& - \ln L(\boldsymbol{\theta} - \mathbf{e}_i + \mathbf{e}_j | \mathbf{y}) + \ln L(\boldsymbol{\theta} - \mathbf{e}_i - \mathbf{e}_j | \mathbf{y}).
\end{aligned} \tag{5.2}
$$

In the equations, e_i and e_j are vectors of the same size as the vector $\boldsymbol{\theta}$, with the ith and jth element respectively set to δ and the remaining elements set to 0 (e.g., Abramowitz & Stegun, 1972; Huber, 2006). The scalar δ controls the step size used to calculate the approximation and should be set to some small value (e.g., 10^{-3}). Alternatively, the step size may be adjusted to scale with the size of each element of $\boldsymbol{\theta}$, a technique used by the function mlecov in MATLAB's Statistics Toolbox, which directly returns the covariance matrix.

Some MATLAB code implementing Equations 5.1 and 5.2 is given in Listing 5.2. For MATLAB code implementing a more refined set of calculations, see Morgan (2000).

Listing 5.2 General Function for Calculating the Hessian Matrix

```
1  function h = hessian(lnLfun,theta,delta, varargin)
2  % The argument lnLfun should be passed as a string
3  %    e.g., 'exGausslnL '
4  % The function expects the free parameters to be
5  %    provided in a single vector theta ,
6  %    and additional arguments (including the data)
7  %    can be passed in varargin (see MATLAB help for
8  %    varargin)
9  % delta is the step size in the Hessian calculations
10
11 % e is the identity matrix multiplied by delta , and  ↩
     is used
12 %    to set up the e_i's and e_j's efficiently;
13 %    we just select the appropriate row in the loop
14 e = eye(length(theta)).*delta;
15 for i=1:length(theta)
16     for j=1:length(theta)
17         C(i,j) = feval(lnLfun, theta+e(i,:)+e(j,:),  ↩
                  varargin{:}) −...
18             feval(lnLfun, theta+e(i,:)−e(j,:),  ↩
                  varargin{:}) −...
19             feval(lnLfun, theta−e(i,:)+e(j,:),  ↩
                  varargin{:}) +...
20             feval(lnLfun, theta−e(i,:)−e(j,:),  ↩
                  varargin{:});
21     end
22 end
23 h = C./(4.*(delta.^2));
```

Likelihood curvature has been used in psychology to quantify uncertainty on parameters for a number of models, including the ex-Gaussian latency distribution (e.g., Ratcliff & Murdock, 1976; Rohrer, 2002), the ROUSE model of short-term priming (Huber, 2006), hidden Markov models (Visser et al., 2000), and multinomial tree models (e.g., Bishara & Payne, 2008; Riefer & Batchelder, 1988). To see the use of the Hessian in practice, let's continue with our old friend, the ex-Gaussian model. MATLAB code for this example is shown in Listing 5.3; the line numbers in the following refer to that listing. Imagine that we have collected a sample of latency observations from a single participant in a single condition in a word-naming task (e.g., Balota et al., 2008; Spieler, Balota, & Faust, 2000). The top panel of Figure 5.3 shows histograms for two representative sets of data; here, we have simply generated 100 (top plot) or 500 (bottom plot of top panel) latency values from an ex-Gaussian distribution with known parameter values $\mu = 500$, $\sigma = 65$, and $\tau = 100$ (in units of milliseconds), thus simulating two hypothetical subjects who participated in 100 or 500 trials, respectively (line 7). Using the methods discussed in Chapters 3 and 4, we minimize $-\ln L$ (note again the sign; we maximize the log-likelihood by minimizing its negative) and obtain the maximum likelihood parameter estimates of $\mu = 503.99$, $\sigma = 56.59$, and $\tau = 95.73$ for $N = 100$ and $\mu = 496.50$, $\sigma = 61.11$, and $\tau = 107.95$ for $N = 500$ (this is line 13 in Listing 5.3). The question now is: What is the variability on these estimates? To determine this, we first obtain the Hessian matrix for the maximum likelihood parameter vector, using Equations 5.1 and 5.2 (line 16):

$$
\begin{array}{c}
\begin{array}{ccc} \mu & \sigma & \tau \end{array} \\
\begin{array}{c} \mu \\ \sigma \\ \tau \end{array}
\begin{bmatrix}
0.0128 & -0.006 & 0.0064 \\
-0.006 & 0.0152 & 0.0020 \\
0.0064 & 0.0020 & 0.0087
\end{bmatrix}.
\end{array}
$$

The positive numbers along the diagonal tell us that the surface is curving upwards as we move away from the ML parameter estimates along each of the parameter dimensions, confirming that we have indeed minimized the negative log-likelihood (note that this is different from Figure 5.2, which shows the plots for log-likelihood, not negative log-likelihood). We now take the inverse of this matrix (e.g., using the `inv` command in MATLAB; line 17 in Listing 5.3)[4] to obtain the covariance matrix:

$$
\begin{array}{c}
\begin{array}{ccc} \mu & \sigma & \tau \end{array} \\
\begin{array}{c} \mu \\ \sigma \\ \tau \end{array}
\begin{bmatrix}
216.18 & 103.32 & -184.2 \\
103.32 & 116.95 & -103.3 \\
-184.2 & -103.3 & 275.80
\end{bmatrix}.
\end{array}
$$

The off-diagonal elements tell us about the covariance between each of the parameters. We can see that μ and σ are positively related (covariance = 103.32) and that μ and τ are negatively correlated (covariance = -184.2). This accords with the simulation results of Schmiedek et al. (2007), who found that MLEs of μ and σ tended to be positively correlated and those for μ and τ tend to be negatively correlated. As noted by Schmiedek et al., this set of correlations is partly due to trade-offs between parameters: μ and τ both affect the mean of the distribution and will not be independent, and since σ and τ both affect the variance, an indirect relationship is introduced between μ and σ.

The cells along the main diagonal of the covariance matrix tell us about the variance of the parameter estimates and can be used to obtain standard errors (ignoring the parameter covariance) by taking the square root of these numbers: This gives us standard errors on μ, σ, and τ of 14.70, 10.81, and 16.61, respectively. If we multiply these standard errors by 1.96 (the .975 quantile of the normal distribution, to give a 95% confidence limit at either end; a brief review of 95% confidence intervals is in order if this doesn't make sense to you), this gives us confidence limits on μ, σ, and τ; these are plotted in Figure 5.3 for the two sample sizes, with the parameter values used to generate the data shown as horizontal lines. As we'd expect, having more data means our standard errors are smaller, and we have less uncertainty about the "true" values of the parameters.

Listing 5.3 An Example of Estimating Parameters and Calling the Hessian Function to Obtain a Hessian Matrix and From That a Covariance Matrix

```
 1  function [x, fVal,hess, cov] = myHessianExample
 2
 3  rand('seed ',151513);
 4  randn('seed ',151513);
 5
 6  N=100;
 7  y = normrnd(500,65, [N 1]) + exprnd(100, [N 1]);
 8
 9  % find MLEs for ex−Gaussian parameters
10  % use inline specification of function to be minimized
11  %    so we can pass parameters and data
12
13  [x,fVal] = fminsearch(@(x) exGausslnL(x,y), [500  65  ↩
            100])
14
15  % find Hessian for MLEs
16  hess = hessian(@exGausslnL,x,10^−3, y);
17  cov = inv(hess);
18
19  end
20
21  function fval = exGausslnL(theta, y)
22
```

```
23 mu = theta(1);
24 sigma = theta(2);
25 tau = theta(3);
26
27 fval = log(1./tau)+...
28     (((mu-y)./tau)+((sigma.^2)./(2.*tau.^2)))...
29     +log(.5)...
30     +log(1+erf((((y-mu)./sigma)-(sigma./tau))./sqrt(2)));
31 fval = -sum(fval); % turn into a summed negative ↵
       log-likelihood for minimization
32 end
```

5.1.3   Bootstrapping

A final method to obtain confidence limits is by using resampling procedures such as the bootstrap (e.g., Efron & Gong, 1983; Efron & Tibshirani, 1994). Bootstrapping allows us to construct a sampling distribution for our statistic of interest (in our case, model parameters) by repeatedly sampling from the model or from the data. For the purposes of constructing confidence limits on model parameters, a favored method is parametric resampling, where samples are repeatedly drawn from the model. Specifically, we generate T samples by running T simulations from the model using the ML parameter estimates. Each generated sample should contain N data points, where N is the number of data points in the original sample. We then fit the model to each of the T generated samples. The variability across the T samples in the parameter estimates then gives us some idea about the variability in the parameters. The process for generating the bootstrap parameter estimates is depicted graphically in Figure 5.4.

Let's go through an example of using bootstrapping to construct confidence limits on parameter estimates. We will take a break from the ex-Gaussian and return to a model we examined in Chapter 4, the SIMPLE model (G. D. A. Brown et al., 2007). We will examine SIMPLE's account of people's performance in the free recall task, a standard episodic memory task in which participants are asked to recall the items (usually words) from a list in any order they choose (in contrast to the serial recall we examined in the last chapter in which output order was prescribed). A common way of examining free recall performance is to plot proportion correct for each item in the list according to its serial position. An example of such a serial position function is shown in Figure 5.5, which plots (using crosses) the proportion correct by serial position for a single participant in one of the conditions from an experiment conducted by Murdock (1962).[5] Also shown in the figure is the ML fit of SIMPLE to the data. The model has been adapted slightly from the earlier application to serial recall in order to reflect

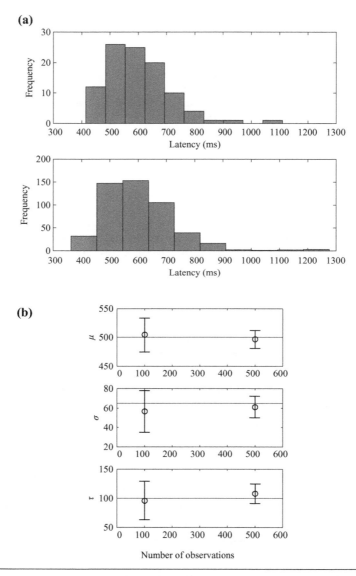

Figure 5.3 Top panel: Histograms for two samples from the ex-Gaussian function. The top histogram summarizes a smaller sample ($N = 100$), and the bottom histogram plots frequencies for a larger sample ($N = 500$). Bottom panel: ML parameter estimates for the ex-Gaussian parameters μ, σ, and τ for the two samples, along with their 95% confidence intervals calculated from the log-likelihood curvature. The solid line in each plot shows the true parameter value (i.e., the value used to generate the data).

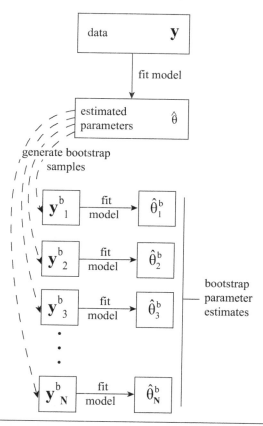

Figure 5.4 The process of obtaining parameter estimates for bootstrap samples. Working from top to bottom, we first fit our model to the original data (in vector $\mathbf{y}$) to obtain maximum likelihood parameter estimates (in vector $\hat{\boldsymbol{\theta}}$). These parameter estimates are then fed into the model to simulate new bootstrap data sets ($\mathbf{y}_k^b$) of the same size as $\mathbf{y}$. The model is then fit to each of these bootstrapped data sets to obtain bootstrap parameter estimates $\hat{\boldsymbol{\theta}}_k^b$, such that each bootstrapped data set provides a vector of parameter estimates.

the changed experimental methodology. The primary change is that we use an omission threshold that was not used in serial recall. This omission threshold is implemented as

$$p_{correct}(i) = \frac{1}{1 + \exp\left(-s\left(D_i - t\right)\right)}, \tag{5.3}$$

where D_i is equal to

$$\frac{1}{\sum_k \eta_{ik}}, \tag{5.4}$$

which was previously used to directly calculate proportion correct (see Equation 4.10). Equation 5.3 is a logistic function and implements the assumption that

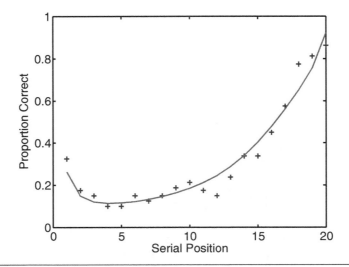

Figure 5.5 Proportion correct by serial position for a single participant from a free recall experiment of Murdock (1962). Crosses show the participant's data; the line shows the ML predictions of the SIMPLE model.

there is an increasing "S-shaped" function between D_i—the distinctiveness of item i—and the probability that the item will be correctly recalled. The equation represents the assumption that there is some chance that no item will be sufficiently accessible in response to a probe, such that no response will be forthcoming (G. D. A. Brown et al., 2007). In Equation 5.3, t is the threshold, and s is a scaling factor that determines the sensitivity of recall to the distinctiveness of items. In addition, in free recall, an item is scored correct irrespective of the position in which it is recalled. Accordingly, we assume that participants cue for each item separately and that the probability of recall of an item is equal to the sum of the probabilities of its recall under each cue (to a maximum probability of just under 1; allowing this to be exactly 1 causes problems with calculation of the binomial probability when the empirical probability is below 1). As in the previous chapter, the model was fit by minimizing the negative log-likelihood, using the binomial function as the data model. Listing 5.4 gives the log-likelihood function for this version of SIMPLE applied to free recall; the parameters are passed in a single vector theta, and the calculation of the binomial log-likelihood (line 22) takes advantage of the simplifications of the binomial and multinomial log-likelihoods introduced in Chapter 4. Listing 5.5 gives code for fitting SIMPLE to the data in Figure 5.5, along with the procedure for constructing the bootstrap confidence interval.

Listing 5.4 The SIMPLE Model Applied to Accuracy in Free Recall

```
1  function [dev, p] = SIMPLEfreeBino(theta, data, ↵
       recTime, presTime, N)
2
3  c = theta(1);
4  t = theta(2);
5  s = theta(3);
6
7  p = zeros(1,length(data));
8  lnL = zeros(1,length(data));
9
10 dist = log(recTime-presTime);
11
12 for i=1:length(data)
13     for j=1:length(data)
14         d(j) = (exp(-c*abs(dist(i)-dist(j))))./sum
15                          ((exp(-c*abs(dist-dist(j))))));
16     end
17     p(i) = sum(1./(1+exp(-s*(d-t))));
18     if (p(i)>1-eps)
19         p(i)=1-eps;
20
21     end
22     lnL(i) = data(i).*log(p(i)) + ↵
           (N-data(i)).*log(1-p(i));
23 end
24
25 dev = sum(-lnL);
```

Having obtained a reasonable fit as displayed in Figure 5.5, with ML estimates of $c = 20.39$, $t = 0.64$, and $s = 10.25$, what is the variability on the parameters? Let's use the bootstrap to find out. The first step is to generate a number of samples from SIMPLE. One feature of SIMPLE is that it is a deterministic model: Every time we simulate the model with the same parameters, we will obtain the same output. In order to generate random samples, we can take the proportion correct at each serial position predicted by the model under the ML parameter estimates and then sample an "observed" proportion correct at each position from the binomial mass function (Equation 4.12) with $N = 80$, the number of trials. Having generated a number of samples (e.g., $T = 1,000$), we then fit SIMPLE back to each of those generated data samples. The result is a unique value for the SIMPLE parameters c, s, and t for each sample. Histograms of the parameter values from a particular set of 1,000 samples from the ML estimates for the data in Figure 5.5

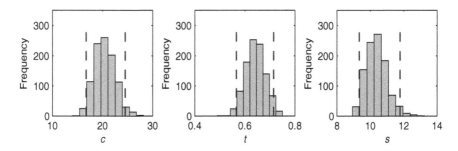

Figure 5.6 Histograms of parameter estimates obtained by the bootstrap procedure, where data are generated from the model and the model is fit to the generated bootstrap samples. From left to right, the histograms correspond to the c, t, and s parameters from the SIMPLE model. Also shown are the 95% confidence limits obtained by calculating the .025 and .975 quantiles of the plotted distributions (dashed lines).

are shown in Figure 5.6. To find our confidence limits on each parameter, we need to find those values of the parameters that cut off 2.5% of the scores at either end of each sampling distribution. That is, we need to find the .025 and .975 quantiles of the data, to give a total of .05 cut off at the ends corresponding to our α level of .05. To do this, we can either use the `quantile` function in the MATLAB Statistics Toolbox or determine these manually by ordering the values for each parameter and finding the score that cuts off the bottom 25 scores (obtained by averaging the 25th and 26th scores) and the score that cuts off the top 25 scores. When we do so, we find 95% confidence limits around $c = 20.39$ of 16.73 and 24.50; for $t = 0.64$, the limits are 0.57 and 0.72; and for $s = 10.25$, the limits are 9.35 and 11.78. These quantiles are marked off in Figure 5.6 by the dashed vertical lines.

Of course, this procedure isn't specific to the SIMPLE model. If we wanted to generate new samples from the ex-Gaussian, for example, this would be straightforward: As per the assumptions of the ex-Gaussian, each observation would be a sample from a normal distribution with parameters μ and σ, plus an independent sample from an exponential distribution with parameter τ. As mentioned earlier, Schmiedek et al. (2007) adopted such an approach to examine the correlations between ex-Gaussian parameter estimates, although they did not use MLEs from fits to participants' data to generate the bootstrap samples.

One thing you might be thinking right now (besides "gosh I'm exhausted!") is that there doesn't seem to be anything about the bootstrap procedure that dictates using it in the ML framework. This is indeed the case. The bootstrap procedure just outlined can equally be used using any measure of discrepancy, including RMSD and χ^2 (see Chapter 2). Indeed, the fact that very few assumptions need to be made when carrying out the bootstrap procedure means it is a popular method for obtaining sampling distributions and confidence limits from models across the sciences.

Listing 5.5 Function to Fit SIMPLE to Free Recall Data and Obtain Bootstrapped Confidence Intervals

```
1  function [theta, fVal, quants] = bootstrapExample
2
3  rand('state',14141);
4  randn('state',151515);
5
6  data = [40, 28, 13, 11, 11, 10, 6, 11, 17, 8, 14,...
7       14, 13, 14, 22, 43, 53, 70, 71, 74];
8  N = 80;
9
10 % some assumed experimental parameters
11 Ti = 1:20;
12 Tr = 30; % we assume retrieval time is fixed here
13
14 % information and initialization for the bootstrap ↩
       procedure
15 bootSamples = 1000;
16 samplePhat = zeros(bootSamples, 3);
17
18 % MLE of parameters
19 [theta, fVal] = fminsearch(@(x) SIMPLEfreeBino(x, ↩
       data, Ti, Tr, N), [2 .1 20]);
20
21 % run the model one last time to get the parameters
22 [temp, pred] = SIMPLEfreeBino(theta, data, Ti, Tr, N);
23
24 % now do the bootstrapping
25 for i=1:bootSamples
26
27     if mod(i,100)==0
28         disp(i);
29     end
30     % the binornd function is from the Statistics ↩
           Toolbox
31     sampData = binornd(80, pred);
32     [samplePhat(i,:)] = fminsearch(@(x) ↩
           SIMPLEfreeBino(x, sampData, Ti, Tr, N), theta);
33 end
34
35 % the quantile function comes from the MATLAB ↩
       Statistics Toolbox
36 quants = quantile(samplePhat,[.025 .975]);
```

5.1.4   What Do Confidence Limits Tell Us?

Interpretation of the standard errors and confidence limits presented in this section depends on the method we use and the data entering into the likelihood function. The methods give us some estimate of variability on a parameter estimate: If we ran the same experiment again, where might we expect the parameter estimate for that new data set to lie? However, we must be careful in our definition of "the same experiment." If we calculate a standard error by looking at the variability in the estimated parameter across participants, we are asking what reasonable range of parameter values we would expect if the experiment were run on a different set of participants; this is the variability we are usually interested in, as we will be concerned with making inferences from a sample of participants to the population. However, calculating standard errors using the Hessian matrix or bootstrapping does not necessarily provide us with this information. Specifically, if we calculate a standard error on the basis of a single participant's data, we cannot estimate the variability between participants that is integral to inferential statistics. In this case, the standard errors only tell us where we would expect the parameter value to lie if we ran the experiment *on the same (one) participant*. If the bootstrapping or likelihood curvature procedure is performed on the data aggregated across participants, then we can legitimately use the standard error as an inferential tool.

One caution is that producing confidence limits as well as parameter estimates can lead us into a false sense of understanding. Not only do we have "best" estimates, we also have some idea about where the true parameters might reasonably lie—isn't that great? Remember, though, that these estimates and confidence intervals (CIs) are conditional on the specific model being examined and don't provide any guarantees about the appropriateness of our model. Very wrong models can produce convincing-looking ML parameter estimates and CIs, although they fundamentally miss important features of the data. In the case of the ex-Gaussian above, it would be straightforward to fit a normal distribution to data generated from an ex-Gaussian process with a large τ and obtain estimates and CIs for μ and σ, although the normal distribution would miss the large positive skew characterizing models like the ex-Gaussian. The remainder of this chapter addresses this very issue: How confident are we that Model X is the best model for our data?

5.2   Introduction to Model Selection

So far we have been concerned only with uncertainty about the parameters of a given model: Recall that our full likelihood specification is conditional on both the observed data and the specific model whose parameters we are estimating (see Section 4.2). This would be fine if we had absolute certainty that our model of choice really is a close approximation to the actual process that generated the data of interest. Although the proponents of a particular model may be more than enthusiastic about its merits, there is yet another level of uncertainty in our reasoning with models—namely, uncertainty about the models themselves. This uncertainty lies at the central question we often ask as theorists in psychology: Which of a number of given candidate models lies closest to the true underlying processes that actually generated the observed data?

In some cases, the superiority of one model over the other is apparent even from visual inspection of the predictions of the models. For example, Figure 5.7 shows the fits of the Generalized Context Model (GCM) and another model of categorization, General Recognition Theory (GRT; e.g., Ashby & Townsend, 1986), to the categorization responses from six participants examined by Rouder and Ratcliff (2004). In each panel, observed categorization probabilities from four different conditions (labeled *stimulus* in the panels) are shown along with the predictions of GCM (dashed lines) and GRT (solid lines). Although the evidence is a little ambiguous to the eye in some cases, for three of the participants (1, 4, and 5), the superior fit of GCM is clear from visual inspection.

An even clearer example of model comparison by eye comes from the paper by Lewandowsky et al. (2009) discussed in Chapter 2. Recall that Lewandowsky et al. compared the predictions from a Bayesian model without any parameters to the data from participants who had to estimate variables such as the length of reign of a pharaoh. Figure 2.6 shows that the model does a very convincing job of predicting the data. Actually, Lewandowsky et al. also tested another model, the $\text{Min}K$ model, which assumes that participants make these judgments not by integrating across the entire distribution of possibilities (as in the Bayesian approach) but on the basis of only a few instances in memory. Although these models sound like they might be difficult to clearly distinguish (as a few samples from a distribution already provide a fair bit of information about the entire distribution, particularly the average of that distribution), Lewandowsky et al. found that the $\text{Min}K$ did a poor job of accounting for their data. Figure 5.8 shows that the $\text{Min}K$ model deviates substantially from the data, in a way that is apparent just from visual inspection.

Although the predictions of different models often diverge visibly, in other cases, the distinction may not be so clear. Consider Participants 2, 3, and 6 in Figure 5.7: Although it looks like GCM more accurately predicts the data, it has only a fine edge over the GRT model. Would we be confident in these cases in saying that these fits provide evidence for the GCM? For another example, take a look back at Figure 1.5. Recall that the data purport to show the ubiquitous "power law of practice." However, as can be seen in that figure, there is actually a

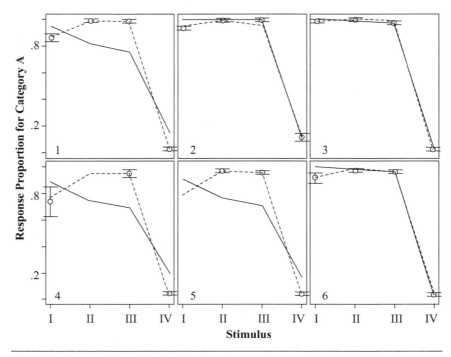

Figure 5.7 Fits of the GCM (dashed lines) and the GRT (solid lines) to data from four probability conditions in Experiment 3 of Rouder and Ratcliff (2004). Figure reprinted from Rouder, J. N., & Ratcliff, R. (2004). Comparing categorization models. *Journal of Experimental Psychology: General, 133,* 63–82. Published by the American Psychological Association; reprinted with permission.

plausible alternative to the power function as a descriptor of the data: an exponential function. We can see that both functions behave pretty similarly: They drop off quickly to begin with and then shallow out over later trials. If we were simply going by the qualitative fit to the data, either of these models is probably an acceptable candidate; in fact, a whole family of versions of these models might also be considered (Heathcote et al., 2000), as well as a number of more detailed psychological models (e.g., J. R. Anderson, Fincham, & Douglass, 1999; Logan, 1988; Rickard, 1997).

Another example comes from time-series analysis, where we are concerned with modeling the statistics of sequences of events. Although experimental psychologists tend to treat successive trials as being completely independent, dependencies between trials are in fact often observed (e.g., Farrell, Ratcliff, Cherian, & Segraves, 2006; Ratcliff, Van Zandt, & McKoon, 1999; Stewart, Brown, & Chater, 2002) and reveal a form of memory that is arguably of theoretical interest

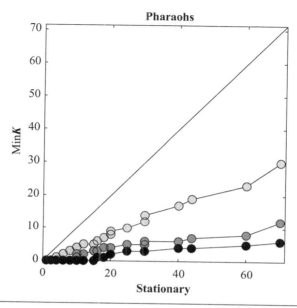

Figure 5.8 Snapshot of results from the Min$K$ model, for comparison with Figure 2.6. The ordinate plots quantiles of the predicted distribution, and the abscissa plots the obtained quantiles. The different levels of gray correspond to different values for K: light gray, $K = 2$; medium gray, $K = 5$; black, $K = 10$. Figure from Lewandowsky, S., Griffiths, T. L., & Kalish, M. L. (2009). The wisdom of individuals: Exploring people's knowledge about everyday events using iterated learning. *Cognitive Science, 33,* 969–998. Copyright by the Cognitive Science Society; reprinted with permission.

(e.g., Fecteau & Munoz, 2003; Gilden, 2001; M. Jones, Love, & Maddox, 2006; Lewandowsky & Oberauer, 2009; Wagenmakers, Farrell, & Ratcliff, 2004). One question we might ask in this vein is whether a fast response tends to be followed by another fast response (Laming, 1979). Specifically, we will assume that there is some dependency between trials in a time estimation task (e.g., Gilden, 2001; Laming, 1979; Wagenmakers, Farrell, & Ratcliff, 2004) and ask more specifically whether this form of memory (or multiple forms; e.g., Wagenmakers, Farrell, & Ratcliff, 2004) extends beyond the previous trial.

For the time estimation task (repeatedly estimating 1-second intervals by pressing a key when 1 second has passed), there is no variation in the stimulus across trials (or indeed there is no stimulus at all; Gilden, 2001). We are asking a very simple question: How far back does participants' memory for their own responses go, such that those memories have effects on time estimation on the current trial? To answer this question about the range of dependence in this task, we will look at two ARMA (Auto-Regressive Moving Average) models. ARMA models predict the future based on two processes: an autoregressive component (basically, a linear regression where the predictors are events on previous trials) and a moving average component. Both of these models base their predictions only on the responses of the participants and do not take into account the stimuli from the previous trial. Let's compare a simpler ARMA(1,1) model, which bases its predictions on only the last response, and the ARMA(2,2) model, which looks at the previous two responses. How can we compare the performance of these two models? On one hand, we might examine the predictions from the models on individual trials by looking at what has happened previously and making predictions about the future. However, Figure 5.9 shows that this doesn't really accomplish much. The figure shows a single series of 750 successive observations from a participant,[6] along with the trial-by-trial predictions of the ARMA(1,1) model (middle panel) and the ARMA(2,2) model (bottom panel). It is quite a challenge to distinguish these predictions from each other, let alone determine which more closely matches the behavior of the participant. Figure 5.10 shows a slightly more discriminating analysis, which plots an autocorrelation function (ACF) for the data and models as a function of lag. For each lag, the ACF gives the correlation between the series and a version of itself lagged by that many trials (for more detail, see Brockwell & Davis, 1996; Wagenmakers et al., 2004). For example, the correlation at lag 5 in the data is around 0.4, indicating that the estimate on the current trial will be correlated with that on the trial five trials back (where the correlation is performed across all current trials where it is possible to look five trials back in the trial history). The two models make slightly different predictions in this analysis, but their qualitative and quantitative behavior is very similar, and we would be hard-pressed to make some distinction between the models on the basis of their visual fit to the data (cf. Figure 1.5).

In these and many other cases, we need some way of comparing the models with respect to their fit to the data. This is where we come to a key concept, that of quantifying evidence. Model selection is really about determining which model is most consistent with data by comparing a number of models on their fit to the data. Although we've seen that a number of measures exist to calculate the discrepancy between the model and the data, we will again focus on the log-likelihood. We will explain below why the log-likelihood has some terrific properties that make it an ideal measure of goodness of fit. However, we don't want to base our decision solely on the fit of the model; as we discussed in Chapter 1, a more complex model is guaranteed to fit a set of data better than a simpler model even if the extra assumptions that the complicated model incorporates are extraneous and bear little or no relation to the underlying processes. Accordingly, the approach to model comparison we will discuss has two concurrent goals: find the *best* and *simplest* model.

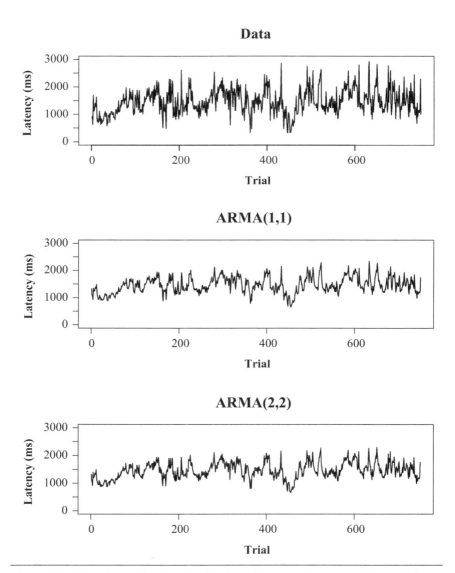

Figure 5.9 Three time series of estimation times in an experiment requiring participants to repeatedly press a key after 1 second has passed (Wagenmakers et al., 2004). Top panel: A series of 750 observations from a single participant. Middle panel: The trial-by-trial predictions of the ARMA(1,1) model under ML parameter estimates. Bottom panel: The predictions of the more complex ARMA(2,2) model.

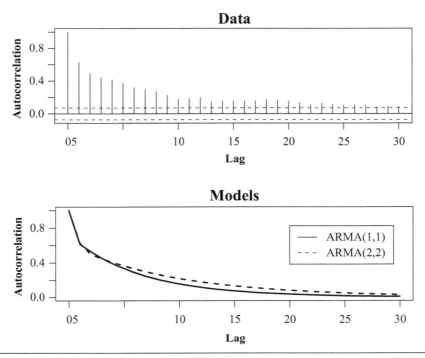

Figure 5.10 Autocorrelation functions for the data (top panel) and the two ARMA models (bottom panel) displayed in Figure 5.9. Each function shows the correlation between trials separated by the number of trials along the *Lag* axis; *Lag* = 0 corresponds to correlating the series with an unshifted version of itself and therefore gives a correlation of 1. The top panel also shows estimated confidence limits around the null autocorrelation value of 0 (corresponding to an uncorrelated series).

You might find it reassuring to know that the general principles of model selection aren't so different from those you've probably already encountered in statistics. Researchers (and graduate students in statistics classes) often confront the problem of deciding which combination of predictors to include in a multiple regression model. In the case of psychological models—such as those we've covered in the last few chapters—the models will be more heterogeneous than different multiple regression models, but the general problem remains the same. Indeed, the methods we will discuss below apply equally to models developed for the purpose of data description, process characterization, and process explanation (see Chapter 1). Moreover, many statistical methods (e.g., logistic regression, multilevel regression, and generalized linear modeling) rely on the likelihood tools we develop in the following.

5.3   The Likelihood Ratio Test

The two sets of models whose predictions are plotted in Figures 1.5 and 5.10 both highlight the need to quantitatively assess their competing fits. There is one important difference between the two sets, which is relevant for the type of model selection we can perform. One relevant feature of ARMA(1,1) and ARMA(2,2) models is that they are *nested* models. The ARMA(1,1) model is a reduced version of the ARMA(2,2) model, and we obtain an ARMA(1,1) model from the ARMA(2,2) model by setting the parameters weighting the two-back prediction to zero. Nested models allow the use of a model selection technique analogous to the process of hierarchical linear regression: If we compare two models that are identical except for one mechanism or assumption that differs between them, any difference between the models in their account of the data can be attributed to that mechanism. In the case of ARMA, we can assess the contribution of the two-back prediction by quantifying the difference in fit between the ARMA(1,1) and ARMA(2,2) models.

By contrast, the exponential and power functions plotted in Figure 1.5 are not nested models: There is no way of fixing one or more parameters in the exponential function to turn it into a power function or vice versa. The power versus exponential case reflects the common case in psychology that models are not nested. In the case where we want to compare two different, nonnested models, model selection also offers some useful tools based on the likelihood framework.

Let's first consider the case of nested models. Again, the fundamental requirement is that one of the models is a reduced version of the other model, obtained by clamping one or more free parameters in the general model to some "null" value at which it has no effect (e.g., 0 if the parameter is additive or 1 if it is multiplicative). In a process model, this will have the effect of "turning off" one or more mechanisms of theoretical interest such that they have no effect on the model's behavior. We are then interested in determining whether the improvement in fit gained by allowing those parameter(s) to be free is warranted.

If we are using the log-likelihood as a measure of goodness of fit, we can take advantage of a fortuitous relationship between the deviance ($-2\ln L$) and the χ^2 statistic. This is that the asymptotic (i.e., large sample) distribution for the difference in $-2\ln L$ between two nested models is the χ^2 distribution. This means that if we take a model that we have fit to some data via MLE and then generalize that model by allowing an additional parameter to freely vary and fit it once again, the change in $-2\ln L$ will be approximately χ^2 distributed if there is no real difference between the two versions.

More generally, if we have K extra free parameters in the more general of two nested models, the difference in $-2\ln L$ between the models will be approximately distributed as a χ^2 with K degrees of freedom. To be clear, this

χ^2 distribution represents the sampling distribution of $-2\ln L$ under the null hypothesis of no difference between the models, except for the extra flexibility in the more complicated model allowing it to fit only noise above and beyond the systematic fit represented in the reduced model. This means that we can assess the contribution of the extra free parameters by calculating the $-2\ln L$ difference between the models,

$$\chi^2 \approx -2\ln L_{specific} - (-2\ln L_{general}), \qquad (5.5)$$

where *general* refers to the general version of the model and *specific* the restricted version with some parameters fixed. We can then compare this obtained χ^2 to the critical value on the χ^2 distribution with K degrees of freedom given our α level (which will usually be .05). This is called the likelihood ratio test, as we are examining whether the increased likelihood for the more complex model (i.e., the smaller $-2\ln L$; due to the relationship between the logarithm and the expo- nential, a ratio in likelihoods translates into a difference in log-likelihoods) is merited by its extra parameters. You might recognize this test from Chapter 2, where we presented the G^2 statistic as a measure of discrepancy between a model and a set of discrete data and noted that it too is asymptotically distributed as χ^2.

As an example of the application of the likelihood ratio test (LRT), the $-2\ln L$ for the ARMA(1,1) and ARMA(2,2) models for the data shown in Figure 5.9 is 10872.08 and 10863.2, respectively. The difference of 8.88 is significant when compared to the critical χ^2 of 5.99 on 2 degrees of freedom,[7] where those extra degrees of freedom relate to the parameters for two-back prediction in both the autoregressive and moving average components of the ARMA model. Although the models appear to behave quite similarly in Figures 5.9 and 5.10, the ARMA(2,2) model provides a significantly better fit to the data: The addition of those two extra parameters is warranted by the increase in quantitative fit. We can then infer that the memory process that carries information between trials to produce the dependencies in time estimation performance operates over larger ranges than simply between successive trials (see, e.g., Thornton & Gilden, 2005; Wagenmakers, Farrell, & Ratcliff, 2004, 2005, for more about the implications of these types of models).

This example again emphasizes the importance of modeling to inform and test our intuitions about a situation. For example, you may be puzzled by the fact that models that operate only over a window of one or two trials can generate the extended ACFs seen in Figure 5.10, with correlations remaining between obser- vations lagged by up to 25 trials. The answer is that the ARMA model works in part by incorporating the history of previous trials; specifically, the autoregressive component of these models states that an observation is obtained by adding noise onto a decayed version of the previous observation (or previous several observations). Accordingly, although the current observation is not based directly on the data from 20 trials back, the effects of the history are carried through intervening trials (trial t is dependent on trial $t - 1$, which in turn is dependent on trial $t - 2$, which in turn is dependent on trial $t - 3 \dots$).

5.4   Information Criteria and Model Comparison

The LRT is a standard and useful method to distinguish between mathematical models on the basis of their fit to some data. However, there are limitations on the LRT that curtail its application as a general model comparison tool. The first is that the LRT is only appropriate for nested models. If our models are not nested, then we simply cannot employ this approach, as the χ^2 sampling distribution applies to the null hypothesis that the two models (general and restricted) are identical. A second argument against using the LRT—even for nested models—is that it rests on the null hypothesis testing approach, in which we a priori assume one model (null hypothesis) and require that there is sufficient evidence to reject this model (hypothesis) in favor of a more complicated alternative model (alternative hypothesis).

A number of problems associated with null hypothesis testing argue against its use for making inferences from models (Wagenmakers, 2007). In particular, although there are practical reasons for using null hypothesis testing when running t tests and ANOVAs (e.g., Howell, 2006; Pawitan, 2001; although see Wagenmakers, 2007), when examining models of psychological processes, we would like to be able to provide support for models as well as find evidence against them, regardless of whether or not they are nested. We will now turn to a discussion of *information criteria*, which are measures of the fit of models to data that apply to nested *and* nonnested models, and which provide us with a measure of the relative strength of evidence for each model in our set of models being compared.

5.4.1   Kullback-Leibler Distance and Akaike's Information Criterion

We have already shown that the likelihood relates to the concepts of information and uncertainty (see Burnham & Anderson, 2002, for a discussion). Exciting as this bridging is in itself, Akaike (1973, 1974) showed that we can use this relationship to treat our minimized $-2 \ln L$ values as evidence about models, not just about parameters. Specifically, we can relate log-likelihoods to the Kullback-Leibler distance, a measure of how well a known model (e.g., SIMPLE, or the ex-Gaussian model) matches the "true" process that we as scientists are really attempting to model. From here on, we call the model that we are concerned with the "known" model and compare it against the unknown state of reality, which we call the "true" model or reality.

The Kullback-Leibler (K-L) distance is a measure of how much information is lost when we use one model to approximate another model. Our interest lies in the case where we use a known model to approximate the "true" model, or reality. The Kullback-Leibler distance for continuous data is given by

$$KL = \int R(x) \log \frac{R(x)}{p(x|\theta)} dx, \tag{5.6}$$

where $R(x)$ is the probability density function for the true model, and $p(x|\theta)$ is the probability density function for our known model and parameters that we are using to approximate reality. In the case of discrete variables, the K-L distance is obtained by

$$KL = \sum_{i=1}^{I} p_i \log \frac{p_i}{\pi_i}, \tag{5.7}$$

where i indexes the I categories of our discrete variable, and p_i and π_i are, respectively, the "true" probabilities and the probabilities predicted by the known model.

The K-L distance shown in Equations 5.6 and 5.7 measures how much the predicted probabilities or probability densities deviate from the "truth."[8] The use of this quantity as a measure of information becomes clearer when we rewrite Equation 5.6 as follows:

$$KL = \int R(x) \log R(x) dx - \int R(x) \log p(x|\theta) dx. \tag{5.8}$$

The first term in Equation 5.8 tells us the total amount of information there is in the "true" model. This information is actually a measure of the entropy or uncertainty in reality. The more variability there is in reality, the more information can be provided by an observation, in that it is harder to predict the next value of x we might observe. The second term in Equation 5.8 quantifies the uncertainty in reality that is captured by the model. The difference between these tells us about the uncertainty that is left over after we have used our model to approximate reality. In the limit, where our model is a perfect match to reality, the two terms will be identical, and there will be no uncertainty in reality that is not reflected in our model: The K-L distance will be 0. As our model gives a poorer and poorer approximation of reality, the K-L distance increases.

One thing to note about Equation 5.8 is that the first term, the information in the "true" model, is insensitive to our choice of approximating model. As a consequence, "truth ... drops out as a constant" (Burnham & Anderson, 2002, p. 58; see also, e.g., Bozdogan, 1987): We can ignore this term and use the second term $(-\int R(x) \log p(x|\theta)dx)$ as a measure of relative distance, or how well our model is doing with respect to reality. The second and important thing to note is that this second term is simply the expected (i.e., weighted average of) $\ln L(\theta|x)$, the log-likelihood of θ given the data and the model. This is even more explicit in Equation 5.7: This is just the formula for the G^2 statistic we mentioned in Chapter 2 (Equation 2.4) but with the observed probabilities replaced by the "true" probabilities and without the number of observations N (which is specific to a particular sample and not a property of the model). As we have more data, the observed probabilities will converge to the "true" probabilities, and the log-likelihood will be an estimate of the K-L distance for a given model and parameter value(s).

The relationship between the K-L distance and likelihood promises to give us a principled framework in which to perform model comparison. However, one important detail we have skipped over so far in discussing K-L distance is that we haven't really said anything about θ, our parameter(s). In Chapters 3 and 4, we confronted a fundamental issue in quantitative modeling: The parameter values of a model are generally not provided to us but must be estimated from the data. This introduces some circularity when we come to determine the goodness of fit of the fitted model: We estimated the parameters of the model from the data set and then want to evaluate the fit of the model for that same data set using the same parameters!

Akaike recognized this very problem with using likelihoods as an estimate of K-L divergence. The general problem is illustrated in Figure 5.11. The panel on the left shows what we ideally want to obtain: the K-L distance between each of our candidate models $M_1, M_2, M_3 \ldots$ and reality, "R" (see Burnham & Anderson, 2002, for a more detailed graph for a specific model, the gamma). However, we are confounded by the situation shown on the right, which shows that the K-L distance will also vary within each model as a function of the parameter(s) θ. Ideally, we would use the log-likelihood corresponding to the ML parameter estimates (marked as $\hat{\theta}$ in Figure 5.11). However, Akaike recognized that the maximized log-likelihood is a biased estimate of the K-L distance because the same data are used to obtain the ML estimates $\hat{\theta}$ and to calculate the K-L distance. That is, we use the data to determine the parameter values that bring us closest to the "true" model, as represented by the data, in K-L space. Using some regularity assumptions about the likelihood surface (as we did above when calculating confidence intervals from the Hessian matrix), Akaike (1973) showed that this bias could be quantified and arrived at a corrected K-L distance measure based solely on the maximum likelihood. For an explanation of this derivation, see Bozdogan (1987), Burnham and Anderson (2002), and Pawitan (2001).

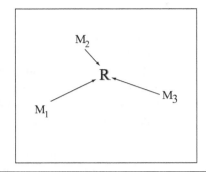 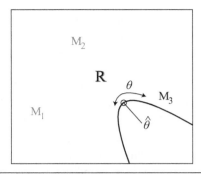

Figure 5.11 K-L distance is a function of models and their parameters. Left panel: Three models and their directed K-L distance to reality, R. Right panel: Change in K-L distance as a function of a parameter θ in one of the models shown in the left panel. The point closest to reality here is the ML estimate of the parameter, $\hat{\theta}$.

This corrected measure, the AIC (Akaike's Information Criterion, although Akaike originally intended this to be simply An Information Criterion), is calculated as

$$AIC = -2\ln L(\theta|y, M) + 2K, \qquad (5.9)$$

where M refers to our particular model (remember how we briefly introduced M in Chapter 4 but then omitted it for the remainder of the discussion; here, we reintroduce it because we now consider multiple models and their differentiation becomes crucial). The first term is simply the deviance $-2\ln L$ that we are now familiar with. The second term corrects for the bias in the minimized negative log-likelihood and is simply twice the number of parameters in our model, K. This simple relationship takes us to the ideal situation plotted in the left of Figure 5.11, where the AIC represents an unbiased estimate of the expected K-L distance between a model and the data, where the model is actually a family of models varying in their specific parameter values (right panel; see, e.g., Kuha, 2004).

One other useful way of thinking about the AIC is in terms of a trade-off between goodness of fit and model complexity. This trade-off is often called the bias-variance trade-off (e.g., M. R. Forster, 2000). This refers to the necessary fact that if our model is underspecified (i.e., not complex enough), we will miss accounting for important effects in the data: Our model will be biased. However, if our model has too many parameters, we will overfit the data, and our model will be fitting noise as well as real effects. This important (and troublesome) issue of overfitting will be taken up at length in Chapter 6. The AIC can be interpreted as accounting for this trade-off by pitting goodness of fit ($-2\ln L$) against model complexity (the number of parameters, K). Introducing more parameters will improve the fit but will also increase the size of the penalty term. In the AIC, we then have a computational instantiation of the principle of parsimony: to find the *best* and *simplest* model.

Before moving on to another well-used information criterion, we mention that a number of statisticians have noted that the AIC does not perform very well when models have a large number of parameters given the number of data points being fit (e.g., Hurvich & Tsai, 1989; Sugiura, 1978). A correction to the AIC has been suggested in the case where regression and autoregression models are fit to small samples; this corrected AIC, called AIC$_c$, is given by

$$AIC_c = -2 \ln L(\theta|y, M) + 2K \left(\frac{N}{N - K - 1} \right), \qquad (5.10)$$

where N is the number of data points. Burnham and Anderson (2002) recommend using this statistic whenever modeling the behavior of small samples (i.e., when the number of data points per parameter is smaller than 40).

5.4.2   Bayesian Information Criterion

An alternative to the AIC is a related measure called the Bayesian Information Criterion (BIC). An outline of the BIC was originally given by Schwarz (1978), who was looking for a correction term analogous to the $2K$ term in the AIC but one motivated by Bayesian theory and thus in some sense optimal. The aim of Bayesian model selection is to obtain the posterior probability of the model given the data, $p(M|y)$. We can use Bayes' theorem (Equation 4.5) to calculate this as

$$p(M|y) = \frac{p(y|M)p(M)}{p(y)}, \qquad (5.11)$$

with $p(M)$ being the prior probability of the model. One complication is that the probability of the data given the model, $p(y|M)$, depends on the selection of the parameter values. We can remove that dependence by working out the probability of the data under all possible parameter values weighted by their prior probabilities:

$$p(y|M) = \int p(y|\theta, M)p(\theta, M)d\theta, \qquad (5.12)$$

where $p(\theta)$ is the prior probability distribution across the parameter(s). This is a complicated procedure for most models, and we can appreciate why Schwarz (1978) and others wanted a quick and simple approximation! Under some reasonable default assumptions about the prior distribution on the model parameters (see, e.g., Kass & Raftery, 1995; Kuha, 2004; Schwarz, 1978), we can approximate full-scale Bayesian model selection by correcting our maximized log-likelihood and obtaining the Bayesian Information Criterion. The BIC is calculated as

$$BIC = -2 \ln L(\theta|y, M) + K \ln N, \qquad (5.13)$$

N being the number of data points on which the likelihood calculation is based. The general form of the AIC and BIC is similar, but you can see that the BIC will provide a greater punishment term whenever $\ln N > 2$—that is, whenever $N > 7$—which will usually be the case. This weighted punishment of complexity means that the BIC has a greater preference for simplicity (e.g., Wagenmakers & Farrell, 2004).

The BIC does not receive the same interpretation of K-L distance as the AIC. Unlike the AIC, a single BIC doesn't have any useful interpretation. However, a comparison of BICs for different models can tell us which model has the highest posterior probability given the data, and we will shortly see how BIC can be used to obtain posterior probabilities for models in a set of candidate models.

5.4.3   Model Comparison With the AIC and BIC

As implied by Figure 5.11, if we have a number of models, we can minimize $-2 \ln L$ for each model and then compute an AIC or BIC value based on each of those likelihoods and the respective number of free parameters in each model. In doing so, we must ensure that the likelihood we have calculated is based on the full likelihood function.

In Chapter 4, we noted that any terms in the log-likelihood function that did not vary with the parameters could be removed, as they do not affect ML estimation of the parameters. However, when we come to comparing different models, we must leave those terms in unless they are shared by all models. For example, the ex-Gaussian density function and the Weibull density function (also used to describe latencies; e.g., Cousineau, Brown, & Heathcote, 2004) each have their own constants that are not shared between the models. In this case, we should leave those constants in if we want to compare log-likelihoods (and AIC or BIC) between those two models. By contrast, suppose we are comparing the SIMPLE model of serial recall to another model (e.g., the primacy model; Page & Norris, 1998b) and we were using the multinomial log-likelihood function (Equation 4.21) to connect both models to the data. In this case, the models will share several constants in the multinomial log-likelihood, and these constants can be discarded (but must be discarded for both models in that case). This is not really an issue for nested models as they will tend to contain the same constants in the likelihood function.

The most obvious next step is to pick the "winning" model as the model with the smallest AIC or BIC. In the case of the AIC, this model is the model with the smallest estimate of the expected K-L distance from the true generating process. In the case of the BIC, the model with the smallest BIC is the model with the highest posterior probability given the data, assuming the models have equal priors (i.e., we a priori consider each model to be equally likely). The winning model can be made more apparent by forming the difference between each AIC (BIC) value and the smallest AIC (BIC) value in our set of models (Burnham & Anderson, 2002). Although not necessary, this can aid in the readability of information criteria, as sometimes these can reach quite large values (on the order of tens of thousands). Looking at AIC (BIC) differences also accounts for the ratio scaling of these information criteria due to the logarithmic transform of the likelihood. This ratio scale means that any *differences* between AIC values are actually *ratios* between the original likelihoods. Hence, a difference between AIC values of 2 and 4 is as large as the difference between AIC values of 2042 and 2044, which is made more explicit by calculating differences. The differences indicate how well the best model (the model with the smallest AIC or BIC) performs compared to the other models in the set. In fact, we can calculate an AIC or BIC difference between any two models and thus quantify their relative corrected goodness of fit.

What do these model differences tell us for the individual criteria? In the case of the AIC, we obtain an estimate of the additional loss in approximation of the "true" model that obtains when we take a particular model, rather than the best model, as the approximating model in the AIC. Burnham and Anderson (2002, p. 70) present a heuristic table for interpreting AIC differences (Δ AIC) as strength of evidence: Δ AIC = 0–2 indicates that there is little to distinguish between the models, 4–7 indicates "considerably less" support for the model with the larger AIC, and > 10 indicates essentially no support for the model with the larger AIC and a great deal of support for the model with the smaller AIC.

The BIC differences can be given a more principled interpretation as the logarithm of the *Bayes factor* for two models. The Bayes factor is the ratio of two models M_1 and M_2 in their posterior probability,

$$B = \frac{p(M_1|y)}{p(M_2|y)}, \tag{5.14}$$

and therefore gives a measure of relative strength of evidence for the models in terms of relative probability. On the basis of this relationship, guidelines for interpreting BIC differences have been suggested along similar lines as those for the AIC (Jeffreys, 1961; Kass & Raftery, 1995; Wasserman, 2000).

Some of these interpretations rely on the more natural interpretation of the Bayes factor rather than the BIC (log Bayes factor). The Bayes factor can be obtained from a BIC difference as

$$B = \exp\left(-\frac{1}{2}\Delta BIC\right), \tag{5.15}$$

where $\Delta BIC = BIC(M_1) - BIC(M_2)$. To clarify, this relationship holds because $\ln(B) = ln(p(M1|y)) - ln(p(M2|y)) = BIC1 - BIC2$. Because we multiplied by 2 in the calculation of the BIC (to follow standard conventions as for the AIC), we need to multiply the ΔBIC by $\frac{1}{2}$ in Equation 5.15.

Wasserman (2000) suggests interpreting the Bayes factor we get from Equation 5.15 in terms of original guidelines outlined by Jeffreys (1961), whereby a Bayes factor in the range of 3 to 10 gives moderate evidence in favor of Model 1 (M_1, the model in the numerator of the Bayes factor), while a Bayes factor greater than 10 indicates strong evidence in favor of that model. If the Bayes factor is below 1, this indicates evidence in favor of the model in the denominator (M_2); in this case, interpretation is made easier by swapping the models and putting the superior model in the numerator.

The Bayes factor is useful in that it not only tells us which is the best model but also tells us the extent to which the evidence favors that model over the others. This is valuable information to know, especially as we have a higher chance of picking an inferior model by accident as we increase the number of models in our comparison set (Zucchini, 2000). We can make the information in these ratios even more interpretable by calculating Bayesian *model weights*. The model weight w_M for model M is given by

$$w_M = \frac{\exp(-\frac{1}{2}\Delta BIC_M)}{\sum_i \exp(-\frac{1}{2}\Delta BIC_i)}, \tag{5.16}$$

where ΔBIC_M is the BIC difference between the best model and model M, and each ΔBIC_i is the difference between a specific model in our set and the best model. These model weights add up to 1 and tell us the posterior probability of each model given the data, assuming the models in our set are the only candidates for explaining the data. These model weights are usually used to predict future observations from all models at once, by averaging the predictions of all models, but with these predictions weighted by each model's posterior probability (e.g., Kass & Raftery, 1995).

We can give similar interpretations to the AIC, although these are more heuristic and arguably less principled. We can turn the AIC values into model likelihoods: Given an AIC difference ΔAIC between a particular model and the best model in a set of models, we obtain a likelihood as (Burnham & Anderson, 2002)

$$L_i \propto \exp\left(-\frac{1}{2}\Delta AIC_i\right).$$ (5.17)

Because Equation 5.17 is based on the AIC, which in turn corrects for the free parameters in our model, we can treat Equation 5.17 as the likelihood of the model given the data, $L(M|y)$ (Burnham & Anderson, 2004). The likelihood is only proportional to the expression in Equation 5.17 because it is expressed relative to the other models in the set; changing the models in the set will change the value obtained from the equation even though the K-L distance for the specific model i is fixed. This isn't a problem, as our real interest in Equation 5.17 is in determining the relative strength of evidence in favor of each model in the set. To this end, Equation 5.17 gives us a likelihood ratio: the ratio between the likelihood for the best model and the likelihood for model i. Just as for the model likelihood ratios discussed in the context of nested models in Section 5.3, this model likelihood ratio tells us about the relative evidence for two models. More generally, we can also calculate Akaike weights as an analog to Bayesian model weights. This is accomplished by using Equation 5.16 and replacing ΔBIC with ΔAIC; that is,

$$w_M = \frac{\exp(-0.5\Delta AIC_M)}{\sum_i \exp(-0.5\Delta AIC_i)}.$$ (5.18)

As for Bayesian model weights, the Akaike weights are useful for model presentation and model inference because they quantify the relative success of each model in explaining the data. Burnham and Anderson (2002) suggest a specific interpretation of Akaike weights as the weight of evidence in favor of each model being the best model in the set ("best" meaning that it has the smallest expected K-L distance to reality). Note that regardless of whether we obtain Akaike weights or Bayesian weights, our inferences are relative with respect to the specific set of models we have fit to the data and are now comparing. This means that we should not compare AIC and BIC values or related statistics for different data sets and that the likelihood ratios, Bayes factors, and model weights are also specific to the set of models that is being compared.

Listing 5.6 provides MATLAB code to calculate AIC, BIC, and their differences and model weights. The information needed (passed as arguments) are three vectors containing, respectively, the minimized negative log-likelihoods, the number of free parameters in each model, and the number of observations involved in calculating the log-likelihood.

The AIC and BIC have been used in many areas of psychology to compare quantitative models of cognition and behavior (Hélie, 2006; Wagenmakers & Farrell, 2004). These include applications to models in the following areas:

- Categorization (e.g., Farrell et al., 2006; Maddox & Ashby, 1993; Nosofsky & Bergert, 2007)

Listing 5.6 MATLAB Code to Calculate Information Criteria Statistics From Minimized Negative Log-Likelihoods

```
 1 function [AIC, BIC, AICd, BICd, AICw, BICw] = ↵
       infoCriteria(nlnLs, Npar, N)
 2 % Calculate information criteria (AIC; BIC),
 3 %    IC differences from best model (AICd; BICd),
 4 %    and model weights (AICw, BICw)
 5 %    from a vector of negative lnLs
 6 % Each cell in the vectors corresponds to a model
 7 % Npar is a vector indicating the
 8 %    number of parameters in each model
 9 % N is the number of observations on which
10 %    the log-likelihoods were calculated
11
12 AIC = 2.*nlnLs + 2.*Npar;
13 BIC = 2.*nlnLs + Npar.*log(N);
14
15 AICd = AIC-min(AIC);
16 BICd = BIC-min(BIC);
17
18 AICw = exp(-.5.*AICd)./sum(exp(-.5.*AICd));
19 BICw = exp(-.5.*BICd)./sum(exp(-.5.*BICd));
```

- Memory (e.g., Farrell & Lewandowsky, 2008; Jang, Wixted, & Huber, 2009; Lewandowsky & Farrell, 2008a)
- Spike trains from single-cell recording (e.g., Bayer, Lau, & Glimcher, 2007; S. Brown & Heathcote, 2003)
- Developmental patterns (Kail & Ferrer, 2007)
- Perception (Kubovy & van den Berg, 2008; Macho, 2007; Ploeger, Maas, & Hartelman, 2002)
- Decision and response latencies (e.g., Ratcliff & Smith, 2004), including time-accuracy functions (Liu & Smith, 2009)
- Serial correlations and sequential transitions (e.g., Torre, Delignières, & Lemoine, 2007; Visser, Raijmakers, & Molenaar, 2002; Wagenmakers, Farrell, & Ratcliff, 2004)

Some examples of the use of Akaike or Bayesian weights to discriminate between models can be found in Farrell and Lelièvre (2009), Liu and Smith (2009), Wagenmakers et al. (2005), and Kail and Ferrer (2007); see Wagenmakers and Farrell (2004) for a general introduction for psychology.

5.4.4   An Example of Model Comparison Using AIC and BIC

Let's look at a specific example. Ratcliff and Smith (2004) compared a number of models of choice latency. They considered the Wiener diffusion model (Ratcliff, 1978), the Ornstein-Uhlenbeck (OU) model (e.g., Busemeyer & Townsend, 1993), and accumulator models. The accumulator models examined by Ratcliff and Smith (2004) involve stochastic accumulation (in contrast to the deterministic LBA model discussed earlier in this chapter) and rely on one of two mechanisms to accumulate information: Either variable amounts of information arrive at regular points in time (e.g., P. L. Smith & Vickers, 1988), or fixed amounts of information are accumulated at randomly sampled intervals (i.e., the Poisson countermodel; e.g., Pike, 1973).

Table 1 of Ratcliff and Smith (2004) shows fits for six models to correct and error response quantiles from a discrimination experiment. Whereas those authors examined χ^2 and BIC values, we will look at the AIC and the BIC for their model results.[9] Table 5.1 presents values related to the AIC for six different models: the diffusion model, the OU model with fixed decay (decay parameter $\beta=4$), an accumulator model with incoming evidence sampled from a rectangular probability density, an accumulator model with evidence sampled from an exponential density, a Poisson counter model with times separating evidence counts sampled from a rectangular density, and the Poisson counter model with a geometric distribution of arrival times.[10] Because their models were computationally demanding, Ratcliff and Smith (2004) fit aggregate data constructed by averaging response proportions and the quantiles of the empirical latency distributions across participants (see Section 3.2.4 in Chapter 3 for more on quantile averaging).

The first two columns in Table 5.1 show the models and their associated $-2\ln L$ values—that is, the fit of each model irrespective of its number of parameters. The number of parameters is given in the next column (K). The fourth column gives AIC values; as you can see, the AIC values are all very large, and it is hard to distinguish between them in this presentation. The next column makes these AIC values more readable by presenting AIC differences (ΔAIC). The ΔAIC values suggest that there are two models "in the running": the exponential accumulator model (the best-fitting model, with ΔAIC=0) and the Wiener diffusion model, with ΔAIC= 1.58. The next column presents the likelihood ratio for each model (with respect to the best model), calculated using Equation 5.17,[11] and the final column presents the Akaike model weights, calculated using Equation 5.18, with the best model's weight in bold font.

If we take the Akaike model weights as being the weight of evidence in favor of each model being the best model (in terms of K-L distance from the true generating process; Burnham & Anderson, 2002), we can conclude that there is some evidence in favor of the exponential accumulator model and that we

Table 5.1 AIC Values and Associated Quantities for the Models in Table 1 of Ratcliff and Smith (2004)

Model[a]	K	$-2\ln L$	AIC	ΔAIC	LR	w
Wiener	10	8084.68	8104.68	1.58	0.453	0.308
OU	10	8091.43	8111.43	8.34	0.015	0.011
Rect acc	12	8167.69	8191.69	88.60	0.000	0.000
Exp acc	12	8079.09	8103.09	0.00	1.000	**0.681**
Rect Poisson	12	8192.89	8216.89	113.80	0.000	0.000
Geom Poisson	12	8101.69	8125.69	22.60	0.000	0.000

[a]Wiener = Wiener diffusion model; OU = Ornstein-Uhlenbeck model; Rect acc and Exp acc = accumulator model with evidence sampled from rectangular or exponential distributions, respectively; Rect Poisson and Geom Poisson = arrival times of evidence sampled from Poisson and Geometric distributions, respectively.

cannot discount the Wiener model. The other models in the set are far beyond these two models in their estimated expected K-L distance. Nevertheless, comparisons within these relatively inferior models may still be informative about the underlying psychological processes. For example, we can take the AIC difference between the rectangular and geometric Poisson models and calculate a heuristic likelihood ratio as $\exp(-.5(8216.89 - 8125.69))$, which gives a very large value ($> 10^{19}$). This tells us that although both versions of the Poisson counter model give a relatively poor account of the data, the data greatly favor the version of the model in which incoming evidence is sampled from a geometric distribution.

Table 5.2 summarizes model comparisons using the BIC. The BIC values were calculated with the number of observations equal to 2304 (i.e., $\ln N = 7.62$); this N was obtained by determining the mean number of trials per participant that were used to calculate response proportions and latency quantiles. The major change in the pattern of results from Table 5.1 is that the BIC almost exclusively favors the Wiener diffusion model (Ratcliff & Smith, 2004). The Bayes factors (B) show that the next best model, the exponential accumulator model, is much less likely than the Wiener model to have generated the data ($B=.007$). We can reexpress this Bayes factor by putting the Wiener model in the numerator and the exponential accumulator in the denominator of Equation 5.14; this works out as $\exp(-.5(8162.1 - 8172))$, approximately equal to 141. That is, the posterior probability of the Wiener model given the data is around 141 times that of the exponential accumulator model. The Bayesian weights in the final column, calculated using Equation 5.16, confirm that the Wiener process stands out as having the highest posterior probability in this set of models.

Table 5.2 BIC Values and Associated Quantities for the Models in Table 1 of Ratcliff and Smith (2004)

Model[a]	K	$-2 \ln L$	BIC	ΔBIC	B	w
Wiener	10	8084.68	8162.10	0.00	1.000	**0.960**
OU	10	8091.43	8168.86	6.76	0.034	0.033
Rect acc	12	8167.69	8260.60	98.50	0.000	0.000
Exp acc	12	8079.09	8172.00	9.90	0.007	0.007
Rect Poisson	12	8192.89	8285.80	123.70	0.000	0.000
Geom Poisson	12	8101.69	8194.60	32.50	0.000	0.000

[a]See note in Table 5.1 for description of models.

5.4.5   Choosing Between AIC and BIC

The previous example highlights the usefulness of model criteria such as the AIC and BIC when comparing a number of computational models. However, it also highlights one of the problems with using the AIC and BIC in practice: The AIC and BIC can point to different winning models and differing strengths of evidence in favor of each model. Some discussion has been given to this in the statistical literature (e.g., Burnham & Anderson, 2002; Kass & Raftery, 1995; Kuha, 2004), with some authors expressing a strong preference for either the AIC (Burnham & Anderson, 2002) or BIC (Kass & Raftery, 1995) on a number of grounds. The AIC is argued to be overly liberal and inconsistent (Kuha, 2004; Wagenmakers & Farrell, 2004) and does not properly take parameter uncertainty into account. There is also debate about whether these criteria—particularly the BIC—assume the "true" model is in the set of candidate models being compared (e.g., Burnham & Anderson, 2004; Wagenmakers & Farrell, 2004; Zucchini, 2000). The BIC, because it is derived in the Bayesian framework, also requires making assumptions about prior distributions on the parameters (specifically, a multivariate normal distribution with a covariance matrix equivalent to that for the expected Hessian matrix for a single observation; Weakliem, 1999). The AIC can equally be cast as Bayesian model selection under the assumption of some fairly informative priors (Kass & Raftery, 1995). Generally, the differences between AIC and BIC should not be surprising given the two criteria were derived to solve different problems (Burnham & Anderson, 2004; Kuha, 2004; Wasserman, 2000).

Irrespective of such debates, we can point to the major consideration that will be of interest to most computational modelers in psychology (Liu & Smith, 2009). This is that the BIC will usually give greater punishment to models with more parameters. If there is a premium on simplicity, the BIC is probably a more appropriate measure. This is particularly the case when the models are nested. For example, if two nested models differ by a single parameter (i.e., the more general model has one additional free parameter), the maximum possible difference in AIC between the two models is 2. This is because the more general model will fit at least as well as the simpler model; hence at worst (for the general model), the $-2 \ln L$ values are identical for both models, and the maximum possible AIC difference would be given by $0 - 2 \times K$, which is 2 for a single parameter ($K = 1$). This means we can never find strong evidence in favor of the simpler model using the AIC.

In contrast, the punishment given to more complex models by the BIC scales with the (log of the) number of observations, meaning that we can find strong evidence for the simpler model with large N. In addition, given that the BIC may tend to conservatism, any evidence against the simpler model in a nested comparison provides good grounds for concluding that the data favor the more complex model (Raftery, 1999). In this respect, BIC appears to be the preferable, though by no means necessary, alternative.

5.5   Conclusion

Putting this all together, model comparison proceeds something like the following. First, we specify a probability density function or probability mass function for each model, perhaps involving the specification of a data model to link the model and the data. Second, we fit the models to the data using maximum likelihood parameter estimation. Third, we use AIC or BIC to point to one or more preferred models, in two ways. The first is to give some indication of which model, out of our set, gives the best account of the data in that it has the smallest estimated expected K-L distance to the data (AIC) or the highest posterior probability given the data (BIC). The second is to quantify model uncertainty; that is, how much does the winning model win by, and how competitive are the remaining models? Another way of looking at this second point is in terms of strength of evidence, which is captured in relative terms by a variety of statistics, such as Bayes factors and model weights. Finally, for the preferred models (and any other models of interest in our set of candidates), we calculate standard errors and confidence intervals on the parameter estimates, to give some idea about the uncertainty in those estimates, especially in those cases where the estimated parameter values are to receive some theoretically meaningful interpretation.

You now have the tools to carry out all of those steps. Of course, there is always more to learn, and there are many papers and tutorials in the literature that will complement or refine what you have learned here. For interesting discussions of the use of likelihoods as measures of uncertainty and evidence, see Edwards (1992), Royall (1997), and Pawitan (2001). For further reading on model selection and model comparison, see Burnham and Anderson (2002), Kass and Raftery (1995), Hélie (2006), Myung and Pitt (2002), and two recent special issues of the *Journal of Mathematical Psychology* devoted to model selection (Myung, Forster, & Browne, 2000; Wagenmakers & Waldorp, 2006).

Before we close this chapter, there are two final and important issues to discuss. The first relates to the notion of *model complexity*. So far we have defined model complexity very generally as the number of free parameters a model uses to fit a specific set of data. The AIC and BIC both rely on this definition, as well as general assumptions about the free parameters, to correct the log-likelihood for model complexity. Recent work has shown that this is only a rough metric and that even models with the same number of free parameters may differ in their complexity, and thus their flexibility in accounting for the data, due to their functional form (Pitt & Myung, 2002).

Computational modelers are becoming increasingly aware of the need to assess model flexibility when comparing different models on their account of data (for a review, see Pitt & Myung, 2002). There are several methods available for surveying and quantifying the flexibility of one or several models, including the extent to which these models are able to mimic each other. These methods include minimum description length (e.g., Myung et al., 2000; Pitt & Myung, 2002), landscaping (e.g., Navarro, Pitt, & Myung, 2004), parameter space partitioning (Pitt, Kim, Navarro, & Myung, 2006), and parametric bootstrapping (Wagenmakers, Ratcliff, Gomez, & Iverson, 2004).

Minimum description length (MDL) is intriguing here because it makes explicit a necessary trade-off between parameter uncertainty and model uncertainty. MDL has a similar form to AIC and BIC but measures model complexity as the sensitivity of model fit to changes in the parameters based on the Hessian matrix for the log-likelihood function (Myung & Pitt, 2002). The more peaked the log-likelihood function at the ML parameter estimates, the more sensitive the fit is to our specific selection of parameter values, and thus the more complex the functional form of the model. As we saw earlier, a more peaked log-likelihood function (quantified using the Hessian matrix) tells us that our parameter estimates are more accurate. This means that a more peaked log-likelihood function makes us more confident in our parameter estimates for the model but less confident that the model is not just overly flexible and fitting the noise in our data. We return to this issue in the next chapter.

A second, related point is that goodness of fit, whether it is corrected for complexity or not, is only partially informative. Papers and book chapters on this topic can often make model selection sound like placing gladiators in an arena and forcing them to fight to the death. After many tortuous simulations and calculations, a single model arises victorious from the gore of accumulation rates and activation functions, triumphantly waving its maxed likelihood in the air! Although there is a temptation to halt proceedings at that point, it is critical that we translate this model success into some theoretically meaningful statement. Although goodness of fit may sometimes be a legitimate end point for a model-fitting exercise, in many cases a complete focus on goodness of fit may disguise a plethora of issues, including a simple failure of the authors to understand the behavior of their model. In addition, as models become more complex in order to handle increasing numbers of data sets, or to account for increasingly complex data, these models are likely to move into territory where they are less useful as theories because they are not comprehendible by humans, even highly educated scientists (see our discussion of Bonini's paradox in Chapter 2).

As experimental psychologists, we are primarily interested in *why* this model won. What features of this model were critical for its success in explaining the data? What aspects of the data did the model handle particularly well? What about the failing models? Why did those models perform so poorly? Is there some common characteristic that led to their downfall? Are there models that failed to capture the individual data points but nonetheless capture the general trend in the data (Shiffrin & Nobel, 1997)? As we will discuss in the next few chapters, these are important questions to ask and resolve.

Notes

1. We will use the terms *model selection* and *model comparison* interchangeably. Although the term *model selection* is most commonly used in the literature, it can create the false impression that our sole aim is simply to pick a model as being the best. Regardless of which term we use, we are always referring to the procedure of comparing models and using their relative performance to tell us useful information about underlying principles or mechanisms.

2. Interested readers may be intrigued to know that this relation can also be obtained through Taylor series expansion around the log-likelihood function; see, for example, Chapter 2 of Pawitan (2001).

3. If we have minimized the deviance $(-2 \ln L)$, then we need to multiply the Hessian matrix by .5 before inverting it.

4. Remember, if we had maximized the log-likelihood, we need to multiply the Hessian matrix by -1 before taking the matrix inverse.

5. Specifically, this is the 20-1 condition, in which participants were presented with 80 lists of 20 words, each word being presented for 1 second. The data were obtained from the Computational Memory Lab website: http://memory.psych.upenn.edu/.

6. Specifically, this series shows the last 750 observations from Participant 2 in the EL condition of Wagenmakers et al. (2004).

7. The critical χ^2 can be obtained using the `chi2inv` function in MATLAB's Statistics Toolbox or by consulting a χ^2 table available in the back of most behavioral sciences statistics textbooks.

8. The K-L distance is not symmetric: The distance between the model and reality is not necessarily equal to the distance between reality and the model. For this reason, some authors prefer to refer to this quantity as the K-L discrepancy (see, e.g., Burnham & Anderson, 2002).

9. Ratcliff and Smith (2004) did not present $-2 \ln L$ values, numbers of parameters, or number of data points. We have estimated these based on their Tables 1–4 (i.e., from the BIC values, differences in numbers of parameters implied by the df in their Table 1, and apparent numbers of parameters in Tables 1–4) and description in the text, with some clarifying details provided by Phil Smith and Roger Ratcliff, for which we are grateful.

10. Ratcliff and Smith (2004) actually looked at two versions of the OU model that differed in their fixed decay parameter β. We examine only a single version of the OU model here, for ease of exposition, and because of one debatable issue. The issue is this: Because Ratcliff and Smith (2004) examined two different versions of the OU model, each with a fixed decay parameter, they effectively treated the decay parameter as a free parameter in calculating their BIC value for that model. Because the decay parameter was not allowed to be entirely free, the BIC for that model would have been quite approximate, as the derivation of the BIC assumes the likelihood is the fully maximized (using the K free parameters) likelihood for that model. This is not troublesome for Ratcliff and Smith's conclusions: They found that the OU model could only give a competitive fit by allowing the decay parameter to be 0, which turned the model into the Wiener diffusion model, a restricted version of the OU model.

11. This is not the same as the likelihood ratio statistic that we looked at in Section 5.3 earlier. Remember that the likelihood ratios in Table 5.1 are calculated using the AIC as a corrected measure of the log-likelihood. We present them here as they are an intermediate step on the way to calculating model weights.

6

Not Everything That Fits Is Gold: Interpreting the Modeling

We have shown you how to fit models to data and how to select the "best" one from a set of candidates. With those techniques firmly under our belt, we can now take up three issues that are important during interpretation of our modeling results.

First, we expand on the notion of "goodness of fit" and how it relates to the properties of our data. What exactly does a good fit tell us? Is a good fit necessarily good? What is a "good fit," anyhow?

Second, suppose that our model fits the data well; we need to ask whether it *could* have been bad—that is, can we be sure that our model was falsifiable? We already touched on the issue of falsifiability in Chapters 1 and 2, and we now provide formal criteria for establishing a model's testability and falsifiability. Does it make sense to even consider models that cannot be falsified? What do we do if we cannot identify a model's parameters?

Finally, we discuss the conclusions and lessons one can draw from modeling. We show how exploration of a model, by examining its behavior in response to manipulations of the parameters, can yield valuable theoretical insights. We then expand on the notions of sufficiency and necessity that were introduced in Chapter 2.

6.1 Psychological Data and the Very Bad Good Fit

We begin by considering the properties of our data. Without data, there would be no modeling, and any cognitive modeler must therefore also be cognizant of the nature of our data. What characterizes psychological data? That's right—they are noisy. No matter how hard you may try, your data will be subject to a variety of sources of error or noise. For example, your measurement tools may be subject to error, as anyone can confirm who has ever used a voice-activated key to measure response latencies. Even if your tools are maximally precise, your subjects won't be. They may daydream on a portion of trials, their chair may collapse (as has been witnessed by one of the authors), and above all they will all differ from each other. Even if subjects stay on task, there is mundane variability in responding between trials that is an inherent feature of human behavior and cannot be eliminated.

As psychologists, we are so used to this fact that we tend to ignore it; for example, we bet that you did not bat an eyelid in Chapter 2, when we superimposed a regression line onto the speech rate data of Hulme and Tordoff (1989). We have reproduced both the data and the regression line in the left panel of Figure 6.1.

Maybe you should start batting an eyelid when you look at the remaining two panels; they show the same data together with a fit of a third-order (i.e., $y = p_1x^3 + p_2x^2 + p_3x + p_4$) and a fifth-order polynomial, respectively. The root mean squared deviations (RMSDs; see Equation 2.2) for the three fits are .062, .037, and (virtually) .0, respectively. Does this tell us that the data are best described by the equation $y = p_1x^5 + p_2x^4 + p_3x^3 + p_4x^2 + p_5x + p_6$? After all, that model provides a perfect fit, so why not accept it? Yet, we would be surprised if you did not feel some discomfort at the prospect of accepting the model in the right-most panel. Why?

The answer is that as experimental psychologists, we know that our data are noisy, and we therefore have a strong intuition that the "kinks" in the function relating memory to speech rate are the result of noise rather than reflecting a deep relationship that is captured by a fifth-order polynomial. This potential problem, that we may inadvertently give the data more credit than their level of noise warrants, is known as overfitting and has been the subject of considerable concern and research efforts (e.g., Pitt & Myung, 2002).

6.1.1 Overfitting

How serious is the overfitting problem, and what can we do about it? Pitt and Myung (2002) reported a simulation study that illustrated the magnitude of the problem. Their basic approach, known as model recovery, is sufficiently important and general to warrant a bit of explanation.

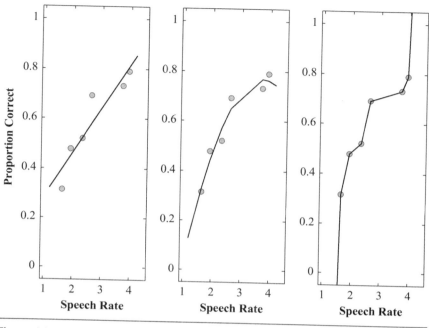

Figure 6.1 The effects of speech rate on recall for 7- and 10-year-olds. The data are identical across panels and are represented by gray circles, whereas the solid lines are various statistical models fit to the data (a regression line on the left, a third-order polynomial in the middle, and a fifth-order polynomial on the right). Data taken from Hulme, C., & Tordoff, V. (1989). Working memory development: The effects of speech rate, word-length, and acoustic similarity on serial recall. *Journal of Experimental Child Psychology, 47*, 72–87. See text for details.

Figure 6.2 explains the process underlying all recovery techniques. A known model (called M_x in the figure) is used to generate a sample of data. For example, in Pitt and Myung's case, data were generated from a one-parameter model $y = (1 + t)^{-a}$ (where $a = 0.4$) by adding some sampling noise to 100 values of y obtained for a range of ts. Note that these "data" are not data in the strict sense (i.e., obtained from participants in an experiment) but are simulated data with a known origin (namely, the model M_x). We already used this technique earlier, in Section 3.1, when generating data for our introductory linear regression example; see Listing 3.1.

The second stage of the recovery procedure, shown in the bottom of Figure 6.2, consists of fitting a number of candidate models (M_y, M_z, ...) to the simulated data. Only one of those models actually generated the data, M_x, and the question is whether it fits (its own) data better than the other competitors. Perhaps surprisingly, Pitt and Myung found in their simulations that in 100% of all

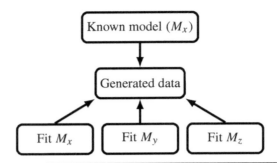

Figure 6.2 Overview of the model recovery procedure. We start with a known model (M_x) and use it to generate data at random (sometimes we may additionally "contaminate" the data with suitably aberrant observations). We then fit a variety of candidate models (M_y, M_z, etc.) to those generated data and examine which one fits best. Ideally, the best-fitting model should always be M_x, the model that generated the data. However, there are instances in which other models may fit even better; see text for details.

cases, the data were better accommodated—as measured by RMSD—by an alternative three-parameter model, $y = (b + ct)^{-a}$, than by the one that generated the data. Thus, the model that generated the data spectacularly failed to be recovered. Why?

The answer is that the competing three-parameter model, being more flexible than its one-parameter cousin that generated the data, was able to fit the "noise" in addition to the true underlying process, thus being favored on the basis of a conventional goodness-of-fit criterion. Unlike the extreme example in Figure 6.1 that involved a rather exotic fifth-order polynomial, the models compared by Pitt and Myung (2002) were all plausible candidates for the data under consideration. Thus, in their scenario, no alarm bells would have been triggered based on the nature of the models themselves, and in practice, the good fit of the more complex one might have been accepted. Given that we seek models that explain how the mind actually works, to rephrase the title of Pitt and Myung's paper, a good fit can sometimes be bad indeed.

6.1.2 Generalizability Versus Goodness of Fit

If we acknowledge that overfitting can be a serious problem, how can we deal with it? To answer this question, we must first decide on a practical criterion that lets us determine when overfitting has *not* occurred. The preceding demonstration was based on simulation results and hammered home the severity of the problem; but in practice, when the true data-generating process is unknown, how do we even know if we have a problem?

We can resolve this conundrum by redefining the problem "as one of assessing how well a model's fit to one data sample generalizes to future samples generated by that same process" (Pitt & Myung, 2002, p. 422). In other words, if we fit a model to one set of noisy data, our fears about possible overfitting can be allayed if the same parameter estimates successfully accommodate another data set within the purview of our model. Generalizing to another data set alleviates the problem because the new data set is guaranteed to be "contaminated" by a different set of "noise" from the first one; hence, if both can be accommodated by the same model, then this cannot be because the model fit any micro-variation arising from error.

There are two main approaches to establishing generalizability of a model. The first is statistical and relies on some of the techniques already mentioned (i.e., in Chapters 4 and 5). Although we did not dwell on this at the time, several model selection techniques have statistical properties that provide at least some safeguard against overfitting. This safeguard is greatest for minimum-description length (MDL) approaches (Grünwald, 2007), which are, however, beyond our scope.

The second approach is more empirical and involves a variety of techniques that are broadly known as "cross-validation" (e.g., Browne, 2000; Busemeyer & Wang, 2000; M. R. Forster, 2000). Cross-validation is sufficiently important to warrant further comment. The basic idea underlying cross-validation is simple and has already been stated: Fit a model to one data set and see how well it predicts the next one. Does this mean we must replicate each experiment before we can fit a model to the data? No; in its simplest form, cross-validation requires that the existing data set be split in half (at random) and that the model be fit to one half (called the calibration sample) and its best-fitting predictions be compared to the data in the other half (the validation sample). This technique is illustrated in Figure 6.3 using the data from the study by Hulme and Tordoff (1989).

We arbitrarily split those observations into a calibration sample ($N = 3$) and a validation sample ($N = 3$). Following standard cross-validation techniques (see, e.g., Browne, 2000; Stone, 1974), we fit three competing models (polynomials of first, fourth, and eighth order, respectively) to the calibration sample; the solid lines in the panels show the resulting predictions.

There is an obvious lesson that can be drawn from the figure: Although the most complex model (an eighth-order polynomial) fits the calibration sample perfectly, it fails quite miserably at fitting the validation sample—quite unlike the linear regression, which does a moderately good job of accommodating both samples. Had these been real data, the cross-validation would have revealed a severe case of overfitting for the most complex candidate model (and also for the intermediate model), and the modeler would have likely chosen the simplest

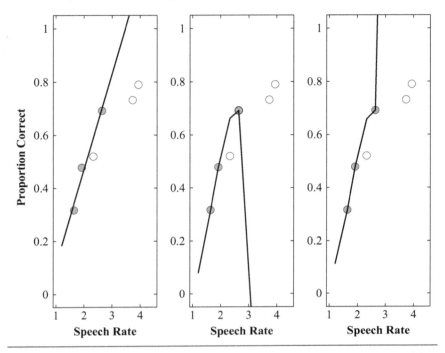

Figure 6.3 The effects of speech rate on recall for 7- and 10-year-olds. The data are identical across panels and are taken from Hulme, C., & Tordoff, V. (1989). Working memory development: The effects of speech rate, word-length, and acoustic similarity on serial recall. *Journal of Experimental Child Psychology, 47*, 72–87. The data in each panel are arbitrarily split into two samples: a calibration sample represented by gray circles and a validation sample represented by open circles. The solid lines in each panel represent various statistical models that are fit to the calibration sample only (a regression line on the left, a fourth-order polynomial in the middle, and an eighth-order polynomial on the right). See text for details.

model—notwithstanding its slightly inferior fit to the calibration sample—as the most appropriate way to describe these data.

We must add some important clarifications: First, the example just presented is highly unrealistic. Statistically, it makes little sense to fit only three data points, and no one would attempt a cross-validation on such a limited set of numbers (we did this only for illustrative purposes). In reality, one would need a much larger sample before splitting it into the two sets. Moreover, in reality, the process would likely be repeated and multiple calibration samples would be drawn, each being fitted by the candidate models and compared to the validation sample.

One drawback of this two-sample approach to cross-validation is that it is quite wasteful because only half the data are involved in calibration. Accordingly, more sophisticated cross-validation techniques involve a "leaving one out at a time" approach, which involves partitioning of a sample of size N into a calibration sample of size $N - 1$ and a single observation for validation. This process is repeated N times, such that each observation serves as the "validation sample" once while also contributing to calibration on the other $N - 1$ occasions (for details, see Browne, 2000; Stone, 1974). The average performance of a model across those N different validations is then used as an index of its generalizability.[1]

A common element of all cross-validation techniques is the reliance on a *single* sample of data (or replications using an identical or nearly identical methodology). Another, more powerful tool to establish a model's generalizability involves the "generalization criterion methodology" developed by Busemeyer and Wang (2000). Like cross-validation, this method relies on fitting the model to a calibration sample before extending it to a validation sample; however, the method designs the validation sample not at random but by systematically seeking extrapolation conditions that can differentiate between alternative models. This approach has several advantages. First, it deals with the fact that as sample size increases, cross-validation becomes useless (because in the limit, if $N \rightarrow \infty$, parameter estimates based on a randomly chosen calibration sample will not differ from those obtained with the validation sample).

The generalization criterion methodology instead partitions the available data into sub*designs*: a calibration *design* and a validation *design*. The distinction between design and sample becomes obvious if we consider an example: DeLosh, Busemeyer, and McDaniel (1997) compared various models in their ability to predict people's extrapolation performance during function learning. In function learning, a continuous stimulus value X (such as the dosage of a drug or driving speed) is related to a continuous response variable Y (such as the response to the drug or stopping distance), and people must discern their interrelationship [e.g., $Y = 210 - (x - 50)^2/12$] across a number of discrete learning episodes. On each trial, some value of X is presented, and the participant's response ($\hat{Y}$) is followed by corrective feedback (Y). Typically, all quantities ($X, \hat{Y}, Y$) are presented in graphical form (e.g., by the length of a bar), and across numerous trials people are able to learn a variety of functions, including the quadratic just mentioned, such that $\hat{Y} \approx Y$ at the end of training. DeLosh et al. (1997) fit several competing models to the data; what is important here is that the models were fit to the training data, and their performance was then assessed on the extrapolation data. That is, in the same way that people were trained on some range of values of X (30–70 in this specific instance) before being confronted with novel values (i.e., 0–29 and 71–100) without feedback, the models' parameters were estimated with respect to the training data, but their performance was examined with respect to the generalization data. Thus, the training stimuli constituted the calibration design and the extrapolation stimuli the validation design. Any overfitting to the training data would have become apparent as a failure to extrapolate; Busemeyer and Wang (2000) report two illustrative examples that make this point very clearly. In both examples, an overly complex model was shown to handle the calibration design particularly well (akin to the polynomial in the right panel of Figure 6.1), whereas a less complex but more principled model handled the validation design far better. Thus, overfitting was revealed by the validation design.

Let us recapitulate. We have shown that overfitting can be a serious problem when models are fit to a single data set. One characteristic difficulty with overfitting is that it cannot be detected by analyzing the data set, the preferred model, and its goodness of fit in isolation. One solution to overfitting involves cross-validation, whereby a model is fit to a subset of the data, and its success at predicting the remainder is assessed. A number of different cross-validation techniques can assist in the detection of overfitting.

A final technique for the detection of overfitting is, simply, to replicate the phenomenon under study and to fit the models to a number of experiments, each slightly different from the preceding one: Any overfitting will reveal itself in the same way that it is revealed by cross-validation—namely, by a failure to fit the new data or by undue variations in parameter values when the fit is repeated across different experiments.

6.2   Parameter Identifiability and Model Testability

Thus far, we have at least tacitly assumed that our models may fail—that is, we acknowledged that they might in principle at least turn out to mispredict data. Perhaps surprisingly, not all models conform to this expectation. For some models, there exists no conceivable experimental outcome with which the model would not be consistent. Those models are called *nontestable* or *unfalsifiable* (Bamber & Santen, 2000).

There are other models that, while testable, are not identifiable: Models are unidentifiable when there is no unique mapping between any possible data pattern and a corresponding set of parameter estimates (Batchelder & Riefer, 1999). That is, an experimental outcome is consistent not with one but with (potentially infinitely) many parameter values.

We take up those twin issues in turn, beginning with a discussion of identifiability. We prefix our discussion by noting that in reality, considerations of identifiability and testability usually arise at the model design stage, rather than after a model has been fit. However, conceptually, those issues pertain to the interpretability of a model fit, and hence they are discussed here, after basic modeling techniques have been introduced.

6.2.1   Identifiability

In Chapter 1, we touched on the issue of *model* identifiability, which refers to the question of whether behavioral data are ever sufficiently constraining to permit a unique process model to be identified from among a set of infinitely many other candidates. Here we address a slightly different question, which is whether for a given model, one can uniquely identify its parameter values.

Suppose you are shown the letters *K L Z*, one at a time, and a short while later you are probed with another letter, and you must decide whether or not it was part of the initial set. So, if you are shown *Z*, you respond with "yes" (usually by pressing one of two response keys), and if you are shown *X*, you respond "no." How might this simple recognition memory task be modeled? Numerous proposals exist, but here we focus on an early and elegant model proposed by Sternberg (e.g., 1975). According to Sternberg's model, performance in this task is characterized by three psychological stages: First, there is an encoding stage that detects, perceives, and encodes the probe item. Encoding is followed by a comparison stage during which the probe is compared, one by one, to all items in the memorized set. Finally, there is a decision-and-output stage that is responsible for response selection and output.[2] This model can be characterized by three temporal parameters: the duration of the encoding process (parameter a), the comparison time per memorized item (b), and the time to select and output a response (c). A crucial aspect of this model is the assumption that the probe is compared to *all* memorized items, irrespective of whether or not a match arises during the scan.

The model makes some clear and testable predictions: First, the model predicts that the time taken to respond should increase with set size in a linear fashion; specifically, each additional item in memory should add an amount b to the total response time (RT). Second, owing to the exhaustive nature of the scan, the set size effect must be equal for old (*Z*) and new (*X*) probes, and hence the slopes relating set size to RT must be parallel for both probe types. In a nutshell, the model would be challenged if RT were not a linear function of set size or if the slope of the set size function were different for old and new probes.[3] As it turns out, the data often conform to the model's expectations when considered at the level of mean RT. Performance is typically characterized by the descriptive regression function:

$$RT = t_{op} + b \times s, \tag{6.1}$$

where s refers to the number of memorized items, and b represents the comparison time parameter just discussed. Across a wide range of experiments, estimates for b converge on a value of approximately 35 to 40 ms (Sternberg, 1975), and the estimates are indistinguishable for old and new items. The intercept term, t_{op}, varies more widely with experimental conditions and tends to range from 380 to 500 ms.

You may have discovered the problem already: We describe the data using two parameters, b and t_{op}, whereas the psychological model has three parameters (a, b, and c). The value of parameter b is given by the data, but all we can say about a and c is that their sum is equal to t_{op}. Alas, beyond that constraint, they are not identifiable because there are infinitely many values of a and c that are compatible with a given estimate of t_{op}. Hence, the relative contributions of encoding and decision times to the total RT remain unknown.

This example illustrates a few important points: First, the model is clearly testable because it makes some quite specific predictions that could, in principle, be readily invalidated by contrary outcomes. Second, even though the data are in accord with the predictions, they are insufficient to identify the values of all the model's parameters. Several questions immediately spring to mind: What are the implications of the lack of identifiability? How can we respond if a model turns out not to be identifiable? Can we ascertain identifiability of a model ahead of time?

6.2.1.1   Implications of Nonidentifiability

What does it mean if a model is not identifiable? Can a nonidentifiable model still be of use? Frequently, the answer is no. The reasons for this are most readily apparent for descriptive models, such as the function describing practice effects in skill acquisition (see Chapter 1), whose entire purpose is to summarize the data by the model's parameters—clearly, if those parameters cannot be identified, the models are of limited value (Batchelder & Riefer, 1999).

There are, however, some exceptions to this general conclusion. First, in some instances, even nonidentifiable models—provided they are testable—may yield valuable psychological insights (Bamber & van Santen, 1985; Van Santen, J. P., & Bamber, D., 1981). For example, if the just-described model of recognition were found to be at odds with the data, this could be highly informative because it would compromise the notion of an exhaustive serial scan. The fact that the model was not identifiable is of little concern in this context.

Moreover, even though nonidentifiability implies that we cannot use the data to identify a *unique* vector of parameter values, it does not necessarily follow that the data provide *no* information about the parameters. In fact, the data may nonetheless provide partial information about parameter values. For example, Chechile (1977) discusses situations in which a model can be "posterior probabilistically identified" even though its parameters escape identification by conventional maximum likelihood means. On Chechile's approach, the data can be used to constrain the likely parameter values, with a sometimes dramatic reduction in uncertainty. For example, given a parameter with range [0-1], if one assumes that the distribution of its possible values is uniform before the data are collected, the variance of this distribution is 1/12. [Because for a uniform distribution, $\sigma^2 = 1/12(b-a)^2$, where a and b are the limits of the range; so for a unit interval, $\sigma^2 = 1/12$.] Chechile provides an example of a multinomial tree model $(\epsilon, \beta, \gamma$; see Figure 1.6 for the general form of such a model) whose posterior distribution—computed in light of the data by Bayesian means—has variances 1/162, 1/97, and 1/865. Thus, notwithstanding the nonidentifiability of parameters, uncertainty about their value has been reduced by a factor of up to 72. Moreover, the mean of the parameters' posterior distribution can be taken as point estimates of their values, thus providing quasi-identifiability in some situations in which conventional identifiability is absent. The quasi-identifiability of parameters is illustrated in Figure 6.4, which shows the posterior probability density for two parameters, β and ϵ, for a multinomial tree model (for simplicity, we omit the third parameter). The solid horizontal line in the figure represents the prior probability density of parameter values; it is obvious how much more is known about the likely parameter values in light of the data (the lines labeled β and ϵ) than is known a priori, where any possible parameter value is equally likely.

Putting aside those exceptions, however, nonidentifiability is often a serious handicap that imperils a model's applicability. Fortunately, if a model turns out to be unidentifiable, there are several ways in which identifiability can be restored.

6.2.1.2 Dealing With Nonidentifiability

One way in which identifiability can be restored is by reparameterization of the model. Consider again the above Sternberg model of the recognition task: If we reexpress the model as consisting of two stages, one involving comparison (and governed by parameter b) and another one that subsumes all other processes involved in the task, then the model becomes identifiable (Bamber & van Santen, 2000). Upon reparameterization, there is one parameter, t_{op}, that captures all other processes plus the comparison parameter, b, and we have already shown how the model's estimation is possible (namely, as the intercept and slope, respectively, in a simple linear regression). Of course, the reparameterization is not without cost: In this instance, information about the relative contribution of encoding versus response selection is lost if there are no longer separate parameters describing each process. However, it is not necessary for reparameterization to involve a tangible loss of information: For example, if model parameters are estimated for multiple response categories, such as in an identification experiment, it is not uncommon to constrain those parameters to sum to some value, thus effectively reducing their number by one (thus J response categories are modeled by $J - 1$ parameters; see, e.g., Batchelder & Riefer, 1999). Equivalently, one of a set of

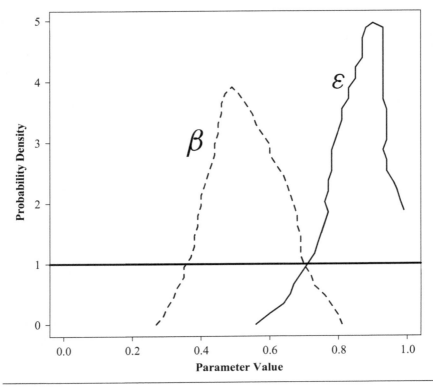

Figure 6.4 Prior probability (solid horizontal line) and posterior probabilities (lines labeled β and ϵ) for two parameters in a multinomial tree model that are "posterior probabilistically identified." Figure adapted from Chechile, R. A. (1977). Likelihood and posterior identification: Implications for mathematical psychology. *British Journal of Mathematical and Statistical Psychology, 30*, 177–184.

parameters can be set to a fixed value, as in the case of Luce's (1959) choice model (see Bamber & van Santen, 2000, for a discussion of the identifiability of Luce's model).

An alternative to reparameterization involves the elimination of parameters by experimentally induced constraints (Wickens, 1982). For example, suppose a model contains a parameter that represents the preexperimental familiarity of the material in a memory experiment. That parameter can be eliminated (e.g., by setting it to 0) if an experiment is conducted in which the to-be-remembered material is entirely novel (e.g., nonsense syllables or random shapes) and thus cannot have any preexperimental familiarity. Upon elimination of one parameter, the model may now be identifiable within the context of that experiment.

Relatedly, identification of a model may be achievable by collecting "richer" data (Wickens, 1982). For example, a model that is not identifiable at the level of simple yes and no responses in a recognition memory experiment may become identifiable when people also provide confidence ratings in the same experiment—we return to this issue below, when discussing models that are identifiable but not testable (Section 6.2.4).

6.2.1.3   Identifying Nonidentifiability

Thus far, we have tacitly assumed that the identifiability of models (or lack thereof) is either obvious or known. Indeed, identifiability was obvious upon a moment's reflection for the earlier model of the Sternberg recognition task. However, the identifiability of a model need not be so obvious, which gives rise to the rather pernicious possibility that we continue to work with a model and rely on its parameter estimates even though it may be unidentifiable (e.g., Wickens, 1982). How can we defend ourselves against that possibility? How can we ascertain identifiability?

One approach relies on examination of the standard results from our model fitting. For example, analysis of the covariance matrix of the parameters (we discussed its computation in Section 5.1.2) after the model has been fit to a single data set can reveal problems of identifiability. In particular, identifiability problems are indicated if the covariances between parameters are high relative to the variances. Li et al. (1996) explore the implications of this technique. Similarly, if multiple runs of the model—from different starting values—yield the same final value of the discrepancy function but with very different parameter estimates, then this can be an indication of a lack of identifiability (Wickens, 1982). Of course, this outcome can also arise if there are multiple local minima, and it is not always easy to differentiate between the two scenarios. Finally, an alternative approach that is not tied to the vagaries of estimating parameters establishes a model's identifiability by formal means through analysis of its "prediction function."

Bamber and van Santen (1985, 2000) and P. L. Smith (1998) showed that identifiability of a model can be established by analyzing the Jacobian matrix of the model's prediction function. For this analysis, we first note that any model can be considered a vector-valued function, call that $f(\theta)$, that maps a parameter vector, θ, into an outcome vector, r. That is, unlike a conventional scalar function, a model produces not a scalar output but an entire vector—namely, its predictions, expressed as point values.

It turns out that the properties of the model, including its identifiability, can be inferred from the properties of the Jacobian matrix, J_θ, of that prediction function. Briefly, the Jacobian matrix describes the orientation of a tangent plane to a vector-valued function at a given point. Thus, whereas scalar-valued functions are characterized by a *gradient*, which is a vector pointing in the direction of steepest descent, vector-valued functions, by extension, are analogously characterized by the Jacobian matrix. This is analogous to the vector of first partial derivatives that we discussed in Chapter 5, where we were talking about changes in the log-likelihood rather than (predicted) data points themselves. In the present context, it is important to note that each column of the Jacobian contains a vector of partial derivatives with respect to one of the model's parameters (and each row refers to a different predicted point). P. L. Smith (1998) showed that if the rank of the Jacobian matrix (i.e., the number of its columns that are linearly independent) is equal to the number of parameters, then the model is identifiable. In other words, if the partial derivatives with respect to the various parameters are all linearly independent, then all parameters can be identified.[4] Conversely, if the rank of the Jacobian is less than the number of parameters, the model is not identifiable.

How, then, does one compute a model's Jacobian matrix? It turns out that this computation is fairly straightforward. Listing 6.1 shows a function, called quickJacobian, that relies on a quick (albeit not maximally accurate) algorithm to compute the Jacobian matrix. The function is of considerable generality and requires a minimum of three arguments: a vector of parameter values (x), the predictions of the model at that point (y), and the name of the function that computes the predictions of the model. Any additional arguments, when present, are passed on to the function that computes the model predictions. The only requirements of the function that computes the model predictions are (1) that the first (though not necessarily only) argument is a vector of parameter values and (2) that it returns a vector of predictions. Beyond that, the function can require any number of further arguments, and its design and workings are completely arbitrary and of no interest to quickJacobian.

Listing 6.1 Computing the Jacobian

```
 1  function [Jac] = quickJacobian(x, y, varargin)
 2  Np = length(x);
 3  Nd = length(y);
 4  Jac = zeros(Nd,Np);
 5  epsilon = sqrt(eps);
 6
 7  % Iterate over parameters to estimate columns of
 8  % Jacobian by finite differences.
 9  for i=1:Np
10      x_offset = x;
11      x_offset(i) = x_offset(i) + epsilon;
12
13      % get model predictions for offset parameter vector.
14      f_offset = ↩
            feval(varargin{1},x_offset,varargin{2:end});
15      Jac(:,i) = (f_offset - y)/epsilon;
16  end
```

To put the use of this function into context, consider the very first modeling example that we presented in Chapter 3. You may recall that we used `fminsearch` to compute the parameters for a simple linear regression, using the program in Listing 3.1. If you run this program and get the best-fitting parameter estimates, you can get information about the model's Jacobian by entering the following three commands into the MATLAB command window:[5]

    y=getregpred(finalParms,data);

This command calls the model to get predictions, using the function shown in Listing 3.3, and stores those predictions in the variable `y`.

    J=quickJacobian(finalParms,y,@getregpred,data)

This command calls the function just presented (Listing 6.1), passing as arguments (1) the final parameter estimates (the listings in Chapter 3 explain how the variable `finalParms` was generated), (2) the vector of predictions created by the immediately preceding command, (3) the name of the function that generates predictions (note the "@," which denotes the parameter as a function handle), and (4) the original data. Note that the last argument is optional from the point of view of the function `quickJacobian`, but it is required by the function `getregpred`, and thus it is passed on to the latter function by `quickJacobian`.

When the command has been executed, the Jacobian matrix is in the variable `J`, and so all that is needed is to type

    rank(J)

at the command prompt, and the single value that is returned is the rank of the model's Jacobian matrix computed at the point of the best-fitting parameter estimates. Of course, in the case of the regression model, the rank is 2, which is equal to the number of parameters—hence, as we would expect, the model is identifiable.[6]

It turns out that the Jacobian matrix is also intimately involved in determining a model's testability; hence, computing the Jacobian helps us in more ways than one.

6.2.2 Testability

We provided a fairly thorough conceptual treatment of the issue of testability (or, equivalently, falsifiability) in Chapter 1. In particular, we have already established that a model is testable if "there exists a conceivable experimental outcome with which the model is not consistent" (Bamber & van Santen, 2000, p. 25).[7] Unfortunately, however useful this in-principle definition of testability might be, it begs the question of whether *this particular model that I am currently designing* will turn out to be testable. Given the paramount emphasis on testability in most circumstances, advanced knowledge of whether one's model is testable is an important consideration when deciding whether to invest further effort into model development.

6.2.2.1   Determining Testability

All notions of determining testability are invariantly tied to the number of free parameters in a model: We saw in Chapter 1 that if the number of parameters is (very) large, a model can even "fit" an elephant (Wei, 1975). We also noted at the same time that the number of parameters required to fit an elephant is far greater than the proverbial four (or five if the trunk is to wiggle; Dyson, 2004). So how many parameters is too many? How many parameters can a model have and still be testable? Traditionally, this question has compared the number of parameters to the number of to-be-fitted data points: If there were as many or more independent free parameters than independent data points, then a model was thought to be untestable. This view represents a simplification that does not always hold. Bamber and van Santen (1985) showed that under certain circumstances, a model could have *more* parameters than data points and still be testable. Not surprisingly, this analysis again involved the model's Jacobian matrix: what matters to testability is not the number of parameters but the rank of the Jacobian matrix. If its *rank* is less than the number of to-be-fitted independent data points, then a model is testable (Bamber & van Santen, 1985). Because the rank can be less than the number of parameters, there are situations in which a model is testable despite having more parameters than data points—although if that situation arises, the model is also nonidentifiable as discussed in the preceding section. (Remember, if the Jacobian is not of full rank, then the model is not identifiable.)

6.2.3   Putting It All Together: Deciding the Identifiability and Testability of a Model

Our discussion of identifiability and testability can be condensed into the simple flowchart in Figure 6.5. First, we examine whether a model is identifiable, based on the Jacobian criteria just reviewed. If the model is unidentifiable because the Jacobian rank (r) is less than the number of independent free parameters (m), it may nonetheless be testable if the rank is also less than the number of data points (n) that are to be fitted. Conversely, if the model is identifiable because the Jacobian is of full rank, it is testable only if the number of parameters is less than the number of data points.

Although the flowchart summarizes a fairly straightforward sequence of steps that can be applied quite readily, it warrants at least one cautionary note and one explanatory comment. First, application of all three "rules" must take note of their detailed underpinnings and requirements, and they are best understood as

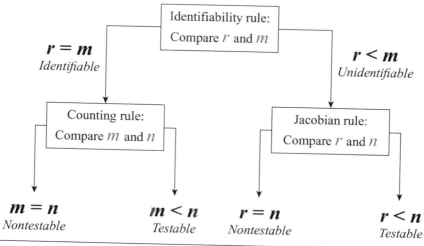

Figure 6.5 Flowchart to determine a model's identifiability and testability based on analysis of the Jacobian matrix, J_θ, of its prediction function. Here r denotes the maximum rank of J_θ, m denotes the number of independent free parameters, and n denotes the number of independent data points that are being fitted. If a model is determined to be "nontestable," weaker forms of testability may nonetheless persist; see text for details. Adapted from Bamber, D., & van Santen, J. P. H. (2000). How to assess a model's testability and identifiability. *Journal of Mathematical Psychology, 44,* 20–40. Reprinted with permission from Elsevier.

being "conjectural" rather than lawful (see Bamber & van Santen, 1985, 2000) for further details). Second, we must clarify the implications of a model being identified as "nontestable" by those rules. Principally, the implication is that the model cannot be tested at a rigorous quantitative level; however, the possibility remains that even a "nontestable" model can be found to be at odds with *some* outcome, albeit not at a quantitative level. For example, even though the model may be (quantitatively) nontestable, it may nonetheless predict inequalities among data points that can be falsified by the data (see Bamber & van Santen, 1985, 2000, for further details).

6.2.4 Models That Are Identifiable but Not Testable

We have already seen that a model can be unidentifiable but nonetheless testable; here we consider the opposite scenario—namely, a model whose parameters are uniquely identifiable but that is nonetheless untestable. Having just discussed ways in which testability can be ascertained, one might well ask why such untestable models ever make it out of the designer's workshop into the public domain. The answer is that models that are not testable can nonetheless be quite useful—in fact, they are quite common.

This becomes obvious if we consider a "model" consisting of the sample mean; we can clearly always identify its single parameter—namely, the sample mean—but we will never be able to "falsify" it. Lest you think that this is a trivial example with no practical relevance, consider the common practice of computing a measure of sensitivity (d') and a criterion (e.g., β) from hits and false alarm rates in a detection or a recognition memory experiment (e.g., Hicks & Marsh, 2000). Those two parameters are always identifiable; that is, any imaginable experimental outcome will always yield one and only one set of values for d' and β. It is common to interpret those parameters as reflecting, respectively, a bias-free measure of the "strength" of evidence underlying people's judgments and the nature of people's response bias. It is perhaps less common to realize that this interpretation is tied to acceptance of a very specific underlying model of the decision process—namely, that the evidence distributions (noise and signal-plus-noise) are Gaussian and have equal variance.[8] Interpretation of the parameters (in particular, the presumed independence of d' and β) is therefore model bound—and therein lies a problem because the model is not falsifiable in the situation just described. That is, there exists no combination of a hit rate and a corresponding false alarm rate that would be incompatible with the signal detection model. Thus, rather than being able to confirm the adequacy of a model before interpreting its parameters, computation of d' and β from a single set of hits and false alarms does the opposite—we *presume* the adequacy of the model and interpret the parameters in light of that model. Is this necessarily inappropriate? No, not at all. In other disciplines, such as physics, it is not uncommon to presume the applicability of a model (e.g., Ohm's law; see Bamber & van Santen, 2000, for an example) and to identify parameters on its basis without being concerned about a lack of testability. In psychology, somewhat greater caution is advised, and interpretation of parameter values must consider the full intricacies of the situation if a model is not testable (see, e.g., Pastore et al., 2003; Wixted & Stretch, 2000).

That said, in many situations, lack of testability *can* present a problem. This problem is particularly pernicious when the exact role of a model has become blurred, for example, when it is no longer totally clear to readers (or even writers, for that matter) whether the model under consideration is being tested, whether support for its assumptions is being adduced, or whether it is presumed to be true in order to imbue the parameter estimates with psychological validity. We illustrate this problem with an identifiable but untestable model that experienced a rash of popularity some time ago.

There has been much fascination with the finding that amnesic patients, who by definition suffer from extremely poor memories, do not appear to differ from normal control participants on *indirect* tests of memory. For example, when asked to recall a word from a previous list given the cue WIN___, amnesic patients perform much more poorly than control subjects. However, when given the same word stem cue with the instruction to complete it "with the first word that comes to mind," patients show the same increased tendency to report a list item (rather than another nonstudied option) as do normal control subjects. This dissociation in performance between direct and indirect memory tests (also known as "explicit" and "implicit" tests, respectively) has been at the focus of intense research activity for several decades (for a comprehensive review, see Roediger & McDermott, 1993), in particular because performance on indirect tests is often said to involve an "unconscious" form of memory that does not involve recollective awareness (e.g., Toth, 2000). The latter claim is beset with the obvious difficulty of ensuring that people are in fact unaware of relying on their memories when completing a word stem. How do we know that a person who completed the stem with a list item did not think of its presence on the list at that very moment? Jacoby (1991) proposed an elegant and simple solution to this "conscious-contamination" problem. The solution is known as the "process dissociation procedure" (PDP), and it permits an empirical estimate of the conscious and unconscious contributions to memory performance. For the remainder of this discussion, we illustrate the procedure within the domain of recognition memory, where the distinction between "conscious" and "unconscious" forms of memory has been adopted by the family of dual-process models (for a review, see Yonelinas, 2002).

At the heart of the PDP is the notion that conscious recollection (R), but not unconscious activation (U), is under the subject's control. In recognition memory experiments that build on this notion, two distinct lists—which we call M and F—are presented for study. Following study of both lists, people are tested first on one and then on the other list. For simplicity, we focus here on the test of List M, where people are asked to respond yes to items from M but *not* to those from List F. For test items from List M, these instructions are creating what is known as an "inclusion" condition because conscious *and* unconscious forms of memory can cooperatively drive a response (namely, "yes"). For test items from List F, by contrast, these instructions create an "exclusion" condition in which conscious recollection is brought into opposition to unconscious activation. That is, on one hand, successful recollection of a test item will mandate a "no" response (because F items are to be excluded). On the other hand, if recollection fails, then unconscious activation arising from the prior study will mistakenly result in a "yes" response. The resultant differences between inclusion and exclusion conditions can be exploited to estimate the relative contribution of the two memorial processes using the logic shown in Figure 6.6.

For the List M items, R and U act in concert, and the probability of a yes response is thus given by $P(Inclusion) = P(R) + P(U) \times [1 - P(R)]$: Either a person recollects the presence of the item on List M and says yes on that basis

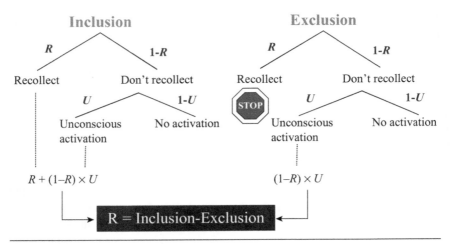

Figure 6.6 Logic underlying the process dissociation procedure. After study of Lists M and F, people are asked to respond "yes" to recognition test items from List M but not those from List F. Thus, items from List M are processed under "inclusion" conditions and those from List F under "exclusion" conditions. It follows that a yes response to M items arises from the independent contributions of R (conscious recollection) and U (unconscious activation). For F items, by contrast, any conscious recollection yields a no response; hence, the tendency to endorse an item from List F as old relies on a *failure* of R. An estimate of R can thus be obtained as the simple difference between the two conditions. See text for details.

with probability $P(R)$, or recollection fails but unconscious activation comes to the rescue with probability $P(U) \times [1 - P(R)]$. For List F items, by contrast, a yes response can only occur if R fails but U succeeds, hence $P(Exclusion) = P(U) \times [1 - P(R)]$. It follows that the difference in performance between the two conditions provides an estimate for R:

$$P(R) = P(Inclusion) - P(Exclusion). \qquad (6.2)$$

Once an estimate of R has been obtained, U can be computed by substitution as

$$P(U) = P(Exclusion)/[1 - P(R)]. \qquad (6.3)$$

When the PDP is applied to recognition memory tests, the procedure yields estimates of R and U that are in line with the expectations of dual-process models. To illustrate, Table 6.1 shows the proportion of yes responses to test items in Experiment 1 of Yonelinas (1994). Consider the estimates in the bottom panel of the table, which were obtained by application of Equations 6.2 and 6.3 to the data in the top panel: In line with the expectation of dual-process models, activation-driven responding (captured by U) does not differ with list length, consonant with

Table 6.1 Proportion of Yes Responses on a Recognition Test in Experiment 1 of Yonelinas (1994)

Condition/Estimate of Memory Component	Short List	Long List
Condition		
Inclusion[a]	.78	.70
Exclusion[b]	.22	.30
New test item[c]	.09	.14
Estimate		
Recollection (R)	.56	.40
Activation (U)	.50	.50

Note: In the experiment, people were tested on both lists, and the data in the table are for both tests. For ease of exposition, our description focuses on a single test only, for the list called M.
a. Correct yes responses to items from List M.
b. Erroneous yes responses to items from List F.
c. Erroneous yes responses (i.e., false alarms) to new items.

the notion that an item's presentation boosts its activation by a constant amount irrespective of other factors such as list length. Conversely, recollection-driven responding (R) declines with list length, consonant with the notion that items become harder to retrieve as list length increases.

Similarly, when the PDP is applied to experiments that compare explicit and implicit memory tests, the empirical estimates of R and U are typically in line with theoretical expectations. For example, when a conventional levels-of-processing manipulation (semantic encoding tasks vs. nonsemantic encoding) is applied to the inclusion and exclusion conditions, $P(R)$ varies considerably between encoding conditions, whereas $P(U)$ remains invariant (e.g., Toth, Reingold, & Jacoby, 1994).[9]

Can we therefore conclude that the PDP yields pristine estimates of the contributions of conscious and unconscious forms of memory? Does the PDP solve the "conscious-contamination" problem? To answer this question, we must begin by considering the assumptions underlying the procedure. First, the PDP assumes that the two memory components are independent of each other; this assumption is crucial because Equation 6.3 relies on statistical independence:[10] If other assumptions are made about the relationship between R and U, a very different equation is implied (Buchner, Erdfelder, & Vaterrodt-Plünnecke, 1995; Joordens & Merikle, 1993). Second, the PDP assumes that R cannot be in error (i.e., one cannot erroneously recollect an extra-list item or an item from List M to have been on List F; Ratcliff, Van Zandt, & McKoon, 1995). Third, as already noted, the PDP assumes that the operation of U is unaffected by changes in context or instruction.

Next, at the risk of stating the obvious, we must realize that the PDP is a *model* rather than just "an ingenious methodology to obtain separate estimates of familiarity and intentional recollection within a single paradigm" (Light & La Voie, 1993, p. 223). This realization immediately gives rise to two important issues: Are the model's parameters identifiable, and is the model testable? For this simple model, we can resolve those issues without analysis of the Jacobian. Concerning identifiability, brief inspection of Equations 6.2 and 6.3 reveals that there is a one-to-one mapping between any possible outcome and the parameter values—namely, the estimates of R and U.[11] Hence the model's parameters are identifiable. Is the model testable? Clearly, it is not: The model necessarily yields a perfect fit for any possible set of data with the parameters that are computed from those data. That is, in the same way that one can always compute d' and β within a two-parameter signal detection framework, there will always be estimates of R and U that one can obtain from any given set of data. The implications are clear and were noted earlier in the context of signal detection theory: Interpretation of the parameter values *presumes* the validity of the model. That is, because the two-parameter signal detection model always fits perfectly, it cannot be invalidated on the basis of its failure to fit data—if this sounds like tautology, it is, but it clarifies the point. It is useful to explore the implications of this fact.

Ratcliff et al. (1995) used a variant of the model recovery technique outlined earlier (see Figure 6.2) to test the PDP. Recall that the true origin of the data is known when the model recovery technique is applied, and emphasis is on whether the model under examination fits its own data better than those generated from competing different models. Ratcliff et al. thus used a single-process model (SAM; Raaijmakers & Shiffrin, 1981) and a dual-process model other than the PDP (Atkinson & Juola, 1973) to generate data to which the PDP was applied. SAM was used to simulate the list length results of Experiment 1 of Yonelinas (1994) that are shown in Table 6.1, and Atkinson and Juola's model was used to generate data for a further experiment involving another manipulation (the details are not relevant here). Ratcliff et al. (1995) found that the PDP yielded interpretable parameter estimates in both cases. This is not surprising because we have already seen that any outcome, whether real data or simulation results, yields meaningful estimates of R and U. The difficulty, however, is that in one case, the data were generated by a single-process model that removes any meaning of the R and U parameters—they are simply not psychologically relevant to the situation. In the other case, even though the data were generated by a dual-process model, the PDP recovered estimates of R and U that were very different from the true probabilities with which the two processes contributed to data generation. In neither case did the PDP provide any indication that the data did not conform to its assumptions—quite unlike the SAM model, which failed to account for the data generated by a dual-process model. Those findings imply that "what is learned about conscious versus unconscious processes in recognition is theory dependent, and process dissociation does not provide a theory-independent means of examining memory processes" (Ratcliff et al., 1995, p. 359).

What are the implications for users of the PDP? First, we suggest that the procedure, and other tools like it, can only be used with confidence in situations in which the applicability of its basic assumptions is beyond doubt. Unfortunately, given the present state of knowledge in which single-process models of recognition are strong contenders (Dunn, 2004), those situations are rare. Second, and most important, the PDP can be augmented by incorporating more detailed assumptions about the processes involved. When those assumptions are made and "richer" data are collected (e.g., collecting confidence ratings in addition to yes and no responses; cf. Wickens, 1982), the PDP becomes testable. It is noteworthy to point out the parallels with signal detection theory, which we mentioned earlier in this chapter: Like the PDP, the signal detection model is not testable—despite d' and β being computable—when only hit and false alarm rates are considered. And like the PDP, signal detection theory becomes testable when richer data (i.e., confidence ratings) are collected.

Recent developments of the PDP are therefore on much firmer ground than the original version that we focused on here for pedagogical reasons. For example, Buchner and colleagues (e.g., Buchner et al., 1995; Buchner & Erdfelder, 1996) have developed multinomial measurement models that implement the PDP under more constrained circumstances, Rouder et al. (2008) have developed a variant of the PDP that does not rely on aggregating of data across subjects, and Wixted (2007) and DeCarlo (2008) have tested a (testable) variant of the PDP against various signal detection models. The fact that the latter two tests did not favor the PDP is interesting but not of direct relevance in the present context; what matters is that an untestable but attractive model was made testable by revision of the model in conjunction with enhanced data collection. Our final message, therefore, is that one generally should not settle for an identifiable but untestable model; generally, with some more development effort, testability can be achieved.

6.3   Drawing Lessons and Conclusions From Modeling

Suppose, then, that our model is identifiable, testable, and unlikely to have overfitted the data. What lessons and conclusions can we draw from our efforts? As we discussed in Chapter 5, the goal of formal modeling is not simply to find a winning model. Finding a winning model can tell us an awful lot, but this usually requires some more exploration on the part of the modeler, and the final report will almost certainly require a well-crafted general discussion that converts the results of the modeling into some clear statements about psychological theory. We will now discuss a number of ways in which researchers have used formal models to make arguments about psychological processes. In terms of Figure 2.8, we are moving from the connection between data and predictions (gray area at the bottom) to the purpose of modeling: relating people to models (unshaded area at the top of Figure 2.8).

6.3.1   Explorations of a Model: Effects of Parameters

We begin by considering the way in which a model's parameters may provide psychological insights. Free parameters are valuable tools. First of all, in some descriptive models (see Section 1.4.2) and in process characterization models (see Section 1.4.3), the principal results of the modeling *are* the parameter estimates— for example, in Chapter 1, we used the multinomial tree model to identify the locus of the word frequency effect in serial recall, and our conclusions were entirely based on the pattern of parameter estimates. Parameter estimates can also be of considerable value with process models. In Chapter 5, we discussed the analysis of parameter values to answer questions about the underlying psychological processes that we could not have answered by directly analyzing the data with standard statistics. Analyzing and exploring the behavior of parameters can also give insight into the workings of a model and consequently highlight novel aspects of our data.

6.3.1.1   Analyzing the Model

One reason for the utility of parameters is that they permit further analysis of the model's behavior. For example, manipulation of a parameter can isolate the contribution of a particular process to the model's predictions.

One example comes from Lewandowsky's (1999) dynamic distributed model of serial recall. The model is a connectionist model in which items are stored in an auto-associative network and compete for recall based on their encoding strength and their overlap with a positional recall cue. One assumption made in Lewandowsky's simulations and shared with other models (e.g., Farrell & Lewandowsky, 2002; Henson, 1998; Page & Norris, 1998b) was that recall of items was followed by *response suppression* to limit their further recall. In Lewandowsky's model, this was accomplished by partially unlearning an item once it had been recalled. Following Lewandowsky and Li (1994), Lewandowsky (1999) claimed that response suppression in his model was tied to the recency effect in serial recall, the increase in recall accuracy for the last one or two items on a list. Intuitively, this sounds reasonable: By the time the last few items are

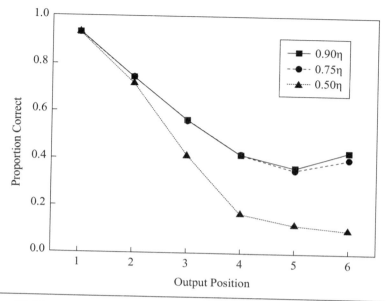

Figure 6.7 The effect of the response suppression parameter η in Lewandowsky's (1999) connectionist model of serial recall. Figure taken from Lewandowsky, S. (1999). Redintegration and response suppression in serial recall: A dynamic network model. *International Journal of Psychology, 34*, 434–446. Reprinted with permission of the publisher, Taylor & Francis Ltd.

being recalled, most other recall competitors (the other list items) have been removed from recall competition, thereby lending an advantage to those last few list items. To confirm this, Lewandowsky (1999) ran a simulation varying the extent of response suppression. The results, reproduced in Figure 6.7, reinforce the link between response suppression and recency in his model: As the extent of response suppression is reduced, so is recall accuracy for the last few items.

6.3.1.2 Making Predictions

Parameter values may also lead to interesting predictions, simply because their particular best-fitting estimates are suggestive of a specific outcome. Suppose you present people in an experiment with a long list of unrelated pairs of words for study. The pair *green–table* might be followed by *book–city* and so on. Every so often, you test people's memory by presenting them with a probe pair (differentiated from study pairs by being bracketed by "?"s). The probe pairs are either intact (*green–table*) or rearranged (*book–table*), and people must discriminate between them. Surely you would observe more forgetting the longer you delay the test of an intact pair? That is, if we re-present *green–table* after only one or two inter-vening other pairs, surely people are more likely to recognize it as intact than if 10 or even 20 intervening items have been presented?

The (surprising) empirical answer to this question was stimulated by a param-eter estimate. Murdock (1989) conducted a simulation of paired-associate exper-iments, such as the one just described, and found that the estimate of the model's forgetting parameter, α, was close to 1, where $\alpha = 1$ means no forgetting. That is, seemingly unreasonably, the model suggested that paired-associate lists were subject to very little forgetting over time.

This counterintuitive expectation was confirmed in a series of experiments by Hockley (1992). Using the method just described, Hockley showed that perfor-mance in associative recognition declined very little, even when people studied up to 20 intervening new pairs. (And this was not a methodological "bug" because at the same time, memory for single items declined considerably—hence there was something special about the resilience of associations.)

6.3.2   Demonstrations of Sufficiency

As discussed in Chapter 2, a demonstration of sufficiency involves showing that a set of assumptions, implemented in a formal model, is able to either qualitatively or quantitatively account for one or more psychological phenomena. The large majority of modeling exercises in cognitive psychology fall into this category. In particular, journals such as *Psychological Review* and *Psychonomic Bulletin & Review* regularly publish papers in which a model is shown to account for a set of benchmark data from some domain of psychological enquiry.

We noted at the outset (Chapter 2; see in particular Figure 2.2) that demon-strations of sufficiency typically constitute a fairly weak claim. This skeptical attitude is necessary because in principle, there always exist other architectures or assumptions that can produce the same type of behavior as our favored model. That said, there are instances in which merely showing that a model *can* handle the data is impressive and noteworthy. Those instances arise when the model in question is a priori—that is, on the basis of intuition or prior research—*unlikely* to handle the data. We consider two such cases here.

Our first example involves the well-known application of a parallel distributed processing model to word recognition and naming (Seidenberg & McClelland, 1989). Seidenberg and McClelland showed that their connectionist model, in which all knowledge about the mapping of orthography to phonology was assumed to be learned from pairings of printed words and phoneme sequences, could account for a key set of findings in word naming and recognition. In word naming, their model was shown to produce word frequency effects (high-frequency words were named faster than low-frequency words), regularity effects (words with regular pronunciation, such as *MINT*, are named faster than irregular words such as *PINT*), and the interaction between regularity and frequency (the regularity effect is larger for low-frequency words). The model was also shown to account for a number of other aspects of the data, including neighborhood size effects and developmental trends, including developmental dyslexia.

What does this actually tell us? Arguably, the most interesting and important claim to arise from Seidenberg and McClelland's (1989) results is that a model that is not programmed with any rules can nonetheless produce rule-like behavior. It has often been assumed that regularity effects reflect the difference between application of a rule in the case of regular words (e.g., INT is pronounced as in *MINT*) and the use of lexical knowledge to name irregular exceptions (the INT in *PINT*). Seidenberg and McClelland's simulations show that a single process is sufficient for naming regular and irregular words. Similar claims have been made in other areas of development, where it has been shown that apparent stage-like behavior (of the type shown in Figure 3.7) can follow from continuous changes in nonlinear connectionist models (Munakata & McClelland, 2003). Critics have highlighted issues with Seidenberg and McClelland's account of reading more generally (e.g., Coltheart, Curtis, Atkins, & Haller, 1993), arguing that the model does not provide a sufficient account of nonword reading or different types of dyslexia. Issues have also been raised regarding the falsifiability of connectionist models of the type represented by Seidenberg and McClelland's model (e.g., Massaro, 1988). Nonetheless, the model constitutes a useful foil to dual-route models of reading.

Our second example comes from the work on the *remember-know* distinction in recognition memory. Recognition memory looks at our ability to recognize whether we have seen or otherwise encountered an object before, usually in some experimental context. The remember-know distinction taps into an assumed dissociation between two processes or types of information that underlie recognition memory: a process of conscious recollection and a feeling of "knowing" that the object has been encountered before but without any attendant episodic details of that experience (Gardiner, 1988). (Note how this dichotomy resembles the two-process views of recognition considered earlier in this chapter; e.g., Yonelinas, 1994.) The remember-know distinction can be operationalized by asking participants after each recognition response ("Yes, I saw the item on the list," or "No, I did not") whether they "remember" (i.e., have a conscious recollection of) seeing the item or whether they simply "know" that the item has been encountered previously. Evidence for a dissociation comes from the finding that certain variables independently affect the frequency of remember and know responses (e.g., amnesiacs vs. controls: Schacter, Verfaellie, & Anes, 1997; item modality: Gregg & Gardiner, 1994) or can have opposite effects on remember and know responses

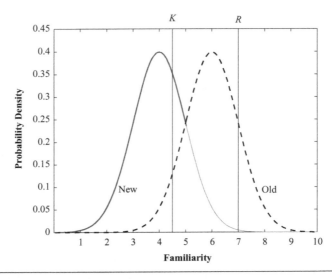

Figure 6.8 A unidimensional signal detection model of remember-know judgments in recognition memory.

(Gardiner & Java, 1990). Although it seems intuitively plausible that the empirical remember-know distinction must be tapping some underlying distinction between recollective and non-recollective processing, it has been demonstrated that a simple signal detection theory (SDT) model of recognition memory can also account for remember-know judgments.

The basics of this model (Donaldson, 1996) are illustrated in Figure 6.8. It is assumed that each time a recognition probe is presented, a measure of familiarity of that probe is calculated. The amount of familiarity depends on whether the item is "old" (was seen in the study phase) or "new." Generally, items previously seen are more familiar. Nonetheless, there is some variability in familiarity, such that there are overlapping distributions (probability density functions or PDFs) for the old and new items. A further assumption is that recognition decisions are made on the basis of criteria, corresponding to remember (R) and know (K) judgments. If the familiarity falls above the R criterion, the participant produces a "remember" response. If the familiarity does not exceed the R criterion but still surpasses the K criterion, then a "know" response is given. Finally, if the familiarity falls below the K criterion, then the item is considered to be new.

The critical feature of the model in Figure 6.8 is that it is a unidimensional model: There is only one dimension of familiarity along which items vary and only one process giving rise to remember-know responses. Several researchers have shown that this simple unidimensional account does surprisingly well at fitting data from the remember-know paradigm (Donaldson, 1996; Dunn, 2004;

Rotello & Macmillan, 2006; Wixted & Stretch, 2004). In particular, Dunn (2004) showed that the model depicted in Figure 6.8 could account for cases where manipulations had selective or opposing effects on remember and know responses by changes in both the separation of the densities in Figure 6.8 and in one or both of the response criteria. For example, Schacter et al. (1997) showed that amnesiacs give fewer "remember" responses to old items than controls but that both groups are roughly equal in their frequency of "know" responses. Dunn's fit of the model showed it to give an excellent quantitative fit to these results, and examination of model parameters showed how the model could account for the hitherto challenging data: The fit to the control data produced a larger d' and larger estimates of the K and R criteria, with a larger change in the K criterion to account for the lack of change in the frequency of K responses. Although this somewhat begs the question of why these groups should differ in their criteria, an argument can be made that the criteria should scale with the quality of an individual's memory (as measured by the difference between the new and old curves in Figure 6.8: Hirshman, 1995).

This is a clear example of a model's success: A model that intuitively might not appear able to account for the data in fact does. One consequence of such successes has been a more careful consideration of what remember and know responses might actually correspond to: Dunn (2004) has presented analyses of the relation of remember and know responses to other possible responses available in the recognition task, and Wixted (2004a) demonstrated the compatibility between the criterion treatment of remember and know responses illustrated in Figure 6.8 and other responses that effectively recruit multiple criteria, such as confidence ratings.

Hirshman and Master (1997) and, later, Hirshman, Lanning, Master, and Henzler (2002) argued that the signal detection account also served a valuable role even if the weight of evidence falls against the theory. Hirshman et al. (2002) were responding to the claim that since some empirical results were clearly problematic for the SDT account of remember-know judgments, the theory should be abandoned. The critics of the SDT account of remember-know judgments hold that the model does not capture the critical qualitative distinction between "remember" and "know" responses (including neurophysiological dissociations), the argued differential extent to which these responses reflect access to conscious awareness and relate to the self (e.g., Conway, Dewhurst, Pearson, & Sapute, 2001; Gardiner & Gregg, 1997). A statement that summarizes the view of SDT from this perspective and that has been subsequently quoted by several studies comes from Gardiner and Conway (1999), cited in Hirshman et al. (2002): "[As] trace strength models will always fall far short of providing anything approaching a full understanding of states of memory awareness, it seems to us that it makes sense to turn to other approaches" (p. 153).

Our fundamental assumption in this book is that no theory is correct; we therefore urge some caution when assessing strong claims such as this. From the perspective we advocate here, and one adopted by many in the modeling community, theoretical development is the continuous refinement of models on the basis of their failures and successes, as well as testing of a variety of theories rather than focusing specifically on the development and testing of a single theory. Hirshman et al. additionally pointed out that even though the SDT account might be "wrong" (i.e., insufficient in its account of a number of key results), it still serves a valuable purpose in showing to what extent a particular set of data specifically support some alternative explanation, such as the dual-process theory usually considered the alternative to the single-process SDT model. In other words, we can use the SDT model to assess claims of necessity (as opposed to sufficiency) from alternative models. If SDT and some other account are equally compatible with the results of an experiment, we should be very careful in then concluding that the data provide support for the alternative.

6.3.3   Demonstrations of Necessity

A stronger claim to be made from formal modeling is that of *necessity*. As the name implies, this involves arguing that a particular assumption or set of assumptions is necessary to the model's success in accounting for the data. Estes (2002) provides a very clear definition of how we can demonstrate this: We need to change the assumptions of the model and show that the changed assumptions lead to an incorrect prediction about the data. In the framework of Figure 2.2, we need to show that there are no other explanations for our target data and that there is a one-to-one mapping between the model and the data.

One way of achieving this is by use of the model selection methods outlined in Chapter 5. Recall that statistics such as the Akaike Information Criterion (AIC) and Bayesian Information Criterion (BIC), as well as their associated Akaike and BIC weights, give us valuable information about the comparative success of the models (if you don't remember, now would be a good time to go back and refresh). By implication, the model weights tell us about the evidence that each model's assumptions are necessary for accounting for the data. What the model weights tell us depends on the exact pattern of weights. Often, we will find that one model has a weight close to 1 and that all other models have weights close to 0. In this case, we have good evidence that the mechanisms built into the winning model are necessary to explaining the data, in the context of the set of models being compared. On the other hand, we will sometimes find that there is some uncertainty in the modeling results, where two or more models have nontrivial weights. In some cases, this can still provide strong evidence in favor of a particular assumption.

As an example, Table 6.2 shows model selection results from Liu and Smith's (2009) examination of time accuracy functions obtained from a response signal task. In this task, participants were given a stimulus about which they needed to make a decision (e.g., whether a Gabor patch is oriented to the left or right; Carrasco & McElree, 2001) and were signaled to respond at various time points after onset of the stimulus. The resulting time accuracy functions have a characteristic shape that resembles an exponential function. Accordingly, common practice is to fit an exponential function to the data, as a purely descriptive model, and estimate values for three parameters: the intercept of the function (the signal delay time where accuracy exceeds chance levels), the asymptote of the function, and the rate at which asymptote is approached. The rate of the exponential is of greatest theoretical interest, as it is taken as a measure of the rate of visual information processing.

In this framework, we can ask whether a specific manipulation affects the rate, asymptote, intercept, or some combination of these variables. For example, Carrasco and McElree (2001) gave participants a visual search task, in which observers were to determine whether a stimulus composed of a pattern of lines—the target—was tilted to the left or right; other distractors on the screen were composed of similar line patterns but were vertically oriented. Carrasco and McElree (2001) examined whether pre-cueing the location of the target (by placing a cue at the target location before target onset) had effects on rate, asymptote, or intercept (or some combination of these) by fitting a time accuracy function to their data. They found that the pre-cue affected both the discriminability of the target (as captured by the asymptote of the exponential) and the rate of approach to asymptote (i.e., the rate of information extraction). To illustrate the procedure of model selection with this family of models, Liu and Smith (2009) fit eight models to some hypothetical response signal data. The eight models all represented the same exponential model for the time accuracy function but varied in whether various aspects of the exponential were affected by the pre-cue. Specifically, Liu and Smith (2009) factorially varied whether each parameter (rate, asymptote, or intercept) was fixed between cued and uncued locations or was allowed to vary. With a few exceptions, these models are not nested within each other. Accordingly, the AIC or BIC is an appropriate model comparison tool to use; following Liu and Smith (2009), we consider the BIC here.

Table 6.2 shows the results of their model fitting. The first column labels the models A, R, and I, respectively, which stand for asymptote, rate, and intercept, and 1 versus 2 indicates where a single parameter was shared between cued and uncued locations (1) or whether that parameter was allowed to freely vary

Table 6.2 BIC Differences and BIC Weights for the Eight Time Accuracy Models of Liu and Smith (2009)

Model	ΔBIC	w_{BIC}
1A-1R-1I	26.36	0.00
2A-1R-1I	2.18	0.18
1A-2R-1I	8.42	0.01
1A-1R-2I	12.36	0.00
2A-2R-1I	2.96	0.12
2A-1R-2I	0	0.53
1A-2R-2I	10.68	0.00
2A-2R-2I	2.39	0.16

between the two (2). The next column shows BIC differences—from the smallest value of BIC—calculated from Liu and Smith's (2009) Table 2, and the final column shows the BIC weights calculated from the BIC differences. Although there is one model that stands out (2A-1R-2I), the evidence for that model is not strong. Several other models have nontrivial BIC weights: the 2A-1R-1I model, the 2A-2R-1I model, and the 2A-2R-2I model. All these models have in common the assumption that the asymptote differs between cued and uncued locations, although they differ in whether they additionally allow changes in rate or intercept or both. Notwithstanding their heterogeneity, when considered jointly, the models provide convincing evidence for a change in asymptote. The higher weight for the 2A-1R-2I model provides some additional evidence about changes in the other two parameters, but this aspect of the evidence is less strong than the clearly identified changes in asymptote.

Of course, sometimes the evidence is less clear for a particular assumption or set of assumptions, or some further investigation might be needed. McKinley and Nosofsky (1995) compared a number of models of people's ability to categorize stimuli where the categories were ill-defined (see their Figure 6 for an illustration of their complicated category structure). One model examined by McKinley and Nosofsky was a deterministic version of the Generalized Context Model (GCM) (Nosofsky, 1986). This is the same GCM model we discussed in Chapter 1, and we'll talk more about the deterministic version of that model in Chapter 7. McKinley and Nosofsky also examined four versions of decision-bound theory, in which participants are assumed to carve up the stimulus space into categories using decision boundaries.

Table 6.3 shows BIC weights for individual participants and the group average for the five models fit to McKinley and Nosofsky's (1995) Experiment 2; these values were calculated from McKinley and Nosofsky's Experiment 2, taking into account the number of trials modeled (300). The mean BIC weights

Table 6.3 BIC Weights for Five Categorization Models From McKinley and Nosofsky (1995)

Participant	GCQ(7)	GCM(D)(6)	QNET (10)	GDQC (12)	QUARB (15)
1	0.00	0.99	0.00	0.01	0.00
2	0.00	0.00	0.08	0.80	0.12
3	0.00	0.00	0.00	0.34	0.66
4	0.00	0.99	0.00	0.01	0.00
5	0.01	0.00	0.72	0.27	0.00
6	0.00	0.00	0.00	0.00	1.00
7	0.00	0.34	0.00	0.65	0.01
8	0.00	0.92	0.00	0.01	0.07
9	0.00	0.13	0.00	0.86	0.00
10	0.00	0.69	0.00	0.31	0.00
11	0.00	0.00	0.00	0.01	0.99
mean	0.00	0.37	0.07	0.30	0.26

Note. The numbers in brackets after model names are the number of free parameters for that model. GCQ = general quadratic classifier (Ashby, 1992a); GCM(D) = deterministic version of the generalized context model (Ashby & Maddox, 1993; Nosofsky, 1986); QNET = quartic network model; GDQC = general double quadratic classifier; QUARB = quadratic polynomial decision boundary.

show that there is no model that gives a particularly outstanding account of the data. Although the GCM is technically the "best" model, two of the decision-bound models—the GDQC (general double quadratic classifier) and the QUARB (quadratic polynomial decision boundary)—are only slightly worse in their relative fit. Unlike the previous example, it turns out that there is little in common between these three superior models, assumption-wise, and as it stands, we don't seem to have enough information from this data set to reach any general theoretical conclusions. Although this might seem like a negative conclusion, we have actually benefited from the model selection approach by requiring that data link to a specific set of assumptions and showing that this condition is not met.

In any case, McKinley and Nosofsky (1995) explored their fits in more detail and found some further consistencies that clarified the story considerably. Inspection of Table 6.3 shows that a single model often does particularly well for a particular participant; however, which specific model this is varies between participants. McKinley and Nosofsky noted that the participants who performed particularly well on their task (Participants 1, 4, 7, 8, and 10) garnered greater support for GCM. (In practice, this might be a situation to explore the clustering techniques considered in Section 3.2.3.) McKinley and Nosofsky suggested that the poor performance of many of their participants reflected some fundamental limitations on human category learning and that the better fit of the decision-bound models to the data of those participants reflected the greater flexibility of those models.

6.3.3.1   Local Necessity

A weaker form of necessity can be demonstrated by turning assumptions on and off inside a model, as implied in Estes's (2002) formulation. Most models constitute a formal implementation of some theoretical principles together with some ancillary assumptions that are needed for pragmatic reasons (see Chapter 2). As models aim to handle a wider range of phenomena or a specific set of phenomena in more detail, they will almost certainly become more and more complicated, especially when entering a different domain that might require some additional ancillary assumptions. In addition to the danger of our model becoming too complicated to serve any theoretically useful purpose (Bonini's paradox; see Chapter 5), making a model more complicated raises concerns about which assumptions are core to the model's qualitative or quantitative account of the data; Lewandowsky (1993) referred to this as the irrelevant specification problem. In particular, there is a danger that the importance of ancillary assumptions is underestimated; in an extreme case, it may be those ancillary assumptions that are doing most of the work in allowing the model to fit the data! Accordingly, it is often a good idea to specifically remove or modify parts of a model and determine their importance in accounting for the data.

As an example, Lewandowsky, Duncan, and Brown (2004) were interested in how information is forgotten over time in a short-term memory task. One particular theory tested in their paper was a modified version of the SIMPLE model (G. D. A. Brown et al., 2007) that we have discussed in previous chapters (e.g., Section 4.3.2). The main modification was to supplement the time-based forgetting that is at the heart of SIMPLE with a mechanism representing forgetting due to output interference that is independent of time. By implementing two forms of forgetting in SIMPLE, Lewandowsky et al. (2004) were able to make a controlled comparison between those forms of forgetting within the same architecture. Specifically, Lewandowsky et al. (2004) compared the full, modified version of SIMPLE with two restricted versions: one in which time-based forgetting was turned off (by restricting attention to the temporal dimension to 0) and one in which interference-based forgetting was eliminated (by setting the parameter controlling output interference to 0). Across two experiments, the model with time switched off differed little in its fit from the full model, indicating that time per se contributed little to forgetting in Lewandowsky et al.'s short-term memory task. In comparison, turning output interference off led to a significantly worse fit for 15 of their 21 participants. This result indicated that output interference was a significant contributor to the fit of the model to the participants' data and supports the claim that output interference is a major contributor to forgetting from short-term memory, compared to the relatively minor role played by time-based forgetting.

Why doesn't every modeling paper go through such procedures to demonstrate necessity? In the case of within-model comparisons, it is often fairly obvious how a model does or does not handle the data, or it is not possible to turn off an assumption without fundamentally changing the model. For example, the phonological loop model that we implemented in Chapter 2 makes the assumption that traces decay over time. There isn't much point turning decay off in the model since it has no recourse to any other source of forgetting, particularly one that is sensitive to word length, and without forgetting recall would necessarily be perfect. Similarly, we can be confident that the logarithmic compression of time in SIMPLE (Chapters 4—in particular Section 4.3.2—and 5) causes it to produce more recency than primacy because items at different serial positions are otherwise treated identically. In many cases, modelers may go through this process to satisfy themselves of the relationship between the model and the data but leave these additional simulations unreported. In addition, some models are computationally intensive and may not permit model selection; until recently, it has been standard practice in the area of short-term memory to estimate parameters "by eye" (e.g., G.D.A. Brown et al., 2000; Burgess & Hitch, 1999; Farrell & Lewandowsky, 2002; Henson, 1998; Page & Norris, 1998b) because fitting the models to data using the methods in Chapters 4 and 5 would have been unfeasible.

Finally, it must be noted that demonstrations of necessity are always *relative*, in that they are tied to the set of alternative models considered. For example, if McKinley and Nosofsky (1995) had examined only the four decision boundary models in modeling their categorization data (unlikely, given that they are proponents of an exemplar account of categorization), they might have concluded that only a complicated quadratic decision-bound model is able to account for the data. Although this appears to be the case with respect to the decision-bound models examined, the existence of a quite different exemplar account suggests this assumption to be merely sufficient. It follows that a claim of necessity will be strengthened if the set of models being compared is (a) large and (b) heterogeneous. It also highlights that a claim of absolute necessity is not really tenable. Can we ever be confident that we have explored all possible models and all possible variants of those models? No. The best we can do is identify existing alternative models that might offer an account of our data and compare those models. One rewarding aspect of science is that it is continually "under construction," and major developments in a field usually come from a researcher introducing a new theory or spotting an explanation for a phenomenon that has not previously been considered.

6.3.4   Summary

In the end, your goal as a modeler is not only to fit one or more models to some data, and perhaps perform some model selection, but also to communicate the implications of these results to others. Explaining to your reader why a particular model was able to account for the data—and why other models failed to do so—will be essential if you want to convince that reader of the role of a particular mechanism, process, or representation; we assume that's why you want to do modeling, right? When doing this, it is especially important to keep in mind that your reader will not necessarily be familiar with the model(s) you are discussing or even with modeling generally. Even if the technical details of your work are opaque to such readers, in an area such as psychology, it is imperative that the implications of your work are apparent to modelers and nonmodelers alike; remember that the latter group will likely constitute the majority of your readership.

Above all, we encourage you to avoid the overly simplistic "winner-takes-all" perspective ("my model fits better than yours, and therefore the assumptions I make are more appropriate") and to adopt a more sophisticated stance ("my model fits better than yours for these reasons, and this is what that tells us about cognition").

Notes

1. It turns out that the "leaving one out at a time" approach is asymptotically identical to model selection based on the Akaike Information Criterion (AIC) that we discussed in Chapter 5 (provided some specific conditions are met; see Stone, 1977, for details).

2. For simplicity, the latter stage lumps together response *selection* and response *output* even though those two processes could quite possibly be considered as separate stages.

3. To illustrate, suppose the comparison process stopped whenever a match was found between the probe and a memorized item. In that case, on the assumption that items from all list positions are tested equally often, the slope for old items would be half of the slope for new items (because on average, only half of the list items would have to be scanned to find a match when the probe is old, whereas a new probe could only be rejected after all items had been scanned).

4. Identifiability follows because a function is invertible if its derivative is invertible—and for that to be the case, the Jacobian has to be full rank; for details, see Bamber and van Santen (1985) and P. L. Smith (1998). Fortunately, for most models, this analysis of the Jacobian can be conducted at *any* arbitrarily chosen θ and then holds for the model overall; for details of when those generalizability conditions hold, see Bamber and van Santen (1985, p. 458).

5. You could also put those commands into an m-file and then execute that program. This achieves the same result, but doing it interactively is more straightforward for simple groups of commands like this.

6. As an exercise, we suggest that you repeat this analysis with three parameters. Specifically, similar to the case of the Sternberg model discussed at the outset, we suggest you replace the intercept, `parms(2)` in Listing 3.3, with *two* values, such that line 4 in that listing now reads as follows: `preds = (data(:,2).* b) + a2+a:`, where a2 is a third free parameter (in `parms(3)`). This will compute seemingly sensible parameter estimates (e.g., we obtained .52, −.43, and .48 in one of our runs, thus yielding an intercept of around zero), but the rank of the Jacobian will be one less (2) than the number of parameters (3), thus confirming the obvious lack of identifiability.

7. The issue of testability can be further subdivided into "qualitative" versus "quantitative" testability (Bamber & van Santen, 1985, 2000). We do not flesh out this distinction here other than to note that quantitative testability is a more stringent criterion and involves models that make exact predictions—as virtually all models considered in this book do. We therefore implicitly refer to *quantitative* testability, as defined by Bamber and van Santen (1985, 2000), throughout our discussion.

8. Strictly speaking, other models can be presumed, but for the present discussion, we assume the equal-variance Gaussian model and focus on β as the chosen descriptive measure of the criterion. We also assume that only a single set of hit and false alarm rates is used to compute the model parameters; the situation is very different when multiple such rates exist and computation of receiver operating characteristic (ROC) curves becomes possible (see, e.g., Pastore, Crawley, Berens, & Skelly, 2003, for details).

9. The principal support for the PDP consists of the broad range of such findings, where R and U behaved as expected on the basis of prior theory, a pattern known as "selective influence." Hirshman (1998) pointed to the flaws in that logic, and Curran and Hintzman (1995) additionally showed that those patterns can be an artifact of data aggregation; however, more recently, Rouder, Lu, Morey, Sun, and Speckman (2008) provided a hierarchical model of the PDP that can circumvent the aggregation problems.

10. Recall that we defined and discussed independence in probability theory in Chapter 4.

11. This statement is a slight oversimplification: If recollection is perfect, $P(Exclusion)$ goes toward 0, in which case $R \simeq 1$ and hence U is undefined.

7

Drawing It All Together: Two Examples

This chapter draws together the entire material presented so far in two detailed examples. The first example involves the WITNESS model of eyewitness identification (Clark, 2003) and in particular its application to the "verbal overshadowing effect" reported by Clare and Lewandowsky (2004). The second example involves a head-to-head comparison of some models of categorization, thereby illustrating the concepts of model selection developed in Chapter 5.

These two examples illustrate several important contrasts: First, WITNESS is based on a stochastic simulation involving a large number of replications, whereas the categorization models are based on analytic solutions and hence provide predictions that are not subject to sampling variability. Second, WITNESS considers the data at the aggregate level because each subject in an eyewitness identification experiment provides only a single response, and response proportions are thus only available in the aggregate, whereas the categorization models can be fit to the data from individuals. Third, the WITNESS example is based on a descriptive approach relying on a least squares criterion (i.e., root mean squared deviation [RMSD]; see Chapter 3), whereas the comparison of the categorization models involves maximum likelihood estimation and model comparison (see Chapters 4 and 5).

7.1 WITNESS: Simulating Eyewitness Identification

In 1979, a Catholic priest, Father Bernard Pagano, was on trial in New Jersey on multiple charges of armed robbery. The prosecution's case was supported by the fact that the defendant had been positively identified by seven (7!) independent eyewitnesses. After the prosecution had presented its case, the actual perpetrator, a Mr. Ronald Clouser, came forward and confessed to the crimes after having been identified and located by a former FBI agent. The charges against Father Pagano were dropped (see Searleman & Herrmann, 1994, for a recounting of this intriguing case). How could so many eyewitnesses have mistakenly identified an innocent person? Lest one dismiss this as an isolated case, Wells et al. (1998) presented a sample of 40 cases in which wrongfully convicted defendants were exonerated on the basis of newly available DNA evidence. In 90% of those cases, eyewitness identification evidence was involved—in one case, a person was erroneously identified by five different witnesses.

Not surprisingly, therefore, the study of eyewitness behavior has attracted considerable attention during the past few decades. In eyewitness identification experiments, subjects typically watch a (staged) crime and are then presented with a lineup consisting of a number of photographs of people (for an overview, see Wells & Seelau, 1995). The lineup typically contains one individual who committed the (staged) crime, known as the perpetrator, and a number of others who had nothing to do with the crime, known as foils. Occasionally, "blank" lineups may be presented that consist only of foils. There is little doubt that people's performance in these experiments is far from accurate, with false identification rates— that is, identification of a foil—in excess of 70% (e.g., Clare & Lewandowsky, 2004; Wells, 1993). The laboratory results thus confirm and underscore the known problems with real-world identification evidence.

The first computational model of eyewitness identification, appropriately called WITNESS, was proposed by Clark (2003). WITNESS provided the first detailed description of the behavior of eyewitnesses when confronted with a police lineup or its laboratory equivalent, and it has successfully accounted for several diagnostic results (Clark, 2003, 2008).

7.1.1   WITNESS: Architecture

WITNESS belongs to the class of direct-access matching models of memory (Clark & Gronlund, 1996), in which recognition decisions are based on direct comparisons between the test items—that is, the people in the lineup—and the contents of memory. In WITNESS, the only relevant content of memory is assumed to be the face of the perpetrator. WITNESS is based on the following architectural principles:

(1) All stimuli are represented as random vectors $(f_1, f_2, \ldots, f_k)$ with features drawn from a uniform distribution with mean zero (and range $-.5$ to $+.5$). One of those vectors represents the perpetrator, whereas the others represent the foils in the lineup.

(2) Encoding into memory is assumed to be imperfect, such that only a proportion s ($0 < s < 1$) of features are veridically copied into a memory vector (called M) when the perpetrator is witnessed during commission of the crime. The value of s is typically estimated from the data as a free parameter.[1] The remaining $1 - s$ features are stored incorrectly and hence are replaced in memory by another sample from the uniform distribution.

(3) At the heart of WITNESS's explanatory power is its ability to handle rather complex similarity relationships between the perpetrator and the foils in a lineup, which vary with the way foils are selected (see Clark, 2003, for details). For the present example, we simplified this structure to be captured by a single parameter, sim, which determined the proportion of features ($0 < sim < 1$) that were identical between any two vectors, with the remainder ($1 - sim$) being randomly chosen from the same uniform distribution (range $-.5$ to $+.5$). Thus, all foils in the lineup resembled the perpetrator to the extent determined by the sim parameter.

(4) At retrieval, all faces in the lineup are compared to memory by computing the dot product between the vector representing each face and M. The dot product, d, is a measure of similarity between two vectors and is computed as

$$d = \sum_{i=1}^{N} g_i M_i, \tag{7.1}$$

where N is the number of features in each vector and i the subscript running over those features. The greater the dot product, the greater the similarity between the two vectors. In WITNESS, the recognition decision relies on evaluating the set of dot products between the faces in the lineup and M.

(5) The complete WITNESS model differentiates between three response types: an identification of a lineup member ("it's him"), a rejection of the entire lineup ("the perpetrator is not present"), and a "don't know" response that was made when there was insufficient evidence for an identification (Clark, 2003). For the present example, we simplified this decision rule by eliminating the "don't know" category in accordance with the experimental method to which we applied the model. This simplified decision rule reduces to a single comparison: If the best match between a lineup member and memory exceeds a criterion, c_{rec}, the model chooses that best match as its response. If all matches fell below c_{rec}, the model rejects the lineup and records a "not present" response.

Because each participant in an eyewitness identification experiment provides only a single response, the data are best considered in the aggregate. In particular, the data consist of the proportion of participants in a given condition who identify the perpetrator or one of the foils, or say "not present." The model predictions are likewise generated by aggregating across numerous replications, each of which involved a different set of randomly constructed stimulus vectors. Each replication can be taken to represent a unique participant who catches a uniquely encoded glimpse of the perpetrator.[2]

7.1.2   WITNESS and Verbal Overshadowing

A common task of eyewitnesses is to provide police with a verbal description of the perpetrator, in the hope that this may lead to the apprehension of a suspect for subsequent identification from a lineup. Although providing a verbal description is standard police procedure, Schooler and Engstler-Schooler (1990) reported an unexpected adverse side effect of verbal descriptions. In their study, subjects viewed a staged crime and then either provided a verbal description of the perpetrator (verbalization condition) or completed an irrelevant filler task (control condition). Following this manipulation, witnesses attempted to identify the perpetrator from a photo lineup. The verbalization condition yielded significantly fewer correct identifications than the control condition. Schooler and Engstler-Schooler termed this adverse influence of verbalization on identification the *verbal overshadowing* effect. This initial study was followed by much research activity, and a meta-analysis of a large number of published and unpublished studies by Meissner and Brigham (2001) confirmed the presence of a small, but significant, negative effect of verbalization on identification accuracy. How might one explain the verbal overshadowing effect? Why would verbalization disrupt one's visual memory of a person's face?

There are several candidate explanations for verbal overshadowing, and the example below is using the WITNESS model to differentiate between them. We focus on two candidates, which for brevity we refer to as the *memory* and *criterion* explanation, respectively. According to the memory explanation, the verbalization harms and disrupts one's memory for the perpetrator, for example, when the verbal description inadvertently entails generation of incorrect elements. According to the criterion explanation, by contrast, verbalization does not alter the memory of the perpetrator but adjusts one's response criterion upward. That is, owing to the subjective difficulty most people experience during an attempt to describe a person, they become more reluctant to choose someone subsequently from the lineup—thus giving rise to the *appearance* of impaired recognition accuracy.

The two explanations can be empirically differentiated by manipulating the type of lineup and the decision required of subjects: First, in a forced-choice situation, in which people *must* identify someone from the lineup, the criterion explanation predicts that no verbal overshadowing should occur. If a choice is mandatory, then a response criterion does not matter. The memory explanation, by contrast, predicts the presence of verbal overshadowing even with forced-choice lineups.

Second, in an optional-choice situation, in which people may make a "not there" response, both explanations expect verbal overshadowing to be present; however, the criterion explanation expects the effect to arise from an increase in (erroneous) "not there" responses, whereas the memory explanation expects the effect to involve primarily an increase in false identifications (of a foil) from the lineup.

Third, if the perpetrator is not present in an optional-choice lineup (which corresponds to a situation in which the police have apprehended the wrong person), then the criterion explanation predicts an *increase* in accuracy after verbalization. If verbalization renders people more conservative, thus making an identification less likely, accuracy in perpetrator-absent lineups should be enhanced. The memory explanation, by contrast, expects overshadowing to have a detrimental effect even with perpetrator-absent lineups because an impaired memory should impair accuracy irrespective of whether or not the perpetrator is presented.

Clare and Lewandowsky (2004) reported three experiments that sought to differentiate between those explanations. The results of all studies clearly confirmed the predictions of the criterion explanation and, by implication, rejected the memory explanation. We focus on two of their studies (their Experiments 1 and 2) that involved an optional-choice lineup in which the perpetrator either was or was not present (Experiment 1) and a forced-choice lineup in which the perpetrator was always present (Experiment 2). Table 7.1 summarizes the results from those two studies.

In each experiment, there were three conditions: a control condition in which people had to perform a verbal task that was unrelated to eyewitness identification and two verbalization conditions that differed only with respect to what people were to emphasize in their descriptions—namely, holistic aspects of the face (i.e., traits such as intelligence, friendliness, etc.) or featural aspects (i.e., hair color, shape of nose, skin tone, etc.). In Experiment 2, in which an identification was mandated, identification rates did not differ between the three conditions, exactly as predicted by the criterion explanation. In Experiment 1, where an identification was optional, the verbal description conditions differed considerably from the control condition, but the direction of the effect was reversed with lineup type. When the perpetrator was present, people were less accurate after providing a description, whereas when the perpetrator was absent, people were more accurate—but in both instances, this change in accuracy reflected a common tendency to be less likely to identify someone (and, correspondingly, to be more likely to respond "not there") after verbalization.

The data clearly seem to favor the criterion explanation. However, there are at least two reasons why modeling is advisable before the explanation can be accepted: First, we must demonstrate that the explanation *can* be instantiated in a model and that the model can quantitatively handle the data (recall the surprising

Table 7.1 Eyewitness Responses in Two Experiments Reported by Clare and Lewandowsky (2004)

Lineup [a]	Decision	Response Type [b]	Verbalization Condition		
			Control	Holistic	Featural
		Experiment 1			
PP	Optional choice	Hit	.80	.57	.69
		False ID	.13	.06	.12
		Miss	.07	.36	.19
PA	Optional choice	CR	.23	.52	.52
		False ID [c]	.77	.48	.48
		Suspect	.04	.20	.00
		Foil	.73	.28	.48
		Experiment 2			
PP	Forced choice	Hit	.86	.81	.84
		False ID	.14	.19	.16

a. PP = perpetrator present; PA = perpetrator absent.
b. Hit = correct identification; False ID = identification of foil; Miss = erroneous "not there" response; CR = correct rejection.
c. False IDs with the perpetrator-absent lineup are further broken down by "suspect" versus the other foils.

difficulties we faced in Chapter 2 when we tried to instantiate the phonological loop model). Second, we must rule out the possibility that some variant of the memory explanation might handle the data after all. We now present the modeling that resolved both of those issues.

7.1.3   WITNESS in MATLAB

Clare and Lewandowsky (2004) applied WITNESS to the data from all three of their experiments using six free parameters. For this example, we focus on their Experiments 1 and 2 and rely on a slightly simpler five-parameter version of WITNESS that was fit to both studies simultaneously. We begin by presenting the criterion explanation within WITNESS.

Table 7.2 summarizes the parameters and their best-fitting estimates (which you will be able to reproduce by the time you have worked through the MATLAB programs that we discuss next).

The first three parameters are exactly as discussed in Section 7.1.1. The last two parameters, $c_{rec}(H)$ and $c_{rec}(F)$, instantiate the criterion explanation and

Table 7.2 Free Parameters in WITNESS

Parameter		Best-Fitting Estimate
Encoding strength	s	.27
Similarity	sim	.29
Baseline criterion	$c_{rec}(C)$	1.20
Holistic criterion	$c_{rec}(H)$	1.84
Featural criterion	$c_{rec}(F)$	1.64

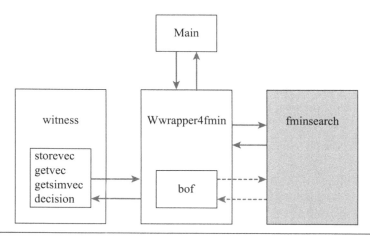

Figure 7.1 The relationship between the MATLAB functions used in the WITNESS simulation. The names in each box refer to the function name(s) and file names. Boxes within a box represent embedded functions. Arrows refer to exchanges of information (via function calls and returns or global variables). Solid arrows represent information exchanges that are managed by the programmer, whereas broken arrows represent exchanges managed by MATLAB. Shading of a box indicates that the function is provided by MATLAB and does not need to be programmed. See text for details.

represent, respectively, the value of the response criterion after holistic and featural verbalization. Aside from altering the setting of the criterion, verbalization has no further effect within this version of WITNESS.[3]

7.1.3.1   *The Calling Sequence*

Our example adheres to the schema introduced in Chapter 3 (Figure 3.2). To guide our presentation, we show the relationship among our various programs in Figure 7.1. The figure is nearly identical to the earlier schema (Figure 3.2) except that the names of the functions have changed to reflect the current situation.

We now present and discuss the various programs, beginning with the function that implements WITNESS and that is called from within `bof`, the function that computes badness of fit. We present the main program and the `Wwrapper4fmin` function later.

7.1.3.2   The WITNESS Function

We begin by presenting in Listing 7.1 the core of the function that implements WITNESS. The function takes a single input argument that contains the current parameter values, and it returns the associated predictions in a single array. In addition, the function uses a "global" variable—defined immediately below the function header—to communicate with other MATLAB programs and functions that are part of the simulation package. Variables that are declared global in MAT-LAB are accessible from within all functions in which they appear in a global statement; this provides another convenient avenue of communication between parts of a large program that does not require input or output arguments.

Listing 7.1 The WITNESS Function

```
 1 function predictions = witness (parms)
 2 % Implementation of the WITNESS model for
 3 % "Computational Modeling in Cognition: Principles ↩
      and Practice"
 4
 5 global consts;
 6
 7 rand ('state', consts.seed)
 8
 9 s    = parms(1);
10 sim  = parms(2);
11 ssp  = sim;
12 paSim= sim;
13 ppSim= sim;
14
15 predictions = zeros (consts.nCond, 3);
16 for reps=1:consts.nRep
17     %obtain perpetrator and perform holdup
18     perp=getvec(consts.n);
19     m=storevec (s, perp);
20
21     %get an innocent suspect
22     inSus=getsimvec(ssp, perp);
23     %create both types of lineup
24     paLineup (1,:)= inSus;
25     ppLineup (1,:)= perp;
```

```
26      for i=2:consts.lSize
27          paLineup (i,:) = getsimvec (paSim, perp);
28          ppLineup (i,:) = getsimvec (ppSim, perp);
29      end
30
31      %eyewitness inspects lineup
32      for i=1:consts.lSize
33          paMatch(i) = dot(paLineup(i,:), m);
34          ppMatch(i) = dot(ppLineup(i,:), m);
35      end
36
37      %witness responds
38      for iLineup=1:consts.nCond
39          if any(iLineup==consts.fChoice)
40              criterion=0;
41          else
42              criterion=parms(consts.ptToCrit(iLineup));
43          end
44          if any(iLineup==consts.paLineup)
45              useMatch = paMatch;
46          else
47              useMatch = ppMatch;
48          end
49          resp = decision (useMatch, criterion);
50          predictions (iLineup, resp) = ↵
                predictions(iLineup, resp) + 1;
51      end
52  end %rep loop
```

Preliminaries. First consider the statement in line 7, which calls the random-number generator with two arguments that reset its state to the value provided by the variable `consts.seed`.[4] Note that this usage of `consts.seed` identifies the global variable `consts` to be a "structure." A structure is a very useful construct in MATLAB because it allows you to refer to many variables (known as "structure members") at the same time, in much the same way that checking in a single suitcase is far preferable to carrying numerous socks and shirts to the airport. Structure members are identified by appending their names to the structure's name, separated by a period (".").

Because the `consts` structure contains several important variables that govern the simulation, we summarize all its members and their values in Table 7.3. We will show later how those structure members are initialized; for now, we can take their values for granted as shown in the table. The structure members that are identified by an asterisk will be explained further in the following; the others are self-explanatory.

Table 7.3 Members of the `consts` Structure in WITNESS

Member Name	Explanation	Value
`consts.seed`	Seed for random generator	21335
`consts.lSize`	Size of lineup	6
`consts.nRep`	Number of simulation replications	1000
`consts.n`	Number of features in vectors	100
`consts.nCond`	Number of conditions modeled	7
`consts.fChoice`	Forced-choice conditions*	[7 8 9]
`consts.paLineup`	Conditions without perpetrator*	[4 5 6]
`consts.ptToCrit`	Pointer to appropriate criterion*	[3 4 5 3 4 5]
`consts.maxParms`	Maximums for parameters*	[1 1 inf inf inf]

The reseeding of the random generator ensures that the sequence of random numbers provided by MATLAB's rand function is identical every time the `witness` function is called. In consequence, there are no uncontrolled random variations across calls of the function during parameter estimation, thus minimizing the disturbance of the error surface that is associated with stochastic simulation models (see Chapter 3).[5]

The subsequent lines (9–13) assign the first two entries in the parameter vector to more mnemonic variable names. Thus, we create a variable s that contains the current value of the encoding parameter, s, and a variable sim for the parameter of the same name. (In case you are wondering how we know that those two parameters take the first two slots in the parameter vector, the answer is that the order of parameters in the vector corresponds to their order of presentation in Table 7.2; this order was determined by us, the programmers.) We then assign the same value of sim to three other variables that represent the specific similarities within the simulation—namely, between the perpetrator and an innocent suspect (i.e., the person that takes the perpetrator's place on perpetrator-absent lineups; variable ssp) and between the perpetrator and all foils on the perpetrator-present (ppSim) and perpetrator-absent (paSim) lineups. The reason we use different variable names here even though all are assigned the same value is to leave open the possibility that in future simulations, the different similarities may take on distinct values.

The core components. The core of the function begins in line 16 with a loop that accumulates predictions across the multiple replications. Within the loop, each replication first involves a holdup (or some other heinous crime), which is modeled in line 19 by storing in memory an image of the perpetrator (generated in the line immediately above). The two functions getvec and storevec form part of the WITNESS simulation package (as foreshadowed in Figure 7.1) and are presented later; for now, it suffices to know that they generate a random vector and store a vector in memory, respectively.

The holdup is immediately followed by lineup construction. First, an innocent suspect is obtained for the perpetrator-absent lineup using another embedded function—namely, `getsimvec` (Line 22). The two lineup types are then created by placing the perpetrator or innocent suspect in the first lineup position (lines 24 and 25) and the foils in the remaining positions (lines 26–29). At this point, your training in experimental design should kick in, and you should balk at the idea that the first lineup position is always taken up by the perpetrator (when present). Surely this important variable must be randomized or counterbalanced? Yes, if this were a behavioral experiment involving human subjects whose decisions are subject to all sorts of biases, then it would be imperative to determine the position of the perpetrator at random. Fortunately, however, WITNESS does not suffer from such biases and considers all lineup positions exactly equally. For that reason, we can fix the perpetrator's position, which turns out greatly to facilitate scoring.

You might also wonder why we created two separate lineups, rather than just a single set of foils that is presented either with the perpetrator or an innocent suspect in the first position. Does the use of different foils for the perpetrator-present and perpetrator-absent lineups not introduce an unnecessary source of variation? The answer is that in reality, foils are selected by police officers in order to match the apprehended person of interest—who may or may not be the perpetrator (for details, see Clark & Tunnicliff, 2001). It follows that in order to be realistic, the foils should differ between the two lineup types. However, because `ppSim` and `paSim` are set to the same value, there should be no systematic differences between foils in the two lineup types.

Once created, the witness inspects the lineups, and a match between memory and each lineup member is computed (lines 32–35). In contrast to human witnesses, who can only be assigned to one lineup type or the other—but not both—the model can consider two completely different conditions without any bias or carryover effects. This means that although it looks like we are testing the same witness under different conditions, we are actually testing different simulated participants in line with the experimental design. The match is computed by calling the MATLAB function dot, which returns the dot product between two vectors.

Response selection and scoring. WITNESS then selects a response in the manner dictated by the experimental methodology and in line with the criterion explanation. This crucial segment, which implements the experimental methodology underlying the data in Table 7.1, involves the loop beginning in line 38.

At this point things get to be somewhat intricate, and to facilitate understanding, we present the mapping between experimental conditions and the program variables in Figure 7.2.

Experiment	1						2		
Lineup	PP			PA			PP		
Condition	Control	Holistic	Featural	Control	Holistic	Featural	Control	Holistic	Featural
iLineup	1	2	3	4	5	6	7	8	9
consts.ptToCrit	3	4	5	3	4	5	n/a	n/a	n/a
criterion	parms (3)	parms (4)	parms (5)	parms (3)	parms (4)	parms (5)	0	0	0
any(iLineup==consts. paLineup)	0	0	0	1	1	1	0	0	0
any(iLineup==consts. fChoice)	0	0	0	0	0	0	1	1	1

Figure 7.2 Mapping between experimental conditions (shaded part at the top) and program parameters in our simulation (bottom part). PP = perpetrator-present lineup; PA = perpetrator-absent lineup. See text for details.

The shaded cells at the top of the figure summarize the data that we want to simulate: There are two experiments, there are two lineup types, and there are three conditions for each lineup type in each experiment. Now consider the bottom (unshaded) panel of the figure, which lists the values of the program variables that, in lines 38 through 51, instantiate this experimental setup, thus ensuring that WITNESS selects responses in the manner appropriate for the experiment, condition, and lineup type being modeled. Turning first to Experiment 2, the response criterion is disabled by setting it to zero (line 40) whenever the loop index iLineup matches one of the elements of consts.fChoice, which is an array that points to the conditions that comprise Experiment 2 (see Table 7.3 and Figure 7.2). Note that the criterion explanation cannot differentiate between the three conditions within a forced-choice methodology, which implies that to the extent that there are differences between the conditions in Experiment 2, this will necessarily increase the misfit of the model.

For the remaining optional-choice conditions from Experiment 1, two choices must be made: The appropriate criterion must be selected from the parameter vector, and the appropriate lineup must be chosen. The criterion is chosen in line 42 using the array consts.ptToCrit. The first three rows in the bottom panel of Figure 7.2 clarify the mapping between the loop index (iLineup) and the decision criterion that is being selected from the parameter vector. The lineup type is determined in line 44, using the array consts.paLineup. The second-last row in Figure 7.2 shows the outcome of the expression in line 44, which is equal to 1 (i.e., true) whenever the value of the loop index (iLineup) matches one of the perpetrator-absent conditions.

Finally, once the criterion and lineup type have been selected, a response is returned by the decision function, which we will discuss in a moment. The returned responses are counted in the `predictions` array (line 50), which keeps track of the number of occurrences of each response type for each condition.

To summarize, within each replication, WITNESS encounters a perpetrator and then selects a response under all conditions being modeled—that is, two lineup types (perpetrator present or absent), two decision types (optional choice or forced choice), and three experimental conditions (control, holistic, and featural). Once all replications are completed, the counted responses are converted to predicted proportions (not shown in listing) and are returned as the model's predictions.

You may have noted that a seemingly disproportionate amount of program (and description) space was devoted to vaguely annoying matters of bookkeeping, such as identification of the appropriate parameters and lineups for the various conditions. Comparatively little space seemed to be devoted to doing the actual simulation, for example, the encoding of the perpetrator's face. This is not at all unusual: In our experience, the majority of programming effort tends to be devoted to instantiating important details of the experimental method and to keeping track of simulation results.

Embedded functions. Let us now turn to the various embedded functions that are required to make WITNESS work. Listing 7.2 shows the remaining segment of the `witness` function; as indicated by the line numbers, this listing involves the same file shown above in Listing 7.1.

Listing 7.2 Embedded Functions for WITNESS

```
54
55
56 %——— miscellaneous embedded functions
57 %get random vector
58     function rv = getvec (n)
59         rv = (rand(1,n)-0.5);
60     end
61
62 %take a vector and return one of specified similarity
63     function outVec=getsimvec (s, inVec)
64         a = rand(1,length(inVec)) < s;
65         outVec = a.*inVec  + ~a.*getvec(length(inVec));
66     end
67
68 %encode a vector in memory
69     function m=storevec (s, inVec)
70         m = getsimvec(s, inVec);
71     end
72
73 %implement the decision rules
74     function resp = decision(matchValues, cRec)
```

(Continued)

(Continued)

```
75            %if all lineup members fall below cRec, then ↩
                 reject
76            if max(matchValues) < cRec
77                resp=3;
78            else
79                [c,j]=max(matchValues);
80                if j == 1     %suspect or perp always ↩
                        first
81                    resp=1;
82                else
83                    resp=2;
84                end
85            end
86       end
87 end
```

The first embedded function in line 58, getvec, is simplicity itself: It creates a vector of uniform random numbers that are centered on zero and range from −.5 to +.5. All stimulus vectors in this simulation are ultimately generated by this function.

The next function, getsimvec in line 63, also returns a random vector, but in this instance, the new vector is of a specified similarity to another one that is provided by the input argument inVec. Specifically, the function returns a vector in which a random proportion s of features are drawn from inVec, and the remainder is sampled at random.

To encode the perpetrator in memory, we use the function storevec in line 69: As it turns out, this function simply calls getsimvec, thus instantiating WITNESS's assumption that only part of the perpetrator image is stored correctly, whereas the remaining encoded features are sampled at random. (In fact, we could have omitted this function altogether and used getsimvec to do the encoding. However, by using a separate function, we leave open the door for possible future modifications of the encoding process.)

Finally, we must examine how WITNESS selects a response. This selection is made by the function decision, which is defined in lines 74 through 86. The function receives an array of dot products that represent the match between memory and the lineup members (input argument matchValues) together with a response criterion (cRec). If all matches fall below the criterion (line 76), then a response type "3" is returned. Alternatively, the lineup member with the largest match is returned as the response. If that largest match is in Position 1 (line 80), then we know that we have identified the perpetrator (or innocent suspect, in perpetrator-absent lineups), and the function returns a response type "1." (Remember how we said earlier that placing the perpetrator in Position 1 facilitates scoring—now you know why.) Alternatively, if the largest match is in any other position, we return response type "2," which means that a foil has been mistakenly identified. To summarize, the decision function returns a single variable that can take on values 1, 2, or 3 and classifies the response, respectively, as (1) an identification of the perpetrator, (2) an identification of a foil, or (3) the rejection of the lineup. Recall that those response types are counted separately across replications (refer back to line 50 in Listing 7.1).

This, then, completes the presentation and discussion of the central part of the simulation—namely, the witness function and all its embedded auxiliary functions. Within the structure in Figure 7.1, we have discussed the box on the left. We next turn to the main program shown in the box at the top of that figure.

7.1.3.3 The Main Program

The compact main program is presented in Listing 7.3 and is explained quite readily. Lines 6 through 13 initialize the consts structure with the values shown earlier in Table 7.3. Note how those values were available inside the witness function because consts was declared to be global both here and inside the function.

Listing 7.3 Main Program for WITNESS Simulation

```
1  % Program to estimate parameters for WITNESS
2  % for Lewandowsky and Farrell's
3  % "Computational Modeling in Cognition: Principles ↵
       and Practice"
4  global consts;
5
6  consts.seed = 2135; %for random generator
7  consts.lSize=6;      %lineup size
8  consts.nRep=1000;    %number of reps at each call
9  consts.n=100;        %number of features in vectors
10 consts.nCond=9;      %number of conditions modeled
11 consts.fChoice=[7 8 9];   %forced-choice conditions
12 consts.paLineup=[4 5 6];  %paLineup conditions
13 consts.ptToCrit=[3 4 5 3 4 5]; %slots in parameters
14
15 %Data Exp 1 & 2 of Clare & Lewandowsky (2004),
16 %columns are: Suspect, Foil, and Reject
17 data = [.80, .13, .07;    %PP control
18         .57, .06, .36;    %PP holistic
19         .69, .12, .19;    %PP featural
20         .05, .72, .23;    %PA control
21         .20, .28, .52;    %PA holistic
22         .00, .48, .52;    %PA featural
```

(Continued)

(Continued)

```
23         .86, .14, .00;   %Exp 2 control
24         .81, .19, .00;   %Exp 2 holistic
25         .84, .16, .00];  %Exp 2 featural
26
27 %initialize parameters in order:
28 %   s
29 %   sim
30 %   crec -control
31 %   crec -holistic
32 %   crec -featural
33 disp ('Starting values of parameters')
34 startParms = [0.2942    0.3508    1.0455    2.0930    ↩
        1.8050]
35 consts.maxParms = [1. 1. inf inf inf];
36
37 [finalParms,fVal] = Wwrapper4fminBnd(startParms, ↩
        data);
38
39 %print final predictions
40 predictions = witness(finalParms)
```

The next few lines (17–25) initialize a matrix with the to-be-fitted data that were shown earlier in Table 7.1. You will note that all numbers in the table are also shown here, albeit in a slightly different arrangement (e.g., the columns represent response types rather than conditions) that simplifies the programming. Note also that the order of conditions, from top to bottom, is the same as their order, from left to right, in Figure 7.2. This is no coincidence because it means that the predictions returned by function witness share the layout of the data.

We next set the starting values for the parameters (line 34) and determine their maximum values (line 35) to ensure that they do not go out of bounds during estimation (e.g., *sim* must not exceed 1 because the similarity between two vectors cannot be greater than identity). Finally, Wwrapper4fminBnd is called to estimate the parameters (line 37). This part of the code is virtually identical to the example presented earlier (in Section 3.1.2) and does not require much comment. We therefore now turn to the remaining function, represented by the central box in Figure 7.1, which coordinates the parameter estimation.

7.1.3.4   Estimating the Parameters

Using MATLAB's standard search function. The function Wwrapper4fmin in Listing 7.4 should be quite familiar from the earlier chapters. Indeed, with the exception of specifying some options (in lines 4 and 5) and dealing with boundary conditions (line 9), this listing is nearly identical to Listing 3.2.

Listing 7.4 Parameter Estimation Function for WITNESS Simulation

```
1  function [x, fVal] = Wwrapper4fmin(parms, data)
2  global consts;
3
4  defOpts = optimset ('fminsearch');
5  options = optimset (defOpts, 'Display', 'iter', ←
      'MaxFunEvals', 400)
6  [x,fVal,dummy,output] = ←
      fminsearch(@bof,parms,options,data)
7
8      function rmsd=bof(parms, data)
9          if (min(parms) < 0) || (min(consts.maxParms − ←
             parms) < 0)
10             rmsd = realmax;
11         else
12             sd=(witness (parms)−data).^2;
13             rmsd=sqrt (sum(sum(sd))/numel(data));
14         end
15     end
16 end
```

The test for boundary conditions in line 9 is noteworthy: If any of the parameters are out of bounds, the function bof returns the maximum number that MATLAB can represent (realmax), thus signaling Simplex not to go anywhere near those values. Only if the current parameter values are within bounds are the predictions of WITNESS computed and compared to the data by computing the standard RMSD (Equation 2.2). We used RMSD as the discrepancy function for comparability with Clare and Lewandowsky (2004); because the data consist of counts (i.e., number of subjects who make a certain response), we could equally have used a χ^2 discrepancy function (which was employed by Clark, 2003).

Improving boundary checks. One limitation of the boundary check in Listing 7.4 is that it creates a "step" function, such that any legitimate parameter value, no matter how close to the boundary, is left unpenalized, whereas any out-of-bounds value, no matter how small the transgression, is given an equally large penalty. These problems can be avoided by using the fminsearchbnd function, which is not part of a standard MATLAB installation but can be readily downloaded from MATLAB Central.

Listing 7.5 shows an alternative parameter estimation function, called Wwrapper4fminBnd, which uses fminsearchbnd and passes the lower and upper bounds of the parameters as additional arguments (lines 4 and 5). Owing to the use of fminsearchbnd, the code has also become more compact because the boundary check did not have to be programmed explicitly.

Listing 7.5 Using `fminsearchbnd` for WITNESS Simulation

```
1  function [x, fVal] = Wwrapper4fminBnd(parms, data)
2  global consts;
3
4  [x,fVal,dummy,output] = ↵
      fminsearchbnd(@bof,parms,zeros(size(parms)),
5          consts.maxParms)
6
7      function rmsd=bof(parms)
8          sd=(witness (parms)-data).^2;
9          rmsd=sqrt (sum(sum(sd))/numel(data));
10     end
11 end
```

There is one other noteworthy aspect of `Wwrapper4fminBnd`: The embedded function `bof` accesses the data not as a function argument (as in Listing 7.4) but by referring to a variable `data` that was passed to the surrounding function. We already discussed this valuable ability of embedded functions to automatically inherit variables from the surrounding function in Section 3.1.2; if this sounds cryptic, you may wish to reread that earlier section. For didactic reasons, we used the inheriting regime in one of our functions while using function arguments in the other.

7.1.4 WITNESS Simulation Results

Our modeling seeks to answer two questions: First, does the criterion explanation as embodied in WITNESS account for the data of Clare and Lewandowsky (2004) at a quantitative level? Second, can an alternative memory explanation be constructed within WITNESS to handle those data?

7.1.4.1 The Criterion Explanation

The simulation as just described was run three times, with a different set of starting values for the parameters on each run. The best-fitting estimates reported in Table 7.2 are based on the run that yielded the smallest RMSD (.0498), suggesting that the average deviation between model predictions and data was on the order of 5%.

Can we be certain that this solution reflects a global rather than a local minimum? There can be no complete assurance that the observed minimum is indeed global, but several facts raise our level of confidence in the solution. First, the different runs converged on very similar RMSDs—namely, .0498, .0511, and

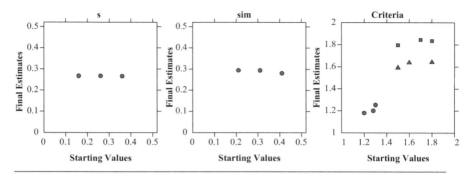

Figure 7.3 Final parameter estimates as a function of their starting values for three fits of the WITNESS model to the data of Clare and Lewandowsky (2004). From left to right, the panels show the values of s, sim, and the recognition criteria, respectively. In the rightmost panel, circles, squares, and triangles refer to $C_{rec}(C)$, $C_{rec}(H)$, and $C_{rec}(F)$, respectively.

.0509, respectively. Second, the final parameter estimates were remarkably similar, notwithstanding considerable variation in their starting values. This is illustrated in Figure 7.3, which shows the final parameter estimates as a function of their starting values. The figure shows that there is very little variability along the ordinate (final estimates) even though the values differ quite noticeably along the abscissa (starting values). The fact that the three simulation runs converged onto nearly indistinguishable best-fitting estimates bolsters our confidence that we have reached a global minimum.

How well does the model capture the data? Figures 7.4 and 7.5 show the data from Experiments 1 and 2, respectively, together with the model predictions.

It is clear from the figures that the model handles the main trends in the data and provides a good quantitative fit of both experiments. By varying the decision criterion, WITNESS captures the effects of verbalization on identification performance for both optional-choice and forced-choice lineups and for perpetrator-absent as well as perpetrator-present lineups. This result lends considerable support to the criterion explanation of verbal overshadowing. What remains to be seen is whether a memory-based alternative explanation may also handle the results.

7.1.4.2 An Alternative Memory Explanation

Clare and Lewandowsky (2004) also examined whether WITNESS might handle the results by assuming that memory is modified during verbalization. Specifically, to instantiate a memory explanation, Clare and Lewandowsky assumed that verbalization partially overwrites the perpetrator's image in memory. This was modeled by a reduction in the encoding parameter s because reducing s is

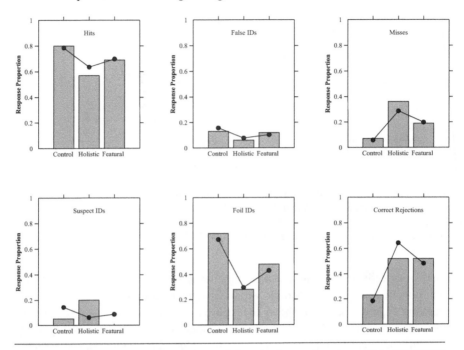

Figure 7.4 Data (bars) and predictions of the criterion explanation within WITNESS (points and lines) for Experiment 1 (optional-choice lineups) of Clare and Lewandowsky (2004). The top row of panels represents the perpetrator-present lineup and the bottom row the perpetrator-absent lineup. Data from Clare, J., & Lewandowsky, S. (2004). Verbalizing facial memory: Criterion effects in verbal overshadowing. *Journal of Experimental Psychology: Learning, Memory, & Cognition, 30,* 739–755. Published by the American Psychological Association; adapted with permission.

equivalent to unimpaired encoding followed by overwriting of the encoded features.

We instantiated the same idea in our simulations. To conserve space, we do not show the modified source code, although it is available at the book's supporting webpage (http://www.cogsciwa.com). In a nutshell, the criterion parameter (c_{rec}) was kept constant across all conditions, whereas the encoding parameter (s) differed between the control, holistic, and featural conditions. This version of WITNESS failed to handle the data, as shown in Figure 7.6. The figure shows predictions with the best-fitting parameter estimates reported by Clare and Lewandowsky (2004). We do not present the fit to Experiment 2 as it does not deviate appreciably from that of the criterion explanation.

Unlike the criterion explanation, the memory explanation cannot handle the effects of verbal overshadowing, presumably because it cannot simultaneously explain the improved performance for perpetrator-absent lineups and the

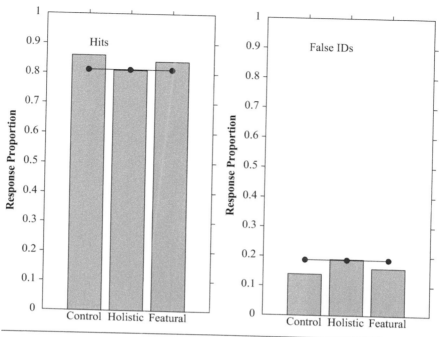

Figure 7.5 Data (bars) and predictions of the criterion explanation within WITNESS (points and lines) for Experiment 2 (forced-choice lineup) of Clare and Lewandowsky (2004). Data from Clare, J., & Lewandowsky, S. (2004). Verbalizing facial memory: Criterion effects in verbal overshadowing. *Journal of Experimental Psychology: Learning, Memory, & Cognition, 30*, 739–755. Published by the American Psychological Association; adapted with permission.

detriment to performance with perpetrator-present lineups. We invite you to modify the source code just presented in order to instantiate the memory explanation and to reproduce the results in the figures. If you encounter difficulties or obtain surprising results, you can consult the information at our webpage. Clare and Lewandowsky (2004) applied the model to all three of their experiments simultaneously, and they estimated parameters only based on perpetrator-present lineups; you will get different results if you fit two experiments only or if you fit all conditions.

7.1.4.3   Conclusions From the Modeling

What conclusions can we draw from the modeling involving WITNESS? First, the modeling shows that the verbal overshadowing effect arguably reflects a criterion adjustment rather than an impairment of memory after verbalization. When this

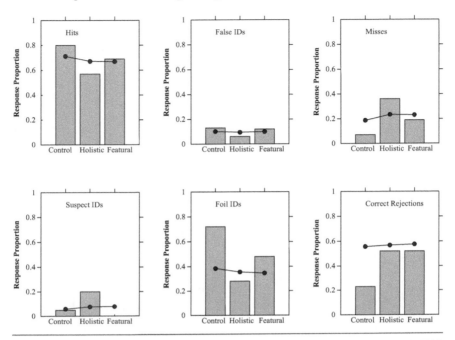

Figure 7.6 Data (bars) and predictions of the memory explanation within WITNESS (points and lines) for Experiment 1 (optional-choice lineups) of Clare and Lewandowsky (2004). The top row of panels represents the perpetrator-present lineup and the bottom row the perpetrator-absent lineup. Data from Clare, J., & Lewandowsky, S. (2004). Verbalizing facial memory: Criterion effects in verbal overshadowing. *Journal of Experimental Psychology: Learning, Memory, & Cognition, 30,* 739–755. Published by the American Psychological Association; adapted with permission.

criterion explanation is instantiated in WITNESS, the model can predict both the presence and absence of verbal overshadowing (or indeed a beneficial effect for perpetrator-absent lineups) depending on the type of decision that is expected of participants. Second, the modeling showed that the data are not readily modeled by an explanation based on alteration or overwriting of memory during verbalization. Although this second finding does not rule out a memory-based explanation because we did not explore all possible instantiations of that alternative, the fact that the criterion explanation handles the data quite parsimoniously makes it an attractive account of the phenomenon.

In the context of verbal overshadowing, Clark (2008) drew attention to the fact that the mere label for the effect—namely, "verbal *overshadowing*"—is not theory neutral but, simply by its name, "implies the memory impairment explanation that has been the dominant explanation ... since the original results were reported" (pp. 809–810). Thus, merely giving an effect a name can create the *appearance* of an explanation: Far from being an advantage, this erroneous appearance may bias subsequent theorizing and may retard corrective action (cf. Hintzman, 1991). One of the uses of computational modeling is to provide *substantive* explanations that necessarily go beyond labeling of an effect. Thus, although we refer to the "criterion explanation" by name, this is a name not for a phenomenon but for a fully instantiated process explanation.

One limitation of the example just presented is that we only considered a single model (albeit in two different variants). In general, stronger inferences about cognitive processes are possible if several competing models are compared in their ability to handle the data. The next example illustrates this situation.

7.2   Exemplar Versus Boundary Models: Choosing Between Candidates

One central aspect of human cognition—and shared with such animals as primates and pigeons (e.g., Fagot, Kruschke, Depy, & Vauclair, 1998; Farrell et al., 2006; Shimp, Long, & Fremouw, 1996)—is the ability to categorize a virtually limitless range of objects in the world into a much smaller number of relevant categories (e.g., Ashby & O'Brien, 2005; Bruner, Goodnow, & Austin, 1956; Lewandowsky, Kalish, & Ngang, 2002; Murphy, 2002; Nosofsky, 1986; Palmeri, Wong, & Gauthier, 2004). Doing so leads to more compact and efficient representations of the world; we can ignore trivial differences between objects and deal with them on the basis of their category. Knowing whether something is a chair or a table is important for determining whether we sit at it or on it; knowing whether it is made of oak or pine is not. Unsurprisingly, a huge wealth of data has been generated about people's learning and use of categories, and this has driven—and been driven by— considerable theoretical development (see, e.g., Figure 1 of Palmeri et al., 2004). The area of categorization is specifically notable in having birthed a number of formal models, including GCM (e.g., Nosofsky, 1986), GRT (e.g., Ashby, 1992b), ALCOVE (Kruschke, 1992), RASHNL (Kruschke & Johansen, 1999), the EBRW model (Nosofsky & Palmeri, 1997), and COVIS (Ashby, Alfonso-Reese, Turken, & Waldron, 1998). You've already seen one of these models, the Generalized Context Model (GCM), and its approach to explaining category learning in Chapter 1.

In the following, we will examine three models of categorization and present code for maximum likelihood estimation of the parameters of those models, along with calculation of the Akaike Information Criterion (AIC) and the Bayesian Information Criterion (BIC) for the purposes of model comparison.

7.2.1   Models of Categorization

Research on categorization has considered a wide variety of category structures of varying dimensionality. Here, we will assume that category members vary along a single dimension. This will simplify the presentation of the models, but it will nonetheless allow us to make some very diagnostic inferences based on a unidimensional categorization experiment that we will discuss a little later.

7.2.1.1   Generalized Context Model: GCM

You've already been presented with the basics of GCM in Chapter 1. Because that was a while ago, and so that you can easily refer back to this material when reading about the application of GCM below, we'll briefly summarize the model again. GCM's main claim is that whenever we have an experience about an object[6] and its category, we store a localist, unitary representation of that object and its category: an exemplar. For the example we are looking at here, the experimental stimuli only vary along a single dimension, and so only a single feature is relevant.

When we come across an object in the world and wish to determine its category (e.g., edible vs. inedible), the GCM postulates that we match that object to all exemplars in memory and categorize the object according to the best match to existing exemplars. This matching process relies on a calculation of the distance between the object i and all the stored exemplars $j \in \mathfrak{J}$:

$$d_{ij} = |x_i - x_j|. \tag{7.2}$$

Note the simple form of this equation compared to the earlier Equation 1.3. We've been able to simplify this because here we only have a single stimulus dimension. This means we do not need to sum across several dimensions, and it also means that we can leave out the generalization to different types of difference metric: For a single dimension, $|a - b| = \sqrt{(a - b)^2}$. This distance is then mapped into a measure of similarity (i.e., match) between the new stimulus and each exemplar:

$$s_{ij} = exp(-c \cdot d_{ij}). \tag{7.3}$$

Remember that the c in Equation 7.3 scales the drop-off in similarity with increasing distance. When c is small, a stimulus will match a wide range of exemplars (i.e., a slow drop-off with distance), and when c is large, the stimulus will only match exemplars within a very narrow range (i.e., a fast drop-off with distance). Finally, the similarity values are added up separately for exemplars in each category and used to determine the categorization probability for the new stimulus:

$$P(R_i = A|i) = \frac{\left(\sum_{j \in A} s_{ij}\right)}{\left(\sum_{j \in A} s_{ij}\right) + \left(\sum_{j \in B} s_{ij}\right)}. \tag{7.4}$$

7.2.1.2 General Recognition Theory: GRT

The fundamental assumption of the GCM is that all past experiences with category members are stored as exemplars in memory. This assumption permits the model to explain the relationship between categorization and recognition memory as discussed in Chapter 1. General recognition theory (GRT; Ashby, 1992a; Ashby & Gott, 1988), by contrast, takes a very different tack. The GRT assumes that what is represented in memory is an abstraction of the category structure rather than the exemplars themselves. Specifically, GRT assumes that the stimulus space is carved into partitions by decision boundaries. All that needs to be stored in memory in order to classify new exemplars is some specification of the placement of the boundaries. In multidimensional space, this can get quite complicated to conceptualize, as the boundaries can have any form, although they are usually assumed to be specified by linear or quadratic equations.[7] In the case of stimuli that vary along only a single dimension, things are very easy: A category boundary is a single point along the stimulus dimension.

Categorization errors are assumed to follow from trial-by-trial variability in the perception of the stimulus (Alfonso-Reese, 2006). This means that on one trial, a stimulus may appear to fall on one side of the boundary, whereas on another trial, it appears to fall on the other side. GRT assumes that this variability takes the form of a normal probability density function (PDF) centered on the true value of the stimulus and with standard deviation σ. An example is shown in the top panel of Figure 7.7: The circle shows the actual stimulus value, and around that is drawn the normal PDF.

Given the normal density around the stimulus and the placement of the boundaries, what is the probability of categorizing the stimulus as belonging to a particular category? This can be worked out using concepts we discussed in Chapter 4 with reference to probability functions. Recall that in the case of a PDF, the probability that an observation will fall within a specific range involves finding the area under the curve within that range. That is, we need to integrate the PDF between the minimum and maximum values defining that range. Take a look again at the top panel of Figure 7.7. The portion of the PDF shaded in gray shows the area under the curve to the left of the boundary; this area under the PDF is the probability that the perceived stimulus value falls below the boundary and therefore corresponds to the probability that the stimulus i will be categorized as an 'A,'

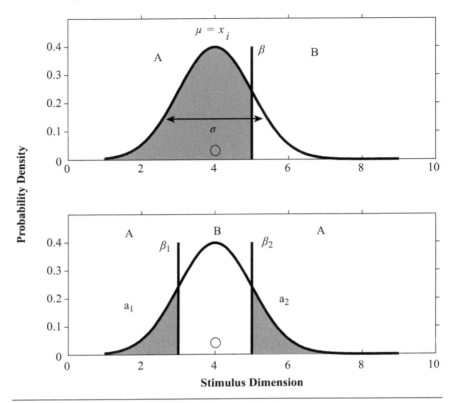

Figure 7.7 Depiction of one-dimensional categorization in GRT. Both panels show a normal PDF reflecting the variability in perception of the stimulus; the stimulus itself has a value of 4 and is shown as a circle. The vertical lines in each panel (labeled β) show the category boundaries. In the top panel, only a single boundary exists, and the probability of categorizing the stimulus as being in Category A is the area under the normal density to the left of the boundary. The bottom panel shows a more complicated example with two boundaries; in this case, the probability of categorizing the stimulus as an 'A' is the area under the curve to the left of the left-most boundary (β_1) plus the area to the right of the right-most boundary (β_2).

$P(R_i = A|i)$. In the top panel, we need to find the integral from the minimum possible stimulus value up to the boundary value (β). Let's assume that the stimulus dimension is unbounded, so that the minimum possible value is $-\infty$. This means we need to calculate

$$P(R_i = A|i) = \int_{-\infty}^{\beta} N(x_i, \sigma), \qquad (7.5)$$

where N is the normal PDF with mean x_i and standard deviation σ. To calculate this integral, we can use the normal cumulative distribution function (CDF). As we discussed in Chapter 4, the CDF is the integral of a PDF and can therefore be used to integrate across segments of the PDF. Using the integral of the normal CDF, Φ, we can rewrite Equation 7.5 as

$$P(R_i = A|i) = \Phi\left(\frac{\beta - x_i}{\sigma}\right),\tag{7.6}$$

where the integration is assumed to be taken from $-\infty$. The argument passed to the normal CDF, $(\beta - x_i)/\sigma$, expresses the boundary as a z score of the normal density around the stimulus because the normal CDF function assumes a mean of 0 and a standard deviation of 1.

We can also use this method to obtain predicted probabilities from GRT for more complicated examples. The bottom panel of Figure 7.7 shows a case where there are two boundaries, β_1 and β_2. Stimuli below β_1 and above β_2 belong to Category A, whereas stimuli between the two boundaries belong to Category B; such a category structure might arise when determining whether some milk is safe to feed to an infant given its temperature. The predicted probability of categorizing a stimulus i as being an 'A' is then the probability that either the perception of the stimulus falls below β_1 or that it falls above β_2. These two probabilities are mutually exclusive (unless it is quantum event, the stimulus cannot simultaneously both fall below β_1 and above β_2), so following the rules of probability in Chapter 4, the probability of either event happening can be obtained by adding up the individual probabilities; that is, we sum the gray areas in Figure 7.7. The first area is obtained in a similar manner to the top panel, by integrating from $-\infty$ to β_1:

$$P(R_i = a_1|i) = \Phi\left(\frac{\beta_1 - x_i}{\sigma}\right).\tag{7.7}$$

The second region, to the right of β_2, requires only a little more thinking. The CDF gives the integral from $-\infty$ up to some value, so we can use it to obtain the integral up to β_2. To work out the area above β_2, we can calculate the integral up to β_2 and subtract it from 1: Remember that probabilities must add up to 1, and if the perceived stimulus doesn't fall to the left of β_2, it must fall to the right (we are assuming that the perceived stimulus cannot fall directly on the boundary). Written as an equation, it looks like this:

$$P(R_i = a_2|i) = 1 - \Phi\left(\frac{\beta_2 - x_i}{\sigma}\right).\tag{7.8}$$

The probability of making an 'A' response is then:

$$P(R_i = A|i) = P(R_i = a_1|i) + P(R_i = a_2|i).$$

Although we can determine the optimal placement of boundaries, we cannot a priori specify the boundaries a participant is actually using. Accordingly, boundary placement will be usually specified by free parameters. In the case of unidimensional stimuli, each boundary will be captured by a single free parameter, and there will be an additional free parameter for σ, the variability in perception.

7.2.1.3 Deterministic Exemplar Model: DEM

Much research has been directed at discriminating between GCM and GRT as competing explanations for human (and animal) categorization (e.g., Farrell et al., 2006; Maddox & Ashby, 1998; McKinley & Nosofsky, 1995; Nosofsky, 1998; Rouder & Ratcliff, 2004). Ashby and Maddox (1993) and Maddox and Ashby (1993) noted that one difficulty with comparing GCM and GRT directly is that such a comparison confounds the representations involved in categorizing a stimulus and the processes required to turn the resulting information into an overt categorization response. That is, not only do GCM and GRT obviously differ in the way category information is represented, but they also differ in the way in which responses are generated. In GCM, responses are probabilistic (by virtue of the use of the Luce choice rule, Equation 7.4), whereas GRT's responses are deterministic: If a stimulus is perceived to fall to the left of the boundary in the top panel of Figure 7.7, it is always categorized as an 'A.'

To partially deconfound these factors, Ashby and Maddox (1993) presented a deterministic exemplar model (DEM). This model is identical to the standard GCM model, with the exception that the response rule is deterministic. DEM replaces Equation 7.4 with a modified version of the Luce choice rule:

$$P(R_i = A|i) = \frac{\left(\sum_{j \in A} s_{ij}\right)^{\gamma}}{\left(\sum_{j \in A} s_{ij}\right)^{\gamma} + \left(\sum_{j \in B} s_{ij}\right)^{\gamma}}. \tag{7.9}$$

The modification is that the summed similarities are raised to the power of a free parameter γ. This parameter controls the extent to which responding is deterministic. If $\gamma = 1$, the model is identical to GCM. As γ gets closer to 0, responding becomes more and more random, to the point where $\gamma=0$ and Equation 7.9 works out as $1/(1+1)$: Responding is at chance and isn't sensitive to the actual stimulus presented. As γ increases above 1, responding gets more and more deterministic. This is because γ acts nonlinearly on the summed similarities, and if $(\sum_{j \in A} s_{ij})^{\gamma}$ is greater than $(\sum_{j \in B} s_{ij})^{\gamma}$, then increasing γ will increase $(\sum_{j \in A} s_{ij})^{\gamma}$ more than it increases $(\sum_{j \in B} s_{ij})^\gamma$. For a very large value of γ, the model will respond deterministically: If $(\sum_{j \in A} s_{ij}) >> (\sum_{j \in B} s_{ij})$, the model will always produce an 'A' response.

7.2.2   A Probabilistic Feedback Experiment

How, then, can the boundary and exemplar models be teased apart? Can they be unambiguously differentiated? Rouder and Ratcliff (2004) approached this problem with an ingenious paradigm in which stimuli varied along a single dimension. Rouder and Ratcliff (2004) presented their participants with a 640 × 480 grid of pixels, with each pixel being colored white, black, or gray. Rouder and Ratcliff varied the proportion of nongray (black or white) pixels that were white and asked participants to categorize each grid as being light or dark. Following Rouder and Ratcliff, we call this single-stimulus dimension *luminance* from here on.

The critical feature for telling apart boundary and exemplar models was that category membership was probabilistic: The same stimulus x_i was sometimes designated as being in Category A by feedback during training and sometimes as being in Category B. The top panel of Figure 7.8 shows the category structure for Rouder and Ratcliff's Experiment 1. The black dots on the solid line refer to the locations, in luminance space, of the eight training stimuli that we number 1 through 8 (from left to right). Stimuli at either end of the stimulus space (i.e., 1, 2, 7, and 8) were presented as members of Category A on 60% of the trials. Stimuli in the middle region of the stimulus space either belonged to Category A 100% of the time (stimuli 3 and 4) or were always Category B members (i.e., never Category A; stimuli 5 and 6).

The bottom two panels show representative predictions from boundary and exemplar theories and show how the experiment can discriminate between the different theories. The middle panel shows predictions from GRT, under the assumption that people place the boundaries more or less optimally. Although participants cannot reach perfect accuracy in this task given its probabilistic nature, they can nonetheless maximize performance by inserting a boundary at each point at which the probability of belonging to Category A in the top panel shifts from above .5 to below .5. That is, the best strategy would be to place one boundary between stimuli 4 and 5 and another one between stimuli 6 and 7. Although there is a shift in probabilities between stimuli 2 and 3, placing a boundary here would be suboptimal because it would lead to a tendency for participants to classify stimuli 1 and 2 as being in Category B, whereas they are more likely to belong to Category A.

Under these assumptions about boundary placement, the middle panel shows that GRT predicts a function that dips in the middle and is monotonically

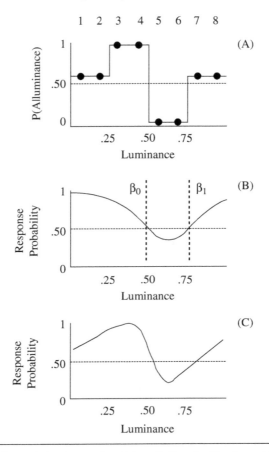

Figure 7.8 Experimental structure and model predictions for Rouder and Ratcliff's (2004) probabilistic categorization experiment. The top panel shows the proportion of times each stimulus value was designated as belonging to Category A by experimental feedback; the integers above the plot number the stimuli from 1 to 8. The middle panel shows representative predictions from GRT under the assumption that a boundary is placed wherever the membership probability crosses 0.5. The bottom panel shows representative exemplar model predictions, from DEM. Figure reprinted from Rouder, J. N., & Ratcliff, R. (2004). Comparing categorization models. *Journal of Experimental Psychology: General, 133,* 63–82. Published by the American Psychological Association; reprinted with permission.

increasing as one moves away from the dip in either direction. In contrast, the bottom panel shows that an exemplar model (DEM) will predict a more complicated function. Although the same dip occurs for stimuli 5 and 6, there is a second dip at the bottom end of the stimulus space.

Why do the two models make different predictions? Exemplar theory predicts that response probabilities should track the feedback probabilities. As we move down the stimulus dimension in the lower half of the space (i.e., from stimulus 4 down to stimulus 1), the proportion of exemplars in memory that belong to Category A drops from 1.0 to 0.6. This means that the summed similarity for Category A will also drop, and since the summed similarity feeds directly into the predicted responses via Equation 7.4 or Equation 7.9, the response proportions are also expected to drop. The extent of this drop will depend on the parameter settings and on the particular model: GCM will show a strong tendency to track the feedback probabilities, while DEM, with its ability to respond deterministically, may show responding that is more deterministic (Farrell et al., 2006). GRT, by contrast, predicts that as we move away from a stimulus boundary the more likely a stimulus is to be classified as corresponding to that category. Although the membership probability decreases as we move to the left of the top panel of Figure 7.8, all GRT is concerned with is the placement of the boundaries; as we move to the left, we move away from the boundary, and the predicted probability of classifying the stimuli as 'A's necessarily increases in a monotonic fashion. A defining characteristic of GRT is that it cannot predict non-monotonicity in response proportions as the absolute distance of a stimulus from the boundary increases.

Figure 7.9 shows the results from the last three sessions for the six participants from Rouder and Ratcliff's (2004) experiment, along with the feedback probabilities reproduced from Figure 7.8 (in gray). The participants in the left and middle columns of Figure 7.9 (SB, SEH, BG, and NC) qualitatively match the predictions of GRT, particularly in the monotonic shape of their response probability functions in the left-hand size of the stimulus space. Participant VB (top right panel) behaves more or less as predicted by GRT, but with a small downturn for the smallest luminances as predicted by exemplar theory. Finally, participant LT (bottom right panel) behaves as predicted by exemplar theory, with a very clear downturn in 'A' responses.

Following Rouder and Ratcliff (2004), we next apply exemplar and decision-bound models to the data from the six participants shown in Figure 7.9. We will use maximum likelihood estimation (MLE) to fit the models to the data and obtain standard errors on the parameter estimates for each participant. Finally, we will use AIC and BIC to compare the models on their account of the data.

7.2.3   MATLAB Code for ML Parameter Estimation for GCM, DEM, and GRT

Let's start with the code for the log-likelihood functions from GCM, DEM, and GRT. We will then move on to look at how we use this code to compare models.

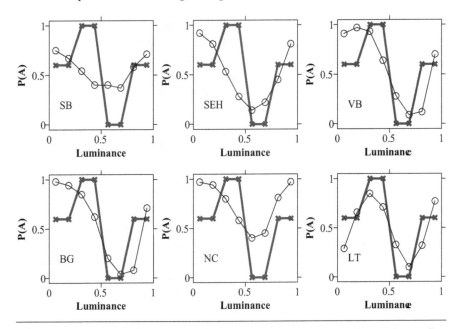

Figure 7.9 Proportion of trials on which stimuli were categorized as belonging to Category A, for six participants (separate panels). Feedback probabilities from the training session are shown in gray. Figure adapted from Rouder, J. N., & Ratcliff, R. (2004). Comparing categorization models. *Journal of Experimental Psychology: General, 133,* 63–82. Published by the American Psychological Association; reprinted with permission.

7.2.3.1   GCM and DEM

Listing 7.6 provides the code for calculation of the negative log-likelihood for GCM and DEM. Recall that GCM is simply the DEM model with γ set to 1. Accordingly, we can use the DEM code to run both GCM and DEM, as long as we remember to set γ equal to 1 when running GCM. The first several lines are comments to tell us what the input arguments are. The first input argument is the parameter vector theta, which contains c as the first element (line 9) and γ as the second element (line 10). The second argument x is a vector containing the luminance values for the eight possible stimuli. The third argument feedback specifies how many times each stimulus was designated to be an 'A.' Specifically, feedback has two columns, one giving the number of times A was given as feedback for each stimulus and a second column giving the number of times B was designated as feedback. The fourth argument data contains the frequencies of A responses from the participant for each stimulus, and the vector N contains the total number of trials per stimulus in a vector.

Listing 7.6 Negative Log-Likelihood Function for GCM and DEM

```
1  function [lnL, predP] = DEMlnL(theta, x, feedback, ↩
      data, N)
2  % gives the negative log-likelihood
3  % for response frequencies from a single participant ↩
      (data)
4  % given the DEM parameters (in vector theta), the ↩
      stimulus values in x,
5  % the number of times each stimulus was an `A' in ↩
      feedback
6  % the number of times `A' was selected as a response ↩
      (data)
7  % and the total number of test trials for each ↩
      stimulus (N)
8
9  c = theta(1);
10 gamma = theta(2);
11
12 for i=1:length(x)
13     s = exp(-c.*abs(x(i)-x));
14     sumA = sum(s.*feedback(1,:));
15     sumB = sum(s.*feedback(2,:));
16     predP(i) = (sumA^gamma)/(sumA^gamma + sumB^gamma);
17 end
18
19 lnL = -sum(data.*log(predP) + (N-data).*log(1-predP));
```

The GCM/DEM calculations are contained in lines 12 to 17. The loop goes through each of the stimuli, i, and for each stimulus calculates the predicted proportion of 'A' responses, `predP(i)`. Line 13 instantiates Equation 7.3, using the simple absolute distance measure in Equation 7.2. Line 13 is in a vectorized form: It calculates the similarity between each x_j and x_i in one go and returns a vector of similarities as a result. Lines 14 and 15 calculate summed similarity values. Rather than considering each exemplar individually, lines 14 and 15 take advantage of the design of the experiment in which there are only eight possible stimulus values. Since identical stimulus values will have identical similarity to x_i, we can calculate the summed similarity between x_i and all the exemplars with a particular value x_j by simply multiplying s_j by the number of exemplars with that particular value of x_j. Again, we don't refer explicitly to s_j in the code because the code is vectorized and processes all js at once. Line 16 feeds the summed similarity values into the Luce choice rule with γ-scaling to give a predicted proportion correct (Equation 7.9).

The final line in Listing 7.6 calculates the negative log-likelihood based on the predicted proportions and observed frequencies. Do you recognize the form of line 19? If not, turn to Section 5.4. Otherwise, right! It's the binomial log-likelihood function we discussed in Chapter 4 and that we used to obtain probabilities from SIMPLE in Chapter 5. The function takes the observed frequencies, the total number of trials, and the predicted proportions to calculate a log-likelihood value for each stimulus (in vectorized form). We then sum the $\ln L$ values and take the negative so we can minimize the negative log-likelihood.

One issue that deserves mention is that we are using the simplified version of the binomial log-likelihood function and have omitted some of the terms from the full function (see Section 4.4). This has implications for calculation of AIC and BIC, as discussed in Chapter 5. This won't be a problem here, as we will use the same binomial data model for all three categorization models and will therefore be subtracting the same constant from AIC and BIC values for all three models.

Finally, to avoid confusion, it should be noted that Rouder and Ratcliff (2004) fit DEM to their data but called it GCM. This is because a number of authors treat DEM not as a model separate from GCM but as a version of GCM with response scaling. The differentiation between GCM and DEM is maintained here because of the possible importance of the decision process in the probabilistic nature of this experiment; in many circumstances, the nature of the response process will be a side issue separate from the main theoretical issue of concern.

7.2.3.2   GRT

Comprehensive code for the GRT is available in a MATLAB toolbox presented in Alfonso-Reese (2006). We will look at simpler code here that is aimed specifically at the experiment of Rouder and Ratcliff (2004). The MATLAB code for GRT is given in Listing 7.7 and has a similar structure to the MATLAB code for GCM. The first argument is a vector containing values for GRT's free parameters, which are extracted in the first bit of the code. The code opens assignment of the three elements of theta to boundary1, boundary2 and sd. The function assumes that the first element in theta is the lower bound β_1 and that the second element is the upper bound β_2 and includes an if statement that performs a sanity check to ensure that the upper boundary is indeed greater than the lower boundary; if not, a large log-likelihood is returned. Lines 19 and 20 implement Equations 7.7 and 7.8. These calculations make use of the embedded function normalCDF, which makes use of the error function erf in MATLAB. The error function computes an integral that is related to the normal CDF by

$$\Phi(x) = \frac{1}{2}\mathrm{erf}\left(\frac{x}{\sqrt{2}}\right). \qquad (7.10)$$

This relationship is used to obtain the normal CDF in the embedded function `normalCDF` and was also used in Chapter 5 for the ex-Gaussian model, which also contains the normal CDF.[8] Line 21 adds the two areas `a1` and `a2` together to obtain predicted proportions, and line 23 implements the same binomial data function as was used in the GCM code. Notice that lines 19 to 21 are written in a vectorized format: At each step, the result is a vector whose elements correspond to specific stimulus values.

Listing 7.7 Negative Log-Likelihood Function for GRT

```
1  function [lnL, predP] = GRTlnL(theta, x, data, N)
2  % gives the negative log-likelihood
3  % for response frequencies from a single participant ↵
      (data)
4  % given the GRT parameters (in vector theta),
5  % the stimulus values in x,
6  % the number of times `A' was selected as a response ↵
      (data)
7  % and the total number of test trials for each ↵
      stimulus (N)
8
9  bound1 = theta(1);
10 bound2 = theta(2);
11
12 if bound1 >= bound2
13     lnL = realmax;
14     predP = repmat(NaN, size(N));
15 end
16
17 sd = theta(3);
18
19 a1 = normalCDF((bound1−x)./sd);
20 a2 = 1 − normalCDF((bound2−x)./sd);
21 predP = a1 + a2;
22
23 lnL = −sum(data.*log(predP) + (N−data).*log(1−predP));
24
25 %% normalCDF
26 function p = normalCDF(x)
27
28 p = 0.5.*erf(x./sqrt(2));
```

7.2.4   Fitting the Models to Data

The code in Listings 7.6 and 7.7 takes a parameter vector, participant data, and other details about the experiment and returns the $-\ln L$ for the parameters given the data and the predicted proportion correct for each stimulus value given the parameters. This is sufficient to carry out parameter estimation and model selection. Listing 7.8 provides a script to fit each of the models and provides statistics for model comparison and further interpretation.

7.2.4.1   Setting Up

The first thing the script does is to assign the proportion of 'A' responses from the six participants to the variable data. The data are structured so that the rows correspond to participants (in the same order as in Figure 7.9), and each column corresponds to a stimulus i.

Listing 7.8 Code for MLE and Model Selection for the Categorization Models

```
1  % script catModels
2  clear all
3  close all
4
5  dataP = [0.75,0.67,0.54,0.4,0.4,0.37,0.58,0.71;
6         0.92,0.81,0.53,0.28,0.14,0.22,0.45,0.81;
7         0.91,0.97,0.93,0.64,0.28,0.09,0.12,0.7;
8         0.98,0.94,0.85,0.62,0.2,0.037,0.078,0.71;
9         0.97,0.94,0.8,0.58,0.4,0.45,0.81,0.97;
10        0.29,0.66,0.85,0.71,0.33,0.1,0.32,0.77];
11
12  % number sessions x 10 blocks x 96 trials /(n stimuli)
13  Ntrain = ((5*10*96)/8);
14  pfeedback = [.6 .6 1 1 0 0 .6 .6];
15  Afeedback = pfeedback .* Ntrain;
16  feedback = [Afeedback; Ntrain-Afeedback];
17
18  Ntest = ((3*10*96)/8);
19  N = repmat(Ntest,1,8);
20
21  dataF = ceil(Ntest.*(dataP));
22
23  stimval = linspace(.0625, .9375, 8);
24
25  %% Maximum likelihood estimation
26  for modelToFit = {'GCM','GRT','DEM'};
27
28      for ppt=1:6
29          switch char(modelToFit)
30              case 'GCM'
31                  f=@(pars) DEMlnL([pars 1], stimval, ↩
                        feedback, dataF(ppt,:), N);
32                  [theta(ppt,:),lnL(ppt),exitflag(ppt)]↩
```

```
33                              =fminbnd(f, 0, 100);
34              case 'GRT'
35                  f=@(pars) GRTlnL(pars, stimval, ↩
                        dataF(ppt,:), N);
36                  [theta(ppt,:),lnL(ppt),exitflag(ppt)]↩
37                          =fminsearchbnd(f,[.3 .7 .1], ↩
                                [-1 -1 eps], [2 2 10]);
38              case 'DEM'
39                  f=@(pars) DEMlnL(pars, stimval, ↩
                        feedback, dataF(ppt,:), N);
40                  [theta(ppt,:),lnL(ppt),exitflag(ppt)]↩
41                          =fminsearchbnd(f,[5 1], [0 ↩
                                0], [Inf Inf]);
42              otherwise
43                  error('Unknown model');
44          end
45
46          [junk, predP(ppt,:)] = f(theta(ppt,:));
47
48          hess = hessian(f,theta(ppt,:),10^-3);
49          cov = inv(hess);
50          thetaSE(ppt,:) = sqrt(diag(cov));
51      end
52
53      figure
54      pptLab = {'SB','SEH','VB','BG','NV','LT'};
55
56      for ppt=1:6
57          subplot(2,3,ppt);
58          plot(stimval, dataP(ppt,:), '-+');
59          hold all
60          plot(stimval, predP(ppt,:), '-.*');
61          ylim([0 1]);
62          xlabel('Luminance');
63          ylabel('P(A)');
64          title(char(pptLab{ppt}));
65      end
66      set(gcf, 'Name', char(modelToFit));
67
68      t.theta = theta;
69      t.thetaSE = thetaSE;
70      t.nlnL = lnL;
71      eval([char(modelToFit) '=t;']);
72      clear theta thetaSE
73  end
74
75
76  for ppt=1:6
```

(Continued)

(Continued)

```
77    [AIC(ppt,:), BIC(ppt,:), AICd(ppt,:), ←
         BICd(ppt,:), AICw(ppt,:), BICw(ppt,:)] = ...
78    infoCriteria([GCM.nlnL(ppt) GRT.nlnL(ppt) ←
         DEM.nlnL(ppt)], [1 3 2], ←
         repmat(Ntest*8,1,3));
79 end
```

Line 13 works out an approximate number of training trials (i.e., number of exemplars per stimulus) based on details provided in Rouder and Ratcliff (2004): There were between four and six (i.e., approximately five) learning sessions per participant, each session containing 10 blocks of 96 trials that were shared between the eight stimuli. Line 14 assigns the category assignment probabilities in the top panel of Figure 7.8 to the variable pfeedback, and these are then multiplied with the number of trials stored in Ntrain to work out the number of trials on which the feedback indicated each stimulus belonged to Category A; this is assigned to the variable Afeedback. The variable feedback is then constructed in accordance with Listing 7.6, with one column for frequency of 'A' feedback and a second column for the frequency of 'B' feedback (these two values adding up to Ntrain for each luminance value).

Line 18 uses a similar procedure to line 13 to work out the number of test trials per stimulus. Rouder and Ratcliff (2004) analyzed the data from the last three sessions for each participant, by which time performance had stabilized. As for line 13, this is combined with the number of blocks per session (10) and the number of trials per block (96), along with the number of stimulus values (8) to determine the number of test trials per stimulus value per participant. It is important that this is exact, as these numbers will feed into the binomial log-likelihood function, which is sensitive to the overall number of trials (1,000 trials are more informative than only 10 trials and will sharpen the log-likelihood surface). These are then multiplied by the proportions stored in dataP to calculate dataF, the number of trials on which each participant responded 'A' for each stimulus value. The resulting value is then replicated eight times to make a vector N holding Ntest for each stimulus value.

The final piece of setting up is in line 23, which assigns the eight stimulus values (linearly spaced in the range .0625–.9375, with increments of .125) to the variable stimval. In line with Rouder and Ratcliff (2004), we assume that the physical luminance values (the proportion of nongray pixels that are white) map directly into psychological luminance values. However, it is possible that there may be some nonlinear relationship between the actual and perceived stimulus. Methods such as multidimensional scaling (Kruskal & Wish, 1978) are available to extract the underlying psychological dimension based on similarity ratings and confusability data. Rouder and Ratcliff (2004) compared a number of functions mapping physical luminance to perceived luminance and found all gave comparable results, including a function assuming a linear relationship between actual and perceived luminance. In providing the physical luminance values as perceived luminance, we are assuming a deterministic (i.e., noise-free) linear relationship between physical and perceived luminance.

7.2.4.2   Fitting the Models

The loop beginning at line 26 and finishing at line 73 does the hard graft of fitting each model to the data from each participant. We start off by setting up a loop across the models; each time we pass through the loop, we will be fitting a different model whose name will be contained in the variable modelToFit as a string. Within that loop is another loop beginning at line 28, which loops across participants, as we are fitting each participant's data individually, indexed by the loop variable ppt. The next line looks at modelToFit to work out which model's code to use in the fitting. This uses a switch statement, which matches char(modelToFit) to a number of possible cases ('GCM','GRT','DEM'), and otherwise reverts to a default catch statement, which here returns an error message. The switch statement uses char(modelToFit) rather than modelToFit directly because the set of values for modelToFit is provided in a cell array (being enclosed in curly braces), so the current value of modelToFit must be turned into a string using the function char before it can be matched to the string in each case statement.

Within each possible case, there are two lines. The first line (e.g., line 31) constructs an *anonymous function* (see the MATLAB documentation for further details). Anonymous functions are functions that are adaptively created on the fly and do not require their own function files in MATLAB. We are using anonymous functions here because, as we will see, we end up calling the same function several times. By using the anonymous function, we will simplify our code and make it easier to read. The main purpose of line 31 is to create a new on-the-fly function called f that takes only a single argument, a parameter vector called pars. Inside this function, all that happens is that we call DEMlnL and pass it pars, along with the other information needed by DEMlnL. Remember that GCM is DEM with γ fixed at 1; the first argument to DEM is therefore a vector joining together the free parameter c and the fixed value of 1 for γ. Going from left to right, we next have stimval, the luminance of each stimulus; [feedback; Ntrain−feedback], a matrix containing one row for the number of times 'A' was given as feedback and a second row containing the number of times 'B' was given as feedback; the frequency of 'A' responses for the participant of current interest; and N, a vector specifying how many trials in total were tested for each stimulus. No feedback information is provided to the anonymous function for GRT because GRT does not require this argument. All this information from `stimval` onwards doesn't change within the participant loop; by using the anonymous function, we can specify it the one time and ignore it for the rest of the code, focusing instead on the parameter vector, which will need to change during the parameter estimation.

The second line within each case passes the anonymous function `f` to a minimization routine to find the ML parameter estimates (remember, we are minimizing the negative log-likelihood). GCM has only a single parameter to be estimated (*c*); accordingly, we use the built-in MATLAB function `fminbnd`, which performs unidimensional function minimization. This function does not need a starting point and only requires the minimum and maximum possible values for the parameter; we've set these to 0 and 100, respectively. For GRT and DEM, the models incorporating at least two free parameters, we use the `fminsearchbnd` function that was introduced in Section 7.1. This function requires a starting vector and vectors of lower and upper bounds on the parameters. These can be inspected in lines 37 and 41.

The result of what we've discussed so far is that for a given model (indexed by `modelToFit`), the code loops across participants, and for each participant, the anonymous function is reconstructed and passed to code that minimizes the appropriate negative log-likelihood function (contained in `f`) using a minimization routine. When each minimization attempt is finished, the ML parameter estimates, the minimized $- \ln L$, and the exit flag (giving information about whether or not the minimization was successful) are respectively placed in variables `theta`, `lnL`, and `exitflag`.

Having found the ML parameter estimates, line 46 runs the model a final time using the MLEs to obtain the predictions of the model under the MLEs; these predicted proportions of 'A' responses are stored in the matrix `predP`.

7.2.4.3   Obtaining Standard Errors on Parameter Estimates

After ML estimation has been performed, the next section of code (lines 48–50) finds the standard errors on the parameter estimates. Because we rewrote each log-likelihood function into the anonymous function `f`, we can use the same code for all three models. Line 48 passes the anonymous function and MLEs to the `hessian` function provided in Chapter 5, along with the δ parameter required by that function. The following two lines convert the resulting Hessian matrix `hess` into standard errors by taking the matrix inverse of the Hessian matrix to obtain a covariance matrix and then taking the square root of the values along the diagonal of this matrix to obtain the standard error on the ML parameter estimates.

The ML parameter estimates and their estimated standard errors are given in Tables 7.4, 7.5, and 7.6 for GCM, GRT, and DEM, respectively. We will refer back to these after discussing the model comparison results.

Table 7.4 ML Parameter Estimates and Associated Standard Errors for the GCM Fits to the Data in Figure 7.9

Participant	c	$SE(c)$
SB	2.29	0.36
SEH	5.29	0.32
VB	9.32	0.38
BG	9.43	0.38
NV	5.91	0.36
LT	10.28	· 0.41

Table 7.5 ML Parameter Estimates and Associated Standard Errors for the GRT Fits to the Data in Figure 7.9

Participant	β_1	$SE(\beta_1)$	β_2	$SE(\beta_2)$	σ	$SE(\sigma)$
SB	0.29	0.01	0.80	0.01	0.29	0.01
SEH	0.33	0.01	0.82	0.01	0.17	0.00
VB	0.92	0.01	0.46	0.01	0.16	0.00
BG	0.45	0.01	0.92	0.01	0.13	0.00
NV	0.43	0.01	0.69	0.01	0.15	0.00
LT	0.12	0.07	1.26	0.17	0.78	0.17

Table 7.6 ML Parameter Estimates and Associated Standard Errors for the DEM Fits to the Data in Figure 7.9

Participant	c	$SE(c)$	γ	$SE(\gamma)$
SB	2.44	0.90	0.95	0.26
SEH	4.89	0.43	1.13	0.11
VB	4.39	0.22	3.38	0.18
BG	4.65	0.21	3.24	0.16
NV	0.86	0.07	5.81	0.23
LT	13.51	1.19	0.69	0.07

7.2.4.4 Model Predictions

Lines 53 to 66 plot the predictions of the model currently specified by `modelToFit` given the ML parameter estimates. These plots are shown in Figures 7.10 to 7.12. GCM, whose predictions are shown in Figure 7.10, gives a visually poor fit to the data in most cases. GCM qualitatively misses the pattern in the data for participants SB, SEH, BG, and NV and apparently quantitatively

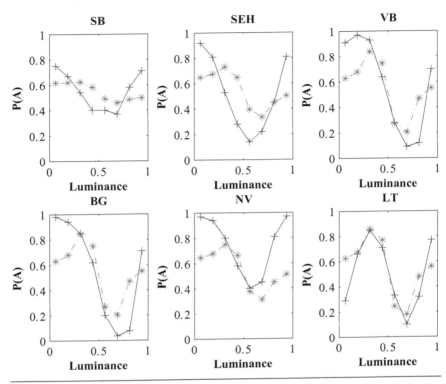

Figure 7.10 Proportion of 'A' responses predicted by GCM under ML parameter estimates. The data are plotted as crosses connected by solid lines, and the model predictions are plotted as asterisks connected by dashed lines.

misses the data of VB. The one participant for whom GCM appears to give a reasonable fit is participant LT in the bottom-right panel, who showed a very clear drop in 'A' responses with lower luminance values (stimuli 1 and 2). The predictions of GRT, shown in Figure 7.11, are much more in line with the data. The one exception is participant LT, for whom GRT predicts a nearly flat function that does little to capture the large changes in responses across luminance values for that participant. Finally, the predictions of DEM are shown in Figure 7.12. These predictions are similar to those of GCM (Figure 7.10), with DEM giving visually better fits in some cases (VB and BG). DEM generally appears to be inferior to GRT, with two exceptions. For participant VB, GRT and DEM appear to give equally good fits, and for participant LT, GRT is clearly inferior to DEM.

7.2.4.5 Model Comparison

Let's use the model selection methods presented in Chapter 5 to compare the three models. Although GRT looks like it gives a better fit to the data in some cases, this

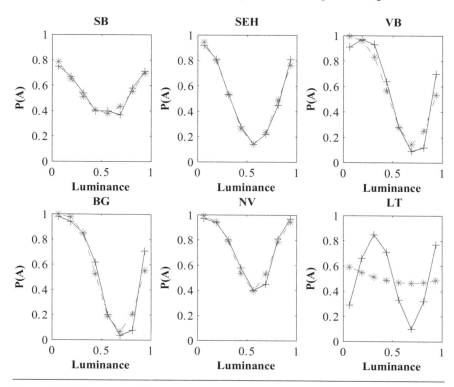

Figure 7.11 Proportion of 'A' responses predicted by GRT under ML parameter estimates.

may simply follow from the fact that it has more free parameters than both GCM and DEM. Similarly, DEM appears to give a better account of the data than GCM, but to what extent is this due to its extra parameter γ picking up nonsystematic residual variance?

Lines 68 to 72 prepare the results of the model fitting for model comparison by storing the results of each model's fit in a separate structure. Line 71 uses the eval function to assign the modeling results, collected in the temporary structure t in the preceding few lines, to a structure named either GCM, GRT, or DEM. Line 72 deletes a few variables because they differ in size between the different models and would return an error otherwise.

The last part of Listing 7.8 calls the function infoCriteria from Chapter 5 to obtain AIC and BIC values, AIC and BIC differences, and model weights for each participant. The AIC and BIC differences calculated by this code are shown in Table 7.7, and the corresponding model weights are shown in Table 7.8. For participants SB, SEH, BG, and NV, the model differences and model weights bear out the superior fit of the GRT suggested in the figures, with the model

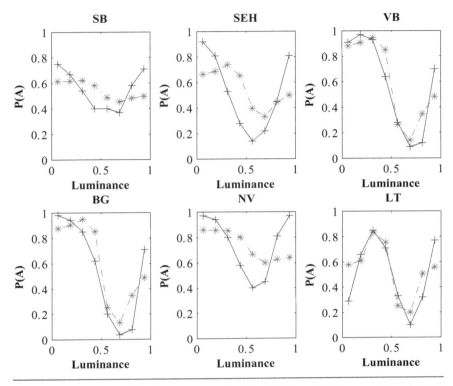

Figure 7.12 Proportion of 'A' responses predicted by DEM under ML parameter estimates.

weights for GRT indistinguishable from 1 for these participants. The information criterion results for VB are more informative. Recall that the fits for GRT and DEM looked similar in quality for VB. Tables 7.7 and 7.8 show that GRT nonetheless gives a statistically superior fit to VB's data, even when the extra parameter in the GRT is accounted for via the correction term in the AIC and BIC. Finally, Tables 7.7 and 7.8 show that LT's data are better fit by an exemplar model, particularly the DEM. Not only does DEM provide a superior fit to GRT in this case, but the information criteria point to DEM also being superior to GCM in its account of the data, indicating that the extra parameter γ is important for the exemplar model's account for this participant. Inspection of the ML parameter estimates in Table 7.6 is instructive for interpreting DEM's success. The row for LT shows that the estimated c was very large compared to the other participants and that the γ parameter was below 1. The large c for DEM (and, indeed, GCM, as shown in Table 7.4) means that stimuli only really match exemplars with the same luminance in memory, leading the model to strongly track the feedback probabilities. However, the $\gamma < 1$ means that the model undermatches those feedback

Table 7.7 AIC and BIC Differences Between the Three Models GCM, GRT, and DEM

	ΔAIC			Δ BIC		
	GCM	GRT	DEM	GCM	GRT	DEM
SB	178.42	0.00	180.38	166.49	0.00	174.42
SEH	715.39	0.00	715.83	703.46	0.00	709.87
VB	413.26	0.00	43.53	401.33	0.00	37.57
BG	703.67	0.00	337.16	691.74	0.00	331.20
NV	990.71	0.00	581.08	978.78	0.00	575.12
LT	18.78	527.95	0.00	12.82	533.92	0.00
sum	3020.23	527.95	1857.99	2954.61	533.92	1828.16

Note. Differences are calculated for each participant individually, and summed differences are shown in the bottom row.

Table 7.8 AIC and BIC Weights for the Three Models GCM, GRT, and DEM

	ΔAIC			Δ BIC		
	GCM	GRT	DEM	GCM	GRT	DEM
SB	0.00	1.00	0.00	0.00	1.00	0.00
SEH	0.00	1.00	0.00	0.00	1.00	0.00
VB	0.00	1.00	0.00	0.00	1.00	0.00
BG	0.00	1.00	0.00	0.00	1.00	0.00
NV	0.00	1.00	0.00	0.00	1.00	0.00
LT	0.00	0.00	1.00	0.00	0.00	1.00
mean	0.00	0.83	0.17	0.00	0.83	0.17

Note. Model weights are calculated for each participant individually, and mean weights are shown in the bottom row.

probabilities, which pulls the predicted proportion of 'A' responses back to the baseline of 0.5.

7.2.5 What Have We Learned About Categorization?

The results of the model fitting just presented lie heavily in favor of the GRT model. If we assume that all participants' performance was based on a single model, we can examine the summed AIC/BIC differences in Table 7.7, or the average model weights in Table 7.8, and conclude that the data as a whole are most consistent with the GRT model, and by quite a margin. However, the data plotted in Figure 7.9, along with the modeling results in Tables 7.7 and 7.8, suggest that one participant, LT, is using a different set of representations or processes to perform this task. The most obvious conclusion based on the modeling results is that LT's performance is supported by matching to stored exemplars. However, that conclusion may be premature. Although the results correspond more to the ML predictions of GCM and DEM, notice that although LT's observed probability of giving an 'A' response changes dramatically between stimuli 1 and 2 (and, indeed, between 7 and 8), GCM and DEM's predictions change little between the same stimuli. Arguably, GCM and DEM are still failing to capture an important aspect of these data. Rouder and Ratcliff (2004) noted another possible explanation for these results: that LT was relying on boundaries (as in GRT) to categorize the stimuli but had inserted a third boundary somewhere around the lowest luminance stimulus despite this being a nonoptimal approach. Rouder and Ratcliff (2004) fit GRT with three boundaries to the data of LT and found it to give the best fit of all models and that it was able to produce the large change between stimuli 1 and 2 seen in LT's data. We leave implementation of that model as an exercise for you, but note that this reinforces the overall consistency between GRT and the data.

What does it mean to say that GRT is the "best" model? The main message is that under conditions of uncertainty, and with stimuli varying along a single dimension, people partition the stimulus space using boundaries and use those boundaries to categorize stimuli observed later on. We know it isn't simply that GRT assumes deterministic responding: The DEM model, an exemplar-based model with deterministic responding, failed to compete with the GRT in most cases.

One interesting note to sign off on is that hybrid models have become increasingly popular in accounting for categorization. For example, the RULEX model of Nosofsky and Palmeri (1998) assumes that people use rules to categorize stimuli but store category exceptions as exemplars. The COVIS model of Ashby et al. (1998) assumes that participants can use both explicit rules and implicit representations learned procedurally to categorize stimuli. Rouder and Ratcliff (2004) found that in some circumstances, their participants appeared to use exemplars to perform similar probabilistic categorization tasks and shifted between using boundaries and exemplars depending on the discriminability of the stimuli. This fits well with another hybrid model, ATRIUM (Erickson & Kruschke, 1998), in which rules and exemplars compete to categorize and learn each new object. ATRIUM has been shown to account for a variety of categorization experiments, particularly ones where participants appear to switch between strategies or mechanisms (e.g., Yang & Lewandowsky, 2004). Nonhybrid models of the types considered here are still useful for determining what type of model is predominantly in use in a particular task; nonetheless, a comprehensive model of categorization will need to explain how participants appear to be using quite different representations depending on the nature of the task and stimuli (e.g., Ashby & O'Brien, 2005; Erickson & Kruschke, 1998).

7.3   Conclusion

We have presented two detailed examples that build on the material from the preceding chapters. If you were able to follow those examples and understand what we did and why, then you have now gathered a very solid foundation in the techniques of computational and mathematical modeling.

Concerning future options for exploring the implementation and fitting of models, two directions for further study immediately come to mind: First, we suggest you explore Bayesian approaches to modeling and model selection. Bayesian techniques have recently become prominent in the field, and the material in this book forms a natural and solid foundation for further study in that area. Second, we suggest you investigate hierarchical (or multilevel) techniques. We touched on those techniques in Chapter 3 but were unable to explore them further in this volume. Many good introductions to both issues exist, and one particularly concise summary can be found in Shiffrin, Lee, Kim, and Wagenmakers (2008).

We next present a final chapter that moves away from the techniques of modeling and considers several general frameworks that have been adopted by modelers to explain psychological processes.

Notes

1. Note that our notation and symbology correspond to that used by Clare and Lewandowsky (2004) rather than by Clark (2003).

2. The fact that each replication involves different stimulus vectors (in addition to encoding of a different subset of features of the perpetrator) also implies that each replication involves a different set of faces in the lineup. This is desirable because it generalizes the simulation results across possible stimuli, but it does not reflect the procedure of most experiments in which a single lineup is used for all participants.

3. There are some minor differences between the simulations reported by Clare and Lewandowsky (2004) and those developed here, which were introduced to make the present example simple and transparent. The parameter estimates and model predictions reported here thus differ slightly (though not substantially) from those reported by Clare and Lewandowsky (2004).

4. In fact, we also select a method by which random numbers are selected, but we ignore this subtlety here for brevity.

5. If the number of replications is small, reseeding the random generator carries the risk that the model may capitalize on some chance idiosyncrasy in the random sequence. The

number of replications should therefore be ample (minimum of 100, preferably 1,000 or more).

6. We use *object* to refer to a collection of feature values; these features could be any of the dimensions defining a potentially highly multidimensional space, such as brightness, nose length, tone frequency, or time.

7. This follows from the assumption that members of a category are distributed as a multivariate Gaussian. The optimal boundary in such a case is a multidimensional plane (i.e., a manifold) tracing out those regions of space where the two adjacent categories are equally plausible, which for multivariate Gaussian distributions is mathematically described by a quadratic equation (Ashby, 1992a).

8. Alternatively, you can use the function `normcdf` in the MATLAB Statistics Toolbox.

8

Modeling in a
Broader Context

Earlier in this book, in Section 2.6, we considered what it actually means to have an "explanation" for something. We discovered that explanations exist not in a vacuum but within a psychological context; that is, they must be *understood* in order to have any value (if this sounds mysterious, you may wish to refer back to Section 2.6.3 before proceeding). We then introduced material in the next five chapters that is required for the construction of satisfactory psychological explanations. Most of our discussion, including the detailed examples in the preceding chapter, involved models that were formulated to provide a process explanation (see Section 1.4.4).

The purpose of this final chapter is to present several additional avenues to modeling that inherit most of the techniques we have presented but that formulate explanations at different levels. We begin by covering Bayesian approaches, which assume that human cognition is a mirror of the environment. We then turn to neural networks (also known as connectionist models), which provide a process explanation of cognition with the added claim of neural plausibility. We next briefly touch on theorizing that is explicitly "neuroscientific" and that strongly appeals to the brain's architecture or indicators of its functioning for validation. In a final section, we introduce cognitive architectures: large-scale models that are best understood as a broad organizing framework within which more detailed models of cognition can be developed.

Each of the sections provides a thumbnail sketch of the approach and, where possible, links to material presented in the earlier chapters. However, we cannot possibly do justice to the complexity and richness of each approach in a single chapter, and we therefore conclude each section with pointers to the relevant literature for follow-up research.

8.1   Bayesian Theories of Cognition

In the previous chapters, we have made reference to the advance of Bayes' theorem into psychology. In Chapters 4 and 5, we touched on the contribution of this theorem to scientific reasoning and its ability to transform the conditional probability of the *data given a model* into the probability of a *model given the data*, thus allowing us to quantify the evidence that a data set provides for various alternative hypotheses. For example, the Bayesian Information Criterion (BIC) was shown to deliver an estimate of the probability of the model given the data (Chapter 5).

It turns out that Bayes' theorem also provides a straightforward and exciting model of how humans reason and behave, by treating humans as statisticians who make inferences about their world. One key idea is that we can explain people's behavior with reference to the statistics of their environment. A recent example comes from R. Baddeley and Attewell (2009), who considered the use of lightness terms (light, dark, gray) in the context of information transmission: A person observes an object of a certain lightness and then must use language to communicate that information to another person. R. Baddeley and Attewell noted that the amount of information in the visual signal is limited because the perception of lightness depends not only on the reflectance of the object but also on variable lighting conditions. Additionally, there will be some variability introduced by imperfect memory of the observer. Using measures of both of these sources of variability—obtained by respectively taking recordings of reflectances from different environments (D. Attewell & Baddeley, 2007) and testing people's memory for gray patches varying in reflectance—R. Baddeley and Attewell were able to specify the *channel capacity* of the communication system, the maximum amount of information that could possibly be transmitted. R. Baddeley and Attewell found this value to approach $\log_2(3)$ bits for modern interior environments and used this to explain why most languages have only the terms *black*, *white*, and *gray* for lightness and why qualifier terms such as *light gray* are used relatively infrequently: Because the channel capacity is around $\log_2(3)$ bits (in fact, less in cases where the terms are not used equally frequently)—which corresponds to three terms—any further terms would be redundant, as they would not (indeed could not) provide any further information.

R. Baddeley and Attewell's (2009) example shows how cognition appears to be adapted to—and mirrors—the world. Such demonstrations provide an important foundation for the application of Bayes' theorem to cognition. A particularly strong example of the adaptationist view was provided by J. R. Anderson and Schooler (1991), who argued that the standard forgetting curve (the amount of information retained as a function of time since its presentation and encoding) reflected the change in *usefulness* of information over time. Intuitively, it makes sense that a piece of information we have just learned is more likely to be immediately relevant than one that was learned several years ago. Hence, recent information is more useful than older information, and according to J. R. Anderson and Schooler (1991), the shape of the forgetting function conforms to the objective utility of information in the environment.

To demonstrate that this is the case empirically, J. R. Anderson and Schooler (1991) tabulated the probability of the appearance of a piece of information (a word in the headline of the *New York Times*, a word in child-directed speech, and the sender of an email message to the author, J. R. Anderson) as a function of the amount of time since that piece of information had last appeared (e.g., how many days ago did that word last appear in the *New York Times* headline?). J. R. Anderson and Schooler found that in all cases, the "probability of reappearance" function was well described by a power function similar to that used to characterize the forgetting function in human memory (e.g., Wickelgren, 1974; Wixted & Ebbesen, 1991).

In other words, human forgetting and the objective need for information in the environment proceeded in lock-step. This remarkable parallelism between human information processing and the information structure of the real world forms the basis of Anderson's view (e.g., J. R. Anderson et al., 2004) that cognition is fundamentally "rational"; that is, it is optimally adapted to the environment in a Bayesian sense. We will revisit this particular notion of rationality later in this chapter, when considering cognitive architectures (Section 8.4).

Bayesian theory allows us to go even further, by feeding the known statistical properties of the environment into Bayes' theorem to make precise quantitative predictions about human behavior. This approach may sound familiar, as we have already discussed a Bayesian theory of cognition, in Chapter 2 (Section 2.5.1). There, we discussed an account of how people make predictions about the future under impoverished circumstances: Specifically, how long will an event last given it has been going on for t minutes/hours/years so far? For example, if you know that a movie has been running for 90 minutes already, how long do you think its total runtime will be? Or if a pharaoh has been reigning for 8 years, how long do you expect his total reign to last? The Bayesian account holds that people base their prediction of the total time on prior knowledge about the distribution of total times for the event under consideration. In equation form:

$$p(t_{total}|t) \propto p(t|t_{total})p(t_{total}). \tag{8.1}$$

In this equation, which has been reproduced from Chapter 2 for convenience, $p(t_{total})$ is the actual prior distribution of total times, as, for example, observable from a historical database that records the reigns of Egyptian pharaohs. Supposing that people have access to this prior distribution from their lifelong experience with the world, in the absence of any other information, it can be used to make a fairly good guess about how long an event from the same family (e.g., runtime of a movie or reign of a pharaoh) would be expected to last.

However, in the example from Lewandowsky et al. (2009), participants had some additional information—namely, the amount of time that the event in question had already been running. Lewandowsky et al. assumed that participants treat this information as the likelihood $p(t|t_{total})$—that is, the probability of observing an event after t time units given that it runs for t_{total} units altogether. This likelihood was assumed to follow a uniform distribution between 0 and t_{total}, reflecting the assumption that there is a constant probability with which one encounters an event during its runtime.

As briefly discussed in Chapter 4, the magic of Bayes' theorem is that it allows us (as statisticians and as organisms behaving in the world) to reverse the direction of a conditional. In Lewandowsky et al.'s (2009) case, it provides the machinery to turn the probability of t given t_{total}, provided by the stimulus value (t) in the experiment, into the probability of t_{total} given t, the prediction that participants were asked to make.

The conceptual framework usually adopted in Bayesian theory is that the prior distribution is updated by the likelihood [the incoming evidence, in this case $p(t|t_{total})$] to obtain a posterior distribution that represents our expectations about the environment in light of the newly obtained information. Be clear that $p(t_{total}|t)$ is a posterior *distribution*: A person's expectations about the future are represented by an assignment of probability to all possible states of the environment—or, in the case of a continuous variable such as time, by a probability density function.

Using Bayes' theorem as per Equation 8.1, Lewandowsky et al. (2009) were able to obtain people's posterior distribution $p(t_{total}|t)$. Moreover, using a procedure called *iterated learning*, in which a person's responses are fed back to him or her later in the experiment as stimuli, Lewandowsky et al. were able to exploit the fact that after many such iterated learning trials, people's final posterior distribution converges onto their prior distribution. That is, Griffiths and Kalish (2007) showed mathematically that in an iterated learning procedure, people's estimates ultimately converge onto *their* prior distribution—that is, their preexperimental knowledge of the quantities under consideration. In a nutshell, this arises because each prediction results from a combination of the prior probability and a likelihood, where the likelihood is obtained from the presented stimulus. If responses are then re-presented as stimuli later in the experiment, the posterior distribution comes to resemble the prior distribution more and more because the impact of specific stimuli "washes out." As illustrated in Figure 2.6, Lewandowsky et al. (2009) found that the actual prior probability of quantities in the environment (on the ordinate) closely matched the prior distributions apparently used by people (the "Stationary" distribution on the abscissa), which were obtained using the iterated learning procedure just described.

One concept often associated with Bayesian theory is that of optimality: Individuals' perception (e.g., Alais & Burr, 2004; Weiss, Simonvelli, & Adelson, 2002; Yuille & Kersten, 2006), cognition (Lewandowsky et al., 2009; Norris, 2006; Tenenbaum, Griffiths, & Kemp, 2006), and action (e.g., Körding & Wolpert, 2006) are adapted to their environment, and their predictions or expectations about the environment are in some sense optimal. Bayesian theory does indeed provide an unambiguous definition of optimality; if the prior distribution and the likelihood are both known, and if the posterior distribution matches the predictions of people in that same environment, then there is a firm basis for concluding that those participants are acting optimally. In some areas, particularly perception, the Bayesian model serves as an "ideal observer" model that describes the best possible performance on a task in light of the inherent uncertainty in the environment, or in the "noisiness" of perception. In the example by Lewandowsky et al. (2009) just discussed, the prior distribution was independently known (e.g., by examining historical data about Egyptian pharaohs), and hence there is little ambiguity in interpreting the outcome as showing that "whatever people do is equivalent to use of the correct prior and sampling from the posterior" (p. 991).

In other cases, however, the model describing the likelihood function might only be assumed, or the prior distribution might be specified by the researcher without necessarily measuring the environment. In these cases, any claims of optimality are less grounded: Correspondence of the model's predictions with human behavior may be down to the specification of the prior or the likelihood, which are effectively free parameters in the model. An additional implication is that optimality is only expressed with respect to a given prior distribution and likelihood function, meaning that our definition of optimality may change depending on how we conceptualize a task or environment (Courville, Daw, & Touretzky, 2006). For example, one feature of many Bayesian theories is that they assume the world to be static, meaning that each previous observation is given equal weighting in making future predictions. However, this model will not be optimal if the world is changing (as in the J. R. Anderson and Schooler example above), and the optimal model will instead be one that explicitly recognizes the temporal uncertainty in the environment. One outstanding issue is whether Bayesian theories provide enough detail to describe theories at a process level (see Section 1.4.4).

Perhaps a better way to think about Bayesian theory is that it describes cognition at a process characterization level (see Section 1.4.3), by identifying general lawful properties of human behavior without describing, say, the memory processes that represent the prior distribution. Having said that, Bayesian concepts can be incorporated into models that provide a process explanation for various cognitive phenomena (e.g., J. R. Anderson, 1996; Dennis & Humphreys, 2001; J. McClelland & Chappell, 1998; Norris, 2006; Shiffrin & Steyvers, 1997).

Although Bayesian theories are relatively new in psychology, there is no question that they are gaining in popularity and that they are here to stay. Our brief discussion of the Bayesian approach barely scratches the surface of the considerable promise of the approach. To gain further information about these models, a good place to start are recent special issues of *Trends in Cognitive Sciences* (Chater, Tenenbaum, & Yuille, 2006c) and *Developmental Science* (e.g., Shultz, 2007).

8.2   Neural Networks

One critical feature of Bayesian theory is that many interesting aspects of human behavior arise from the characteristics of the environment. The same can be said of our next framework, neural network modeling (also called connectionism).

The fundamental feature of neural network models is that they treat cognition and behavior as resulting from learning about the environment, thus creating a reflection of regularities in the environment in our behavior. Neural network models are also notable for their treatment of cognition as resulting from the massively parallel operation of simple processes, a characteristic that connectionist modelers point out is also a fundamental feature of the brain. Connectionist models also generated much excitement in the 1980s and 1990s following demonstrations that the models formed their own internal representations based only on regularities in the input. Those "emergent properties" that are seemingly generated by the model without being known beforehand contribute much to the continued popularity of these models. We present an example of emergent properties after presenting the basics of neural networks.

8.2.1   Basic Architecture and Operation

The basic assumption of neural network models is that cognition is carried out by the passing of activation between simple, interconnected processing units. An example of a neural network is shown in Figure 8.1.

The circles in the figure represent simple, primitive processing units. Depending on the type of network, these units can represent items in the world (an object,

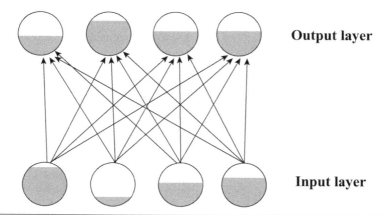

Output layer

Input layer

Figure 8.1 An example of a neural network model. Each circle is a processing unit ("neuron"), and the arrowhead lines between them are the weighted connections. Also schematically depicted in the figure are the activation values of the units: The more activated a unit, the more it is filled with dark shading.

a word, or a category), meaningful features of objects (color or size), or abstract features that are not directly interpretable (more on this below). Regardless of the representational scheme, the overall pattern of activations across input or output units represents a meaningful stimulus or event in the world. This pattern may be as simple as activating a single unit to represent an item, as is assumed in *localist* models (e.g., J. L. McClelland & Rumelhart, 1981; Page & Norris, 1998a; see Page, 2000, for a review). In that case, each unit directly represents an item or object. Alternatively, as discussed below, in a *distributed* representation, a number of units (or indeed all units) are activated to some extent, and the meaningfulness derives from the overall pattern, similar to the way in which the overall ensemble of pixels in a digital camera yields a meaningful image (but no individual pixel on its own does).

The units are connected by weights that pass activation, and thus information, between the units to an extent determined by their values (hence the name *weights*). Larger weight values mean more activation is passed from one unit to the other.

One characteristic of the network shown in Figure 8.1 is that the units are separated into two layers, an input layer and an output layer. This characteristic applies to most standard neural networks and reinforces the learning-directed nature of these models: The model's task is to learn associations, such that when some input is presented, the output that has been previously associated with it appears at the output layer. How, then, are those weights set to enable the network to successfully solve a task? In most cases, the weights are updated by

mathematical learning rules in response to the stimuli (and responses) to which
the network is exposed; that is, the network learns about its environment. We consider two types of such learning algorithms within two classes of networks that
have been highly influential during the past 30 years.

8.2.2   Hebbian Models

We begin by considering a class of models that—for reasons that will soon become
apparent—are named after the great Canadian psychologist Donald Hebb. These
"Hebbian" models generally assume that items are represented in a *distributed*
fashion. As already noted, a distributed representation is one in which the identity
of an item cannot necessarily be determined from the activation of any particular unit because several items may assign it the same activation, in the same way
that a given pixel in a digital image may coincidentally be identically activated by
multiple different images. Instead, the activation values of all the units jointly represent items. For this reason, items are usually coded as vectors, with each vector
element representing the activation of a particular unit.

There is often no necessary correspondence between items being presented
to participants in an experiment and the coding of those items in the confines of
the model. For example, in several models of memory, list items are created by
generating vectors of random numbers (e.g., G. D. A. Brown et al., 2000; Farrell
& Lewandowsky, 2002; Murdock, 1982). If there is some similarity structure in
the stimuli, this can be incorporated by making the item vectors more or less
similar to each other by introducing covariations in the activation values across
items (e.g., G. D. A. Brown et al., 2000; Lewandowsky & Farrell, 2008a). Note
that all these assumptions are, to a large extent, external to the operation of the
model itself: The core task of the model is to learn associations between input
patterns and output patterns.

How are these associations learned? The learning process in Hebbian models
was inspired long ago by Hebb (1949), who made the simple—yet fundamental—
suggestion that if two units are coactivated, then the connection between those
units should be strengthened. Although Hebb was talking about hypothetical neurons in the brain, the same principle gave rise to a mathematical formulation of
what is now called the generalized Hebb rule of learning, which is expressed formally as

$$\Delta w_{ij} = \eta f_i g_j, \tag{8.2}$$

where w_{ij} is the weight between input unit f_i and output unit g_j, and the Δ sign
indicates that we are updating the weight with whatever is on the right-hand side
of the equation. This turns out to simply be the product of the activations of the

input unit and output unit, scaled by a parameter η that controls the strength of learning.

It should be clear how this is analogous to Hebb's verbal proposal: If f_i and g_j are both large and positive, then the weight between them will increase proportionally to both units' activation.

By thus using the weights to track the co-firing of input and output units, Hebbian learning provides a mechanism for learning associations between whole items. If an activation pattern is presented across the input units (vector $\mathbf{f}$, represented by elements f_i in the above equation) and a separate activation pattern presented across the output units ($\mathbf{g}$), then adjusting the weights amounts to learning an association between those two activation patterns. In other words, the memory in the network is in the weights! Critically, the weights by themselves do not mean or do anything: Memory in a neural network is the effect of past experience on future performance via the weights, which determine how activation is passed from the input units to the output units. In addition, and in departure from alternative viewpoints such as the cognitive architectures discussed below, there are no separate memories: All associations are stored in the one weight matrix, such that memories are superimposed in this "composite" storage. That is, the learning rule in Equation 8.2 applies irrespective of the identity of items $\mathbf{f}$ and $\mathbf{g}$, and the same weight w_{ij} may be updated multiple times by different pairs of items.

The effects of changing the weights can be seen by considering how a Hebbian network retrieves information. Let us imagine that the network has learned several input-output pairs and that we now present some input pattern as a cue and ask the network for a response. That is, we ask the network, What output pattern was paired with this input pattern? To do so, we present a cue, $\mathbf{c}$, and activate the input units accordingly. The activation of output unit j in this test situation, r_j, is then simply the sum of each input activation multiplied by the weight between that input unit and the output unit j:

$$r_j = \sum_i c_i w_{ij}. \tag{8.3}$$

The effects of learning become apparent when we substitute the weight change resulting from the association between a particular input-output pair $\mathbf{f}$-$\mathbf{g}$ from Equation 8.2 into the activation rule in Equation 8.3:

$$r_j = \sum_i \eta c_i f_i g_j. \tag{8.4}$$

There are two things to note about this equation. The first is that the bigger the input activations (c_i) or the larger the weight values overall, the larger the output activation values will be. The second, less trivial feature of Equation 8.4 is that the learned output g_j will be elicited as the activation for the output unit j to the extent that the activation pattern $\mathbf{c}$ matches the learned input $\mathbf{f}$. In the case of an extreme match, where $\mathbf{c}$ is the same as $\mathbf{f}$, the product following η is given by $f_i^2 g_j$, which, when applied for all output units, will produce the best match to $\mathbf{g}$. In practice, there will usually be a number of associations stored in the weights, and each output pattern $\mathbf{g}(k)$ will be elicited to the extent that the cue matches the corresponding input pattern $\mathbf{f}(k)$, where the match is measured by the dot product (see Equation 7.1). As a consequence, if the cue matches more than one input pattern, the output of the network will be a blend—a weighted sum of the learned outputs.

Hebbian models are well suited to modeling memory. For example, they are able to generalize to new cues based on previous knowledge: Several models of serial recall (see Chapter 4) assume that people remember the order of elements in a list by forming a Hebbian association between each list item and some representation of its timing (G. D. A. Brown et al., 2000) or position (Lewandowsky & Farrell, 2008a). Critically, the vectors representing neighboring positions (or times) are assumed to overlap. This means that cueing for an item at a particular position (time) will elicit a blend of list items, with the target item highly weighted, and neighboring items activated to a lesser extent. This similarity-based generalization during retrieval explains the common fact in serial recall that when items are recalled out of order, they are nonetheless recalled in approximately the correct position (rather than in a random position; e.g., Henson et al., 1996).

Hebbian learning also plays an important role in autoassociative models, in which recurrent weights projecting from a single layer of units feed back into that same layer. By implication, updating weights using Hebbian learning means that an item is associated with itself—hence the name *autoassociator*. This probably sounds ridiculous—what good can such a mechanism be in practice? It sounds as though the associative component is redundant because all it supplies is the item that has to be available as a cue in the first place! However, autoassociative models come into their own when we consider the situation of having only partial information about an item. If I have some knowledge about an object (e.g., I can see the lower half of a person's face, and I need to identify the person), I can present this information to the autoassociative network and let it fill in the gaps. This works because the weights, which connect together different units in the same single layer, effectively store information about the correlations between units. If two units tend to fire together, and I know that one of the units is on, a justifiable inference (from the network's perspective) is that the other unit should also be on. Hence, an autoassociator provides a powerful tool for a process known as "redintegration," whereby a complete item can be reconstructed from partial and/or degraded information in the cue.

In reality, it turns out that a single pass through the network rarely suffices for complete redintegration because what is produced at output will be a blend of the items that have been learned by the network. Accordingly, most autoassociative models use an iterative procedure, in which the output activations from one iteration serve as the input for the next iteration (e.g., J. A. Anderson, Silverstein, Ritz, & Jones, 1977; Lewandowsky & Farrell, 2008b; O'Toole, Deffenbacher, Valentin, & Abdi, 1994). Over iterations, the strongest item in the blend will come to dominate; since, according to Equation 8.4, items will be more strongly represented in the blend at output if they more strongly match the input, and since the input on one iteration is simply the output from the previous iteration, this process serves as an amplification device that will eventually converge on a single representation. For this reason, autoassociative networks have been used as "clean-up" mechanisms that take the blended output from a standard associator and disambiguate this to obtain a pure representation of a single item (e.g., Chappell & Humphreys, 1994; Lewandowsky, 1999; Lewandowsky & Farrell, 2008b). They have also been applied to such areas as perceptual learning (J. A. Anderson et al., 1977) and face recognition (O'Toole et al., 1994).

8.2.3   Backpropagation Models

Attractive as Hebbian models are, they have clear and well-understood mathematical limitations that prevent them from learning more complicated sets of associations (for a discussion, see Chapter 2 of Elman et al., 1996). Those limitations are circumvented by another class of networks, known as backpropagation models. Backpropagation models extend the basic framework outlined so far by introducing a third, "hidden" layer of units in between the input and output units. When a pattern of activation is presented across the input layer, the hidden units update their activation based on the activation transmitted from the input units across the first layer of weights and then pass the updated activations through the next set of weights to the output layer. Although the presence of an intermediate layer of weights may appear trivial at first glance, it actually has profound implications that we flesh out in the following.

The presence of a hidden layer is tied to the further assumption that learning and processing are nonlinear. To illustrate, the activation of units is calculated according to Equation 8.3, but with an additional step in which the activations are "squashed" using a so-called logistic function:[1]

$$r_j = \frac{1}{1 + \exp(-\sum_i w_{ij} f_i)}.$$
(8.5)

A key feature of backpropagation models is that they learn via error correction. That is, weights are updated not simply on the basis of the output values—as in

Hebbian learning—but rather based on the difference between the "correct" output value and the output actually produced when the input pattern is used as a cue. In fact, the backpropagation learning algorithm works to minimize the error between the desired and obtained output $E = \sum(r_j - g_j)^2$. The algorithm minimizes this error using a gradient descent algorithm that, for a particular learning episode, adjusts the weights so as to reduce E as much as possible. This is precisely analogous to the error minimization routines discussed in Chapter 3, except that the "parameters" being optimized are the weights in the network rather than conventional model parameters.

Although this might seem to imply that backpropagation models are thus incredibly flexible, it is important to note that the weights are optimized with respect to the training sequence (stimuli and feedback) rather than with respect to the data; that is, the network is trying best to account for the environment, *not* people's behavior in that environment.

A classic example of a backpropagation model is Hinton's (1990) demonstration of how connectionist networks can learn family trees (see also Hinton, 1986). In Hinton's network, the name of a person and a relationship (e.g., brother, grandmother) were coded and fed in as inputs, with the network tasked to produce a pattern of activation across the output units corresponding to the appropriate response. For example, if Colin and Charlotte are siblings, and "Colin + sister" is given as the input, then the target output is "Charlotte." The network, which used localist representations of people and relationships, was trained on two family trees, one English and one Italian, each involving 12 people spread across three generations (see top panel of Figure 8.2).

Not only did the network learn to produce the outputs appropriate to specific cues, but it also developed some "emergent" internal representations. Those emergent representations become apparent when the weights from the input to hidden units are analyzed. As can be seen in the bottom panel of Figure 8.2, the first unit[2] "represents" the difference between English and Italian, in that the weights to this unit from English people were excitatory, whereas those from Italian people were inhibitory. Note that the network was given no separate information about the language of the people involved; this discrimination emerged by virtue of the fact that only people from the same tree were ever presented to the network as members of a relationship. Figure 8.2 also shows other forms of representation; for example, the second unit appears to code for generation, receiving excitatory weights from grandparents, inhibitory weights from grandchildren, and small positive or negative weights from the middle stratum of the family tree, parents. Again, no information was given about this higher order information, but the model used the statistics of the input (which people are paired with each other and as part of which specific relationship) to extract these higher order relationships.

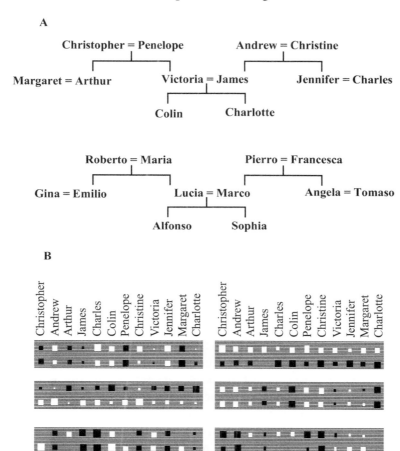

Figure 8.2 Hinton's (1986, 1990) application of a backpropagation network to the learning of familial relations. Panel A shows one of the tree structures used to generate the Person 1–relationship–Person 2 sets that were presented for learning. Panel B shows the size and sign of the weights projecting from each localist unit coding a person to each of six hidden units. Each large box corresponds to a hidden unit, and the top and bottom rows in each box correspond to English and Italian names, respectively. The small squares indicate whether a weight was excitatory (white) or inhibitory (black), with the size of the square indicating the magnitude of the weight. From Hinton, G. E. (1990). Mapping part-whole hierarchies into connectionist networks. *Artificial Intelligence, 46*, 47–75. Published by Elsevier. Reproduced with permission.

A final notable feature of this example is that it highlights the role of the different layers of units: The weights between the input and hidden layers effectively learn to transform or remap the input into new representations that are (more easily) learnable. The hidden-to-output connections then store the associations

between the transformed inputs and the target outputs. It is this ability to transform input space into emergent representations that differentiates backpropagation networks from Hebbian networks, and that has contributed to much of the
excitement about connectionism in general.

One interesting implication of the error-driven learning inherent in backpropagation is that it gives greater weighting to more recent information. In the extreme
case, backpropagation may produce *catastrophic interference*, whereby learning
one set of associations grossly impairs the network's memory for another, previously learned set of associations (McCloskey & Cohen, 1989; Ratcliff, 1990).
Although this problem is largely quantitative, in that modifying various assumptions about the representations and learning algorithm brings the interference
more in line with that seen in human forgetting (e.g., French, 1992; Lewandowsky,
1991), the catastrophic-interference effect usefully illustrates the dynamics of
learning in these models. To see why catastrophic interference might arise, consider the top panel of Figure 8.3, which schematically depicts the progress of
learning as the movement of weights through "weight space," analogous to the
movement of a parameter vector through parameter space in parameter estimation
(see Figure 3.4).

If the network is first trained on one set of associations, B, the weights will
move from their initial setting (A) and, due to the error-driven learning of the
backpropagation algorithm, will eventually settle on a minimum error $Min(X)$
representing a set of weights that adequately captures the associations in B. Now,
if a new set of associations (C) is presented, the error surface will change—
because the already stored knowledge is no longer adequate—and will drive the
weights toward the new minimum $Min(Y)$. In doing so, the weights will move
away from $Min(X)$, producing forgetting of the old set of associations, B.

One way to prevent catastrophic interference is to interleave both sets of information to be learned, such that no one set of information is more recent than the
other. As depicted in the bottom of Figure 8.3, the state of the weights will constantly change direction as one or the other set of information is learned but will
ultimately converge on a minimum $Min(X\&Y)$ that does a reasonable job of
accounting for both sets of associations. Supported by simulations, Farrell and
Lewandowsky (2000) used this reasoning to explain why automating tasks (for
example, in an aircraft cockpit) leads operators to be poor at detecting occasional
failures of the automation. Farrell and Lewandowsky (2000) suggested that when
a task is automated, operators learn *not* to respond to a task, which catastrophi-
cally interferes with their previously learned responses (e.g., to push a button in
order to change radio frequencies when entering a different air space).

It has also been found that repeatedly returning full control of the task to
an operator for a brief period is sufficient to minimize the deleterious effects of
automation on performance. Farrell and Lewandowsky (2000) suggested that this

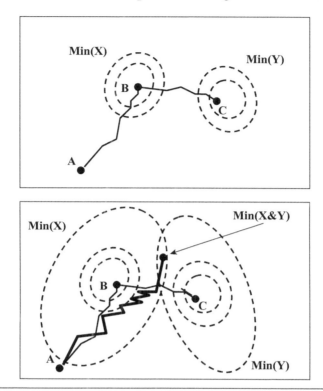

Figure 8.3 Schematic depiction of movement through weight space as learning progresses in a backpropagation network. The top panel corresponds to sequential learning of two sets of information, and the bottom panel corresponds to interleaved presentation of the two sets. From Farrell, S., & Lewandowsky, S. (2000). A connectionist model of complacency and adaptive recovery under automation. *Journal of Experimental Psychology: Learning, Memory, & Cognition, 26,* 395–410. Published by the American Psychological Association. Reproduced with permission.

situation is analogous to the interleaved learning illustrated in the bottom panel of Figure 8.3: Returning temporary control to the operator provides some "rehearsal" of the old associations, preventing the weights from converging on the weight space minimum representing "don't respond."

8.2.4   Summary

We presented two neural networks that have been influential in cognitive psychology during the past few decades. There is a plethora of other networks, and we cannot do this area justice in a single section. Instead, interested readers may wish to choose from the large number of relevant texts to learn more about networks. For example, the book by J. A. Anderson (1995) provides an in-depth treatment of Hebbian networks and autoassociators, whereas Gurney (1997) and Levine (2000) provide other broad overviews.

Irrespective of which network you may choose to apply to a particular problem, the techniques you will use are identical to those outlined in Chapters 2 to 7. In fact, the WITNESS model discussed in Chapter 7 can be considered to be a (albeit miniaturesque) neural network: All stimuli were represented by vectors, thus instantiating a "distributed" representation, and information was retrieved by interrogating memory via a cue, similar to the way information is elicited in a Hebbian net.

Thus, from the preceding chapter you already know that just like any other model, a neural network requires that some parameters (e.g., the learning rate η in Equation 8.2 or the parameters of WITNESS) be estimated from the data. Just like any other model, a network will generate predictions that are then compared to the data—although unlike many other models, a network requires access to the sequence of training stimuli in order to learn the task before it can generate predictions.

8.3   Neuroscientific Modeling

Whereas neural networks tend merely to "borrow" a neural metaphor—by representing their underlying mathematics in a pictorial form that is analogous to the known structure of the brain—another branch of theorizing directly appeals to the brain's architecture, or indicators of its functioning, for validation and test of the theories' assumptions. For example, some variants of the multiple memory systems (MMS) view provide very specific information about the location, within the brain, of the different memory systems: The declarative system, which is responsible for storage and recollection of episodic memories, is said to reside in the medial temporal lobes, whereas the procedural system, which is responsible for the acquisition and retention of routinized skills, is said to reside in other cortical and subcortical structures (for a review, see, e.g., Poldrack & Foerde, 2008).

For lack of a universally acknowledged term for this type of modeling, we call this the "neuroscience approach." Because this approach sometimes reverts to purely verbal theorizing, we first show how the pitfalls of verbal theorizing identified in Chapter 2 apply in equal force to neuroscientific reasoning. We then turn to other instances in which neuroscientific data have been used with considerable success to test and constrain computational models.

8.3.1   The Allure of Neuroscience

We discussed the vexations of the identifiability problem at the beginning of our book (Section 2.6.1). In that earlier discussion, we noted that J. R. Anderson (1990) suggested that the identifiability problem can be resolved by the additional constraint provided by neuroscientific measures—for example, in the form of brain imaging data—and that this has now been achieved or is at least near (J. R. Anderson, 2007). For example, J. R. Anderson (2005) reviewed evidence that provided a mapping between specific brain regions and modules within his cognitive architecture ACT-R (more on that later in Section 8.4), concluding that brain imaging data go a long way toward providing the constraints necessary to identify the presumed components of a complex sequence of cognitive processes that would escape identification by purely behavioral means.

Although we agree that neuroscience has made a notable contribution to cognitive psychology, a thorough examination of its claims appears advisable because neuroscientific data have a powerful—and sometimes problematic—allure, as noted by Weisberg, Keil, Goodstein, Rawson, and Gray (2008): "Something about seeing neuroscience information may encourage people to believe they have received a scientific explanation when they have not" (p. 470). Weisberg et al.'s statement is based on the results of an experiment in which they asked subjects to rate how "satisfied" they were with brief explanations for scientific phenomena. Explanations were either good—namely, designed to explain the phenomena— or bad—namely, mere restatements of the phenomenon. Generally, people were found to be quite sensitive to the quality of the explanations, with one exception: When the explanations were augmented by statements about neuroscience that provided no additional substantive information (e.g., "Brain scans indicate that [phenomenon X] happens because of the frontal lobe brain circuitry known to be involved in [phenomenon X]"), then bad explanations were no longer judged to be bad. That is, the mere mention of neuroscience improved the perceived quality of a bad explanation. This "allure" of neuroscience was found for novice subjects as well as students enrolled in an introductory neuroscience course, although it was *not* detected with expert neuroscientists.

These findings reinforce the earlier discussion (Section 2.6.3) about the fact that some aspects of explanations are inherently psychological. Those psychological aspects of explanations deserve to be taken seriously: Readers who are not expert at neuroscience may thus wish to hone their skepticism when approaching verbal theorizing within a neuroscience framework. Apparently, it is quite easy to be seduced by "bad" explanations merely because they are couched in neuroscientific language! This risk of seduction is greatest when the neuroscientific approach is combined with purely verbal theorizing.

8.3.1.1   Verbal Theorizing and the Risk of Circularity

We noted the pitfalls of verbal theorizing in Chapter 2, but it is worth illustrating them again with an example from neuroscience. Poldrack and Foerde (2008) stated that "the concept of multiple memory systems (MMS) is perhaps one of the most successful ideas in cognitive neuroscience" (p. 197). We focus here on the distinction between two putative systems involved in categorization and memory, respectively—namely, a "procedural" system that can learn to classify stimuli into different categories but cannot form declarative memories, and a declarative system that resides in the hippocampus and medial-temporal lobes and that can form distinct declarative memories (e.g., Knowlton, 1999). We have discussed models of categorization throughout this book (e.g., Chapters 1 and 7), so this final example can be presented quite readily.

A principal pillar of support for the MMS view arises from *dissociations*—some of which we already discussed (Section 6.2.4)—between explicit declarative memory and some other more indirect measure of memory, in this instance category learning performance.

For example, Knowlton, Squire, and Gluck (1994) showed that whereas amnesic patients were impaired when their declarative knowledge was tested, their performance on a probabilistic categorization task was statistically indistinguishable from that of age-matched control subjects. This dissociation has been replicated on several occasions and forms one (of several) pillars of support of the MMS view. There are, however, two problems with this logic.

First, dissociations constitute surprisingly weak evidence for the presence of two memory systems or distinct processes (for details, see, e.g., Dunn & James, 2003; Dunn & Kirsner, 2003; B. R. Newell & Dunn, 2008). That is, the presence of a dissociation is by no means sufficient evidence for the presence of separate memory systems. (The reasons for this are quite involved, and we refer you elsewhere for a full explanation; e.g., B. R. Newell & Dunn, 2008. In a nutshell, dissociations are neither sufficient nor necessary to infer the presence of separate systems or processes. Moreover, dissociations suffer from conventional statistical problems because they often crucially rely on acceptance on a null effect—namely, the absence of a difference between patients and control subjects.)

Second, there is a danger of circularity in the verbally imputed existence of multiple memory systems because whenever further dissociations fail to materialize, despite being expected on the basis of previous results or MMS theorizing, then several quick fixes serve to soften that empirical blow. For example, when a dissociation fails to materialize, the two systems may have "acted in concert" in that situation—indeed, there is no reason that *some* experimental variable might not affect two memory systems in the same way, and hence the occasional failure to observe a dissociation can be expected. Alternatively, performance on one task may be "contaminated" by unwanted involvement of the other memory system, thus obscuring a dissociation that otherwise would have been observed. To illustrate the latter point, consider the study by Hopkins, Myers, Shohamy, Grossman, and Gluck (2004), which compared performance of amnesic patients and control subjects on a probabilistic categorization task. Unlike the studies by Knowlton and colleagues just mentioned, in this instance, the amnesic patients were found to be impaired on the category learning task as well—which is tantamount to a failure to dissociate declarative memory from procedural memory. In interpreting this finding, Poldrack and Foerde (2008) suggested that the reasons for the discrepancy in outcome between the two sets of studies rested with the age-matched control subjects, who were elderly in the studies by Knowlton and colleagues but relatively young in the study by Hopkins et al. Thus, on the further assumptions that (a) the elderly control subjects were likely suffering from some age-related declarative memory loss and (b) that declarative memory *can* contribute to category learning performance, the data can be explained within the MMS view. Although this interpretation is entirely plausible, it also introduces the danger of circularity—which people have difficulty detecting (Rips, 2002)—because the MMS view is no longer testable if any unexpected difference between groups of subjects can be ascribed to unexpectedly good declarative memory of the control participants. (Readers interested in this issue may refer to Keren & Schul, 2009, who provide an incisive and more detailed analysis of the conceptual difficulties underpinning the MMS view, with a particular emphasis on data from reasoning and decision making.)

It is important to clarify that this one example does not invalidate the MMS view, nor does it even touch on the considerable body of other evidence that has been amassed in support of the view. However, the example underscores once again the core theme of our book—namely, that verbal theorizing, even if it involves neuroscientific or neuropsychological evidence, is subject to conceptual fuzziness.

8.3.1.2   *Imaging Data: Constraining or Unreliable?*

The introduction of brain imaging data to cognitive science, in particular from functional magnetic resonance imaging (fMRI), was met with much enthusiasm, and imaging techniques now form a staple tool of investigators in cognitive neuroscience. Henson (2005) provides a particularly eloquent case for the use of fMRI data, arguing convincingly that it can contribute to cognitive understanding under some reasonable assumptions. (For a contrary position, see Page, 2006, who argues that data about the localization of functions are irrelevant to answering the core question about *how* cognitive processes operate.)

We do not reject Henson's conclusions but again provide several notes of caution that must be borne in mind while collecting or interpreting functional imaging data. First, there is some debate concerning the reliability of fMRI signals. The reliability of measurements across repeated trials is central to the entire scientific enterprise: In the extreme case, if repeated measurements are uncorrelated with each other, no meaningful interpretation of the data is possible. In the physical sciences, of course, reliability is high—for example, two consecutive measurements of the length of a fossilized femur are likely to be virtually identical. In the behavioral sciences, reliability is not perfect but still considerable; for example, the reliability of the Raven's intelligence test across repeated applications is around .80 (Raven, Raven, & Court, 1998). What is the reliability of functional imaging measures?

There has been some recent controversy surrounding this issue (Vul, Harris, Winkielman, & Pashler, 2009a, 2009b), with postulated values of reliability ranging from .7 (Vul et al., 2009a) to .98 (Fernandez, 2003). Bennett and Miller (2010) provided a particularly detailed examination of this issue and reported a meta-analysis of existing reliability measures. Reassuringly, Bennett and Miller found that between-subject variability was generally greater than within-subject variation—in other words, the fMRI signals of the same individual performing the same task repeatedly were more similar to each other than the fMRI signals between different individuals on the same single occasion. (The same relationship between within-subject and between-subject variation holds for most behavioral measures; see, e.g., Masson & Loftus, 2003.) On a more sobering note, the average cluster overlap between repeated tests was found to be 29%. That is, barely a third of the significantly activated voxels within a cluster can be expected to also be significant on a subsequent test involving the same person. Other measures of reliability converge on similar results, leading Bennett and Miller to conclude that the reliability of fMRI is perhaps lower than that of other scientific measures. This context must be borne in mind when evaluating fMRI data.

Second, Coltheart (2006) provided a detailed critique of several instances in which the claimed theoretically constraining implications of fMRI results arguably turned out to be less incisive than initially claimed. For example, E. E. Smith and Jonides (1997) reported imaging data that purportedly identified different working-memory systems for spatial, object, and verbal information based on the fact that the different types of information appeared to involve activation of different brain regions. E. E. Smith and Jonides concluded that for "a cognitive model of working memory to be consistent with the neural findings, it must distinguish the three types of working memory" (p. 39). The model said to be favored by their findings was the "working memory" model of A. D. Baddeley (e.g., 1986). Coltheart (2006) rejected those conclusions based on two arguments: First, E. E. Smith and Jonides did not consider alternatives to the Baddeley model, thus precluding any conclusions about the necessity of that particular model (see our earlier discussion about sufficiency and necessity in Section 2.6). Second, Coltheart argued that it was unclear whether any pattern of imaging results *could* have challenged the Baddeley model, given that the model makes no claims about localization of any of its purported modules. Importantly, Coltheart's analysis was not an in-principle critique of the utility of neuroscientific results; rather, it thoroughly analyzed existing claims of interpretation and found them to be wanting. Below, we analyze some further instances that in our view do not suffer from such shortcomings.

8.3.1.3 *From Caveats to Endorsement*

It is important to be clear about what exactly we have critiqued thus far. We have drawn attention to interpretative problems associated with verbal theorizing: Logically, those problems are no more severe for the neuroscientific approach than they are for any other approach—for example, the phonological loop model discussed in Chapter 2. Thus, our discussion of the MMS view applies in equal force to theorizing that is not neuroscientifically inspired; indeed, our arguments concerning the risk of circularity and the weakness of dissociations mesh with those made by Keren and Schul (2009) and McKoon, Ratcliff, and Dell (1986) in the context of purely cognitive verbal theorizing about multiple memory systems. However, owing to the demonstrable allure of neuroscience (Weisberg et al., 2008), perhaps some extra care must be applied when interpreting neuroscientific data.

We have also briefly reviewed some of the known problems associated with neuroimaging data; most of those problems are well known, and they do not seriously compromise the neuroscientific approach. Instead, they just delineate the necessary cautions that apply to the interpretation of neuroimaging results.

Crucially, what we did *not* critique was the utility of neuroscientific data in general, and the indisputable fact that they provide additional constraints on theorizing. We next discuss some examples that illustrate the true promise of neuroscience.

8.3.2 The True Promise of Neuroscience

Given the theme of this book, it will come as no surprise that we suggest that consideration of neuroscientific data offers greatest promise if considered within a modeling context. Specifically, we propose that it is the computational modeling that provides the necessary rigor for a fruitful synergy of behavioral and neuroscientific data. We present some illustrative examples from the area of decision making before returning to the MMS view of categorization.

The first example involves a model that we already discussed in Section 5.1.1—namely, the linear ballistic accumulator (LBA; S. D. Brown & Heathcote, 2008). Recall that in the LBA, all decision alternatives (e.g., whether to say yes or no to a recognition probe) compete in a "race" of evidence accumulation: Specifically, each alternative increases its activation linearly over time until its "accumulator"—that is, the cumulative repository of the information sampled during the decision process—passes a threshold, at which point it is taken as being the "winner" and is given as a response. A desirable property of the LBA is that it can elegantly handle situations in which people must make speeded responses, as for example while playing sports or driving a race car. Whenever speed is of the essence, people are thought to lower their response threshold, such that evidence accumulation leads to an overt response more quickly than it otherwise would. Because faster responding inevitably implies that less evidence is accumulated before a decision is made, speed and accuracy necessarily trade off in this situation.

Forstmann et al. (2008) suggested that the basal ganglia (a group of nuclei at the base of the forebrain, with strong connections to cortical regions) might be involved in the speed-accuracy trade-off. Specifically, the basal ganglia are thought to send tonic inhibition to other brain areas, thus preventing the premature execution of any action. When a response is primed by other cognitive processes—for example, an instruction to forego accuracy in favor of speed—the resulting cortical input to the basal ganglia is thought to suppress the inhibitory signal, thus allowing the response to be made.

Forstmann et al. instructed subjects to respond at one of three different levels of speed (slow, medium, and fast) randomly on each trial of a simple psychophysical detection task. Not surprisingly, a standard speed-accuracy trade-off was obtained, such that speed and accuracy of responding were negatively correlated. Moreover, the LBA was fit to the data of individual subjects, and (not unexpectedly) it was found that a variation in response threshold between speed conditions was sufficient to capture the data at a fine level of detail (including, for example, the shape of the response time distributions). Finally, and most interesting for our purposes, the individual estimates of the response threshold settings correlated significantly with the fMRI signal in two regions of interest in the basal ganglia. Specifically, the more people were put under time pressure, the more two regions of the basal ganglia (namely, the anterior striatum and presupplementary motor area) were activated—and across individuals, the extent of that activation directly mapped into the parameter within the LBA that is responsible for response urgency. Attesting to the selectivity of this result, the activation did not correlate with any other model parameter, and it also correlated only weakly with the response measures. Thus, it was only at the level of model parameters that the individual differences in activation became tractable; the raw data were insufficient for this purpose.

We next turn to an example involving single-cell recordings. Single-cell recordings offer far better temporal resolution than fMRI imaging data, and of course they are also highly localized (namely, to the neuron being recorded). We focus on an example that involves recordings from the superior colliculus (SC) of rhesus monkeys. Ratcliff, Hasegawa, Hasegawa, Smith, and Segraves (2007) trained monkeys to perform a brightness discrimination task by moving their eyes to one or another target in response to a centrally presented stimulus patch. For example, a bright patch might require the monkey to fixate on the target to the right, whereas a dim patch would require a saccade to the left. The use of brightness decoupled the nature of the stimulus—namely, its luminosity—from the decision process and its outcome—namely, the direction in which to move the eyes—thus ensuring that variation in firing rates reflected a decisional component rather than stimulus perception. Only those neurons were recorded that showed no responsiveness to a central visual stimulus but were preferentially active during the period leading up to a right or left saccade, respectively.

Ratcliff et al. fitted both behavioral and neural data with a version of the diffusion model (e.g., Ratcliff, 1978), which we considered briefly in Chapter 5. The diffusion model is related to the LBA, except that its information accumulation over time is stochastic rather than deterministic—that is, the accumulated information during the decision process varies randomly at each time step. Ratcliff et al. first fit the diffusion model to the behavioral data, consisting of the response time distributions and accuracies of the monkey's eye movements. To relate the model to firing rates, they then assumed that proximity to the decision in the diffusion process was reflected in the firing rates of the neurons in the SC—the nearer the process was to a decision criterion, the higher the firing rate. The model was found to capture many—although not all—aspects of the observed firing rates, suggesting that the superior colliculus is a plausible locus of the decision process involved in planning saccades.

The examples just discussed confirm that neuroimaging results and single-cell recordings can inform theorizing and can provide valuable constraints that go beyond those available in behavioral data. However, crucially, it is neither the behavioral data nor the imaging results on their own, and neither is it the combination of the two, that suffice to advance theorizing: It is only by integrating all sources of empirical results within a computational and mathematical model that this becomes possible. When this is done, the potential payoff in terms of additional constraints on models is considerable.

The same conclusion applies to the multiple memory systems view in categorization. Although we noted some potential limitations with the approach at the beginning of this section, those concerns were largely confined to the verbal theorizing that often surrounds the MMS. Ashby, Paul, and Maddox (in press) recently reported a computational instantiation of the MMS view that circumvented at least some of those problems. Ashby et al. applied their model to a single experiment with the aid of more than a dozen parameters; the generality and power of their model thus remain to be ascertained, but the fact that it exists in a computational instantiation is noteworthy. The potential now exists for this computational model to be applied to numerous other phenomena.

As in the earlier case of neural networks, computational neuroscientific modeling as just described involves all the techniques presented in this book. The only difference is that the to-be-modeled dependent measures also include measures such as brain activation or neural activity. Further information about those techniques is available in a number of sources, for example, the book by Dayan and Abbott (2001). Specific programming techniques for MATLAB can be found in Wallish et al. (2009).

8.4   Cognitive Architectures

No discussion of modeling can be complete without considering the cognitive architecture approach, which has been enormously influential during the past 30 years. Unlike the models we have discussed in the first seven chapters, cognitive architectures are designed independently of any particular phenomenon. Thus, whereas models such as GCM or SIMPLE were developed to deal with categorization and memory, respectively, a cognitive architecture is developed to deal with *all* facets of cognition, ranging from attention to categorization to language and problem solving. Several such architectures have been proposed, with SOAR (e.g., A. Newell, 1990) and ACT-R (e.g., J. R. Anderson, 1983; J. R. Anderson et al., 2004) arguably being most prominent among them.

The term *cognitive architecture* was coined by the late Alan Newell and refers to "a theory of the basic principles of operation built into the cognitive system" (J. R. Anderson, 1983, p. ix). Like the architecture of a building, a cognitive architecture relates *structure* to *function*. In the case of a building, the structure involves bricks and posts and so on, and its function is to provide habitation for humans. In the case of cognition, the function of the architecture is to enable cognition, and the structures consist of various modules that are dedicated to different cognitive processes. Although the exact nature of these modules differs between particular architectures, a distinction is commonly made between a relatively static declarative memory, on one hand, and a flexible processing system, on the other hand, that acts on the contents of memory. We illustrate this distinction more fully by describing an architecture that has become—or is about to become—the de facto standard.

8.4.1   Cognitive Architectures: Convergence to a Standard

There are several contemporary architectures that rely on a variety of different approaches—for example, SOAR (A. Newell, 1990), CLARION (e.g., Sun, Slusarz, & Terry, 2005), and ACT-R (e.g., J. R. Anderson, 1996). An efficient overview of these different approaches can be found in Taatgen and Anderson (2008); here, we exploit the claim by Taatgen and Anderson (2009) that the various approaches are perhaps converging onto a modal architecture. We therefore illustrate the notion of architectures using the ACT-R ("Adaptive Control of Thought–Rational") framework developed by John Anderson and colleagues (e.g., J. R. Anderson et al., 2004).

ACT-R rests on three principal components: First, cognition is assumed to be "rational," in the sense of being optimally adapted to the environment (e.g., J. R. Anderson & Schooler, 1991). We already discussed the notion of rationality at the outset of this chapter (Section 8.1). In consequence, when faced with choices between options, ACT-R will choose the one that has the highest utility— that is, the highest expected probability of succeeding and the lowest (cognitive) cost. To illustrate, in a model of forming the past tense (Taatgen & Anderson, 2002), irregular solutions were found to be cognitively optimal for high-frequency words (because the cognitive cost of storing a few exceptions is worth the efficiency gain), whereas regular solutions were preferred for verbs of lower frequency (because storing many exceptions does not pay off, and so the cognitive cost associated with a regular transformation becomes more economical).

Second, like virtually all cognitive architectures, ACT-R differentiates between a declarative memory and a procedural system. The former is a relatively passive repository of information that is associatively organized and functions much like "conventional" long-term memory systems in other models. The latter is more interesting because it involves what is known as a production system. In a nutshell, a production system consists of a large number of condition-action pairs, each of which is known as a "production." At each time step, the current contents of the architecture's various working memory buffers (more on that below) are compared to the "condition" part of all productions: If a condition is met, then the corresponding action is executed. This execution, in turn, will likely alter the contents of memory, and the next cycle will therefore trigger the condition of a different production.

To illustrate, consider the cognitive task of solving the equation $x + 4 + 3 = 13$. The production that fires first, when people scan the equation and consider the x, is given by

IF the goal is to solve an equation and a variable has been read and there are no
   arguments
THEN store it as the first argument.

At the next step, when people consider the + sign, the relevant production is
as follows:

IF the goal is to solve an equation and an operator has been read and there is no
   operator stored
THEN store it as the operator.

J. R. Anderson (1996, Figure 3) shows the overall sequence of productions
that are involved in solving the entire equation, including the time course of each
operation. A crucial component of the production system is that only one production can be chosen for execution at any one time, even though the conditions of
multiple productions may be met: In those situations, the *utility* of a production
determines its probability of being chosen, where the utility reflects the production's past history and records its likelihood of success as well as the cognitive
"cost" of its execution (where cost is typically measured in the anticipated duration of executing the production).

The final component of ACT-R is its modularity, which is illustrated in Figure 8.4. That is, ACT-R involves a number of independent modules, each of which
is dedicated to processing information in a particular modality. For example, there
is a module that deals with visual information, another one that controls manual actions, and so on. Each module "is capable of massively parallel computation to achieve its objectives. For instance, the visual module is processing the
entire visual field and the declarative module searches through large databases"
J. R. Anderson (2005, p. 314). However, each module also encounters a bottle-
neck in the form of a buffer: The buffer enables a module to communicate with the
production system, but its capacity is strictly limited. Figure 8.4 also lists the brain
structures that have been putatively identified as the loci of the various modules;
we return to this neuroscientific angle of ACT-R later.

In summary, ACT-R is a comprehensive theory that combines psychological
and neuroscientific knowledge with developments from artificial intelligence to
produce a powerful general-purpose engine of cognition. Not surprisingly, cognitive architectures have an impressive track record of success.

8.4.2   Cognitive Architectures: Successes, Problems, and Solutions

Some of the successes of architectures are notable because they reach beyond the
confines of the psychological laboratory. For example, R. M. Jones et al. (1999)
used the SOAR architecture—which, like ACT-R, relies on a production system

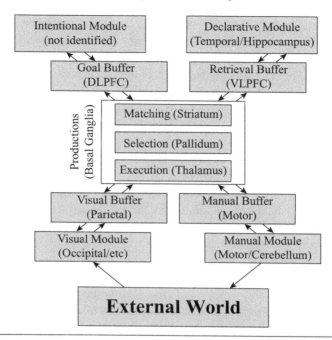

Figure 8.4 The overall architecture of ACT-R. The modules communicate with the production system via buffers: The contents of the buffers are compared to the conditions of productions, and the actions of productions change the contents of the buffers. Where possible, the presumed localization of components in the brain is identified. DLPFC = dorsolateral prefrontal cortex; VLPFC = ventrolateral prefrontal cortex. Figure taken from Anderson, J. R., Bothell, D., Byrne, M. D., Douglass, S., Lebiere, C., & Qin, Y. (2004). An integrated theory of mind. *Psychological Review, 111*, 1036–1060. Published by the American Psychological Association. Reproduced with permission.

as its principal engine—to develop simulated fighter jets that "flew" on their own and interacted with other pilots and air traffic control using a (limited) natural-language vocabulary. In a large-scale military simulation, some 100 simulated aircraft were piloted by SOAR with notable success. At the heart of this application of SOAR were more than 8,000 production rules that imbued the simulated aircraft (or their simulated pilots) with the knowledge necessary to "fly" in a realistic manner. Those productions, in turn, were derived from subject matter experts (such as military pilots) and "textbook knowledge" of military doctrine and tactics. Although this application of SOAR is impressive by the standards of expert systems and artificial intelligence, it also illustrates one of the principal problems of *psychological* applications of cognitive architectures—namely, their reliance on external input that provides the knowledge required to make the architecture work.

Specifically, in the same way that for the jet fighter simulation much intellectual capital was expended on extracting knowledge from domain experts and textbooks, and to convert that knowledge into a form that was palatable to SOAR, in many *psychological* applications, much of the architecture's work is done by the productions that define the particular task being modeled (Taatgen & Anderson, 2008). For example, the ACT-R productions shown above that were required to solve equations are typically provided to the system by the theoretician, and their mere presence thus does not represent an achievement of the architecture—instead, they serve the role of free parameters in other more conventional models (J. R. Anderson et al., 2004).

This, then, points to the fundamental problem of cognitive architectures—namely, that they "make broad assumptions, yet leave many details open" (Sun et al., 2005, p. 616). This problem is well known, and two broad classes of solutions have been explored: The first approach seeks to find ways by which the architecture can acquire its own productions—for example, by processing instructions presented in (quasi-natural) language. Thus, like a human subject, the architecture is presented with task instructions and processes those instructions to develop a set of productions required for the task (J. R. Anderson et al., 2004). When successful, this obviates the need for a task analysis or other interventions by the theoretician to select suitable productions, thus effectively eliminating a large source of (tacit) free parameters in the model. The second approach seeks to connect the cognitive architecture to its presumed neural underpinnings.

8.4.3   Marrying Architectures and Neuroscience

Figure 8.4 identified locations in the brain that are thought to host the various modules of ACT-R. It is informative to consider a study involving children's acquisition of algebra skills that explored this linkage between architecture and brain. In this study (Qin, Anderson, Silk, Stenger, & Carter, 2004), 10 students (ages 11–14) spent 6 days practicing solving equations of the type shown earlier. Not surprisingly, the students solved the equations increasingly more quickly over the 6 days, and overall solution time was found to depend on the number of steps required to reach a solution.

When ACT-R was applied to these data, it was able to reproduce the results with great quantitative precision. In the present context, it is of greater interest to focus on a micro-analysis of the activation of the various modules in ACT-R over time. This analysis is shown in Figure 8.5, which traces the activation of each module in "real" (simulated) time for the solution of the equation $7 * x + 3 = 38$ early in learning (left-hand column) and later in learning (right-hand column).

The complexity of Figure 8.5 is notable, and indeed, "it is hard to justify all those boxes and assumptions on the basis of three simple learning curves"

(J. R. Anderson, 2005, p. 323). Why, then, do we reproduce this bedazzling figure here? The answer is that brain imaging data provide the constraints necessary to confirm some of the assumptions made within ACT-R and the interplay between its various models.

Table 8.1 presents the detailed presumed mapping between ACT-R modules and brain regions, obtained from a number of imaging studies (e.g., J. R. Anderson, 2005, 2007). Under some fairly straightforward assumptions about the temporal characteristics of the blood oxygen–level dependent (BOLD) response measured by fMRI imaging, the mapping in the table permits prediction of brain activations from the simulated activations of the modules shown in Figure 8.5.

Table 8.1 Mapping Between Modules in ACT-R and Brain Regions Identified by Imaging Data

ACT-R Module	Associated Brain Region
(1) Procedural (production)	Caudate
(2) Retrieval	Prefrontal, inferior frontal sulcus
(3) Goal	Anterior cingulate
(4) Imaginal (problem state)	Parietal, border of intraparietal sulcus
(5) Manual (motor)	Central sulcus

J. R. Anderson (2005) showed that once the architecture was fit to the behavioral data (i.e., the learning curves for the various problem types), the simulated pattern of activations of the various modules correlated highly with the activations observed during brain imaging. Those correlations, then, arguably provided the independent verification necessary to justify the complexity of Figure 8.5 (see page 312).

8.4.4   Architectures and Models

At this stage, one might wonder how any of this relates back to the content of the first seven chapters: How do model selection techniques and parameter estimation techniques apply to research involving cognitive architectures? Our answer is twofold.

On one hand, one difference between cognitive architectures and conventional cognitive models is that within architectures, " there is an almost infinite freedom in specifying the initial knowledge and strategies of the model, allowing many different ways to model a single task" (Taatgen & Anderson, 2009, p. 9). We have described two ways in which this excessive flexibility can be constrained—namely, by modeling the processing of instructions and by linking the architecture to brain regions. Nonetheless, concerns about undue flexibility remain and set cognitive architectures apart from the models discussed in the first seven chapters.

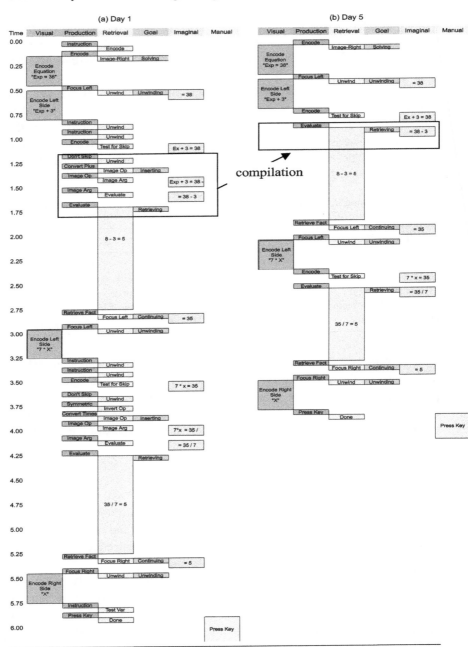

Figure 8.5 Simulated module activity in ACT-R during solution of a two-step equation on Day 1 (a) with a two-step equation on Day 5 (b). In both cases, the equation is $7 * x + 3 = 38$. See text for details. Figure taken from Anderson, J. R. (2005). Human symbol manipulation within an integrated cognitive architecture. *Cognitive Science, 29,* 313–341. Copyright by the Cognitive Science Society; reprinted with permission.

On the other hand, when it comes to specific models developed within an architecture, their application to data is governed by the very same principles outlined in this book. For example, Daily, Lovett, and Reder (2001) applied a model developed within the ACT-R architecture to individual differences in a working memory task. The techniques involved in fitting that model to the data and to estimate parameters do not differ from those employed in any other model application, such as those presented in Chapter 7. Thus, by the time you apply it to data, any particular instantiation of ACT-R is very much like any other model discussed so far—the one exception being that the productions contained in the model must often be considered "invisible" free parameters, and hence care is advisable when using complexity-sensitive model comparison techniques (e.g., AIC, BIC; see Chapter 5).

8.5 Conclusion

This concludes our exploration of the elements of computational and mathematical modeling in cognition. We began by considering some very general conceptual issues regarding the use of models, and we finished by drawing a wide arc to encompass a variety of approaches that are united by their attempt to explain human cognition by quantitative and computational means, thus avoiding the pitfalls that beset purely verbal theorizing.

Where does this leave you, and what future options exist for further study? At the very least, you should now be in a position to apply existing models to your own data. This may initially require some further "coaching" from the model's author(s) or other experts, but we expect you to have acquired the relevant skills by working through the material in this book. We encourage you to practice widely and to use your skills wisely; please remember the conceptual lessons of Chapters 1, 2, and 6.

There are many ways in which you can apply the skills acquired in this book. The approaches we have discussed in this chapter cover only some of the many models that have been applied in cognitive psychology, and the best way to broaden your understanding of computational models of cognition is to read about these models. To give you a head start, in the remaining sections of this chapter, we present pointers to a small sample of models from a number of areas. Each of those models has made a significant contribution to the literature, and you cannot go wrong by exploring any one of them in greater depth.

On our webpage (http://www.cogsciwa.com), you will find an extended version of this listing that we endeavor to keep current and that also includes direct links to code for the models if available. Whatever area of cognition you are specializing in, you will find an attractive model in this list that is worthy of further examination. Begin by working with one of those models; after you have gathered some expertise applying an existing model, there will be little to stop you from designing your own. We wish you the best of luck!

8.5.1   Memory

Retrieving Effectively from Memory (REM; Shiffrin & Steyvers, 1997): a Bayesian model of recognition memory, in which the likelihood of partial episodic traces is calculated in parallel given a presented probe.

Scale-Invariant Memory, Perception and Learning (SIMPLE; G. D. A. Brown et al., 2007): a contemporary model of memory in which items are confused on the basis of their proximity in multidimensional space, with a particular role accorded to temporal proximity.

Search of Associative Memory (SAM; Raaijmakers & Shiffrin, 1980, 1981): a classic dual-store model of episodic memory that specifies the process by which retrieval cues are instantiated and used to search memory.

Serial-Order in a Box (SOB; Farrell & Lewandowsky, 2002; Lewandowsky & Farrell, 2008b): a connectionist model of serial order memory in which learning is gated by the novelty of sequence elements.

Temporal Context Model (TCM; Howard & Kahana, 2002; Sederberg, Howard, & Kahana, 2008): a distributed connectionist model that explains forgetting in episodic memory as a consequence of the evolution of temporal context driven by incoming information.

8.5.2   Language

Bayesian Reader (Norris, 2006): a Bayesian model of word recognition, lexical decision, and semantic categorization.

Saccade Generation With Inhibition by Foveal Targets (SWIFT; Engbert, Nuthmann, Richter, & Kliegl, 2005): an accumulator model of saccade generation during reading, accounting for effects of word length and word frequency on fixation positions and latencies.

Dual-Route Cascade Model of Reading (DRC; Coltheart, Rastle, Perry, Langdon, & Ziegler, 2001): a connectionist model of word recognition and naming that assumes different methods of processing words (variously using semantic, lexical, and graphemic knowledge) are carried out in parallel.

Bound Encoding of the Aggregate Language Environment (BEAGLE; M. N. Jones & Mewhort, 2007): a composite holographic model that builds representations of word meaning and word order from unsupervised experience with natural language.

Word-form Encoding by Activation and VERification (WEAVER; Roelofs, 1997): a model explaining how the passing of activation between localist representations of lexical, syntactic, and morphemic information enacts retrieval of word forms in speech production.

8.5.3   Perception and Action

Model of the Influence of Task on Attention (Navalpakkam & Itti, 2005): the model explains task-specific guidance of visual attention in real-world scenes. Information about the task is stored in working memory and, together with relevant long-term information, biases the visual attention system to perceive relevant features.

Recurrent Model of Sequential Action (Botvinick & Plaut, 2004): a recurrent connectionist model of sequential action that explains context as recurrent feedback from previous network states.

Dynamical Systems Model of Coordination (Haken, Kelso, & Bunz, 1985): a dynamical systems model treating bimanual coordination as a system of coupled oscillators, where qualitative changes in coordinating behavior arise from phase transitions.

The Bayesian Ventriloquist (Alais & Burr, 2004): a Bayesian model of multimodal integration that explains ventriloquism as precise (in terms of spatial location) visual information capturing imprecise auditory information.

Neural Model of Cognitive Control (J.W. Brown, Reynolds, & Braver, 2007): a neurally inspired model that implements two distinct control mechanisms for task switching.

8.5.4   Choice and Decision Making

Diffusion Model (Ratcliff & Rouder, 1998): a diffusion model of two-choice decisions, in which evidence drives a random walk between two decision thresholds until one of the thresholds is crossed.

Leaky Integrator Model (Usher & McClelland, 2001): an accumulator model of decision making, in which the activity of accumulators increases stochastically over time but is limited by leakage from the accumulators and competition (inhibition) between accumulators.

(Linear) Ballistic Accumulator Model (LBA; S. Brown & Heathcote, 2005; S. D. Brown & Heathcote, 2008): a simple, deterministic accumulator model in which latency variability arises from variability in model parameters across trials; different versions do or do not assume inhibition between accumulators.

Decision Field Theory (DFT; Busemeyer & Townsend, 1993): a model of decision making under uncertainty, in which a random walk is driven by samples from possible events and the valence of the outcomes.

8.5.5   Identification and Categorization

Generalized Context Model (GCM; Nosofsky, 1986): an exemplar model of categorization, in which objects in the world are categorized according to their aggregate perceptual match to experienced objects in memory.

Attention Learning and Covering Map (ALCOVE; Kruschke, 1992): a connectionist instantiation of the GCM that implements learning of attention and exemplar-to-category associations.

General Recognition Theory (GRT; Ashby, 1992b): a model of categorization in which the multidimensional space in which items are represented is carved up by decision boundaries, and objects are categorized according to the partition in which they fall.

Supervised and Unsupervised STratified Adaptive Incremental Network (SUSTAIN; Love, Medin, & Gureckis, 2004): an exemplar model in which a new exemplar is stored only if it is sufficiently novel or surprising and explains both supervised and unsupervised learning.

Selective Attention, Mapping, and Ballistic Accumulation (SAMBA; S. D. Brown, Marley, Donkin, & Heathcote, 2008): a model of absolute identification in which perceptual information is accumulated over time, based on comparisons between the stimulus and anchor points set by the participant.

Relative Judgment Model (RJM; Stewart, Brown, & Chater, 2005): a model of absolute identification in which identification is based on comparisons between the current and previous stimuli, as well as feedback from the previous trial.

Notes

1. The backpropagation algorithm also assumes a contribution from bias units that provide a constant input to each hidden and output unit. For conceptual clarity, we do not discuss these units here.

2. There is no meaning to the spatial arrangement of units within a layer (i.e., the units are unordered), and so the numbering of units in Figure 8.2 is completely arbitrary.

References

Abramowitz, M., & Stegun, I. A. (1972). *Handbook of mathematical functions with formulas, graphs, and mathematical tables*. New York: Dover.

Addis, K. M., & Kahana, M. J. (2004). Decomposing serial learning: What is missing from the learning curve? *Psychonomic Bulletin & Review, 11,* 118–124.

Akaike, H. (1973). Information theory and an extension of the maximum likelihood principle. In B. N. Petrov & F. Csaki (Eds.), *Second international symposium on information theory* (pp. 267–281). Budapest: Akademiai Kiado.

Akaike, H. (1974). A new look at the statistical model identification. *IEEE Transactions on Automatic Control, 19,* 716–723.

Alais, D., & Burr, D. (2004). The ventriloquist effect results from near-optimal bimodal integration. *Current Biology, 14,* 257–262.

Alfonso-Reese, L. A. (2006). General recognition theory of categorization: A MATLAB toolbox. *Behavior Research Methods, 38,* 579–583.

Anderson, J. A. (1995). *An introduction to neural networks*. Cambridge, MA: MIT Press.

Anderson, J. A., Silverstein, J. W., Ritz, S. A., & Jones, R. S. (1977). Distinctive features, categorical perception, and probability learning: Some applications of a neural model. *Psychological Review, 84,* 413–451.

Anderson, J. R. (1976). *Language, memory, and thought*. Hillsdale, NJ: Lawrence Erlbaum.

Anderson, J. R. (1983). *The architecture of cognition*. Cambridge, MA: Harvard University Press.

Anderson, J. R. (1990). *The adaptive character of thought*. Hillsdale, NJ: Lawrence Erlbaum.

Anderson, J. R. (1996). ACT: A simple theory of complex cognition. *American Psychologist, 51,* 355–365.

Anderson, J. R. (2005). Human symbol manipulation within an integrated cognitive architecture. *Cognitive Science, 29,* 313–341.

Anderson, J. R. (2007). *How can the human mind occur in the physical universe?* Oxford: Oxford University Press.

Anderson, J. R., Bothell, D., Byrne, M. D., Douglass, S., Lebiere, C., & Qin, Y. (2004). An integrated theory of mind. *Psychological Review, 111,* 1036–1060.

Anderson, J. R., Fincham, J. M., & Douglass, S. (1999). Practice and retention: A unifying analysis. *Journal of Experimental Psychology: Learning, Memory, and Cognition, 25,* 1120–1136.

Anderson, J. R., & Schooler, L. J. (1991). Reflections of the environment in memory. *Psychological Science, 2,* 396–408.

Andrews, S., & Heathcote, A. (2001). Distinguishing common and task-specific processes in word identification: A matter of some moment? *Journal of Experimental Psychology: Learning, Memory, and Cognition, 27,* 514–544.

Ashby, F. G. (1992a). Multidimensional models of categorization. In F. G. Ashby (Ed.), *Multidimensional models of perception and cognition* (pp. 449–483). Hillsdale, NJ: Erlbaum.

Ashby, F. G. (1992b). *Multidimensional models of perception and cognition.* Hillsdale, NJ: Erlbaum.

Ashby, F. G., Alfonso-Reese, L. A., Turken, A. U., & Waldron, E. M. (1998). A neuropsychological theory of multiple systems in category learning. *Psychological Review, 105,* 442–481.

Ashby, F. G., & Gott, R. E. (1988). Decision rules in the perception and categorization of multidimensional stimuli. *Journal of Experimental Psychology: Learning, Memory, and Cognition, 14,* 33–53.

Ashby, F. G., & Maddox, W. T. (1993). Relations between prototype, exemplar, and decision bound models of categorization. *Journal of Mathematical Psychology, 37,* 372–400.

Ashby, F. G., Maddox, W. T., & Lee, W. W. (1994). On the dangers of averaging across subjects when using multidimensional scaling or the similarity-choice model. *Psychological Science, 5,* 144–151.

Ashby, F. G., & O'Brien, J. B. (2005). Category learning and multiple memory systems. *Trends in Cognitive Sciences, 9,* 83–89.

Ashby, F. G., Paul, E. J., & Maddox, W. T. (in press). COVIS. In E. M. Pothos & A. J. Wills (Eds.), *Formal approaches in categorization.* New York: Cambridge University Press.

Ashby, F. G., & Townsend, J. T. (1986). Varieties of perceptual independence. *Psychological Review, 93,* 154–179.

Atkinson, R. C., & Juola, J. F. (1973). Factors influencing speed and accuracy of word recognition. In S. Kornblum (Ed.), *Attention and performance IV* (pp. 583–612). New York: Academic Press.

Attewell, D., & Baddeley, R. J. (2007). The distribution of reflectances within the visual environment. *Vision Research, 47,* 548–554.

Baddeley, A. D. (1986). *Working memory.* New York: Oxford University Press.

Baddeley, A. D. (2003). Working memory: Looking backward and looking forward. *Nature Reviews Neuroscience, 4,* 829–839.

Baddeley, A. D., & Hitch, G. (1974). Working memory. In G. Bower (Ed.), *The psychology of learning and motivation: Advances in research and theory* (Vol. 8, pp. 47–89). New York: Academic Press.

Baddeley, A. D., Thomson, N., & Buchanan, M. (1975). Word length and structure of short-term memory. *Journal of Verbal Learning and Verbal Behavior*, *14*, 575–589.

Baddeley, R., & Attewell, D. (2009). The relationship between language and the environment: Information theory shows why we have only three lightness terms. *Psychological Science*, *20*, 1100–1107.

Balota, D. A., Yap, M. J., Cortese, M. J., & Watson, J. M. (2008). Beyond mean response latency: Response time distributional analyses of semantic priming. *Journal of Memory and Language*, *59*, 495–523.

Bamber, D., & van Santen, J. P. (1985). How many parameters can a model have and still be testable? *Journal of Mathematical Psychology*, *29*, 443–473.

Bamber, D., & van Santen, J. P. (2000). How to assess a model's testability and identifiability. *Journal of Mathematical Psychology*, *44*, 20–40.

Bartels, A., & Zeki, S. (2000). The neural basis of romantic love. *Neuroreport*, *11*, 3829–3834.

Batchelder, W., & Riefer, D. (1999). Theoretical and empirical review of multinomial process tree modeling. *Psychonomic Bulletin & Review*, *6*, 57–86.

Bayer, H. M., Lau, B., & Glimcher, P. W. (2007). Statistics of midbrain dopamine neuron spike trains in the awake primate. *Journal of Neurophysiology*, *98*, 1428–1439.

Bechtel, W. (2008). Mechanisms in cognitive psychology: What are the operations? *Philosophy of Science*, *75*, 983–994.

Bennett, C. M., & Miller, M. B. (2010). How reliable are the results from functional magnetic resonance imaging? *Annals of the New York Academy of Sciences*, *1191*, 133–155.

Bickel, P. J., Hammel, E. A., & O'Connell, J. W. (1975). Sex bias in graduate admissions: Data from Berkeley. *Science*, *187*, 398–404.

Bireta, T. J., Neath, I., & Surprenant, A. M. (2006). The syllable-based word length effect and stimulus set specificity. *Psychonomic Bulletin & Review*, *13*, 434–438.

Bishara, A. J., & Payne, B. K. (2008). Multinomial process tree models of control and automaticity in weapon misidentification. *Journal of Experimental Social Psychology*, *45*, 524–534.

Botvinick, M. M., & Plaut, D. C. (2004). Doing without schema hierarchies: A recurrent connectionist approach to normal and impaired routine sequential action. *Psychological Review*, *111*, 395–429.

Botvinick, M. M., & Plaut, D. C. (2006). Short-term memory for serial order: A recurrent neural network model. *Psychological Review*, *113*, 201–233.

Box, M. J. (1966). A comparison of several current optimization methods, and the use of transformations in constrained problems. *Computer Journal*, *9*, 67–77.

Bozdogan, H. (1987). Model selection and Akaike's Information Criterion (AIC): The general theory and its analytical extensions. *Psychometrika*, *52*, 345–370.

Brockwell, P. J., & Davis, R. A. (1996). *Introduction to time series and forecasting*. New York: Springer-Verlag.

Brown, G. D. A., & Hulme, C. (1995). Modelling item length effects in memory span: No rehearsal needed? *Journal of Memory and Language*, *34*, 594–621.

Brown, G. D. A., & Lewandowsky, S. (2010). Forgetting in memory models: Arguments against trace decay and consolidation failure. In S. Della Sala (Ed.), *Forgetting* (pp. 49–75). Hove, UK: Psychology Press.

Brown, G. D. A., Neath, I., & Chater, N. (2007). A temporal ratio model of memory. *Psychological Review*, *114*, 539–576.

Brown, G. D. A., Preece, T., & Hulme, C. (2000). Oscillator-based memory for serial order. *Psychological Review*, *107*, 127–181.

Brown, J. W., Reynolds, J. R., & Braver, T. S. (2007). A computational model of fractionated conflict-control mechanisms in task-switching. *Cognitive Psychology*, *55*, 37–85.

Brown, S., & Heathcote, A. (2003). QMLE: Fast, robust, and efficient estimation of distribution functions based on quantiles. *Behavior Research Methods, Instruments & Computers*, *35*, 485–492.

Brown, S., & Heathcote, A. (2005). A ballistic model of choice response time. *Psychological Review*, *112*, 117–128.

Brown, S. D., & Heathcote, A. (2008). The simplest complete model of choice response time: Linear ballistic accumulation. *Cognitive Psychology*, *57*, 153–178.

Brown, S. D., Marley, A. A. J., Donkin, C., & Heathcote, A. (2008). An integrated model of choices and response times in absolute identification. *Psychological Review*, *115*, 396–425.

Browne, M. W. (2000). Cross-validation methods. *Journal of Mathematical Psychology*, *44*, 108–132.

Bruner, J. S., Goodnow, J. J., & Austin, G. A. (1956). *A study of thinking*. New York: Wiley.

Buchner, A., & Erdfelder, E. (1996). On assumptions of, relations between, and evaluations of some process dissociation measurement models. *Consciousness & Cognition*, *5*, 581–594.

Buchner, A., Erdfelder, E., & Vaterrodt-Plünnecke, B. (1995). Toward unbiased measurement of conscious and unconscious memory processes within the process dissociation framework. *Journal of Experimental Psychology: General*, *124*, 137–160.

Buckles, B. P., & Petry, F. E. (1992). *Genetic algorithms*. Los Alamitos, CA: IEEE Computer Science Press.

Burgess, N., & Hitch, G. J. (1999). Memory for serial order: A network model of the phonological loop and its timing. *Psychological Review*, *106*, 551–581.

Burnham, K. P., & Anderson, D. R. (2002). *Model selection and multimodel inference: A practical information-theoretic approach* (2nd ed.). New York: Springer-Verlag.

Burnham, K. P., & Anderson, D. R. (2004). Multimodel inference: Understanding AIC and BIC in model selection. *Sociological Methods & Research, 33*, 261–304.

Busemeyer, J. R., & Stout, J. C. (2002). A contribution of cognitive decision models to clinical assessment: Decomposing performance on the Bechara gambling task. *Psychological Assessment, 14*, 253–262.

Busemeyer, J. R., & Townsend, J. T. (1993). Decision field theory: A dynamic-cognitive approach to decision making in an uncertain environment. *Psychological Review, 100*, 432–459.

Busemeyer, J. R., & Wang, Y.-M. (2000). Model comparisons and model selections based on generalization criterion methodology. *Journal of Mathematical Psychology, 44*, 171–189.

Carpenter, R. H. S., & Williams, M. L. L. (1995). Neural computation of log likelihood in control of saccadic eye movements. *Nature, 377*, 59–62.

Carrasco, M., & McElree, B. (2001). Covert attention accelerates the rate of visual information processing. *Proceedings of the National Academy of Sciences USA, 98*, 5363–5367.

Chappell, M., & Humphreys, M. S. (1994). An auto-associative neural network for sparse representations: Analysis and application to models of recognition and cued recall. *Psychological Review, 101*, 103–128.

Chater, N., Tenenbaum, J. B., & Yuille, A. (2006). Probabilistic models of cognition: Conceptual foundations. *Trends in Cognitive Science, 10*, 287–291.

Chechile, R. A. (1977). Likelihood and posterior identification: Implications for mathematical psychology. *British Journal of Mathematical and Statistical Psychology, 30*, 177–184.

Chechile, R. A. (1998). Reexamining the goodness-of-fit problem for interval-scale scores. *Behavior Research Methods, Instruments, & Computers, 30*, 227–231.

Chechile, R. A. (1999). A vector-based goodness-of-fit metric for interval-scaled data. *Communications in Statistics: Theory and Methods, 28*, 277–296.

Chong, E. K. P., & Zak, S. H. (1996). *An introduction to optimization.* New York: Wiley.

Chun, M. M., & Jiang, Y. (1998). Contextual cueing: Implicit learning and memory of visual context guides spatial attention. *Cognitive Psychology, 36*, 28–71.

Clare, J., & Lewandowsky, S. (2004). Verbalizing facial memory: Criterion effects in verbal overshadowing. *Journal of Experimental Psychology: Learning, Memory, & Cognition, 30*, 739–755.

Clark, S. E. (2003). A memory and decision model for eyewitness identification. *Applied Cognitive Psychology, 17*, 629–654.

Clark, S. E. (2008). The importance (necessity) of computational modelling for eyewitness identification research. *Applied Cognitive Psychology, 22*, 803–813.

Clark, S. E., & Gronlund, S. D. (1996). Global matching models of recognition memory: How the models match the data. *Psychonomic Bulletin & Review, 3*, 37–60.

Clark, S. E., & Tunnicliff, J. L. (2001). Selecting lineup foils in eyewitness identification experiments: Experimental control and real-world simulation. *Law and Human Behaviour, 25*(3), 199–216.

Cohen, A. L., Sanborn, A. N., & Shiffrin, R. M. (2008). Model evaluation using grouped or individual data. *Psychonomic Bulletin & Review, 15*, 692–712.

Coltheart, M. (2006). What has functional neuroimaging told us about the mind (so far). *Cortex, 42*, 323–331.

Coltheart, M., Curtis, B., Atkins, P., & Haller, P. (1993). Models of reading aloud: Dual-route and parallel-distributed-processing approaches. *Psychological Review, 100*, 589–608.

Coltheart, M., Rastle, K., Perry, C., Langdon, R., & Ziegler, J. (2001). DRC: A dual route cascade model of visual word recognition and reading aloud. *Psychological Review, 108*, 204–256.

Conway, M. A., Dewhurst, S. A., Pearson, N., & Sapute, A. (2001). The self and recollection reconsidered: How a "failure to replicate" failed and why trace strength accounts of recollection are untenable. *Applied Cognitive Psychology, 15*, 673–686.

Courville, A. C., Daw, N. D., & Touretzky, D. S. (2006). Bayesian theories of conditioning in a changing world. *Trends in Cognitive Sciences, 10*, 294–300.

Cousineau, D., Brown, S., & Heathcote, A. (2004). Fitting distributions using maximum likelihood: Methods and packages. *Behavior Research Methods Instruments & Computers, 36*, 742–756.

Coyne, J. A. (2009). *Why evolution is true.* New York: Viking.

Curran, T., & Hintzman, D. L. (1995). Violations of the independence assumption in process dissociation. *Journal of Experimental Psychology: Learning, Memory, & Cognition, 21*, 531–547.

Daily, L., Lovett, M., & Reder, L. (2001). Modeling individual differences in working memory performance: A source activation account. *Cognitive Science, 25*, 315–353.

David, F. N. (1962). *Games, gods and gambling.* London: Charles Griffin and Co.

Dayan, P., & Abbott, L. F. (2001). *Theoretical neuroscience: Computational and mathematical modeling of neural systems.* Cambridge, MA: MIT Press.

DeCarlo, L. T. (2008). Process dissociation and mixture signal detection theory. *Journal of Experimental Psychology: Learning, Memory, and Cognition, 34*, 1565–1572.

DeGroot, M. H. (1989). *Probability and statistics* (2nd ed.). Reading, MA: Addison-Wesley.

DeLosh, E. L., Busemeyer, J. R., & McDaniel, M. A. (1997). Extrapolation: The sine qua non of abstraction in function learning. *Journal of Experimental Psychology: Learning, Memory, and Cognition, 23*, 968–986.

Dennis, S., & Humphreys, M. S. (2001). A context noise model of episodic word recognition. *Psychological Review, 108*, 452–478.

Donaldson, W. (1996). The role of decision processes in remembering and knowing. *Memory & Cognition, 24*, 523–533.

Dunn, J. C. (2000). Model complexity: The fit to random data reconsidered. *Psychological Research, 63*, 174–182.

Dunn, J. C. (2004). Remember–know: A matter of confidence. *Psychological Review, 111*, 524–542.

Dunn, J. C., & James, R. N. (2003). Signed difference analysis: Theory and application. *Journal of Mathematical Psychology, 47*, 389–416.

Dunn, J. C., & Kirsner, K. (2003). What can we infer from double dissociations? *Cortex, 39*, 1–7.

Dutton, J. M., & Starbuck, W. H. (1971). *Computer simulation of human behavior.* New York: Wiley.

Dyson, F. (2004). A meeting with Enrico Fermi. *Nature, 427*, 297.

Edwards, A. W. F. (1992). *Likelihood* (Expanded ed.). Baltimore, MD: Johns Hopkins University Press.

Efron, B., & Gong, G. (1983). A leisurely look at the boostrap, the jackknife, and cross-validation. *The American Statistician, 37*, 36–38.

Efron, B., & Tibshirani, R. (1994). *Introduction to the bootstrap.* New York: Chapman & Hall.

Eliason, S. R. (1993). *Maximum likelihood estimation: Logic and practice.* Newbury Park, CA: Sage.

Elman, J. L., Bates, E. A., Johnson, M. H., Karmiloff-Smith, A., Parisi, D., & Plunkett, K. (1996). *Rethinking innateness: A connectionist perspective.* Cambridge, MA: MIT Press.

Engbert, R., Nuthmann, A., Richter, E. M., & Kliegl, R. (2005). SWIFT: A dynamical model of saccade generation during reading. *Psychological Review, 112*, 777–813.

Erickson, M. A., & Kruschke, J. K. (1998). Rules and exemplars in category learning. *Journal of Experimental Psychology: General, 127*, 107–140.

Erickson, M. A., & Kruschke, J. K. (2002). Rule-based extrapolation in perceptual categorization. *Psychonomic Bulletin & Review, 9*, 160–168.

Estes, W. K. (1956). The problem of inference from curves based on group data. *Psychological Bulletin, 53*, 134–140.

Estes, W. K. (1975). Some targets for mathematical psychology. *Journal of Mathematical Psychology, 12*, 263–282.

Estes, W. K. (2002). Traps in the route to models of memory and decision. *Psychonomic Bulletin & Review, 9*, 3–25.

Everitt, B. S. (1993). *Cluster analysis* (3rd ed.). London: Edward Arnold.

Fagot, J., Kruschke, J. K., Depy, D., & Vauclair, J. (1998). Associative learning in baboons (Papio papio) and humans (Homo sapiens): Species differences in learned attention to visual features. *Animal Cognition, 1*, 123–133.

Farrell, S. (2010). Dissociating conditional recency in immediate and delayed free recall: A challenge for unitary models of recency. *Journal of Experimental Psychology: Learning, Memory, and Cognition, 36*, 324–347.

Farrell, S., & Lelièvre, A. (2009). End anchoring in short-term order memory. *Journal of Memory and Language, 60*, 209–227.

Farrell, S., & Lewandowsky, S. (2000). A connectionist model of complacency and adaptive recovery under automation. *Journal of Experimental Psychology: Learning, Memory, and Cognition, 26*, 395–410.

Farrell, S., & Lewandowsky, S. (2002). An endogenous distributed model of ordering in serial recall. *Psychonomic Bulletin & Review, 9*, 59–79.

Farrell, S., & Lewandowsky, S. (2008). Empirical and theoretical limits on lag recency in free recall. *Psychonomic Bulletin & Review, 15*, 1236–1250.

Farrell, S., & Lewandowsky, S. (in press). Computational models as aids to better reasoning in psychology. *Current Directions in Psychological Science*.

Farrell, S., & Ludwig, C. J. H. (2008). Bayesian and maximum likelihood estimation of hierarchical response time models. *Psychonomic Bulletin & Review, 15*, 1209–1217.

Farrell, S., Ratcliff, R., Cherian, A., & Segraves, M. (2006). Modeling unidimensional categorization in monkeys. *Learning & Behavior, 34*, 86–101.

Fecteau, J. H., & Munoz, D. P. (2003). Exploring the consequences of the previous trial. *Nature Reviews Neuroscience, 4*, 435–443.

Fernandez, G. (2003). Intrasubject reproducibility of presurgical language lateralization and mapping using fMRI. *Neurology, 60*, 969–975.

Forster, K. I. (1994). Computational modeling and elementary process analysis in visual word recognition. *Journal of Experimental Psychology: Human Perception and Performance, 20*, 1292–1310.

Forster, M. R. (2000). Key concepts in model selection: Performance and generalizability. *Journal of Mathematical Psychology, 44*, 205–231.

Forstmann, B. U., Dutilh, G., Brown, S., Neumann, J., von Cramond, D. Y., Ridderinkhofa, K. R., et al. (2008). Striatum and pre-SMA facilitate decision-making under time pressure. *Proceedings of the National Academy of Sciences USA, 105*, 17538–17542.

Freedman, D., Pisani, R., Purves, R., & Adhikari, A. (1991). *Statistics* (2nd ed.). New York: W. W. Norton.

French, R. M. (1992). Semi-distributed representations and catastrophic forgetting in connectionist networks. *Connection Science, 4*, 365–377.

Fum, D., Del Missier, F., & Stocco, A. (2007). The cognitive modeling of human behavior: Why a model is (sometimes) better than 10,000 words. *Cognitive Systems Research, 8*, 135–142.

Gardiner, J. M. (1988). Functional aspects of recollective experience. *Memory & Cognition, 16,* 309–313.

Gardiner, J. M., & Conway, M. A. (1999). Levels of awareness and varieties of experience. In B. H. Challis & B. M. Velichovsky (Eds.), *Stratification in cognition and consciousness* (pp. 237–254). Amsterdam, Netherlands: John Benjamins Publishing.

Gardiner, J. M., & Gregg, V. H. (1997). Recognition memory with little or no remembering: Implications for a detection model. *Psychonomic Bulletin & Review, 4,* 474–479.

Gardiner, J. M., & Java, R. I. (1990). Recollective experience in word and non-word recognition. *Memory & Cognition, 18,* 23–30.

Gerla, G. (2007). Point-free geometry and verisimilitude of theories. *Journal of Philosophical Logic, 36,* 707–733.

Gilden, D. L. (2001). Cognitive emissions of $1/f$ noise. *Psychological Review, 108,* 33–56.

Glover, S., & Dixon, P. (2004). Likelihood ratios: A simple and flexible statistic for empirical psychologists. *Psychonomic Bulletin & Review, 11,* 791–806.

Goldstone, R. L., & Sakamoto, Y. (2003). The transfer of abstract principles governing complex adaptive tasks. *Cognitive Psychology, 46,* 414–466.

Gopnik, A. (1998). Explanation as orgasm. *Minds and Machines, 8,* 101–118.

Gregg, V. H., & Gardiner, J. H. (1994). Recognition memory and awareness: A large effect of study-test modalities on "know" responses following a highly perceptual orienting task. *European Journal of Cognitive Psychology, 6,* 131–147.

Grider, R. C., & Malmberg, K. J. (2008). Discriminating between changes in bias and changes in accuracy for recognition memory of emotional stimuli. *Memory & Cognition, 36,* 933–946.

Griffiths, T. L., & Kalish, M. L. (2007). Language evolution by iterated learning with Bayesian agents. *Cognitive Science, 31,* 441–480.

Grünwald, P. D. (2007). *The minimum description length principle.* Cambridge, MA: MIT Press.

Gurney, K. (1997). *An introduction to neural networks.* London: UCL Press.

Haken, H., Kelso, J. A. S., & Bunz, H. (1985). A theoretical model of phase transitions in human hand movements. *Biological Cybernetics, 51,* 347–356.

Hayes, K. J. (1953). The backward curve: A method for the study of learning. *Psychological Review, 60,* 269–275.

Heathcote, A. (2004). Fitting Wald and ex-Wald distributions to response time data: An example using functions for the S-Plus package. *Behavior Research Methods, Instruments, & Computers, 36,* 678–694.

Heathcote, A., Brown, S., & Mewhort, D. J. (2000). The power law repealed: The case for an exponential law of practice. *Psychonomic Bulletin & Review, 7,* 185–207.

Hebb, D. O. (1949). *The organization of behavior.* New York: Wiley.

Hélie, S. (2006). An introduction to model selection: Tools and algorithms. *Tutorials in Quantitative Methods for Psychology*, *2*, 1–10.

Helsabeck, F. (1975). Syllogistic reasoning: Generation of counterexamples. *Journal of Educational Psychology*, *67*, 102–108.

Henson, R. N. A. (1998). Short-term memory for serial order: The Start-End model. *Cognitive Psychology*, *36*, 73–137.

Henson, R. N. A. (2005). What can functional neuroimaging tell the experimental psychologist? *Quarterly Journal of Experimental Psychology*, *58A*, 193–233.

Henson, R. N. A., Norris, D. G., Page, M. P. A., & Baddeley, A. D. (1996). Unchained memory: Error patterns rule out chaining models of immediate serial recall. *Quarterly Journal of Experimental Psychology*, *49A*, 80–115.

Hicks, J. L., & Marsh, R. L. (2000). Toward specifying the attentional demands of recognition memory. *Journal of Experimental Psychology: Learning, Memory, & Cognition*, *26*, 1483–1498.

Hinton, G. E. (1986). Learning distributed representations of concepts. In *Proceedings of the eighth annual conference of the cognitive science society* (pp. 1–12). Amherst, MA: Erlbaum.

Hinton, G. E. (1990). Mapping part-whole hierarchies into connectionist networks. *Artificial Intelligence*, *46*, 47–75.

Hinton, G. E., & Shallice, T. (1991). Lesioning an attractor network: Investigations of acquired dyslexia. *Psychological Review*, *98*, 74–95.

Hintzman, D. L. (1980). Simpson's paradox and the analysis of memory retrieval. *Psychological Review*, *87*, 398–410.

Hintzman, D. L. (1991). Why are formal models useful in psychology? In W. E. Hockley & S. Lewandowsky (Eds.), *Relating theory and data: Essays on human memory in honor of Bennet B. Murdock* (pp. 39–56). Hillsdale, NJ: Lawrence Erlbaum.

Hirshman, E. (1995). Decision processes in recognition memory: Criterion shifts and the list-strength paradigm. *Journal of Experimental Psychology: Learning, Memory, and Cognition*, *21*, 302–313.

Hirshman, E. (1998). On the logic of testing the independence assumption in the process-dissociation procedure. *Memory & Cognition*, *26*, 857–859.

Hirshman, E., Lanning, K., Master, S., & Henzler, A. (2002). Signal-detection models as tools for interpreting judgements of recollections. *Applied Cognitive Psychology*, *16*, 151–156.

Hirshman, E., & Master, S. (1997). Modeling the conscious correlates of recognition memory: Reflections on the remember-know paradigm. *Memory & Cognition*, *25*, 345–351.

Hockley, W. E. (1992). Item versus associative information: Further comparisons of forgetting rates. *Journal of Experimental Psychology: Learning, Memory, and Cognition*, *18*, 1321–1330.

Hohle, R. H. (1965). Inferred components of reaction times as functions of foreperiod duration. *Journal of Experimental Psychology*, *69*, 382–386.

Hood, B. M. (1995). Gravity rules for 2-to 4-year olds? *Cognitive Development*, *10*, 577–598.

Hooge, I. T. C., & Frens, M. A. (2000). Inhibition of saccade return (ISR): Spatio-temporal properties of saccade programming. *Vision Research*, *40*, 3415–3426.

Hopkins, R. O., Myers, C. E., Shohamy, D., Grossman, S., & Gluck, M. (2004). Impaired probabilistic category learning in hypoxic subjects with hippocampal damage. *Neuropsychologia*, *42*, 524–535.

Howard, M. W., Jing, B., Rao, V. A., Provyn, J. P., & Datey, A. V. (2009). Bridging the gap: Transitive associations between items presented in similar temporal contexts. *Journal of Experimental Psychology: Learning, Memory, and Cognition*, *35*, 391–407.

Howard, M. W., & Kahana, M. J. (2002). A distributed representation of temporal context. *Journal of Mathematical Psychology*, *46*, 269–299.

Howell, D. C. (2006). *Statistical methods for psychology*. Belmont, CA: Wadsworth.

Hoyle, F. (1974). The work of Nicolaus Copernicus. *Proceedings of the Royal Society, Series A*, *336*, 105–114.

Huber, D. E. (2006). Computer simulations of the ROUSE model: An analytic simulation technique and a comparison between the error variance-covariance and bootstrap methods for estimating parameter confidence. *Behavior Research Methods*, *38*, 557–568.

Hudjetz, A., & Oberauer, K. (2007). The effects of processing time and processing rate on forgetting in working memory: Testing four models of the complex span paradigm. *Memory & Cognition*, *35*, 1675–1684.

Hughes, C., Russell, J., & Robbins, T. W. (1994). Evidence for executive dysfunction in autism. *Neuopsychologia*, *32*, 477–492.

Hulme, C., Roodenrys, S., Schweickert, R., Brown, G. D. A., Martin, S., & Stuart, G. (1997). Word-frequency effects on short-term memory tasks: Evidence for a redintegration process in immediate serial recall. *Journal of Experimental Psychology: Learning, Memory, and Cognition*, *23*, 1217–1232.

Hulme, C., & Tordoff, V. (1989). Working memory development: The effects of speech rate, word-length, and acoustic similarity on serial recall. *Journal of Experimental Child Psychology*, *47*, 72–87.

Hunt, E. (2007). *The mathematics of behavior*. Cambridge, UK: Cambridge University Press.

Hurvich, C. M., & Tsai, C. L. (1989). Regression and time series model selection in small samples. *Biometrika*, *76*, 297–307.

Hutchison, K. A. (2003). Is semantic priming due to association strength or feature overlap? *Psychonomic Bulletin & Review*, *10*, 785–813.

Inglehart, R., Foa, R., Peterson, C., & Welzel, C. (2008). Development, freedom, and rising happiness. *Perspectives on Psychological Science*, *3*, 264–285.

Jacoby, L. L. (1991). A process dissociation framework: Separating automatic from intentional uses of memory. *Journal of Memory and Language, 30,* 513–541.

Jang, Y., Wixted, J., & Huber, D. E. (2009). Testing signal-detection models of yes/no and two-alternative forced choice recognition memory. *Journal of Experimental Psychology: General, 138,* 291–306.

Jaynes, E. T. (2003). *Probability theory: The logic of science.* Cambridge: Cambridge University Press.

Jeffrey, R. (2004). *Subjective probability: The real thing.* Cambridge: Cambridge University Press.

Jeffreys, H. (1961). *Theory of probability.* Oxford: Oxford University Press.

Jiang, Y., Rouder, J. N., & Speckman, P. L. (2004). A note on the sampling properties of the vincentizing (quantile averaging) procedure. *Journal of Mathematical Psychology, 48,* 186–195.

Jones, M., Love, B. C., & Maddox, W. T. (2006). Recency effects as a window to generalization: Separating decisional and perceptual sequential effects in category learning. *Journal of Experimental Psychology: Learning, Memory, and Cognition, 32,* 316–332.

Jones, M. N., & Mewhort, D. J. K. (2007). Representing word meaning and order information in a composite holographic lexicon. *Psychological Review, 114,* 1–37.

Jones, R. M., Laird, J. E., Nielsen, P. E., Coulter, K. J., Kenny, P., & Koss, F. V. (1999). Automated intelligent pilots for combat flight simulation. *AI Magazine, 20,* 27–41.

Joordens, S., & Merikle, P. M. (1993). Independence or redundancy? Two models of conscious and unconscious influences. *Journal of Experimental Psychology: General, 122,* 462–467.

Kaelo, P., & Ali, M. M. (2007). Integrated crossover rules in real coded genetic algorithms. *European Journal of Operational Research, 176,* 60–76.

Kail, R. V., & Ferrer, E. (2007). Processing speed in childhood and adolescence: Longitudinal models for examining developmental change. *Child Development, 78,* 1760–1770.

Kane, M. J., Hambrick, D. Z., & Conway, A. R. A. (2005). Working memory capacity and fluid intelligence are strongly related constructs: Comment on Ackerman, Beier, and Boyle (2005). *Psychological Bulletin, 131,* 66–71.

Kass, R. E., & Raftery, A. E. (1995). Bayes factors. *Journal of the American Statistical Association, 90,* 773–795.

Keren, G., & Schul, Y. (2009). Two is not always better than one: A critical evaluation of two-system theories. *Perspectives on Psychological Science, 4,* 533–550.

Keynes, J. M. (1921). *A treatise on probability.* London: Macmillan.

Kirkpatrick, S., Gelatt, C. D., & Vecchi, M. P. (1983). Optimization by simulated annealing. *Science, 220,* 671–680.

Klein, R. M., & MacInnes, W. J. (1999). Inhibition of return is a foraging facilitator in visual search. *Psychological Science, 10*, 346–352.

Knowlton, B. J. (1999). What can neuropsychology tell us about category learning? *Trends in Cognitive Science, 3*, 123–124.

Knowlton, B. J., Squire, L. R., & Gluck, M. A. (1994). Probabilistic classification learning in amnesia. *Learning and Memory, 1*, 106–120.

Kolda, T. G., Lewis, R. M., & Torczon, V. (2003). Optimization by direct search: New perspectives on some classical and modern methods. *SIAM Review, 45*, 385–482.

Körding, K. P., & Wolpert, D. M. (2006). Bayesian decision theory in sensorimotor control. *Trends in Cognitive Sciences, 10*, 319–326.

Kruschke, J. K. (1992). ALCOVE: An exemplar-based connectionist model of category learning. *Psychological Review, 99*, 22–44.

Kruschke, J. K., & Johansen, M. K. (1999). A model of probabilistic category learning. *Journal of Experimental Psychology: Learning, Memory, and Cognition, 25*, 1083–1119.

Kruskal, J. B., & Wish, M. (1978). *Multidimensional scaling.* London: Sage.

Kubovy, M., & van den Berg, M. (2008). The whole is equal to the sum of its parts: a probabilistic model of grouping by proximity and similarity in regular patterns. *Psychological Review, 115*, 131–154.

Kuha, J. (2004). AIC and BIC: Comparisons of assumptions and performance. *Sociological Methods & Research, 33*, 188–229.

Lagarias, J. C., Reeds, J. A., Wright, M. H., & Wright, P. E. (1998). Convergence properties of the Nelder-Mead simplex method in low dimensions. *SIAM Journal on Optimization, 9*, 112–147.

Lamberts, K. (2005). Mathematical modeling of cognition. In K. Lamberts & R. L. Goldstone (Eds.), *The handbook of cognition* (pp. 407–421). London: Sage.

Laming, D. (1979). Autocorrelation of choice-reaction times. *Acta Psychologica, 43*, 381–412.

Leahey, T. H., & Harris, R. J. (1989). *Human learning* (2nd ed.). Englewood Cliffs, NJ: Prentice Hall.

Lee, M. D., & Webb, M. R. (2005). Modeling individual differences in cognition. *Psychonomic Bulletin & Review, 12*, 605–621. Levine, D. S. (2000). *Introduction to neural and cognitive modeling* (2nd ed.). Mawah, NJ: Lawrence Erlbaum.

Lewandowsky, S. (1986). Priming in recognition memory for categorized lists. *Journal of Experimental Psychology: Learning, Memory, and Cognition, 12*, 562–574.

Lewandowsky, S. (1991). Gradual unlearning and catastrophic interference: A comparison of distributed architectures. In W. E. Hockley & S. Lewandowsky (Eds.), *Relating theory and data: Essays on human memory in honor of Bennet B. Murdock* (pp. 445–476). Hillsdale, NJ: Erlbaum.

Lewandowsky, S. (1993). The rewards and hazards of computer simulations. *Psychological Science*, *4*, 236–243.

Lewandowsky, S. (1999). Redintegration and response suppression in serial recall: A dynamic network model. *International Journal of Psychology*, *34*, 434–446.

Lewandowsky, S., Duncan, M., & Brown, G. D. A. (2004). Time does not cause forgetting in short-term serial recall. *Psychonomic Bulletin & Review*, *11*, 771–790.

Lewandowsky, S., & Farrell, S. (2000). A redintegration account of the effects of speech rate, lexicality, and word frequency in immediate serial recall. *Psychological Research*, *63*, 163–173.

Lewandowsky, S., & Farrell, S. (2008a). Phonological similarity in serial recall: Constraints on theories of memory. *Journal of Memory and Language*, *58*, 429–448.

Lewandowsky, S., & Farrell, S. (2008b). Short-term memory: New data and a model. In B. H. Ross (Ed.), *The psychology of learning and motivation* (Vol. 49, pp. 1–48). London, UK: Elsevier.

Lewandowsky, S., Griffiths, T. L., & Kalish, M. L. (2009). The wisdom of individuals: Exploring people's knowledge about everyday events using iterated learning. *Cognitive Science*, *33*, 969–998.

Lewandowsky, S., & Heit, E. (2006). Some targets for memory models. *Journal of Memory and Langauge*, *55*, 441–446.

Lewandowsky, S., Kalish, M., & Ngang, S. (2002). Simplified learning in complex situations: Knowledge partitioning in function learning. *Journal of Experimental Psychology: General*, *131*, 163–193.

Lewandowsky, S., & Li, S.-C. (1994). Memory for serial order revisited. *Psychological Review*, *101*, 539–543.

Lewandowsky, S., & Oberauer, K. (2008). The word length effect provides no evidence for decay in short-term memory. *Psychonomic Bulletin & Review*, *15*, 875–888.

Lewandowsky, S., & Oberauer, K. (2009). No evidence for temporal decay in working memory. *Journal of Experimental Psychology: Learning, Memory, and Cognition*, *35*, 1545–1551.

Li, S.-C., Lewandowsky, S., & DeBrunner, V. E. (1996). Using parameter sensitivity and interdependence to predict model scope and falsifiability. *Journal of Experimental Psychology: General*, *125*, 360–369.

Light, L. L., & La Voie, D. (1993). Direct and indirect measures of memory in old age. In P. Graf & M. E. J. Masson (Eds.), *Implicit memory. New directions in cognition, development, and neuropsychology* (pp. 207–230). Hillsdale, NJ: Erlbaum.

Little, D. R., & Lewandowsky, S. (2009). Beyond non-utilization: Irrelevant cues can gate learning in probabilistic categorization. *Journal of Experimental Psychology: Human Perception and Performance*, *35*, 530–550.

Liu, C. C., & Smith, P. L. (2009). Comparing time-accuracy curves: Beyond goodness-of-fit measures. *Psychonomic Bulletin & Review*, *16*, 190–203.

Locatelli, M. (2002). Simulated annealing algorithms for continuous global optimization. In P. M. Pardalos & H. E. Romeijn (Eds.), *Handbook of global optimization* (Vol. 2, pp. 179–229). Dordrecht, Netherlands: Kluwer Academic Publishers.

Logan, G. D. (1988). Toward an instance theory of automatization. *Psychological Review*, *95*, 492–527.

Lombrozo, T. (2005). Why adaptationist explanations are so seductive. In B. Bara, B. Barsalou, & M. Bucciarelli (Eds.), *Proceedings of the 27th annual conference of the cognitive science society* (p. 2516). Mahwah, NJ: Lawrence Erlbaum.

Lombrozo, T. (2007). Simplicity and probability in causal explanation. *Cognitive Psychology*, *55*, 232–257.

Love, B. C., Medin, D. L., & Gureckis, T. M. (2004). SUSTAIN: A network model of category learning. *Psychological Review*, *111*, 309–332.

Luce, R. D. (1959). *Individual choice behavior.* New York: John Wiley.

Luce, R. D. (1963). Detection and recognition. In R. D. Luce, R. R. Bush, & E. Galanter (Eds.), *Handbook of mathematical psychology* (Vol. 1, pp. 103–189). New York: Wiley.

Luce, R. D. (1986). *Response times.* Oxford: Oxford University Press.

Luce, R. D. (1995). Four tensions concerning mathematical modeling in psychology. Annual Review of Psychology, 46, 1–26.

Ludwig, C. J. H., Farrell, S., Ellis, L. A., & Gilchrist, I. D. (2009). The mechanism underlying inhibition of saccadic return. *Cognitive Psychology*, *59*, 180–202.

MacCallum, R. C. (2003). Working with imperfect models. *Multivariate Behavioral Research*, *38*, 113–139.

Macho, S. (2007). Feature sampling in detection: Implications for the measurement of perceptual independence. *Journal of Experimental Psychology: General*, *136*, 133–153.

Maddox, W. T., & Ashby, F. G. (1993). Comparing decision bound and exemplar models of categorization. *Perception and Psychophysics*, *53*, 49–70.

Maddox, W. T., & Ashby, F. G. (1998). Selective attention and the formation of linear decision boundaries: Comment on McKinley and Nosofsky (1996). *Journal of Experimental Psychology: Human Perception and Performance*, *24*, 301–321.

Marr, D. (1982). *Vision.* San Francisco: W. H. Freeman.

Massaro, D. W. (1988). Some criticisms of connectionist models of human performance. *Journal of Memory and Language*, *27*, 213–234.

Masson, M. E. J., & Loftus, G. R. (2003). Using confidence intervals for graphically based data interpretation. *Canadian Journal of Experimental Psychology*, *57*, 203–220.

McClelland, J. L., & Chappell, M. (1998). Familiarity breeds differentiation: A subjective-likelihood approach to the effects of experience in recognition memory. *Psychological Review*, *105*, 734–760.

McClelland, J. L., & Rumelhart, D. E. (Eds.). (1986). *Parallel distributed processing: Explorations in the microstructure of cognition.* Cambridge, MA: MIT Press.

McClelland, J. L., & Rumelhart, D. E. (1981). An interactive activation model of context effects in letter perception: Part 1. An account of basic findings. *Psychological Review, 88,* 375–407.

McCloskey, M., & Cohen, N. J. (1989). Catastrophic interference in connectionist networks: The sequential learning problem. *The Psychology of Learning and Motivation, 24,* 109–165.

McKinley, S. C., & Nosofsky, R. M. (1995). Investigations of exemplar and decision bound models in large, ill-defined category structures. *Journal of Experimental Psychology: Human Perception and Performance, 21,* 128–148.

McKoon, G., Ratcliff, R., & Dell, G. (1986). A critical evaluation of the semantic-episodic distinction. *Journal of Experimental Psychology: Learning, Memory, and Cognition, 12,* 295–306.

McNicol, D. (1972). *A primer of signal detection theory.* London: Allen and Unwin.

Meehl, P. E. (1990). Appraising and amending theories: The strategy of Lakatosian defense and two principles that warrant it. *Psychological Inquiry, 1,* 108–141.

Meeter, M., & Murre, J. M. J. (2005). Tracelink: A model of consolidation and amnesia. *Cognitive Neuropsychology, 22,* 559–587.

Meissner, C. A., & Brigham, J. C. (2001). A meta-analysis of the verbal overshadowing effect in face identification. *Applied Cognitive Psychology, 15,* 603–616.

Mitchell, M. (1996). *An introduction to genetic algorithms.* Cambridge, MA: MIT Press.

Miyake, A., Friedman, N. P., Emerson, M. J., Witzki, A. H., & Howerter, T. D. (2000). The unity and diversity of executive functions and their contributions to complex "frontal lobe" tasks: A latent variable analysis. *Cognitive Psychology, 41,* 49–100.

Morey, R. D., Pratte, M. S., & Rouder, J. N. (2008). Problematic effects of aggregation in zROC analysis and a hierarchical modeling solution. *Journal of Mathematical Psychology, 52,* 376–388.

Morgan, B. J. T. (2000). *Applied stochastic modelling.* New York: Oxford University Press.

Mueller, S. T., Seymour, T. L., Kieras, D. E., & Meyer, D. E. (2003). Theoretical implications of articulatory duration, phonological similarity, and phonological complexity in verbal working memory. *Journal of Experimental Psychology: Learning, Memory, and Cognition, 29,* 1353–1380.

Munakata, Y., & McClelland, J. L. (2003). Connectionist models of development. *Developmental Science, 6,* 413–429.

Murdock, B. B. (1962). The serial position effect of free recall. *Journal of Experimental Psychology*, *64*, 482–488.

Murdock, B. B. (1982). A theory for the storage and retrieval of item and associative information. *Psychological Review*, *89*, 609–626.

Murdock, B. B. (1989). Learning in a distributed memory model. In C. Izawa (Ed.), *Current issues in cognitive processes: The Tulane Flowerree symposium on cognition* (pp. 69–106). Hillsdale, NJ: Erlbaum.

Murphy, G. (2002). *The big book of concepts*. Cambridge, MA: MIT Press.

Myung, I. J. (2003). Tutorial on maximum likelihood estimation. *Journal of Mathematical Psychology*, *47*, 90–100.

Myung, I. J., Forster, M. R., & Browne, M. W. (Eds.). (2000). Model selection [special issue]. *Journal of Mathematical Psychology*, *44*.

Myung, I. J., & Pitt, M. A. (2002). Mathematical modeling. In J. Wixted (Ed.), *Stevens' handbook of experimental psychology vol. 4: Methodology in experimental psychology* (pp. 429–460). New York: John Wiley & Sons.

Navalpakkam, V., & Itti, L. (2005). Modeling the influence of task on attention. *Vision Research*, *45*, 205–231.

Navarro, D. J., Pitt, M. A., & Myung, I. J. (2004). Assessing the distinguishability of models and the informativeness of data. *Cognitive Psychology*, *49*, 47–84.

Neath, I. (2000). Modeling the effects of irrelevant speech on memory. *Psycho-nomic Bulletin & Review*, *7*, 403–423.

Neath, I., Bireta, T. J., & Surprenant, A. M. (2003). The time-based word length effect and stimulus set specificity. *Psychonomic Bulletin & Review*, *10*, 430–434.

Nelder, J. A., & Mead, R. (1965). A simplex method for function minimization. *Computer Journal*, *7*, 308–313.

Newell, A. (1990). *Unified theories of cognition*. Cambridge, MA: Harvard University Press.

Newell, B. R., & Dunn, J. C. (2008). Dimensions in data: testing psychological models using state-trace analysis. *Trends in Cognitive Science*, *12*, 285–290.

Norris, D. (2005). How do computational models help us build better theories? In A. Cutler (Ed.), *Twenty-first century psycholinguistics: Four cornerstones* (pp. 331–346). Mahwah, NJ: Lawrence Erlbaum.

Norris, D. (2006). The Bayesian reader: Explaining word recognition as an optimal Bayesian decision process. *Psychological Review*, *113*, 327–357.

Nosofsky, R. M. (1986). Attention, similarity, and the identification-categorization relationship. *Journal of Experimental Psychology: Learning, Memory, and Cognition*, *115*, 39–61.

Nosofsky, R. M. (1989). Further tests of an exemplar-similarity approach to relating identification and categorization. *Perception & Psychophysics*, *45*, 279–290.

Nosofsky, R. M. (1991). Tests of an exemplar model for relating perceptual classification and recognition memory. *Journal of Experimental Psychology: Human Perception and Performance*, *17*, 3–27.

Nosofsky, R. M. (1998). Selective attention and the form of linear decision bound: Reply to Maddox and Ashby (1998). *Journal of Experimental Psychology: Human Perception and Performance, 24*, 322–339.

Nosofsky, R. M., & Bergert, F. B. (2007). Limitations of exemplar models of multi-attribute probabilistic inference. *Journal of Experimental Psychology: Learning, Memory, and Cognition, 33*, 999–1019.

Nosofsky, R. M., & Palmeri, T. (1998). A rule-plus-exception model for classifying objects in continuous-dimension spaces. *Psychonomic Bulletin & Review, 5*, 345–369.

Nosofsky, R. M., & Palmeri, T. J. (1997). An exemplar-based random walk model of speeded classification. *Psychological Review, 104*, 266–300.

Nourani, Y., & Andresen, B. (1998). A comparison of simulated annealing cooling strategies. *Journal of Physics A: Mathematical and General, 31*, 8373–8385.

Oberauer, K., & Kliegl, R. (2006). A formal model of capacity limits in working memory. *Journal of Memory and Language, 55*, 601–626.

Oberauer, K., & Lewandowsky, S. (2008). Forgetting in immediate serial recall: Decay, temporal distinctiveness, or interference? *Psychological Review, 115*, 544–576.

Oberauer, K., Süß, H.-M., Schulze, R., Wilhelm, O., & Wittmann, W. W. (2000). Working memory capacity—facets of a cognitive ability construct. *Personality and Individual Differences, 29*, 1017–1045.

Oberauer, K., Süß, H.-M., Wilhelm, O., & Sander, N. (2007). Individual differences in working memory capacity and reasoning ability. In A. R. A. Conway, C. Jarrold, M. J. Kane, A. Miyake, & J. N. Towse (Eds.), *Variation in working memory* (pp. 49–75). New York: Oxford University Press.

O'Toole, A., Deffenbacher, K., Valentin, D., & Abdi, H. (1994). Structural aspects of face recognition and the other-race effect. *Memory & Cognition, 22*, 208–224.

Page, M. P. A. (2000). Connectionist modelling in psychology: A localist manifesto. *Behavioral and Brain Sciences, 23*, 443–467.

Page, M. P. A. (2006). What can't functional neuroimaging tell the cognitive psychologist. *Cortex, 42*, 428–443.

Page, M. P. A., & Norris, D. (1998a). Modelling immediate serial recall with a localist implementation of the primacy model. In J. Grainger & A. M. Jacobs (Eds.), *Localist connectionist approaches to human cognition* (pp. 227–255). Mahwah, NJ: Lawrence Erlbaum.

Page, M. P. A., & Norris, D. (1998b). The primacy model: A new model of immediate serial recall. *Psychological Review, 105*, 761–781.

Palmeri, T. J. (1997). Exemplar similar and the development of automaticity. *Journal of Experimental Psychology: Learning Memory & Cognition, 23*, 324–354.

Palmeri, T. J., Wong, A. C.-N., & Gauthier, I. (2004). Computational approaches to the development of perceptual expertise. *Trends in Cognitive Sciences, 8*, 378–386.

Pastore, R. E., Crawley, E. J., Berens, M. S., & Skelly, M. A. (2003). "Nonparametric" A' and other modern misconceptions about signal detection theory. *Psychonomic Bulletin & Review, 10*, 556–569.

Pawitan, Y. (2001). *In all likelihood: Statistical modelling and inference using likelihood*. Oxford: Oxford University Press.

Pike, R. (1973). Response latency models for signal detection. *Psychological Review, 80*, 53–68.

Pitt, M. A., Kim, W., Navarro, D. J., & Myung, J. I. (2006). Global model analysis by parameter space partitioning. *Psychological Review, 113*, 57–83.

Pitt, M. A., & Myung, I. J. (2002). When a good fit can be bad. *Trends in Cognitive Science, 6*, 421–425.

Ploeger, A., Maas, H. L. J. van der, & Hartelman, P. A. I. (2002). Stochastic catastrophe analysis of switches in the perception of apparent motion. *Psychonomic Bulletin & Review, 9*, 26–42.

Poldrack, R. A., & Foerde, K. (2008). Category learning and the memory systems debate. *Neuroscience and Biobehavioral Reviews, 32*, 197–205.

Popper, K. R. (1963). *Conjectures and refutations*. London: Routledge.

Qin, Y., Anderson, J. R., Silk, E., Stenger, V. A., & Carter, C. S. (2004). The change of the brain activation patterns along with the children's practice in algebra equation solving. *Proceedings of the National Academy of Sciences, 101*, 5686–5691.

Raaijmakers, J. G. W., & Shiffrin, R. M. (1980). SAM: A theory of probabilistic search of associative memory. In G. H. Bower (Ed.), *The psychology of learning and motivation* (Vol. 14, pp. 207–262). New York: Academic Press.

Raaijmakers, J. G. W., & Shiffrin, R. M. (1981). Search of associative memory. *Psychological Review, 88*, 93–134.

Raftery, A. E. (1999). Bayes factors and BIC: Comment on "A critique of the Bayesian Information Criterion for model selection." *Sociological Methods & Research, 27*, 411–427.

Ratcliff, R. (1978). A theory of memory retrieval. *Psychological Review, 85*, 59–108.

Ratcliff, R. (1979). Group reaction time distributions and an analysis of distribution statistics. *Psychological Bulletin, 86*, 446–461.

Ratcliff, R. (1990). Connectionist models of recognition memory: Constraints imposed by learning and forgetting functions. *Psychological Review, 97*, 285–308.

Ratcliff, R. (1998). The role of mathematical psychology in experimental psychology. *Australian Journal of Psychology, 50*, 129–130.

Ratcliff, R., Hasegawa, Y. T., Hasegawa, Y. P., Smith, P. L., & Segraves, M. A. (2007). Dual diffusion model for single-cell recording data from the superior colliculus in a brightness-discrimination task. *Journal of Neurophysiology, 97*, 1756–1774.

Ratcliff, R., & Murdock, B. B. (1976). Retrieval processes in recognition memory. *Psychological Review, 83*, 190–214.

Ratcliff, R., & Rouder, J. N. (1998). Modeling repsonse times for two-choice decisions. *Psychological Science, 9*, 347–356.

Ratcliff, R., & Smith, P. L. (2004). A comparison of sequential sampling models for two-choice reaction time. *Psychological Review, 111*, 333–367.

Ratcliff, R., Van Zandt, T., & McKoon, G. (1995). Process dissociation, single-process theories, and recognition memory. *Journal of Experimental Psychology: General, 124*, 352–374.

Ratcliff, R., Van Zandt, T., & McKoon, G. (1999). Connectionist and diffusion models of reaction time. *Psychological Review, 106*, 261–300.

Raven, J., Raven, J. C., & Court, J. H. (1998). *Section 2: Coloured Progressive Matrices (1998 edition). Introducing the parallel version of the test, Manual for the Raven's progressive matrices and vocabulary scales.* Oxford, UK: Oxford Psychologist Press.

Reitman, W. B. (1965). *Cognition and thought.* New York: Wiley.

Rickard, T. (1997). Bending the power law: A CMPL theory of strategy shifts and the automatization of cognitive skills. *Journal of Experimental Psychology: General, 126*, 288–311.

Riefer, D., & Batchelder, W. (1988). Multinomial modeling and the measurement of cognitive processes. *Psychological Review, 95*, 318–339.

Rips, L. (2002). Circular reasoning. *Cognitive Science, 26*, 767–795.

Roberts, S., & Pashler, H. (2000). How persuasive is a good fit? A comment on theory testing. Psychological Review, 107, 358–367.

Roediger, H. L., & McDermott, K. B. (1993). Implicit memory in normal human subjects. In F. Boller & J. Grafman (Eds.), *Handbook of neuropsychology* (Vol. 8, pp. 63–131). Amsterdam: Elsevier.

Roelofs, A. (1997). The WEAVER model of word-form encoding in speech production. *Cognition, 64*, 249–284.

Rohrer, D. (2002). The breadth of memory search. *Memory, 10*, 291–301.

Root-Bernstein, R. (1981). Views on evolution, theory, and science. *Science, 212*, 1446–1449.

Rosenbaum, D. A. (2007). *MATLAB for behavioral scientists.* Mahwah, NJ: Lawrence Erlbaum.

Rotello, C. M., & Macmillan, N. A. (2006). Remember-know models as decision strategies in two experimental paradigms. *Journal of Memory and Language, 55*, 479–494.

Rouder, J. N., & Lu, J. (2005). An introduction to Bayesian hierarchical models with an application in the theory of signal detection. *Psychonomic Bulletin & Review, 12*, 573–604.

Rouder, J. N., Lu, J., Morey, R. D., Sun, S., & Speckman, P. L. (2008). A hierarchical process-dissociation model. *Journal of Experimental Psychology: General, 137*, 370–389.

Rouder, J. N., Lu, J., Speckman, P., Sun, D., & Jiang, Y. (2005). A hierarchical model for estimating response time distributions. *Psychonomic Bulletin & Review, 12*, 195–223.

Rouder, J. N., & Ratcliff, R. (2004). Comparing categorization models. *Journal of Experimental Psychology: General, 133*, 63–82.

Rowan, T. H. (1990). *Functional stability analysis of numerical algorithms.* Unpublished doctoral dissertation, University of Texas at Austin.

Royall, R. M. (1997). *Statistical evidence: A likelihood paradigm.* London: Chapman & Hall.

Schacter, D. L., Verfaellie, M., & Anes, M. D. (1997). Illusory memories in amnesic patients: Conceptual and perceptual false recognition. *Neuropsychology, 11*, 331–342.

Schmiedek, F., Oberauer, K., Wilhelm, O., Süß, H.-M., & Wittmann, W. W. (2007). Individual differences in components of reaction time distributions and their relations to working memory and intelligence. *Journal of Experimental Psychology: General, 136*, 414–429.

Schmitt, L. M. (2001). Theory of genetic algorithms. *Theoretical Computer Science, 259*, 1–61.

Schooler, J. W., & Engstler-Schooler, T. Y. (1990). Verbal overshadowing of visual memories: Some things are better left unsaid. *Cognitive Psychology, 22*, 36–71.

Schunn, C. D., & Wallach, D. (2005). Evaluating goodness-of-fit in comparison of models to data. In W. Tack (Ed.), *Psychologie der Kognition: Reden and Vorträge anläßlich der Emeritierung von Werner Tack* (pp. 115–154). Saarbrücken, Germany: University of Saarland Press.

Schwarz, G. (1978). Estimating the dimension of a model. *The Annals of Statistics, 6*, 461–464.

Schweickert, R. (1993). A multinomial processing tree model for degradation and redintegration in immediate recall. *Memory & Cognition, 21*, 168–175.

Schweickert, R., Chen, S., & Poirier, M. (1999). Redintegration and the useful lifetime of the verbal memory representation. *International Journal of Psychology, 34*, 447–453.

Searleman, A., & Herrmann, D. (1994). *Memory from a broader perspective.* New York: McGraw-Hill.

Sederberg, P. B., Howard, M. W., & Kahana, M. J. (2008). A context-based theory of recency and contiguity in free recall. *Psychological Review, 115*, 893–912.

Seidenberg, M. S., & McClelland, J. L. (1989). A distributed, developmental model of word recognition and naming. *Psychological Review, 96*, 523–568.

Severini, T. A. (2000). *Likelihood methods in statistics.* Oxford: Oxford University Press.

Shepard, R. N. (1987). Toward a universal law of generalization for psychological science. *Science, 237*, 1317–1323.

Shiffrin, R. M., Lee, M. D., Kim, W., & Wagenmakers, E. J. (2008). A survey of model evaluation approaches with a tutorial on hierarchical Bayesian methods. *Cognitive Science, 32*, 1248–1284.

Shiffrin, R. M., & Nobel, P. A. (1997). The art of model development and testing. *Behavior Research Methods, Instruments & Computers, 29*, 6–14.

Shiffrin, R. M., & Steyvers, M. (1997). A model for recognition memory: REM—retrieving effectively from memory. *Psychonomic Bulletin & Review, 4,* 145–166.

Shimojo, S., Simion, C., Shimojo, E., & Scheier, C. (2003). Gaze bias both reflects and influences preference. *Nature Neuroscience,* 1317–1322.

Shimp, C. P., Long, K. A., & Fremouw, T. (1996). Intuitive statistical inference: Categorization of binomial samples depends on sampling context. *Animal Learning & Behavior, 24,* 82–91.

Shultz, T. R. (2007). The Bayesian revolution approaches psychological development. *Developmental Science, 10,* 357–364.

Smith, E. E., & Jonides, J. (1997). Working memory: A view from neuroimaging. *Cognitive Psychology, 33,* 5–42.

Smith, J. B., & Batchelder, W. H. (2008). Assessing individual differences in categorical data. *Psychonomic Bulletin & Review, 15,* 713–731.

Smith, P. L. (1998). Attention and luminance detection: A quantitative analysis. *Journal of Experimental Psychology: Human Perception and Performance, 24,* 105–133.

Smith, P. L., & Vickers, D. (1988). The accumulator model of two-choice discrimination. *Journal of Mathematical Psychology, 32,* 135–168.

Spanos, A. (1999). *Probability theory and statistical inference.* Cambridge: Cambridge University Press.

Spieler, D. H., Balota, D. A., & Faust, M. E. (2000). Levels of selective attention revealed through analyses of response time distributions. *Journal of Experimental Psychology: Human Perception and Performance, 26,* 506–526.

Sternberg, S. (1975). Memory scanning: New findings and current controversies. *Quarterly Journal of Experimental Psychology, 27,* 1–32.

Stewart, N., Brown, G. D. A., & Chater, N. (2002). Sequence effects in categorization of simple perceptual stimuli. *Journal of Experimental Psychology: Learning, Memory, and Cognition, 28,* 3–11.

Stewart, N., Brown, G. D. A., & Chater, N. (2005). Absolute identification by relative judgement. *Psychological Review, 112,* 881–911.

Stone, M. (1974). Cross-validatory choice and assessment of statistical predictions. *Journal of the Royal Statistical Society, 36B,* 111–147.

Stone, M. (1977). An asymptotic equivalence of choice of model by cross-validation and Akaike's criterion. *Journal of the Royal Statistical Society, 39B,* 44–47.

Sugiura, N. (1978). Further analysis of the data by Akaike's information criterion and the finite corrections. *Communications in Statistics: Theory and Methods, 7,* 13–26.

Sun, R., Coward, A., & Zenzen, M. J. (2005). On levels of cognitive modeling. *Philosophical Psychology, 18,* 613–637.

Sun, R., Slusarz, P., & Terry, C. (2005). The interaction of the explicit and the implicit in skill learning: A dual-process approach. *Psychological Review, 112,* 159–192.

Taatgen, N. A., & Anderson, J. R. (2002). Why do children learn to say "broke"? A model of learning the past tense without feedback. *Cognition*, *86*, 123–155.

Taatgen, N. A., & Anderson, J. R. (2008). Constraints in cognitive architectures. In R. Sun (Ed.), *The Cambridge handbook of computational psychology* (pp. 170–185). Cambridge: Cambridge University Press.

Taatgen, N. A., & Anderson, J. R. (2009). The past, present, and future of cognitive architectures. *Topics in Cognitive Science*, 1–12.

Tan, L., & Ward, G. (2008). Rehearsal in immediate serial recall. *Psychonomic Bulletin & Review*, *15*, 535–542.

Tenenbaum, J. B., Griffiths, T. L., & Kemp, C. (2006). Theory-based Bayesian models of inductive learning and reasoning. *Trends in Cognitive Science*, *10*, 309–318.

Thompson, D. R., & Bilbro, G. L. (2000). Comparison of a genetic algorithm with a simulated annealing algorithm for the design of an ATM network. *IEEE Communications Letters*, *4*, 267–269.

Thornton, T. L., & Gilden, D. L. (2005). Provenance of correlations in psychological data. *Psychonomic Bulletin & Review*, *12*, 409–441.

Torre, K., Delignières, D., & Lemoine, L. (2007). Detection of long-range dependence and estimation of fractal exponents through ARFIMA modelling. *British Journal of Mathematical and Statistical Psychology*, *60*, 85–106.

Toth, J. P. (2000). Nonconscious forms of human memory. In E. Tulving & F. I. M. Craik (Eds.), *The Oxford handbook of memory* (pp. 245–261). Oxford: Oxford University Press.

Toth, J. P., Reingold, E. M., & Jacoby, L. L. (1994). Toward a redefinition of implicit memory: Process dissociations following elaborative processing and self-generation. *Journal of Experimental Psychology: Learning, Memory, and Cognition*, *20*, 290–303.

Trout, J. D. (2007). The psychology of scientific explanation. *Philosophy Compass*, *2/3*, 564–591.

Tsoulos, I. G. (2008). Modifications of real code genetic algorithm for global optimization. *Applied Mathematics and Computation*, *203*, 598–607.

Turner, M., & Engle, R. (1989). Is working memory capacity task dependent? *Journal of Memory and Language*, *49*, 446–468.

Tversky, A., & Kahneman, D. (1992). Advances in prospect theory: Cumulative representation of uncertainty. *Journal of Risk and Uncertainty*, *5*, 297–323.

Underwood, B. J. (1975). Individual differences as a crucible in theory construction. *American Psychologist*, *30*, 128–134.

Usher, M., & McClelland, J. L. (2001). The time course of perceptual choice: The leaky, competing accumulator model. *Psychological Review*, *108*, 550–592.

Vanderbilt, D., & Louie, S. G. (1984). A Monte Carlo simulated annealing approach to optimization over continuous variables. *Journal of Computational Physics*, *56*, 259–271.

van Santen, J. P., & Bamber, D. (1981). Finite and infinite state confusion models. *Journal of Mathematical Psychology*, *24*, 101–111.

Van Zandt, T. (2000). How to fit a response time distribution. *Psychonomic Bulletin & Review, 7*, 424–465.

Venn, J. (1888). *The logic of chance* (3rd ed.). London: Macmillan.

Verbeemen, T., Vanpaemel, W., Pattyn, S., Storms, G., & Verguts, T. (2007). Beyond exemplars and prototypes as memory representations of natural concepts: A clustering approach. *Journal of Memory and Language, 56*, 537–554.

Verzani, J. (2004). *Using R for introductory statistics.* Boca Raton, FL: CRC Press.

Visser, I., Raijmakers, M. E. J., & Molenaar, P. C. M. (2000). Confidence intervals for hidden Markov model parameters. *British Journal of Mathematical and Statistical Psychology, 53*, 317–327.

Visser, I., Raijmakers, M. E. J., & Molenaar, P. C. M. (2002). Fitting hidden Markov models to psychological data. *Scientific Programming, 10*, 185–199.

Vul, E., Harris, C., Winkielman, P., & Pashler, H. (2009a). Puzzlingly high correlations in fMRI studies of emotion, personality, and social cognition. *Perspectives on Psychological Science, 4*, 274–290.

Vul, E., Harris, C., Winkielman, P., & Pashler, H. (2009b). Reply to comments on "puzzlingly high correlations in fMRI studies of emotion, personality, and social cognition." *Perspectives on Psychological Science, 4*, 319–324.

Wagenmakers, E.-J. (2007). A practical solution to the pervasive problems of *p* values. *Psychonomic Bulletin & Review, 14*, 779–804.

Wagenmakers, E.-J., & Farrell, S. (2004). AIC model selection using Akaike weights. *Psychonomic Bulletin & Review, 11*, 192–196.

Wagenmakers, E.-J., Farrell, S., & Ratcliff, R. (2004). Estimation and interpretation of $1/f^{\alpha}$ noise in human cognition. *Psychonomic Bulletin & Review, 11*, 579–615.

Wagenmakers, E.-J., Farrell, S., & Ratcliff, R. (2005). Human cognition and a pile of sand: A discussion on serial correlations and self-organized criticality. *Journal of Experimental Psychology: General, 134*, 108–116.

Wagenmakers, E.-J., Ratcliff, R., Gomez, P., & Iverson, G. J. (2004). Assessing model mimcry using the parametric bootstrap. *Journal of Mathematical Psychology, 48*, 28–50.

Wagenmakers, E.-J., & Waldorp, L. (Eds.). (2006). Special issue on model selection: Theoretical developments and applications. *Journal of Mathematical Psychology, 50*, 99–214.

Wallish, P., Lusignan, M., Benayoun, M., Baker, T. I., Dickey, A. S., & Hatsopoulos, N. G. (2009). *MATLAB for neuroscientists: An introduction to scientific computing in MATLAB.* Burlington, MA: Academic Press.

Walthew, C., & Gilchrist, I. D. (2006). Target location probability effects in visual search: An effect of sequential dependencies. *Journal of Experimental Psychology: Human Perception and Performance, 32*, 1294–1301.

Wandell, B. A. (1977). Speed-accuracy tradeoff in visual detection: Applications of neural counting and timing. *Vision Research, 17*, 217–225.

Wasserman, L. (2000). Bayesian model selection and model averaging. *Journal of Mathematical Psychology*, *44*, 92–107.

Weakliem, D. L. (1999). A critique of the Bayesian Information Criterion for model selection. *Sociological Methods & Research*, *27*, 359–397.

Wei, J. (1975). Least square fitting of an elephant. *Chemtech, February*, 128–129.

Weisberg, D. S., Keil, F. C., Goodstein, J., Rawson, E., & Gray, J. R. (2008). The seductive allure of neuroscience explanations. *Journal of Cognitive Neuroscience*, *20*, 470–477.

Weiss, Y., Simonvelli, E. P., & Adelson, E. H. (2002). Motion illusions as optimal percepts. *Nature Neuroscience*, *5*, 598–604.

Wells, G. L. (1993). What do we know about eyewitness identification? *American Psychologist*, *48*, 553–571.

Wells, G. L., & Seelau, E. (1995). Eyewitness identification: Psychological research and legal policy on lineups. *Psychology, Public Policy, and Law and Human Behavior*, *1*, 765–791.

Wells, G. L., Small, M., Penrod, S., Malpass, R. S., Fulero, S. M., & Brimacombe, C. A. E. (1998). Eyewitness identification procedures: Recommendations for lineups and photospreads. *Law and Human Behavior*, *22*, 603–643.

Whitley, D. (1994). A genetic algorithm tutorial. *Statistics and Computing*, *4*, 65–85.

Wickelgren, W. A. (1974). Single-trace fragility theory of memory dynamics. *Memory & Cognition*, *2*, 775–780.

Wickens, T. D. (1982). *Models for behavior: Stochastic processes in psychology*. San Francisco: W. H. Freeman.

Wickens, T. D. (2002). *Elementary signal detection theory*. Oxford: Oxford University Press.

Wixted, J. T. (2004a). On common ground: Jost's (1897) law of forgetting and Ribot's (1881) law of retrograde amnesia. *Psychological Review*, *111*, 864–879.

Wixted, J. T. (2004b). The psychology and neuroscience of forgetting. *Annual Review of Psychology*, *55*, 235–269.

Wixted, J. T. (2007). Dual-process theory and signal-detection theory of recognition memory. *Psychological Review*, *114*, 152–176.

Wixted, J. T., & Ebbesen, E. B. (1991). On the form of forgetting. *Psychological Science*, *2*, 409–415.

Wixted, J. T., & Rohrer, D. (1994). Analyzing the dynamics of free recall: An integrative review of the empirical literature. *Psychonomic Bulletin & Review*, *1*, 89–106.

Wixted, J. T., & Stretch, V. (2000). The case against a criterion-shift account of false memory. *Psychological Review*, *107*, 368–376.

Wixted, J. T., & Stretch, V. (2004). In defense of the signal detection interpretation of remember/know judgements. *Psychonomic Bulletin & Review*, *11*, 616–641.

Yang, L.-X., & Lewandowsky, S. (2004). Knowledge partitioning in categorization: Constraints on exemplar models. *Journal of Experimental Psychology: Learning, Memory, and Cognition*, *30*, 1045–1064.

Yechiam, E., Busemeyer, J. R., Stout, J. C., & Bechara, A. (2005). Using cognitive models to map relations between neuropsychological disorders and human decision-making deficits. *Psychological Science, 16,* 973–978.

Yonelinas, A. (1994). Receiver-operating characteristics in recognition memory: Evidence for a dual-process model. *Journal of Experimental Psychology: Learning, Memory, and Cognition, 20,* 1341–1354.

Yonelinas, A. (2002). The nature of recollection and familiarity: A review of 30 years of research. *Journal of Memory and Language, 46,* 441–517.

Yuille, A., & Kersten, D. (2006). Vision as Bayesian inference: Analysis by synthesis? *Trends in Cognitive Sciences, 10,* 301–308.

Zucchini, W. (2000). An introduction to model selection. *Journal of Mathematical Psychology, 44,* 41–61.

Author Index

345

Subject Index

joint probability, *see* probability, joint

Kepler's model, 4, 32
Kullback-Leibler distance, 179–182, 184,
    189, 192
    expected, 192

latency, 114, 151–153, 189
latency distribution, 151, 152
layers, in neural networks, 289, 293
LBA, *see* Linear Ballistic Accumulator
learning, in neural networks, 290–291
lesioning of models, 27–28
lexical decision, 152
lightness, terms for, 284
likelihood, 150, 286
likelihood function, 150, 153, 155
    asymptotic normality, 159
    curvature, 154–157, 170
likelihood ratio, 178, 187, 189
likelihood ratio test, 177–179
likelihood surface, 153
Linear Ballistic Accumulator,
    151, 152, 304
local minimum,global minimum, 85
localist representation, 40, 289, 294
log-likelihood, 181
    ex-Gaussian
    MATLAB code, 154, 162
    maximum, 149, 150
    simplifying, 166, 184
log-likelihood function, 153, 155,
    157, 158
    binomial, 166
    concave, 157
    curvature, 193
    ex-Gaussian, 153
    quadratic, 159
log-likelihood surface, 155, 158
    quadratic, 158
logarithm function, 185
logistic function, 165
LRT, *see* likelihood ratio test
Luce's choice axiom, 22, 24
luminance, 273

MATLAB, 42, 128, 178
matrix inverse, 159, 161

matrix of second derivatives, *see* Hessian
    matrix
maximum likelihood estimation, 151,
    153, 184, 192
    minimization vs. maximization, 158
Min K model, 171
minimum description length, 193
mode, 153
model, 2, 5
    definition, 10–11
    descriptive, 11–16
    elements of, 10–11
    process characterization,
        16–19, 288
    process explanation, 19–24, 287
    quantitative, 3
model architecture, 58
model complexity, 182, 184, 193–194
model flexibility, *see* flexibility
model recovery, 198
model selection, 5, 8, 33, 150, 170–193
model weights, 186–187, 192
models
    classes of, 25
    insights from, 26–27
models, classes of, 283–284
movie running time, 285
multinomial models, multinomial
    processing tree, MPT, 16–19
multinomial processing tree, 159
multiple memory systems, 298–301
multiple regression, 176

nested models, 177–179, 191
neural network, 288–298
    Hebbian, 290
neuroscience, 298
normative behavior, normative
    expectations, 15
null hypothesis, 178, 179

omission error, 165
optimality, 287
optimization, 71
Ornstein-Uhlenbeck model, 189
outcome space, 29
overfitting, 198

taxation, 12
testability, *see* falsifiability
testability,falsifiability, 54, 204
the *Vasa*, 9
threshold, 151, 165, 166
time estimation, 173
time-series analysis, 172–174
transposition error in serial
    recall, 9
truth, 32–33, 180, 181

uncertainty, 149, 150, 153, 170–171, 180,
    192, 193
units, in neural networks, 288–289

variance
    in parameter estimates, 151, 153
verbal overshadowing effect, 238
verbal theorizing, 5, 8
verisimilitude, 67
visual search, 151

weather, 19
weight space, 296
weights, in neural networks, 289, 291
WITNESS model, 236
word frequency, 18
word naming, 27, 152, 161
word-length effect, 36
working memory, 153

About the Authors

Stephan Lewandowsky obtained his PhD at the University of Toronto in 1985 and after serving on the faculty at the University of Oklahoma until 1995, he is now a Winthrop Professor at the University of Western Australia. He currently holds an Australian Professorial Fellowship, which permits him to focus exclusively on his research. His research examines human memory, decision making, and knowledge structures within a modelling framework. To date, he has published over 100 scholarly articles and chapters. Stephan was Associate Editor of the *Journal of Experimental Psychology: Learning, Memory, and Cognition* from 2006 to 2008. He has won several teaching awards and his research has been funded continuously since 1990.

Simon Farrell completed a PhD at the University of Western Australia and then worked as a post-doctoral fellow at Northwestern University. He moved to the Universty of Bristol in 2003, where he is now a Reader in Cognitive Psychology. Simon's work focuses on the application of models in cognitive psychology, particularly in the areas of memory and choice behaviour. He is currently an Associate Editor for *Journal of Memory and Language,* and was recently awarded the Bertelson Award by the European Society for Cognitive Psychology for his outstanding early-career contribution to European Cognitive Psychology.

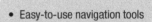